# AI, Cybersecurity, and Next-Generation Mobility in Smart Cities

Mishall H. Al-Zubaidie
https://orcid.org/0000-0002-3149-9129
*University of Thi-Qar, Iraq*

IGI Global
Scientific Publishing
Publishing Tomorrow's Research Today

| | |
|---|---|
| Vice President of Editorial | Melissa Wagner |
| Director of Acquisitions | Mikaela Felty |
| Director of Book Development | Jocelynn Hessler |
| Production Manager | Mike Brehm |
| Cover Design | Jose Rosado |

Published in the United States of America by
IGI Global Scientific Publishing
701 East Chocolate Avenue
Hershey, PA, 17033, USA
Tel: 717-533-8845 | Fax: 717-533-7115
Website: https://www.igi-global.com E-mail: cust@igi-global.com



Library of Congress Cataloging-in-Publication Data

Names: Al-Zubaidie, Mishall H., 1981- editor
Title: AI, cybersecurity, and next-generation mobility in smart cities / edited by Mishall H. Al-Zubaidie.
Description: Hershey, PA : IGI Global Scientific Publishing, 2026. | Includes bibliographical references and index. | Summary: "This book explores how artificial intelligence, cybersecurity, and emerging mobility technologies intersect to shape the future of smart cities. It examines secure, sustainable, and data-driven urban systems, addressing challenges in privacy, transportation, and digital infrastructure while proposing innovative solutions for safer, more efficient, and intelligent urban living"-- Provided by publisher.
Identifiers: LCCN 2025054888 (print) | LCCN 2025054889 (ebook) | ISBN 9798337381336 h/c | ISBN 9798337381343 s/c | ISBN 9798337381350 ebook
Subjects: LCSH: Smart cities--Security measures | Smart cities--Data processing | Transportation--Security measures | Transportation--Data processing | Artificial intelligence--Industrial applications | Computer security | Computer networks--Security measures
Classification: LCC TD159.4 A43 2026 (print) | LCC TD159.4 (ebook)
LC record available at https://lccn.loc.gov/2025054888
LC ebook record available at https://lccn.loc.gov/2025054889

British Cataloguing in Publication Data
A Cataloguing in Publication record for this book is available from the British Library.

To my parents (Hammed and Edaa), who fostered and sowed the germ of knowledge in my head.

To my brothers and sisters, the people who share my pleasures and sufferings, my strength and support, the model of sacrifice, pride, and giving.

For my dear Hawa, who has guided me with her love and support? Our journey together is documented in this book.

To my kids (Haider, Mohammed, and Ayoub), who never stop motivating me to share meaningful stories/goals.

For my friend (Loretta), who became family, my Australian mother.

To the courage of those who dare to change the world.

For each reader who discovers a bit of themselves in these chapters.

To the past that molded me, the present that sustains me, and the future that lies ahead.

To the anxieties, uncertainties, and restless nights, we succeeded.

To the books that were my closest companions on lonely evenings.

To everyone who has offered their prayers for me

This modest book is dedicated to you.

Mishall Al-Zubaidie

# Table of Contents

# Detailed Table of Contents

The opportunity to create sustainable business models that take into account social, economic, and environmental factors is presented by the integration of artificial intelligence (AI) in smart cities. Intelligent transportation networks, waste management programs, and smart grids are some of the key uses. Cutting-edge frameworks for the circular economy, sharing economy platforms, and performance-based models improve recycling procedures, reduce waste, make resource sharing easier, and boost productivity. The useful advantages of AI in promoting urban sustainability are demonstrated by case studies of prosperous AI-driven sustainable business models in international smart cities. Nonetheless, issues including legal frameworks, significant upfront investment expenditures, and data privacy concerns must be resolved. Public-private collaborations, encouraging legislation, and the use of moral AI are some of the solutions. This chapter offers stakeholders a thorough manual for putting AI-enhanced sustainable solutions into practice in urban settings.

This chapter explores the integration of vehicle emission monitoring within intelligent transport systems (ITS) to support the development of a permanent smart city. The real-time data enables the continuous monitoring and control of vehicles by taking advantage of data analytics, IoT sensors, and advanced traffic management technologies. Systems that improve air quality, urban planning, and environmentally friendly mobility solutions have been explored in this chapter. Case studies and emerging innovations are presented to highlight practical implementation and challenges. The future urban ecosystems are emphasized as data-driven policy-making, civil engagement, cross-sector cooperation, and status-comprehensive awareness.



Smart cities are the result of significant innovations like IoT, AI, and 5G, and new forms of cyber threats have appeared. This chapter aims to identify and discuss the major cybersecurity threats, risks, and challenges in smart cities, such as IoT-based threats, privacy and data protection issues, and network-level threats. It also assesses the solutions that have been adopted at the strategic level with a view to managing these risks, including encryption, the use of artificial intelligence in threat detection, and blockchain in matters concerning data authenticity. The study focuses on the need to have policy structures in place, international cooperation, and constant development to meet emerging threats in the field of cybersecurity. As more and more smart cities are being developed, it will become paramount to ensure that there are adequate security measures put in place to safeguard the infrastructure that will be in place as well as the citizens.



Data protection in smart agricultural markets remains a critical area of inquiry amid escalating digital transformations. This chapter examines the challenges and solutions surrounding privacy in agricultural data ecosystems, with particular attention to encryption, blockchain, and federated learning technologies. It also evaluates global legal, ethical, and regulatory frameworks such as the GDPR and CCPA that influence data governance in digital agriculture. As of 2023, over 75% of large-scale farms in developed nations employ IoT and AI-driven tools for data collection, yet only 38% have robust data protection measures in place, exposing vulnerabilities in ownership, consent, and access control. The integration of privacy-preserving mechanisms such as homomorphic encryption, zero-knowledge proofs, and secure multi-party computation is discussed as a pathway to sustainable data security. The findings emphasize the urgent need for interoperable standards and policy-driven frameworks to protect stakeholders, particularly smallholder farmers, within smart agricultural marketplaces.



This chapter explores the integration of smart city infrastructure with innovative drones and small aircraft services operated by Circular Professional Models. Smart cities benefit from advanced technologies to enhance urban efficiency, durability, and quality of life. Drones and small aircraft play major roles in this atmosphere, optimizing logistics, public services, and transportation, and providing solutions. A circular professional model approach guarantees resource efficiency and reduces waste, and this promotes sustainable practices in interconnected systems. It discusses case studies and emerging trends where these technologies are integrated, showing their transformative effect on urban mobility, logistics, and service distribution. By accepting the circular in business strategies, cities can achieve elasticity, economic benefits, and environmental conditions for future smart city developments.



This chapter suggests a Simple and Lightweight Method for Encrypting Images. This combines the Lorenz Chaotic System with DNA coding. This hiding method makes sure that private patient details are kept secret and safe during the study process. Further, it introduces optimal key selection using the Child Drawing Development Optimization Algorithm (CDDOA). This makes the encryption key better, which helps increase the safety. Using these methods together makes a complete way to find out ovarian cancer. It is both very accurate in diagnosis and safe for patient information. The Proposed EfficientNet model achieves an exceptional ovarian cancer classification accuracy of 98.88% and outperforms other existing models also in precision, recall, specificity, and F1 score. The proposed Lightweight Encryption model excels with superior security, entropy 6.9, PSNR 40.5, and remarkable efficiency in encryption and decryption processes. This study opens the way for improvements in research on ovarian cancer and sets a model for safe and fast handling of genetic data in medical situations.



This chapter attempts to present a Post-Quantum Secure Smart City Electricity Data (PQSED) system, which generates a quantum key via the BB84 protocol and digitally signs the data using FALCON, and uses pseudonym technology to add more security and protection to the data and digital signature, and also uses Walrus Optimization Algorithm (WOA) technology to the data to detect any abnormal behavior. The proposed system has been tested against several recently known attacks, such as replay attacks, Sybil attacks, eavesdropping, advanced ransomware attacks, social engineering attacks, and critical infrastructure attacks, and it has been proven to overcome them. In terms of performance evaluation, we obtained an average signature time of about 0.004 MS, an average signature verification time of about 0.006 MS, an average execution time of 0.66 MS, a precision of 96%, a recall of 95%, and an F1-score of 96%, which are good compared to the state-of-the-art research. Thus, our proposed system is highly acceptable for power plant applications.



This chapter explores the transformative potential of blockchain technology in reshaping urban governance. Far beyond its technical capabilities, blockchain challenges traditional, opaque models of municipal administration by offering transparency, auditability, and decentralized control. From land titling to procurement and identity management, tamper-proof records and distributed verification can help restore public trust, particularly in contexts plagued by inefficiency or corruption. Moreover, blockchain enables participatory governance through decentralized applications and smart contracts, allowing citizens to directly engage in urban planning, service oversight, and co-management of infrastructure. The chapter emphasizes the importance of incremental implementation, stakeholder coalitions, and careful integration with existing urban systems. It also calls for adaptive design, interoperability, and open-source development to ensure scalability and citizen accessibility.



Secure communication in urban environments is becoming increasingly vital as cities embrace smart technologies, IoT, and digital infrastructures. This chapter surveys the challenges and innovations associated with ensuring secure communication in modern urban settings. It highlights key issues such as scalability, real-time constraints, and the integration of legacy systems. Furthermore, the chapter discusses emerging solutions like AI-driven threat detection, federated learning, zero trust architectures, and quantum-resistant cryptography. The need for interdisciplinary collaboration is emphasized to tackle both technological and regulatory challenges.

# Foreword

The growth of smart cities depends on the convergence of AI, cybersecurity, and next-generation mobility. Together, these components produce urban environments that are safer, more effective, and sustainable. Public safety, resource management, traffic control, and citizen engagement are all made possible by AI in smart cities. Furthermore, data protection, infrastructure security, resilience against threats, collaboration, and standards are presented in cybersecurity in smart cities. Additionally, next-generation mobility offers smart infrastructure, autonomous vehicles, mobility as a service, and sustainable transportation. System integration, data privacy, public trust, and regulatory frameworks are among the interconnections and challenges. Significant developments in the digital world were brought about by the 21st century. These days, a large portion of our economy is driven by internet applications. Applications for smart cities, artificial intelligence, cybersecurity, and mobility techniques that change how users interact with these apps on a daily basis are examples of more recent smart models. This clever model has proven especially remarkable in the last ten years. In addition to more recent platforms and applications in wireless power transmission and radio frequency energy harvesting, the four main drivers are smart city computing, artificial intelligence, cybercity, and next-generation software-defined mobility.

This book, "AI, Cybersecurity, and Next-Generation Mobility in Smart Cities," is a timely and important addition to the discussion about how cybersecurity, AI, smart cities, and next-generation mobility can all work together to create a safer and more environmentally responsible digital future. It integrates a variety of research, viewpoints, and solutions that address significant problems in cybersecurity, cryptography, and computational efficiency in smart cities.

The book covers a broad range of topics, from fundamental concepts to cutting-edge technology, from reducing security concerns to safeguarding space data and maintaining information privacy in e-banking, e-commerce, e-transportation, and e-governance. One of the most appealing aspects of this book is its practical utility. As more businesses adopt smart city security systems, it is now crucial to strike a balance between performance, efficiency, and security. The discussions in this book are not just theoretical inquiries; they also offer governments, businesses, scholars, and legislators useful road maps for implementing safe and ecologically appropriate cybersecurity frameworks, artificial intelligence, and mobility in smart cities.

I congratulate the editor and contributors for their imaginative curation in putting together this insightful book. The book establishes a dependable digital ecosystem that future generations may build upon by bridging the gap between big data security in smart cities and technological innovation. I think that this book will be an essential tool for academics, researchers, security professionals, and decision-makers, assisting them in building a future where big data security, artificial intelligence, next-generation mobility, and technology coexist. In the age of smart cities, I fervently urge readers to read this book and begin their journey toward long-term information security.

**Mohammad Kaisb Layous Alhasnawi**
*Faculty of Health, Engineering and Sciences, University of Southern Queensland, Australia*

# Preface

## ABOUT THE BOOK TOPIC

Artificial intelligence, next-generation mobility, and smart city applications have brought people closer together at a rate never before seen at the civilizational level. This shift caused some elements to resurface in the form of illegal activities like cybercrime and security breaches, while others became the target of a number of insufficient remedial measures. In this new age, information is precious details, and almost everything is information, particularly identities, personal information, and the intricate relationships between them. Therefore, these are not the only traits of a fully computerized technological society where the boundaries of the earth have little bearing on the active agents of this system, whether they are harmful or not.

The last ten years have demonstrated that security problems are unquestionably the most challenging issue confronting humanity, with sudden changes upending civilization and having a major detrimental impact on politics, the economy, society, and the environment. Security breaches negatively impact societies in a variety of ways. The security of societies and organizations is seriously impacted by this volatility because traditional security technologies do not offer trends, goods, issues, and solutions. Additionally, it causes a disruption that is now almost impossible to control or hide. The Internet of Things (IoT), the most important information highway in many domains, such as e-transport, e-government, e-commerce, e-health, etc., is constantly relied upon by individuals, organizations, and nations. The vast army of unidentified malevolent actors who plot to undermine security in order to obtain any kind of benefit from the misuse of information is inextricably linked to the Internet of Things. Because individuals depend on technology but lack the knowledge to comprehend its various aspects, security being the most crucial, cybersecurity vulnerabilities arise through highly technical behaviors in smart cities, AI, and next-generation mobility.

To enable prompt communication and wise decision-making, the world needs smart cities, AI, next-generation mobility, and advanced, effective technology. However, data from smart cities also needs a robust security against various breaches and invasions. The interaction between these technologies and cybersecurity has become an important topic for research and development in an era where smart cities, artificial intelligence, and cutting-edge cryptography technologies are revolutionizing entire industries. The integration of information security in smart contracts and smart cities is a comprehensive endeavor to explore the relationship between cybersecurity and big data, offering insights into their prospects, challenges, and future directions.

Researchers, scholars, academics, business professionals, legislators, and students who want to comprehend and use trustworthy security tactics and procedures in the smart cities digital, AI, and next-generation mobility era will find this book to be an invaluable resource. In order to maintain a balance between technological advancement and environmental responsibility, it brings together experts from a variety of fields to present state-of-the-art innovations that combine cryptography technologies like blockchain, quantum, and encryption algorithms with security solutions for smart cities.

## THE GOAL

Information security experts find it challenging to stay up to date with the most recent developments in the rapidly developing disciplines of artificial intelligence, cybersecurity, and next-generation mobility in smart cities. In order to give academicians, researchers, and students a firm grasp of the crucial subjects surrounding cybersecurity/information privacy, AI, and next-generation mobility in smart cities, the editor and authors are pleased to present the first edition of "AI, Cybersecurity, and Next-Generation Mobility in Smart Cities" book. This comprehensive standalone edition is filled with the best research and references available. This book's current research and studies provide thorough and in-depth perspectives on cutting-edge ideas and developments in smart city security. This reference is meant to act as a single point of reference for conceptual, methodological, technological, and managerial difficulties in addition to providing insight into recent advancements and the field's potential for smart cities.

## ORGANIZATION THE BOOK

This book guide is divided into 10 chapters and was co-authored by 39 authors from 35 different organizations across 5 countries (India, Iraq, Pakistan, USA, and

Uzbekistan). This substantial involvement allows us to assert a range of perspectives that support the validity of this book. We acknowledge the outstanding efforts of each and every author. Their extensive expertise in the fields of information privacy and smart city security is shown in this book of research. The book is arranged into ten chapters that cover core principles, modern cryptography technologies, security mechanisms of smart cities, and real-world applications across industries in order to provide a logical and systematic progression of themes.

**Chapter 1**: This chapter explores how AI and ML are applied for traffic management and the public transport system, and enable predictive analyses to make real-time decisions. At the same time, using sensor networks, reducing emissions, and enhancing the travel experiences through autonomous systems and mobility-as-a-service platforms.

**Chapter 2**: This chapter offers stakeholders a thorough manual for putting AI-enhanced sustainable solutions into practice in urban settings. The useful advantages of AI in promoting urban sustainability are demonstrated by case studies of prosperous AI-driven sustainable business models in international smart cities. Nonetheless, issues including legal frameworks, significant upfront investment expenditures, and data privacy concerns must be resolved.

**Chapter 3**: This chapter explores the integration of vehicle emission monitoring within intelligent transport systems (ITS) to support the development of a permanent smart city. The real-time data enables the continuous monitoring and control of vehicles by taking advantage of data analytics, IoT sensors, and advanced traffic management technologies. Systems that improve air quality, urban planning, and environmentally friendly mobility solutions have been explored in this chapter.

**Chapter 4**: This chapter aims to identify and discuss the major cybersecurity threats, risks, and challenges in smart cities, such as IoT-based threats, privacy and data protection issues, and network-level threats. It also assesses the solutions that have been adopted at the strategic level with a view to managing these risks, including encryption, the use of artificial intelligence in threat detection, and blockchain in matters concerning data authenticity.

**Chapter 5**: This chapter examines the challenges and solutions surrounding privacy in agricultural data ecosystems, with particular attention to encryption, blockchain, and federated learning technologies. It also evaluates global legal, ethical, and regulatory frameworks such as the GDPR and CCPA that influence data governance in digital agriculture.

**Chapter 6**: This chapter explores the integration of smart city infrastructure with innovative drones and small aircraft services operated by Circular Professional Models. Smart cities benefit from advanced technologies to enhance urban efficiency, durability, and quality of life. Drones and small aircraft play major roles in this atmosphere, optimizing logistics, public services, and transportation, and providing solutions.

**Chapter 7**: This chapter suggests a Simple and Lightweight Method for Encrypting Images. This combines the Lorenz Chaotic System with DNA coding. This hiding method makes sure that private patient details are kept secret and safe during the study process. Further, it introduces optimal key selection using the Child Drawing Development Optimization Algorithm (CDDOA). This makes the encryption key better, which helps increase the safety.

**Chapter 8**: This chapter attempts to present a Post-Quantum Secure Smart City Electricity Data (PQSED) system, which generates a quantum key via the BB84 protocol and digitally signs the data using FALCON, and uses pseudonym technology to add more security and protection to the data and digital signature, and also uses Walrus Optimization Algorithm (WOA) technology to the data to detect any abnormal behavior.

**Chapter 9**: This chapter explores the transformative potential of blockchain technology in reshaping urban governance. Far beyond its technical capabilities, blockchain challenges traditional, opaque models of municipal administration by offering transparency, auditability, and decentralized control. From land titling to procurement and identity management, tamper-proof records and distributed verification can help restore public trust, particularly in contexts plagued by inefficiency or corruption.

**Chapter 10**: This chapter surveys the challenges and innovations associated with ensuring secure communication in modern urban settings. It highlights key issues such as scalability, real-time constraints, and the integration of legacy systems. Furthermore, the chapter discusses emerging solutions like AI-driven threat detection, federated learning, zero trust architectures, and quantum-resistant cryptography.

## A FUTURE PERSPECTIVE

As smart cities and cryptographic technologies continue to transform the cybersecurity landscape, dependable and efficient AI tools, cybersecurity measures, and next-generation mobility solutions are more crucial than ever. This book aims to provide a way to integrate modern encryption technologies with smart cities in order to foster a future where security and performance efficiency coexist. We want to sincerely thank all of the writers, reviewers, and publishing professionals who made this book possible. Their dedication and expertise have helped produce a volume that will inspire academics, researchers, scholars, and business executives to promote information security in smart cities. The goal of this book is to serve as a starting point for a more intelligent, secure, and environmentally responsible digital future.

We hope you find it useful. Enjoy your reading!

The Editor,

**Mishall Al-Zubaidie**

*Department of Computer Sciences and Artificial Intelligence, Education College for Pure Sciences, University of Thi-Qar, Nasiriyah, Iraq*

# Acknowledgment

This book, "AI, Cybersecurity, and Next-Generation Mobility in Smart Cities," would not be possible without God's assistance first and then accumulated/ongoing experiences. Being a leader among outstanding leaders is a blessing, and you have given me the chance to lead a wonderful group of people.

It's as difficult as it sounds to transform an idea into a book. It's a rewarding and internally hard experience. I would really like to express my gratitude to everyone who made this possible.

We would like to express our sincere gratitude to everyone who contributed to the completion of the "AI, Cybersecurity, and Next-Generation Mobility in Smart Cities" book. This book would not have been successful without the dedication, expertise, and support of many people.

We also want to sincerely thank the IGI Global Publishing team for their guidance, technical expertise, and continuous support during this process. Their dedication and expertise have been essential to this project's success. We are also grateful to IGI Global for providing us with the opportunity to edit this book and for the excellent support provided by their team of professionals.

We would especially want to thank father, mother, and my wife for their unwavering patience, love, and support, which have been a constant source of strength. Their support has been crucial to the project's successful completion and has enabled us to continue through its challenges.

People who wish to grow and guide others make the world a better place. Those who donate their time to mentor future leaders are what make it even better. I want to thank everyone who works hard to develop themselves and others.

I would like to express my gratitude to everyone I have had the privilege of leading, being led by, or observing their leadership from a distance for serving as the model and inspiration for The Leadership Manifesto.

Chapter 1

# Smart Urban City Transport Using AI and ML for Next-Generation Mobility Solutions

**Kimsy Gulhane**
https://orcid.org/0009-0006-6791-8651
*School of Management, Ramdeobaba University, Nagpur, India*

**Malathi Narra**
https://orcid.org/0000-0002-6076-1464
*Department of Civil Engineering, Siddhartha Academy of Higher Education, Vijayawada, India*

**Darshna Dalvadi**
*School of Computing and Technology, Institute of Advanced Research, Gandhinagar, India*

**S. Reshma**
https://orcid.org/0000-0002-3584-0021
*Department of Artificial Intelligence and Machine Learning, Dayananda Sagar College of Engineering, Bangalore, India*

**R. Gukendran**
*Department of Mechanical Engineering, Kongu Engineering College, Erode, India*

**S. Saravanan**
https://orcid.org/0009-0004-1899-3239
*SNS Institute of Technology, India*

## ABSTRACT

*The evolution of smart urban city transport is increasingly driven by the integration of artificial intelligence (AI) and machine learning (ML), enabling dynamic, data-based mobility solutions. This chapter explores how AI and ML are applied for traffic management and the public transport system, and enable predictive analyses to make real-time decisions. At the same time, using sensor networks, reducing emissions, and enhancing the travel experiences through autonomous systems and mobility-as-a-service (MAAS) platforms. Deployment and emerging trends are ex-*

DOI: 10.4018/979-8-3373-8133-6.ch001

*plored by case studies. This chapter also addresses the implementation challenges, moral considerations, and strategic planning through AI-powered mobility systems for future smart cities.*

## INTRODUCTION

The rapid pace of urbanization associated with great growth in population and vehicle consumption has led to the need for innovative, scalable, and intelligent urban mobility solutions. In many cities around the world, traditional transport structures are becoming increasingly inadequate to withstand demand, crowds, pollution, and resource barriers. In reply, the concept of smart city has emerged-a vision of the atmosphere that gives digital techniques and data-based decisions to increase the quality of life, operational efficiency, and durability. In this regard, artificial intelligence (AI) and machine learning (ML) are playing a transformative role in shaping the upcoming phase of the urban transport system (Kalusivalingam et al., 2021). Not only do these technologies operate the transport network, but the cities plan, predict, and respond to how the cities plan, predict and respond to the requirements of movements in real-time. AI and ML enable migration from reactive to active mobility management. Unlike traditional systems, which depend on a stable schedule, AI-driven systems can process a large amount of real-time data from various sources to mobilize the flow of GPS, traffic sensors, CCTV cameras, and mobile applications. Machine learning algorithms can learn from patterns and past behaviors to predict traffic congestion, indicate the best ways, and adjust the transportation schedule with minimal human intervention. This data-based intelligence helps cities to better use existing infrastructure without delay, reducing low emissions, improving travel satisfaction, and always without resorting to expensive expansion (Varshney et al., 2021).

One of the most significant applications of AI and ML in Smart City Transport is the intelligent traffic management systems. These systems use real-time traffic data to manage signal time, re-operate vehicles during peak hours, and react more effectively to emergencies. Adaptive traffic signal control, for example, uses machine learning to analyze traffic flow and automatically adjusts the signal period to reduce congestion. This dynamic response is in intense contrast with stable traffic light systems that often contribute to gridlocks and inaccuracies. Moreover, the models of the forecasts operated by AI may expect a crowd before delaying, enabling city organizers and passengers to perform leading actions (Ang et al., 2022a). The public transport system is another area where AI and ML are offering significant improvements. By analyzing rider demand, geographical distribution, weather conditions, and event schedules, transport agencies can predict additional demand, plan over routes, and improve vehicle dispatch. AI-powered chatbots and voice assistants are being integrated into passenger support systems, providing real-time updates, answering questions, and increasing cost. AI also supports the operation of the fleet by monitoring the fuel consumption, vehicle health, driver behavior, and maintenance schedules - fully cost savings and better service reliability (Deep & Verma, 2023).

Perhaps the most disturbing innovation in urban mobility is the emergence of autonomous vehicles (AV) and their ecosystem. Machine learning is the main capability behind AVS vision, forecasting, and decision-making. Through advanced computer vision, sensor fusion, and reinforcement learning, autonomous vehicles can navigate in complex urban environments, identify traffic signals, avoid pedestrians, and make driving decisions based on context. As the technology matures, it is ready to reduce human errors, increase traffic efficiency, and redefine personal and public transport. These effects are distant, touching land use, parking, insurance, and urban design (Mahapatra et al., 2023). Supplementing this progress is the concept of MAAS, which integrates various forms of public transport, ride-sharing, cycling, and walking into a unified digital platform. AI personalized trip planning, dynamic prices, and multimodal routes enable optimization, empowering users to select the most efficient, affordable, and durable travel options. This user-centered model not only promotes behavioral changes away from private car ownership but also allows cities to manage demand more effectively (Makanadar & Shahane, 2023a).

While the benefits are clear, the deployment of AI and ML in urban transport is not without challenges. High-quality data is a lifestyle of intelligent systems, yet in many cities, infrastructure, standardization, and interoperability are still facing gaps. Data privacy and security concerns are supreme, especially when collecting and analyzing location data and individual travel patterns (Razzaq et al., 2025). Moral questions also arise, as algorithms make decisions during accidents or prefer various user groups. Moreover, digital division means that all communities do not have the same access to smart mobility solutions, potentially strengthening social and spatial inequalities if not thoughtfully addressed (Makanadar & Shahane, 2023c). From the point of view of policy and governance, urban transport demands the integration of AI, regulatory structures, public-private partnerships, and engagement. Pilot projects and innovation sandboxes are used to test AI-based mobility solutions in a controlled environment before scaling. As governments, industry leaders, and civil society cooperate, it is necessary to put a clear emphasis on transparency, liability, and civil trust. This is especially important in the age where the decision of the algorithm affects the public structure and daily life (Jagatheesaperumal et al., 2024).

Despite these obstacles, the path to smart transportation is firmly visible. Cities around the world, from Singapore and Helsinki to Dubai and San Francisco, are already taking advantage of AI and ML to increase urban mobility and durability. With the emergence of green mobility, electric vehicle integration, and climate-conscious urban planning, the intelligent transport system will also play a central role in achieving environmental goals. Moreover, the conversion of AI with other emerging technologies such as blockchain, 5G, digital twins, and Internet of Things (IoT) also opens up more transformative possibilities (Mohsen, 2024). Hence, this chapter presents comprehensive research on how AI and ML smart cities are transforming urban transport. It outlines technical bases, real-world applications, case studies, implementation challenges, and strategic approaches for future mobility. As cities face two pressures of rapid urban growth and environmental stability, intelligent transport systems powered by AI and ML give way to not only operational efficiency but also more integrated, elastic, and resilient urban futures (Ogundare, 2024a).

## Objectives

The purpose of this chapter is to explore how AI and ML are revolutionizing the urban transport system in terms of smart city development. The main objectives include the role of AI/ML in traffic optimization, public transport growth, autonomous vehicle systems, and mobility-as-a-service (MAAS) platform. This chapter also intends to highlight predictive analysis and real-time system adaptability, making data-based decisions. Through global case teaching and trend analysis, the purpose is to provide a strategic understanding of how AI and ML contribute to efficient, durable, and user-centered mobility solutions.

## Scope

This chapter covers the application of AI and ML techniques on various aspects of smart urban transport. These include discussions about intelligent traffic management, real-time transit systems, autonomous mobility, multimodal integration, and the role of IoT in enabling the capabilities of prediction. This chapter also searches for current industry methods, deployment challenges, moral considerations, and future innovation ways. While the primary focus is on the urban environment, the chapter refers to the developed and emerging city references to provide a global perspective. It is intended for policies, urban organizers, technology, and researchers interested in the upcoming pay generation mobility system.

# TECHNOLOGICAL FOUNDATIONS FOR SMART URBAN CITIES

The successful realization of smart urban transport systems is basically based on a strong technical backbone. As cities try to be more intelligent, interconnected, and adaptable, technologies such as AI, ML, IoT, and Edge computing make pillars. These technologies not only increase operational efficiency but also enable real-time response to mobility ecosystems, forecasting decisions, and long-term durability. This section searches for key technical capable people running smart urban transportation systems, with a focus on AI, ML, and their integration with IoT and Edge computing infrastructures (Mavlutova et al., 2023). Figure 1 illustrates the Technological foundations for smart urban transport systems.

*Figure 1. Technological foundations for smart urban transport systems*

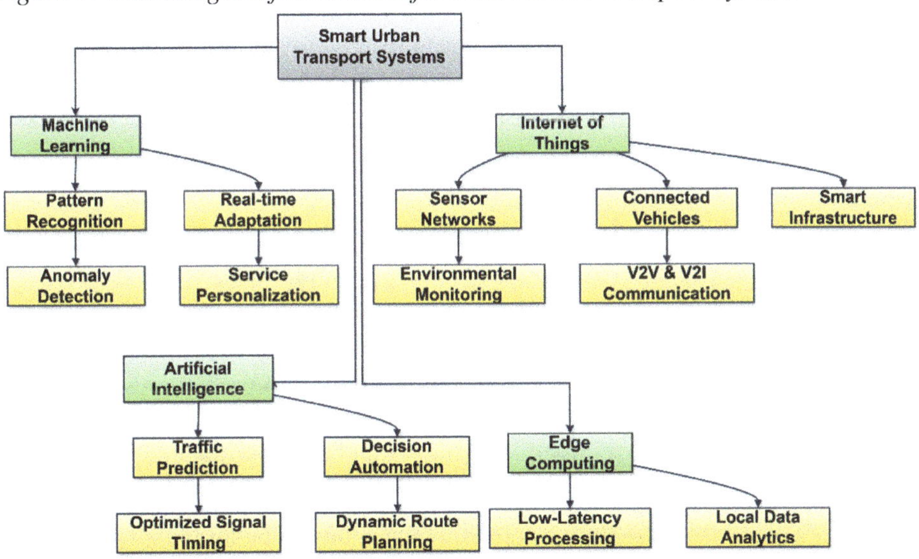


## Artificial Intelligence in Urban Transportation

Artificial intelligence serves as the central nervous system of smart city transportation infrastructure. At its origin, AI enables machines and systems to mimic tasks such as learning, logic, and problem-solving. In the context of Urban Transport, AI emphasizes the systems to process and analyze the large amount of the sexual data produced by vehicles, passengers, infrastructure, and sensors. The result is a transport network capable of optimizing to adaptive, self-regulatory, and real-time operations. Urban dynamics include intelligent traffic control, event investigation, route planning, and demand-responsive transit among AI's main requests (Jha et al., 2024; Sundaramoorthy et al., 2024). For example, AI-powered traffic signal systems use computer vision and real-time traffic flow data to adjust signal time based on current conditions rather than a pre-set cycle. This will reduce waiting time, fuel consumption, and congestion. Similarly, AI is integral for video analytics to enable a rapid emergency response, to detect a violation of AI accidents or traffic (Oladimeji et al., 2023).

AI also plays a crucial role in logistics and delivery networks in cities, especially in terms of e-CE Mars growth and last-mile delivery challenges. Route optimization algorithms reduce travel time and improve fleet efficiency. Moreover, AI-propelled behavioral analyzes help officials to understand passenger patterns and preferences, enabling data-based planning and structural investments. As AI maturity, its integration with other systems - such as autonomous vehicles, smart parking, and environmental monitoring - creates opportunities for holistic urban mobility solutions. These systems work harmoniously to reduce environmental influence, enhance public safety, and ensure an integrated travel experience.

## Machine Learning Algorithms for Traffic and Mobility

Machine learning, an AI subset, focuses on developing algorithms that allow systems to learn from data without being clearly programmed. ML is particularly effective in the transport domain, where sources such as GPS, sensors, mobile devices, social media, and transport cards are constantly producing large quantities of data. In traffic management, ML algorithms are used to predict crowd patterns based on historical rhythmic and real-time data. Observed education models can predict traffic volumes on certain routes, identify high-risk intersections, and indicate the best way. Reinforcement Education-BG ML technology is increasingly used to train traffic signal control systems for making real-time decisions that improve flow efficiency (Savin, 2021).

In public transport, the ML convoy is deployed for maintenance. By analyzing data from the components of the vehicle, machine learning models can identify inconsistencies and alert operators before mechanical failures occur. This reduces downtime and increases the reliability of the service. ML is also integrated into demand prediction. By analyzing rider behavior, time-of-day method, weather conditions, and special events, models can predict ridership demand with high accuracy. This enables a dynamic schedule of buses, metros, or ride-sharing services, where there is capacity to use and improve the satisfaction of the passengers. Moreover, Natural Language Processing (NLP)-The area within ML is used to power conversational interfaces, such as chatbots and voice assistants, which guide passengers, respond to various ways to navigate to urban spaces. The most crucial use of ML is in autonomous driving systems, where algorithms continuously process sensory data to make split-second decisions. These include finding the traffic bug acts, understanding traffic signs, forecasting pedestrian behavior, and running certain navigation commands.

## Integration with IoT and Edge Computing

The IoT serves as the sensory level of the smart city, in which the large ecosystem of physical devices is connected to the traffic cameras and vehicles connected to the smart meter and the pedestrian sensor. These devices collect granular data at various touchpoints in the transportation network, enabling cities to create real-time digital twins of urban mobility. For example, IoT-enabled smart traffic lights can communicate with vehicles to prioritize emergency responses or reduce idling at intersections. Connected parking systems can guide drivers to available locations, facilitate urban congestion, and save fuel. Environmental sensors can stimulate restrictions in high-pollution zones by integrating with real-time traffic data (Burlacu et al., 2022; Ogundare, 2024b). However, the data generated by IoT devices demands the calculation resources close to the scale and motion data source - this is where the same computing comes in the game. Unlike traditional cloud computing that focuses the process in remote servers, the same computing network distributes intelligence to the Edge. This allows Ultra-Law latency and local decision-making, which is important for applications such as autonomous vehicles, real-time traffic control and conflicting systems. Edge pushes analytical capabilities on devices such as traffic cameras or vehicle-mounting processors, ensuring instant response, without depending on a conversion connectivity of AI-AI and Edge computing. This not only improves system elasticity but also addresses concerns around data privacy and bandwidth.

The fusion of IoT, ML, and Edge computing facilitates a closed-loop system where data is constantly sensed, analyzed, and action-making the transport network self-uncomfortable and efficient. The technical bases for smart urban transport are developing rapidly, which is led by progress in AI, ML, IoT, and Edge computing. These technologies enable cities to transition to stable, reactive transport systems from dynamic, forecast, and intelligent mobility ecosystems. By providing real-time data, adaptive algorithms, and decentralized computing, cities can provide safer, more efficient, and durable transportation for all. As the innovation continues to accelerate, the seamless integration of these technologies will be important to achieve the vision of the smart mobility of the upcoming pay general.

# AI/ML-ENABLED TRANSPORTATION APPLICATIONS

AI and ML are running a transformative wave in the urban transport sector. In the mobility systems, pouring the wisdom of prediction and Auto Tomatoes, these technologies are redefining how people and goods move in cities. The following applications show how more efficient, adaptive, and user-centered enabling the next pay-Generation transport solutions, from-to-be AI and ML, from autonomous vehicles to autonomous vehicles and unified mobility platforms (Makanadar & Shahane, 2023b). Figure 2 shows that AI/ML-enabled transportation applications.

*Figure 2. AI/ML-Enabled Transportation Applications*

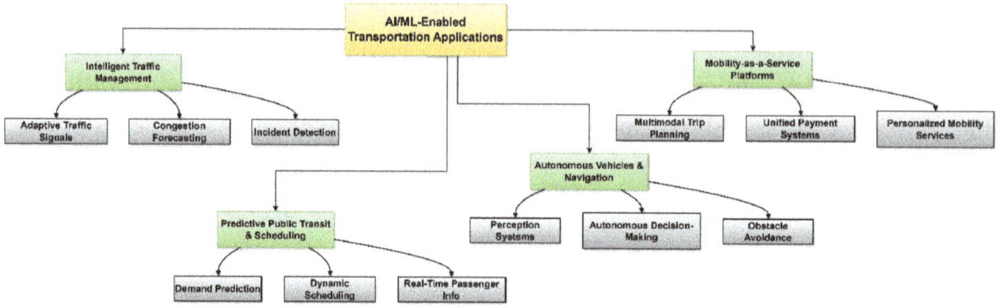


## Intelligent Traffic Management Systems

Urban traffic congestion is the most challenging issue facing modern cities. Traditional traffic systems, usually operated by steady signal times and limited data inputs, are increasingly inadequate in managing dynamic traffic patterns. AI and ML are addressing the issue by introducing intelligent traffic management systems that process real-time data to optimize the flow and reduce delays. Using computer vision, sensors, and connected infrastructure, AI algorithms analyze vehicle volume, pedestrian activity, weather conditions, and accident reports. Based on this information, adaptive signal control systems automatically adjust the green light period and signal phases at the intersection. ML Models, especially reinforcement learning algorithms, continue to learn and adapt based on observed traffic patterns and driver behavior, improving system performance over time (Wallace et al., 2025). In addition, AI-operated surveillance systems enhance traffic monitoring, enabling rapid occurrence investigations and feedback. These systems can automatically identify inconsistencies, such as stuck vehicles or accidents, and trigger appropriate actions, such as sending emergency services. Moreover, AI facilitates long-term traffic forecasts, identifying city planners' obstacles, prioritizing infrastructure investments, and imitating future development. Cities like Los Angeles, Singapore, and Barcelona have applied smart traffic control systems with reduced congestion, improved travel time, and low emissions (Sharma et al., 2024; Sundaramoorthy et al., 2024).

## Predictive Public Transit and Scheduling

AI and ML forecast schedules, real-time decision-making, and data-based services are revolutionizing public transport by enabling optimization. In traditional systems, the transportation schedule is fixed and will not be well adjusted to fluctuations in demand for travel. AI -powered platforms eliminate this rigidity by analyzing large datasets from rental systems, mobile applications, vehicle sensors, and weather forecasts to predict rider demand with high accuracy. Machine Learning Models expect the effect of peak use time, geographical demand concentrations, and external factors such as special events or road closures. Based on these insights, transport officers can dynamically adjust the bus or metro frequencies, rebuild the vehicles, and plan the way to meet real-time demand. For example, during a major concert or sporting event, predictive analyzes can report scaling to the fleet and guide temporary routing changes to reduce disruptions (Khatoon et al., 2022; Makanadar & Shahane, 2023b).

AI also supports real-time passenger information systems, providing live updates on the arrival time of the vehicle, the level of congestion, and service changes. This enhances the travel experience by reducing the uncertainty and the time spent waiting. Natural Language Processing (NLP) Chatbots help more by responding to travel-related questions, providing multilingual support, and improving accessibility by answering travel-related questions. The second key application is in the maintenance of the transport fleet. Forecast component failures before ML algorithms occur by monitoring the functioning of the devices and analyzing the patterns of history. This allows active repairs, reducing vehicle downtime and improving reliability. Cities like London and Stockholm are taking advantage of these capabilities for transit from reactive to responsive public transport operations, resulting in better service quality and operational costs.

## Autonomous Vehicles and Navigation

Autonomous vehicles (AV) represent the most visible and disruptive application of AI and ML in urban transport. A.V. At the root of technology is a sophisticated suite of AI-powered systems that enables vehicles to understand and navigate their surroundings without human intervention. M.L. Algorithms power complex functions. Avoiding Obstacles and Route Planning. Using sensor inputs from leaders, radars, cameras, and GPS, these systems create an extensive understanding of the vehicle's environment. Deep learning models, especially the Conventional Neural

Networks (CNN), process visual data to identify pedestrians, vehicles, traffic signals, and road signals in real time (Ogundare, 2024a, 2024b; Wallace et al., 2025).

In addition to the assumption, A.V. Other ways to make navigation decisions in dynamic environments use prediction models to expect users' actions and reinforcement learning. These decisions must be adjusted to adhere to safety, efficiency, and traffic rules - often complex urban settings include unexpected elements such as emergency vehicles. Outside of private cars, autonomous shuttles and delivery robots are being deployed in a controlled urban environment. These applications can reduce human error, improve fuel efficiency, and increase mobility for the underserved population, such as older and disabled individuals. Nevertheless, pilot projects in cities such as Phoenix and Berlin show promising progress, live in full autonomous transportation and development. Regulatory structures, cyber safety, and public acceptance are crucial challenges for widespread adoption (Dhanalakshmi et al., 2024; Giri et al., 2024; Godwin Immanuel et al., 2024).

## Mobility-as-a-Service Platforms

Dynamics-as-a-Service is an emerging example that integrates multiple modes of transportation into a unified digital platform, including public transport, ride-sharing, bike rental, carpooling, and micro-mentality. AI and ML are central to MAAS, enabling personal travel planning, real-time optimization, and a seamless payment process. The main feature of the mass is Multimodal Trip Planning, which uses AI to recommend the fastest, cheapest, or most durable way by combining various transport options. For example, a single journey can include a ride-share on the bike-share until the metro station, a metro ride, and the final destination, all coordinated by an interface. AI Algorithms optimize based on user preferences, real-time availability, and traffic status to these compounds (Mohsen, 2024; Wallace et al., 2025).

Dynamic prices are another AI-enabled function that helps balance the demand and supply in transport services. ML models analyze consumption trends, fuel costs, and service congestion to adjust values in real time. This not only improves the efficiency of service but also promotes travel behavior. ML user also supports behavioral analysts, enabling MaaS providers to tailor services for personal needs. For example, subscription models are often offered to travelers, while tourists can receive flexible one-day passes or recommendations based on their interests. From the point of view of city management, Mass provides valuable data on travel behavior, peak demand zones, and model shift patterns. This data supports more effective urban mobility planning and policy development. AI and ML are at the center of the urban mobility solutions of the next generation. Through intelligent traffic systems, predicted public transport, autonomous navigation, and a unified MAAS platform, these technologies provide a powerful toolkit to create smarter, more responsive, and integrated cities. Despite technical, regulatory, and moral challenges pending, the ongoing evolution of AI/ML applications promises to redefine urban transport experience - it is not only more efficient and durable, but also addresses the different needs of modern city residents.

*Figure 3. Elements of Data-Driven Decision Making in Smart Urban Transportation*

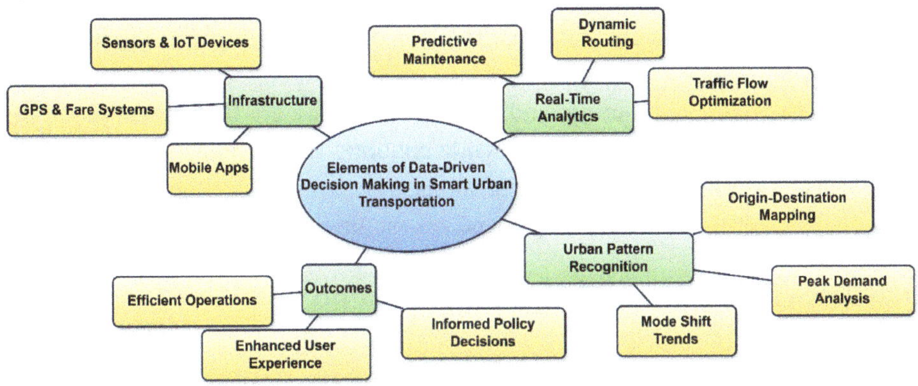


## DATA-DRIVEN DECISION MAKING

In the field of smart urban transportation, data is the lifeblood of intelligent operations and planning. As cities grow more complex and need more diverse mobility options, the ability to make timely, evidence-based decisions becomes crucial. Data-based decisions enable transport officers, service providers, and urban organizers to work with accuracy, efficiency, and precaution. This section finds how data is collected from smart infrastructure, analyzed in real time, and is used to identify urban dynamics patterns that shape policy, performance, and user experience (Sarker, 2022). Figure 3 illustrates the elements of data-driven decision-making in smart urban transportation.

### Data Collection from Smart Infrastructure

Smart infrastructure creates the base level of data storage in urban transport ecosystems. With the proliferation of IoT techniques, cities now deploy a network of devices connected to each other, in which traffic cameras, environmental sensors, GPS trackers, RFID-enabled rental systems, vehicle telemetry units, and smart streetlights produce high volume (Yermachenko et al., 2023). Smart City devices collect various metrics, including reports of traffic flow, public transportation schedules, pedestrian and bicycle movements, air quality, parking availability, and emergency occurrences. This data is securely transmitted to centralized or decentralized repositories, often in real-time (Tameemi et al, 2025). Open data initiatives in smart cities make this information available to developers, researchers, and private mobility providers, promoting innovation and collaborative problem-solving. In addition, mobile applications used for gender, navigation, ticketing, and journey planning serve as a rich source of behavioral and location data, reflecting travel preferences, peak hours, and mode preferences. Privacy-saving data collection protocols, data anonymization, edge computing, and federated learning are being used more and more to protect personal information while enabling further insights. This equips urban transport systems with sensor-tensions and user-contributing data richness and variations for intelligent planning and responding.

## Real-Time Analytics and Dynamic Routing

Real-time analytics powered by AI, ML, and Edge computing enables urban mobility systems to transition from reactive to active and predictive modes. This is crucial for dynamic routing and traffic optimization. AI-powered analytics engines use real-time data of GPS-enabled vehicles, road sensors, and surveillance systems to evaluate road events and environmental factors, enable emergency vehicle routing, dynamic bus route adjustments, and rides (Kandt & Batty, 2021; Zhang et al., 2022).

For example, if a major accident occurs on the central artery route, real-time analytics can identify the affected zone, reroute buses and services, notify users through mobile warnings, and update digital signage for passengers. Similarly, in delivery logistics, companies use real-time data to recreate vehicles on the basis of congestion, where fuel efficiency and delivery time improve. Dynamic routing systems also integrate external data such as weather forecasts, main event schedules, or construction updates to expect potential disruptions. This layered intelligence system improves elasticity and reduces dependence on fixed structural features. Moreover, the analytics platform uses dashboards and visualization to present active insights to the transportation managers and city organizers. These tools support a quick decision in the control centers and help to formulate a long-term strategy based on the trends and view simulation (Broo et al., 2022; Kandt & Batty, 2021).

## Urban Mobility Pattern Recognition

In addition to immediate routing and operation, the accreditation of the AI-powered pattern uncovers the possibility of the history of urban dynamics to reveal the ER radiation of the urban motorcycles. M.L. Models analyze huge datasets over time to highlight the prediction indicators in recurring patterns, inconsistencies, and various modes of transportation (Jha et al., 2024; Sundaramoorthy et al., 2024). The use of O-D mapping helps to understand how people travel, guide structural development, and service deployment. It also helps monitor the transition between transport modes, predict travel time, and identify high-pierced areas. Zone-based traffic modeling helps identify the underutilized corridors and high-demand areas. Socio-demographic split helps to include various population groups using mobility services and promotes mobility (Broo et al., 2022; Kandt & Batty, 2021; Yermachenko et al., 2023). These insights also contribute to widespread urban planning efforts. For example, the validity of the pattern can identify undeterred neighbors through public transport, enabling targeted investments in infrastructure or demand services. Similarly, it can report the placement of electric vehicle (EV) charging stations, bike-sharing hubs, or pedestrian zones based on consumption trends and community needs. In the public health context, analysis of dynamic patterns can help predict the spread of the disease or manage a safe distance during the epidemic. During the COVID-19 pandemic, many cities used overall mobility data to monitor the compliance of lockdowns and adjust public transportation accordingly.

Pattern validity also supports long-term stability goals. For example, finding an increase in cycling activity can justify the conversion of some ways to a permanent bike lane, while the use of cars in the downtown core can promote the expansion of pedestrian plazas and green spaces. Data-based decisions represent an instance shift in urban transport management. Cities can create mobility systems that are not only intelligent but also even and durable, by collecting rich data in smart infrastructure, collecting multi-urinary data in real time, and highlighting long-term behavioral patterns.

## CASE STUDIES AND GLOBAL BEST PRACTICES

The integration of AI and machine learning in urban transport is no longer ambitious - it actively shapes dynamics in progressive cities around the world. When offering technical foundations, successful implementation is based on strategic vision, stakeholder coordination, adaptive policies, and client-centered design. This section presents three case studies that give an example of global best practices: Singapore's extensive AI-powered transportation system, the autonomous transport initiative in the United States, and the leading smart mobility corridor in Europe (Khan & Ivan, 2023; Makanadar & Shahane, 2023d).

## AI-Powered Transport in Singapore

Singapore has been widely recognized as a global leader in Smart City Development. Transport is the foundation of its innovation agenda. Singapore's Land Transport Authority has adopted a holistic, long-term strategy to increase mobility using AI, data analytics, and Auto Tomatoes. The main initiative of Singapore is the intelligent transport system (ITS), which integrates AI-powered traffic signal control, real-time monitoring, and dynamic routing in the island network. Using sensors, Closed-Circuit Television (CCTV) cameras, GPS data, and vehicle investigation systems, the city constantly collects traffic flow data that feeds into forecast models. These models predict over the traffic light cycle and adjust them to real time, significantly reducing the congestion during peak hours (Alwar et al., 2024; Ang et al., 2022b).

The main element of Singapore's AI-enabled mobility is its smart mobility, which promotes a user-centered, forecast, and adaptive transport ecosystem. An innovative project under this scheme is the Express Way Monitoring and Advisory System (EMAS). EMAS uses AI and ML to prevent accidents, stuck vehicles, or other road incidents, and to deploy immediate traffic marshals and emergency response teams. The system automatically updates the digital signage to recreate drivers and reduce traffic disruptions. On the public transport front, Singapore's Public Transport Data Analytics System (PTDAS) analyzes travel behavior, boarding patterns, and trip frequency to optimize bus routes and metro schedules. System Commuter also integrates AI chatbots in mobile apps to provide real-time information and help passengers with multilingual support (Alwar et al., 2024; Wu et al., 2024).

Singapore has also initiated autonomous shuttle trials in areas like Jurong Lake District and Sentosa Island. These driverless shuttles depend on AI to avoid environmental mapping, pedestrian validity, and obstruction. Despite the trial phase, they indicate the commitment to being uniformly integrated into the city's urban landscape. The success of Singapore's AI-powered transportation is attributed to its central regime, investment in digital infrastructure, and active regulatory approach, which provides a model for other urban centers that want to harness AI for mobility change.

## Autonomous Transit Initiatives in the United States

The United States is home to various landscapes of autonomous transport projects, many of which are run by public-private partnerships and innovation clusters. Key urban regions, including Phoenix, San Francisco, and Arlington, are piloting or managing AI-enabled authentic transport systems. Since 2020, Waymo has provided a full driverless ride to people using electric autonomous vehicles equipped with advanced AI algorithms. These vehicles use a combination of leaders, radar, and camera data to navigate the city streets, identify route users, and make real-time decisions. The Waymo AI stack integrates deep learning, potential logic, and real-time mapping to handle complex traffic views with high-level safety (Alwar et al., 2024; Ang et al., 2022b).

In San Francisco, companies such as Cruise (supported by General Motors) and Zoox (owned by Amazon) are testing robotaxi services and delivery bots. Cruise has obtained permission to offer autonomous rides, paying in some parts of the city, gaining AI for dynamic routing, crowding, and coordination of vehicles. Systems are supported by Edge Computing Nodes and Cloud-based neural network training platforms, enabling real-time updates and continuous education. At the Arlington Municipal Level of Texas, one of the first autonomous shuttle pilot programs in the US began to transport people in one of the city's entertainment districts. US Federal and state-level support by agencies such as the Department of Transportation and the National Highway Traffic Safety Administration (NHTSA) has enabled regulatory sandboxes where autonomous transportation techniques can be tested in a real-world environment with controlled risks. This initiative is A.I. U.S.'s decentralized yet innovative approach to based transition, showing a rich approach, emphasizing private sector leadership, technical scaling, and additional regulatory adaptations.

## European Smart Mobility Corridors

Europe's approach to AI in transport emphasizes regional coordination, durability, and mobility integration across borders. Through multinational projects and public-private consortia, the continent is creating a smart mobility corridor that connects cities and countries through the AI-Before Transport Network. One of the main initiatives is the Norway project, which connects Norway, Sweden, Finland, and Denmark by AI-operated vehicle-to-infrastructure (V2I) and vehicle-to-vehicle (V2V) communication (Sundaramoorthy et al., 2024). The use of infrastructure with edge computing and machine learning, vehicles, and large highways shares data about road conditions, accidents, weather changes, and traffic patterns. This allows real-time dynamic routing, safe autonomous driving, and integrated cross-border transport logistics (Alwar et al., 2024; Wu et al., 2024).

Another significant case is a new dynamic in Germany. This project focuses on the test of AI-enabled autonomous and connected vehicle techniques under real traffic conditions. Age AIs interact with AVS to ze pace, units on the side of the road, lane use, and traffic signal synchronization. There is also a test to integrate electric vehicles and smart charging infrastructure. The Amsterdam Smart Mobility Program is for its MAAS integration. City AI uses AI to enable bike-sharing, trams, ferries, ride-hailing, and running in a single digital interface, planning a multimodal tour. AI engine analyzes real-time transit availability, environmental impact, and user preferences to indicate the best trip combinations. Europe's power collaborative innovation, citizens' engagement, and data privacy leadership. The initiative is often co-funded by the Horizon European program of the European Commission and complies with the General Data Protection Regulation (GDPR), ensuring moral AI use and data governance. In addition, the climate targets of Europe under the European Green Deal are more focused on AI-powered mobility with long-term stability goals. This global case study explains that AI-enabled urban mobility is not a single-size-fit-all solution; it should correspond to the local priority, structural maturity, and models of the regime. Central, technical-firm model of Singapore; US innovative, decentralized experiment; And Europe's regionally integrated, durable-centered approach offers every valuable lesson.

## CHALLENGES AND OPPORTUNITIES

While AI and ML offer a transformative possibility for smart urban transport, their deployment is not without significant challenges. These challenges spread to technology, social, legal, and moral domains. In order to successfully adopt AI-powered mobility solutions, they must consider the following critical fields: data privacy and cybersecurity, moral and social effects, technical and structural barriers, and regulatory and policy structures (Alwar et al., 2024; Jagatheesaperumal et al., 2024). Challenges and opportunities in deploying AI/ML in smart urban transport are shown in Figure 4.

*Figure 4. Challenges and opportunities in deploying AI/ML in smart urban transport*

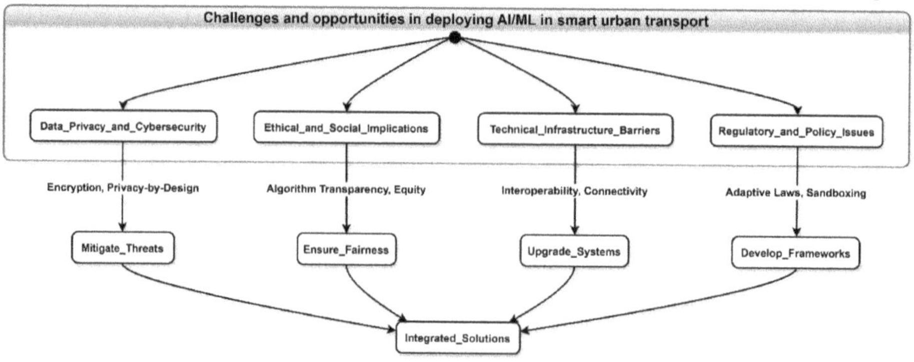

## Data Privacy and Cybersecurity

Data is the foundation of AI-enabled transport systems, but its collection and use raise serious concerns about privacy and security. Smart mobility platforms depend on real-time location, travel behavior, payment details, and sensitive data such as individual identifiers. Strong privacy is at risk of losing abuse, surveillance, and public confidence without protection. Moreover, the integration of connected vehicles, IoT devices, and cloud platforms expands the attack surface for cyber threats. Breach-IT traffic control centers or autonomous vehicle-wide transport operations in any component can disrupt or endanger human life.

## Ethical and Social Implications

AI systems, especially those that make autonomous or algorithmic decisions, raise complex moral questions. In the context of autonomous vehicles, for example, moral dilemmas around decisions in compulsory accident scenarios can arise, which is commonly referred to as a "trolley problem". These challenges require transparent and responsible AI models that can explain and justify their decisions. Social equity is another major consideration. If not designed, AI-enabled systems can expand digital division by marginalizing individuals without digital devices. Particular algorithms can have a disproportionate effect on some communities, especially if trained on non-representative datasets. Algorithmic ness for the same deployment, ensuring the involvement of design and community engagement (Alwar et al., 2024).

## Technical and Infrastructure Barriers

Despite the growing interest, many cities - especially in developing regions - create significant technical and structural barriers. Legacy Transport Infrastructure often lacks digital interfaces or sensor integration to support AI-operated operations. Lack of standardization in data formats, hardware interoperability, and communication protocols further hinders system integration. In addition, effective AI applications require a large amount of high-quality, labeled data, which may not be easily available or compatible. In many urban areas, high-speed connectivity, cloud computing resources, and edge infrastructure face limitations, which are real-time analytics and a prerequisite for making decisions. Integrated investment, capacity building, and phased digital transformation strategy are needed to eliminate these obstacles (Deep & Verma, 2023; Khan & Ivan, 2023; Mahapatra et al., 2023).

## Regulatory and Policy Frameworks

Regulatory uncertainty is a major obstacle to adopting AI-powered urban transport. In many jurisdictions, public infrastructure, autonomous vehicles, or MAAS platform lacks extensive policies addressing the use of AI. This makes it unclear for stakeholders and slows down innovation. Governments must develop adaptive, forward-looking regulatory structures that promote innovation while protecting public interests. Key policy requirements include AV, data governance standards, interoperability mandates, and a structure of liability for the moral AI guide. Pilot programs, regulatory sandboxes, and international collaboration can help enhance regulatory capacity and innovation under a controlled environment (Wallace et al., 2025; Wu et al., 2024). It is necessary to remove these multifaceted challenges for AI's moral, security, and effective integration in urban mobility systems. Balanced approach - innovation with regime, technology with morality and security - it will be important to ensure that smart transportation solutions really benefit all parts of society.

*Figure 5. Future Outlook and Innovation pathways*

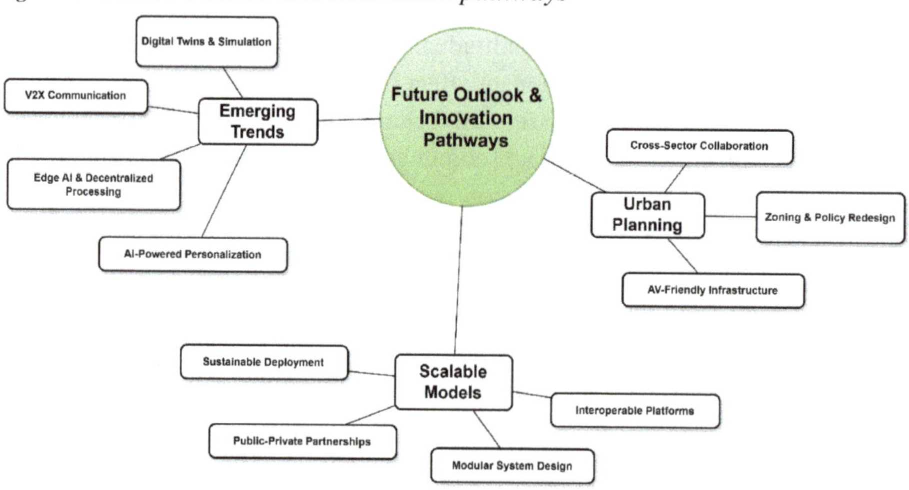


## FUTURE TRENDS AND INNOVATION PATHWAYS

As AI and machine learning have evolved, their role in shaping the future of urban mobility will become increasingly strategic. Smart transportation systems are being transferred from pilot projects to large-scale deployment, enabling cities to become more responsive, efficient, and integrated. This section invents emerging trends, strategies for autonomous ecosystems, and scalable, durable models that will define the next era of intelligent urban transport (Ogundare, 2024a; Wallace et al., 2025; Wu et al., 2024). Figure 5 illustrates the future outlook and innovation pathways.

## Emerging Trends in AI and Mobility

Some emerging trends are redefining the intersection of AI and mobility. There is a growing use of generating AI and digital twins for the imitation of urban transport views before deployment and optimization. These tools allow organizers to model disaster response strategies with infrastructure investments, traffic flows, and unprecedented accuracy. Edge is getting AI traction, enabling the decentralized process on the source, where vehicles, sensors, and traffic cameras-tattoos are more secure and bandwidth-efficient decision-oriented. Meanwhile, vehicle-to-everything (V2X) communication will revolutionize in autonomous coordination, enabling vehicles to communicate with infrastructure, pedestrians, and each other in real time (Wallace et al., 2025).

## Urban Planning for Autonomous Ecosystems

In order to accommodate autonomous and AI -powered transport systems, cities must re -imagine their spatial and policy structure. Future-ready urban planning will need to redesign infrastructure such as streets, intersections and parking zones to support AV, delivery and micromobility vehicles. Zoning policies may need to be developed to allow for mixed use places were AV with traditional transport modes. Can work. Moreover, Municipal Planning Integrating data will help to balance traffic loads, reduce emissions, and improve safety. It will be necessary to create cross-sector collaboration, elastic and adaptive ecosystems between urban organizers, technical providers and transport officials where autonomous technologies bloom (Alwar et al., 2024).

## Scalability and Sustainable Deployment Models

In order to scale AI-powered mobility solutions on a sustainable basis, cities must adopt modular, interoperable systems that can develop technologically. Open APIs, certified data formats, and cloud-native architects will enable seamless integration of new services without extensive overnutritions. Durability should also be the main metric. AI can support the carbon-exhausted transport targets by optimizing the vehicle dispatch, promoting shared mobility, and charging electric vehicle (EV) based on demand forecasts. Cities will benefit from phased implementation strategies, where pilot projects report large rollouts. Funding methods such as public-private partnerships and result-based investments will further support long-term scalability and innovation (Ogundare, 2024a). The future of urban dynamics is in the strategic fusion of AI, infrastructure, policy, and man-centered design. By accepting these innovation routes, cities can create scalable, adaptive, and durable dynamic ecosystems that are ready for tomorrow's problems.

## CONCLUSION

The integration of AI and ML in urban transport systems presents an example of how cities manage mobility, infrastructure facilities, and public services. From intelligent traffic management and predictable public transport to autonomous vehicles and unified MaaS platforms, it enables AI and ML cities to become more adaptive, efficient, and user-centered. Singapore, the United States, and Europe's Case Studies highlight the converting strategy, yet a variety of benefits of AI to eliminate urban mobility challenges. These examples show the importance of collaborative innovations in achieving measures such as real-time data collections, predictive analysis, and reduced congestion, improved safety, and advanced travel satisfaction. However, as the technology matures, a framework that is used by its users is also required. Addressing issues such as data privacy, algorithmic bias, cyber safety, and similar access for responsible deployment. Similarly, eliminating infrastructure limitations and aligning regulatory structures with technological advances will be important for long-term scalability. Looking forward, the future of smart urban dynamics will be shaped by emerging innovations like AI, digital twins, and durable deployment models. In order to develop in cities, they must take a balanced approach, which integrates cutting-edge technology with urban planning, moral regime, and durability targets. After all, AI and ML are not only the tools for optimization, but the catalyst to re-imagine urban dynamics in intelligent, elastic, and man-centered ways. Travel towards smart cities begins with strategic objectives, interdependent cooperation, and the shape of all service transport systems.

## REFERENCES


Alwar, B., Edgardo, H., & Faustino, E. (2024). Integrating IoT and Artificial Intelligence for Sustainable Smart City Development: A Case Study Approach. [Information Technology Engineering Journals]. *ITE Journal*, *9*(2), 80–90.

Ang, K. L.-M., Seng, J. K. P., Ngharamike, E., & Ijemaru, G. K. (2022a). Emerging technologies for smart cities' transportation: Geo-information, data analytics and machine learning approaches. *ISPRS International Journal of Geo-Information*, *11*(2), 85.

Broo, D. G., Bravo-Haro, M., & Schooling, J. (2022). Design and implementation of a smart infrastructure digital twin. *Automation in Construction*, *136*, 104171.

Burlacu, M., Boboc, R. G., & Butilă, E. V. (2022). Smart cities and transportation: Reviewing the scientific character of the theories. *Sustainability*, *14*(13), 8109.

Deep, G., & Verma, J. (2023). Embracing the future: AI and ML transforming urban environments in smart cities. *Journal of Artificial Intelligence*, *5*, 57.

Dhanalakshmi, M., Tamilarasi, K., Saravanan, S., Sujatha, G., Boopathi, S., & Associates. (2024). Fog Computing-Based Framework and Solutions for Intelligent Systems: Enabling Autonomy in Vehicles. In *Computational Intelligence for Green Cloud Computing and Digital Waste Management* (pp. 330–356). IGI Global.

Giri, R. B., N., Alhamad, A. M., Mamidi, P. L., R., S., & Boopathi, S. (2024). Human-Centered Design Approach to Autonomous Electric Vehicles: Revolutionizing Mobility. In *Advances in Logistics, Operations, and Management Science* (pp. 91–109). IGI Global. https://doi.org/DOI: 10.4018/979-8-3693-1862-1.ch006

Godwin Immanuel, D., Solaimalai, G., Chandrakala, B. M., Bharath, V. G., Singh, M. K., & Boopathi, S. (2024). Advancements in Electric Vehicle Management System: Integrating Machine Learning and Artificial Intelligence. In *Advances in Web Technologies and Engineering* (pp. 371–391). IGI Global. https://doi.org/DOI: 10.4018/979-8-3693-1487-6.ch018

Jagatheesaperumal, S. K., Bibri, S. E., Huang, J., Rajapandian, J., & Parthiban, B. (2024). Artificial intelligence of things for smart cities: Advanced solutions for enhancing transportation safety. *Computational Urban Science*, *4*(1), 10.

Jha, S. K., & Beevi, S. J. P., H., Babitha, M. N., Chinnusamy, S., & Boopathi, S. (2024). Artificial Intelligence-Infused Urban Connectivity for Smart Cities and the Evolution of IoT Communication Networks. In *Blockchain-Based Solutions for Accessibility in Smart Cities* (pp. 113–146). IGI Global. https://doi.org/DOI: 10.4018/979-8-3693-3402-7.ch005

Kalusivalingam, A. K., Sharma, A., Patel, N., & Singh, V. (2021). Enhancing smart city development with AI: Leveraging machine learning algorithms and IoT-driven data analytics. *International Journal of Artificial Intelligence and Machine Learning*, *2*(3).

Kandt, J., & Batty, M. (2021). Smart cities, big data and urban policy: Towards urban analytics for the long run. *Cities (London, England)*, *109*, 102992.

Khan, A. F., & Ivan, P. (2023). Integrating machine learning and deep learning in smart cities for enhanced traffic congestion management: An empirical review. *J. Urban Dev. Manag*, *2*(4), 211–221.

Khatoon, N., Dilshad, N., & Song, J. (2022). Analysis of use cases enabling AI/ML to IOT service platforms. *2022 13th International Conference on Information and Communication Technology Convergence (ICTC)*, 1431–1436.

Mahapatra, S., Raj, S., & Badi, M. (2023). Smart transportation based on AI and ML technology. In *Artificial Intelligence and Machine Learning in Smart City Planning* (pp. 281–299). Elsevier.

Makanadar, A., & Shahane, S. (2023a). Smart mobility and cities 2.0: Advancing urban transportation planning through artificial intelligence and machine learning. In *Urban Mobility India* (pp. 23–38). Springer.

Makanadar, A., & Shahane, S. (2023c). Urban mobility: Leveraging ai, machine learning, and data analytics for smart transportation planning-a case study on new york city. *2023 14th International Conference on Computing Communication and Networking Technologies (ICCCNT)*, 1–6.

Mavlutova, I., Atstaja, D., Grasis, J., Kuzmina, J., Uvarova, I., & Roga, D. (2023). Urban transportation concept and sustainable urban mobility in smart cities: A review. *Energies*, *16*(8), 3585.

Mohsen, B. M. (2024). Ai-driven optimization of urban logistics in smart cities: Integrating autonomous vehicles and iot for efficient delivery systems. *Sustainability*, *16*(24), 11265.

Ogundare, E. (2024a). Understanding the mediating role of artificial intelligence in urban transportation planning for smart city development and its implications for the United States. *International Journal of Innovative Science and Research Technology*, *9*, 10–5281.

Oladimeji, D., Gupta, K., Kose, N. A., Gundogan, K., Ge, L., & Liang, F. (2023). Smart transportation: An overview of technologies and applications. *Sensors (Basel)*, *23*(8), 3880. PMID: 37112221

Razzaq, R. H., Tahayur, D. H., & Jebbar, W. A. (2025). Sturdy Blockchain Combined with E-apps Repositories Based on Reliable Camouflaging and Integrating Mechanisms. *IJ Computer Network and Information Security*, *17*(3), 35–53.

Sarker, I. H. (2022). Smart City Data Science: Towards data-driven smart cities with open research issues. *Internet of Things : Engineering Cyber Physical Human Systems*, *19*, 100528.

Savin, G. V. (2021). The smart city transport and logistics system: Theory, methodology and practice. *Upravlenec, 12*(6).

Sharma, M., Sharma, M., Sharma, N., & Boopathi, S. (2024). Building Sustainable Smart Cities Through Cloud and Intelligent Parking System. In *Handbook of Research on AI and ML for Intelligent Machines and Systems* (pp. 195–222). IGI Global.

Sundaramoorthy, K., Singh, A., Sumathy, G., Maheshwari, A., Arunarani, A., & Boopathi, S. (2024). A Study on AI and Blockchain-Powered Smart Parking Models for Urban Mobility. In *Handbook of Research on AI and ML for Intelligent Machines and Systems* (pp. 223–250). IGI Global.

Tameemi, H. A., Shayea, G. G., Khaleel, Y. L., Habeeb, M. A., Hussein, N. A. H. K., & Albahri, A. S. (2025). A Systematic review of metaverse cybersecurity: Frameworks, challenges, and strategic approaches in a quantum-driven era. *Mesopotamian Journal of CyberSecurity*, *5*(2), 770–803.

Varshney, H., Khan, R. A., Khan, U., & Verma, R. (2021). Approaches of artificial intelligence and machine learning in smart cities: Critical review. *IOP Conference Series. Materials Science and Engineering*, *1022*(1), 012019.

Wallace, J., Vukovic, M., Karimovic, T., & Edwards, W. (2025). A High-Performance 5G/6G Framework for Smart Cities Supporting Multi-Level Artificial Intelligence. *2025 2nd International Conference on Advanced Innovations in Smart Cities (ICAISC)*, 1–9.

Wu, P., Zhang, Z., Peng, X., & Wang, R. (2024). Deep learning solutions for smart city challenges in urban development. *Scientific Reports*, *14*(1), 5176. PMID: 38431741

Yermachenko, V., Bondarenko, D., Akimova, L., Karpa, M., Akimov, O., & Kalashnyk, N. (2023). *Theory and practice of public management of smart infrastructure in the conditions of the digital society'development: Socio-economic aspects.*

Zhang, Y., Zhang, Y., Zhang, H., & Zhang, Y. (2022). Evaluation on new first-tier smart cities in China based on entropy method and TOPSIS. *Ecological Indicators, 145*, 109616.

# Chapter 2
# Sustainable Business Models for Smart City Using AI

**Balpreet Singh Madan**
*School of Design, Sharda University, Greater Noida, India*

**M. Chitra**
*Department of Artificial Intelligence and Data Science, PGP College of Engineering and Technology, Namakkal, India*

**Archana Ratnaparkhi**
https://orcid.org/0000-0002-1269-6389
*Department of E&TC, Vishwakarma Institute of Technology, Pune, India*

**T. Santhini**
https://orcid.org/0009-0009-0935-7990
*Department of MCA, Rathinam Technical Campus, Coimbatore, India*

**P. Karthikeyan**
https://orcid.org/0000-0002-9902-1869
*Department of Management Studies, Kongu Engineering College, Erode, India*

**K. Praveenkumar**
https://orcid.org/0009-0007-1807-6643
*KPR Institute of Technology, Coimbatore, India*

## ABSTRACT

*The opportunity to create sustainable business models that take into account social, economic, and environmental factors is presented by the integration of artificial intelligence (AI) in smart cities. Intelligent transportation networks, waste management programs, and smart grids are some of the key uses. Cutting-edge frameworks for the circular economy, sharing economy platforms, and performance-based models improve recycling procedures, reduce waste, make resource sharing easier, and boost productivity. The useful advantages of AI in promoting urban sustainability are demonstrated by case studies of prosperous AI-driven sustainable business models in international smart cities. Nonetheless, issues including legal frameworks, signif-*

DOI: 10.4018/979-8-3373-8133-6.ch002

*icant upfront investment expenditures, and data privacy concerns must be resolved. Public-private collaborations, encouraging legislation, and the use of moral AI are some of the solutions. This chapter offers stakeholders a thorough manual for putting AI-enhanced sustainable solutions into practice in urban settings.*

## INTRODUCTION

Urban problems, including lack of resources, environmental deterioration, and social injustice, are addressed by smart cities. With the growth in cities, sustainable development is becoming increasingly important. Artificial intelligence (AI) is an important technique that can change urban administration and promote sustainability. Smart cities use digital techniques to improve the quality and service functionality of life. Artificial intelligence (AI), which combines robotics, natural language processes, and machine learning, can handle large amounts of data and give a wise verdict. AI can speed up public services, reduce its impact on the environment, and improve resource allocation in smart cities. AI-Power controls smart grids, energy zeal supply and demand, cutting waste and carbon emissions. Traffic management systems with AI capabilities reduce pollution and congestion (Boopathi, 2024a). Smart city and AI integration increase operational effectiveness and create new, durable business models. These models face social and environmental problems. Circular Economy models, sharing economy models, and display-based models come in three extensive groups. Circular economy samples emphasize waste reduction and resource efficiency. AI ensures that the material is reused and the resources are protected by optimizing the recycling processes and predicting lifetime trends. This strategy protects resources and reduces the environmental influence of urban operations (Sonia et al., 2024).

AI-powered economy models match the supply and demand in real time by optimizing the use of property through a shared access case. Because fewer automobiles are operated, this platform reduces pollutants and traffic congestion. Cooperative spaces with AI capabilities make the most of the formation of Office Fissure, which reduces the demand for a new building. Typically, operating petting models are especially good to promote durable habits because they take advantage of AI to improve efficiency and service distribution. These models-smart can improve the method of use by the help of Utility Services-users through energy, and reducing costs. But there are issues that need to be resolved, such as data privacy, high investment costs, and the requirement for strong legal structures. Public-private partnerships can combine resources, knowledge, and regulatory baking to solve these problems. In order to integrate AI in an urban environment, policies protecting public interests while promoting innovation (Sharma et al., 2024).

This chapter has investigated how creative professional models can benefit AI to promote sustainable urban development. It provides information on how AI-powered durable professional models apply to smart cities, emphasizing stakeholders and the best efforts for the upcoming possibilities. It also provides information on how to optimize and promote durable habits. Smart cities are cutting-edge approaches for urban development and planning, including the same technology to enhance lifestyle, durability and efficiency. They deal with issues including social injustice, lack of resources, and environmental deterioration. These cities maximize urban operations and improve the quality of life for their citizens using digital techniques such as AI, Big Data Analytics, and IoT (Malathi et al., 2024).

Smart cities try to limit their negative effects on the environment by promoting effective resource management, low energy pollution consumption, and the use of renewable energy accessories. The city's carbon footprint can be reduced by integrating the smart grid in the composition of its energy room, which allows real-time monitoring and power demand. This energy improves the efficiency and facilitates the integration of renewable energy sources. Smart cities use AI-operated analytics and sophisticated sensor networks to give waste and water management first priority. These devices help protect the resources and cut waste, keeping in view of water quality, leaks, and use. Waste management systems promote a circular economy where materials are constantly used and recycled, recycling storage routes by optimizing and reducing the amount of landfill space (Maguluri, Arularasan, et al., 2023).

Durable urban development can be very helpful, especially with smart city technology in the field of transport. With the use of AI-based technology, traffic can be operated, crowds can be reduced, and motor and public transport can be promoted. This promotes healthy urban settings, reduces greenhouse gas emissions, improves air quality, and reduces the use of private vehicles. Artificial intelligence (AI) is transforming smart cities through data analysis, trend prediction, and decision-making. In real time, it is processed by a large amount of data infrastructure and resource management. AI algorithms can integrate renewable energy sources, improve smart grid operations, and predict the demand for energy, all leading to more economical and environmentally friendly outcomes. In order to ensure that the Energy Zone is delivered throughout the cities, AI can also predict high energy demand times and change the supply (Pachiappan et al., 2024; Rebecca et al., 2024).

By directing autonomous cars and improving traffic signals, artificial intelligence is transforming urban transport and cutting traffic and travel time. Ride-sharing services can be operated by AI-powered systems, reducing the need for vehicles. In the district, safety, surveillance systems, identifying inconsistent activity and risks, facilitate rapid reactions from law enforcement. AI is used by predictive police systems to evaluate crime data and point to higher-risk regions, which enables preventive actions in time. All things are taken into account, AI is improving efficiency and safety while revolutionizing urban travel. The design and administration of smart buildings, which are the original elements of smart cities, depend very much on artificial intelligence(Rebecca et al., 2024; Sharma et al., 2024). Based on professional patterns, weather, and other variables, these buildings increase the use of lighting, HVAC systems, and energy, increasing comfort and energy enthusiasm efficiency. To maintain a healthy urban environment and reduce the effects of climate change, AI-powered sensor is able to monitor air and water quality, identify pollution sources, and provide data for regulatory compliance and public health programs (Sundaramoorthy et al., 2024). AI is essential for the development of smart cities as it makes urban settings elastic, durable, and efficient. It enhances residential quality, service distribution, and resource management. Continuous development and integration of AI technology is essential for the success of smart cities in the future.

## Objectives of the Chapter

Research searches for the use of AI techniques to improve urban operations and quality of life, focusing on durable professional models such as the economy platform and circular economy. It also addresses AI implementation barriers such as data privacy and high investment costs, indicating moral AI deployment and public-private cooperation. The study also introduced the possibility of AI in smart buildings, adaptive urban design, and renewable energy.

# AI AND URBAN SUSTAINABILITY

The ability of urban sites to sustain the well-being of their residents is known as urban stability, which protects the environment, economy, and social resources for future generations. It involves actions and rules to reduce environmental influence, accelerate economic expansion, and improve the standard of living. Three pillars of sustainable development are prosperity, environment, and people (Das et al., 2024; Prasad et al., 2024; Vijaya Lakshmi et al., 2024).

## AI Technologies for Smart Cities

### Machine Learning

A type of artificial intelligence called Machine Learning (ML) enables a computer to learn from data, look for patterns, and make less judgment with no human input. It is essential for smart cities as it maximizes the durability and efficiency of urban processes. Traffic flow predictions M.L. can be done by algorithms, which can improve the signal time and reduce the congestion, resulting in fewer emissions and smoother traffic. In addition, machine learning is used in the maintenance of infrastructure to ensure safety and protect expensive repairs by predicting maintenance requirements from the sensors implanted in buildings, roads, and bridges (Ingle et al., 2023; Zekrifa et al., 2023).

In energy management, machine learning algorithms are used to predict the use of energy, enhance the smart grid performance, and reduce energy waste. In addition, they improve public safety by facilitating the rapid time of rapid law enforcement through civilized surveillance systems. By learning from past data, machine learning (ML) models can also help predict offenses, spending more intelligently to officials and actively targeting high-risk regions.

## Internet of Things (IoT)

The Internet exchanges network data of linked devices called of Things (IoT) and provides real-time information for automation and decisions in smart cities. It has cameras, sensors, and smart meters to monitor water levels, energy access, traffic movement, and air quality. City officials are able to prepare for future requirements, make well-informed choices, and quickly respond to concerns attributed to this constant data (Ali et al., 2024; Upadhyaya et al., 2024; Venkateswaran et al., 2024).

Smart Waste Management Systems employ the Internet of Things (IoT) sensors for tracking garbage levels, improving storage routes, searching for leaks, monitoring water quality, and effectively operating distribution networks. IoT sensors are used in water management to monitor the distribution network and find leaks. IoT devices, public transport vehicles, and traffic signals in the parking lot provide data to improve all traffic flows, reduce congestion, and improve users' overall mobility experiences (S., 2024; Upadhyaya et al., 2024).

## Big Data Analytics

Big data analytics is an essential tool to understand complex urban mobility and streamlined processes in smart cities. In order to facilitate insights and decisions, it processes and evaluates the enormous proportion of data from many sources, including social media, public records, and Internet of Things devices (Dhanya et al., 2023).

Numerous sectors, such as public health, environmental management, urban planning, energy route management, and public safety, depend greatly on large data analytics. It can monitor trends, forecast epidemics, follow the transmission of illness, and provide immediate actions. It can evaluate air and water quality data in environmental management to point out the sources of pollution and estimate the success of the rules. It can be used to guide policy decisions in urban planning through economic indicators, land use patterns, and demographic data analysis. It can predict the time of peak demand, put the demand reaction in action, and reduce the waste of energy in energy management. Smart cities are built on a combination of large data ticks, analytics, IoT, and machine learning, which improve lifestyle, durability, and efficiency. The smarter, more durable cities are being made by machine learning, which maximizes the skills of forecasts, IoT for real-time data, and large data analytics for complete insights.

## Benefits of AI in Sustainable Urban Development

Sustainable urban development, thanks to artificial intelligence (AI), is facing issues including social justice, environmental degeneration, and resource management. It affects many aspects of urban life and improves the standard of living for inhabitants in multiple fields. AI has many benefits for sustainable urban development (Periasamy et al., 2024; Tirlangi et al., 2024).

- **Optimized Resource Management:** Because AI maximizes the management of the resource, it is essential for durable urban development. It can predict consumption trends and predict the overuse of raw materials, water, and energy ponds by analyzing large amounts of data. Artificial intelligence in the smart grid (AI) algorithms can unite renewable energy sources, cut waste, and balance the supply and demand for power. AI can also improve water management by detecting patterns of use, identifying leaks, and guaranteeing effective distribution, all of which save water resources and save operating costs (Koshariya, Khatoon, et al., 2023; Sengeni et al., 2023).
- **Improved Transportation Systems:** Artificial intelligence (AI) is transforming urban transportation to optimize traffic signals, reducing congestion and travel time. As a result, there are fewer emissions and the quality of the air is better. AI contributes to the development of a driverless car, which reduces traffic accidents and improves fuel economy. AI-powered systems can provide over optim, promote environmentally friendly mobility, and reduce the use of private vehicles (Gopal et al., 2024).
- **Enhanced Waste Management:** To optimize collection routes, and recycling more effectively, and monitor the waste level in real-time, using Smart Waste Management Solutions AI and IOT sensors. This promotes a circular economy where the material is reused and recycled, eventually reducing the emission of greenhouse gas and reducing the use of landfills and greenhouse gas emissions (Dhanalakshmi et al., 2024; Vijaya Lakshmi et al., 2024).
- **Sustainable Urban Planning:** AI offers sophisticated equipment for data analysis and modeling, which facilitates durable urban design. It analyzes the

environment, economy, and demographic subject data for patterns and guides choices. Organizers can create elastic settings by upgrading the infrastructure by increasing the use of land, increasing green areas, and handling the expansion of the population, while imitating the views of urban development thanks to AI-powered models (Sundaramoorthy et al., 2024).

- **Improved Public Health and Safety:** Artificial intelligence (AI) increases public health and safety by accelerating monitoring systems, identifying inconsistent activity, and predicting epidemics. In addition, it monitors health trends, illnesses, and resource allocation. In order to create better urban settings, AI can also analyze environmental data to point out the sources of pollution and to evaluate their effects on public health (Boopathi & Khang, 2023; Durairaj et al., 2023).
- **Increased Energy Efficiency:** AI increases the efficiency of EI business in buildings and infrastructure by optimizing HVAC systems based on the spirit of business patterns, weather conditions, and energy. This results in significant savings and operational costs. AI also manages lighting systems, monitors consumption, and energy, indicating a measure for zoning savings, contributing to urban stability.
- **Promoting Social Equity:** AI can improve the social equity picture by assuring that urban services are delivered. An AI-operated platform is capable of enhancing public transport, healthcare, and education delivery by analyzing data. Eliminating inequality and assuring that all citizens consume basic services, this strategy incorporates and promotes similar metropolitan settings.

Artificial intelligence (AI) technologies are essential to improve resource management, transport networks, waste management, urban planning, public health, energy efficiency, and social needs. AI is a crucial tool for more durable cities due to its continued growth and integration, which will help to manage the complex difficulties of urbanization and meet long-term durability goals.

## INNOVATIVE BUSINESS MODELS FOR SMART CITIES

*Figure 1. Innovative business models for smart cities*

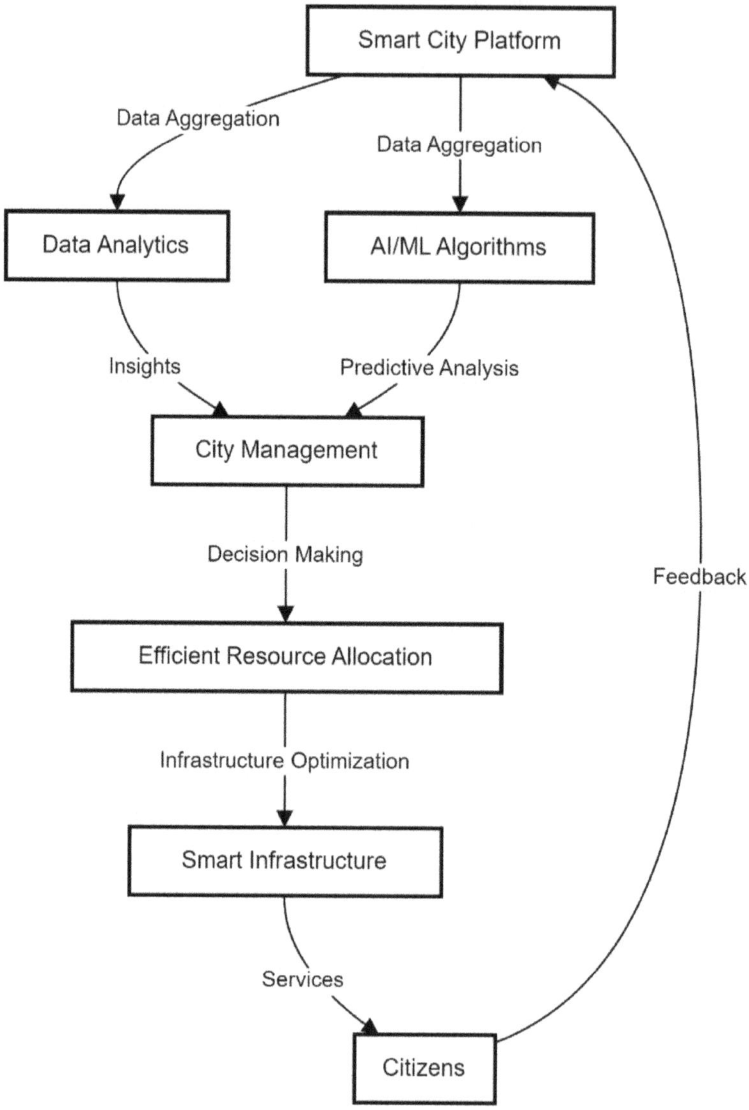


Figure 1 represents a professional model where the smart city platform collects data from various sources in the city. This data is then analyzed using data analytics and AI/ML algorithms to obtain insights for the city management. Infections produced are used to make a decision, which leads to efficient resource allocation and city infrastructure. Ultimately, improved infrastructure and services benefit citizens, who react to the smart city platform, closing the loop for continuous improvement.

## Circular Economy Models

### AI in Waste Management and Recycling

Circular economy samples emphasize recycling and waste management to reduce waste production and improve resource efficiency. AI techniques are required to improve recycling initiatives in metropolitan areas and streamline waste management processes. AI-driven systems provide a collection of ways to collect and detect high waste-generating locations by analyzing data from sensors, cameras, and other sources using sophisticated algorithms. This leads to a decrease in costs, environmental impact, and an increase in operational efficiency (Dhanya et al., 2023; Hanumanthakari et al., 2023).

AI is transforming recycling with elevated processing and rattling capabilities. Traditional features use manual sorting, and it is error-filled and labor-intensive. With sensors and machine learning algorithms at their disposal, AI-driven systems are accurately detecting elements such as paper, metals, and plastic, capable of detecting different elements, increasing the quality of recycled materials, increasing the recycling rate, and reducing contamination.

### Real-time Smart Recycling Systems

Artificial Intelligence (AI) and Internet of Things (IoT) are used to improve recycling through real-time smart recycling systems and make it easier, effective, and environmentally friendly. These systems recognize and identify recyclable items using a smart container equipped with a sensor. Use the collected data to improve the processes and storage schedules after the AI algorithms. The ability of these systems to provide immediate response and incentives to users is one of the main benefits, promoting active involvement in recycling initiatives. Earns appropriate recycling users' points or discounts that can be used to support community efforts or redeemed in the nearest businesses (Boopathi, 2024b; Pachiappan et al., 2024).

Municipalities and waste management companies can monitor recycling trends, non-filling levels, and low partnership rates with the use of real-time smart recycling systems. This data -based strategy has been made possible through recycling rate and low pollution, such as educational campaigns or low pollution, such as educational campaigns or structural upgrades. Artificial intelligence (AI)-Increase the effectiveness of the collection of drain trash management and recycling systems, promote the circular economy in urban settings by increasing sorting accuracy and incorporating locals of recycling initiatives. Artificial intelligence (AI) will be necessary to promote environmental goals and innovation as cities accept the circular economy (Maguluri, Ananth, et al., 2023; Rahamathunnisa et al., 2024).

## Sharing Economy Models

### AI-driven Resource Sharing Platforms

Urban Sharing Economy models operated by AI are improving stability and resource efficiency. These systems reduce waste and maximize the use of wealth by enabling people to effectively share resources such as cars, living spaces, and office spaces. Increases real-time supply and demand matching users' experiences, and resource allocation using AI algorithms. AI is used to predict demand trends through ride-sharing services, more effectively connect drivers and riders, and modify prices dynamically. Artificial intelligence (AI) systems can provide individualized experiences, reduce waiting time, and indicate effective ways by evaluating past data and customer preferences (Naveeenkumar et al., 2024). Co-operative space platform AI is using user communication, facility management, and space use. Artificial intelligence (AI) Algorithms optimize desk assignments, arrange meetings, and provide customized features by evaluating business rates, space usage trends, and user preferences. This user improves community and functionality.

## BEST PRACTICES

### Successful Implementation of AI in Smart Cities

*Figure 2. Implementation process of AI technologies for smart cities*

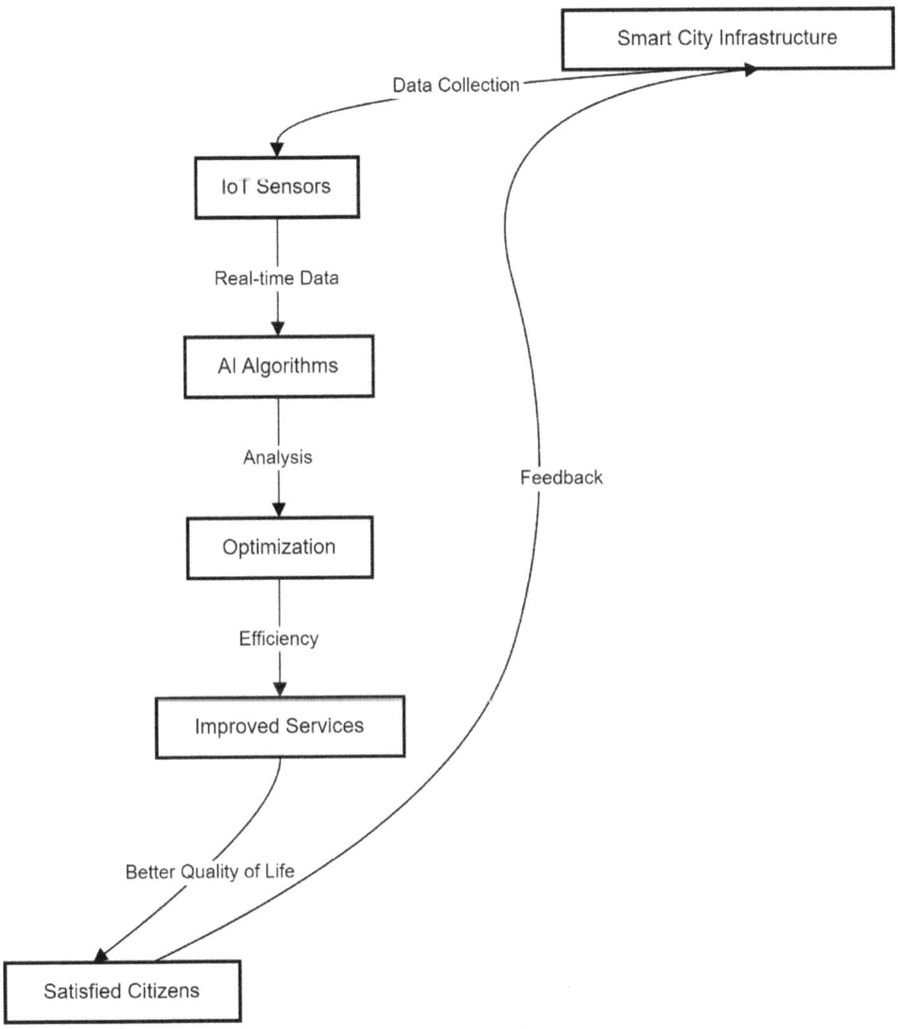


Figure 2 explains the implementation process of AI techniques to create smarter, more efficient, and citizen-centered cities. An IoT sensor collects real-time data on parameters such as traffic, energy consumption, and air quality. Advanced AI algorithms process this data to gain valuable insights. These insights are used to plan the city's operations, such as traffic management and waste management. This increases the efficiency, improves services, and satisfaction in citizens through optimization. The feedback loop allows for continuous improvement in smart city infrastructure. This model shows how AI techniques can be used to create smarter, more efficient, and civil-focused cities (Hussain et al., 2023; Kumar et al., 2023).

- Data Governance and Management: To guarantee the security, privacy, and quality of data used in AI systems, install a strong framework for data governance. Adopt data management processes that provide accommodation, interoperability, and data integrity in various city departments and stakeholders.
- Joint Ventures: Encourage the cooperation between the public and commercial sectors, educational institutions, and tech companies to enhance knowledge, wealth, and credit for artificial intelligence projects. To stimulate innovation and optimize, establish a public-minor partnership that shares risks and benefits and organizes incentives.
- Organize people in planning, creation, and use of AI solutions that accurately reflect the needs and concerns of the common people. Clearly promote openness and responsibility by providing a clear outline of the goals, parameters, and results of the AI initiative and asking for input at each stage of the process.
- Ethical and Responsible AI: Priority to justice, responsibility, transparency, and inclusion when forming and implementing AI systems. Create rules of moral standards and behavior for AI professionals and make sure all applicable laws and regulations are followed.
- Scalability and Interoperability: Create AI systems that can be easily expanded and adapted to different urban conditions and cases of use. Invest in interoperable platforms, open standards, and modular designs to facilitate future growth and evolution, and allow integration with current systems.
- Continuous Monitoring and Evaluation: To guarantee the effectiveness, reliability, and performance of AI systems, place processes for continuous monitoring, assessment, and optimization. Collect and evaluate information about the results of user comments, key performance indicators, and results that require correction, and properly adjust AI models and algorithms.
- Resilience and Security: To protect against potential risks, weaknesses, and attacks, AI offers top priority of cyber safety and elasticity in systems (Jebbar et al., 2024). Put strong security measures in place to protect infrastructure and data from illegal access and guarantee service. These methods include encryption, authentication, and access controls.
- Development Capacity and Knowledge Sharing: Funding training programs and capacity development projects to understand, apply, and make profits

from artificial intelligence (AI) technology to municipal employees, legislators, and the people. Encourage the culture of information and lifelong education to promote creativity and teamwork in the city ecosystem.

- Evidence-based Decision Making: Apply AI to support a decision by offering visual modeling, data-based insights, and predictive analysis to guide resource allocation, policy preferences, and urban planning. Make sure the desired results are established on the response of empirical facts, enemy principles, and stakeholders, to optimize and avoid unwanted effects.
- Planning for the long term and sustainability: Include artificial intelligence (AI) in the long-term durability strategy, and urban development is planned to cope with immediate issues, including lack of resources, social inequality, and climate change. Prioritize funds for activities that will receive observable economic, social, and environmental benefits for both current and future pay generations. Align AI efforts with more common stability goals.

## Analysis of Critical Success Factors

### Governance and Policy Support

The successful use of AI in smart cities is based on strong legislative support and an effective regime. This framework provides direction, rules, and supervision to ensure that AI projects meet strategic goals, adhere to moral principles, and reduce risks. Citizens, companies, and stakeholders are more trusted when there are policies related to data governance, privacy defense, cybersecurity, and algorithmic transparency (Tahayur et al., 2024). Compilation in levels that participate in government agencies, departments, and AI programs is facilitated by strong regime formats. Defining roles, responsibilities, and decision-making processes facilitates resource optimization, reduces duplication, and streamlines performance. The engagement of a citizen is possible through the governance framework supporting responsibility, transparency, and inclusion.

### Public-Private Partnerships

In smart cities, public-private partnerships (PPPs) are required to stimulate innovation, allocate funds, and accelerate AI deployment. In view of difficult urban issues and providing real benefits to society, they take advantage of the skills and experience of both fields to co-build and implement AI solutions. PPPs connect resources and distribute risks, providing capital, skills, and technology from the private sector to advance the government's AI projects. Private sector partners offer market insights, innovative skills, and subjects.

Public-private partnership (PPP) stimulates economic development and competitiveness by promoting cooperation and information exchange between public and private parties. They enable stakeholders to cooperate with shared objectives, including strengthening citizens' involvement, enhancing sustainable development, organizing interests, promoting collaboration and sharing responsibilities, and improving public services. Successful PPPs will have strong regime methods to balance well-planned, adjust specific goals and interests, control risks, and distribute rewards. Open communication, concrete relationships, and trust are needed to overcome obstacles and disputes. Smart City and AI adoption are very dependent on public-private cooperation, legal support, and governance. The government can accelerate the change in the intelligent, durable, and incorporated environment of cities by promoting innovation, investment, and cooperation through the provision of a platform for legal structures, strategic direction, and cooperation.

## CHALLENGES AND SOLUTIONS

### Challenges:

- Data Privacy Issues: Because AI-operated smart city projects combine, store, and process enormous volumes of data, privacy issues arise. People may be reluctant to join if they fear that their personal information will be misused or used without authorization. The danger of violations of data leaks and privacy increases as data is collected from many sources.
- Security Vulnerabilities: Malware, cyberattacks, and data breaches are some security risks that AI systems are sensitive to. Hackers can obtain unauthorized access, interfere with services, or tamper with AI-powered decisions by taking advantage of errors in cloud infrastructure, IoT devices, and AI algorithms. The mistaken results can also be caused by missing or biased data (Koshariya, Kalaiyarasi, et al., 2023; Maguluri, Ananth, et al., 2023).

### Solutions:

- Principles of Privacy-by-Design: Adopt a privacy-design strategy for AI systems, integrate technologies such as anonymity, encryption, and differential privacy to reduce the amount of information that is individually identified on the file, collected on the file, collected on the file, while maintaining data integrity and secrecy. Whenever possible, obtain clear consent from the people and communicate openly about the goals, implications, and extent of data storage and processing.

- Data Minimization and Localization: Reducing the volume and granularity of data, adopting data minimization techniques, and taking all crucial steps to ensure the security of the AI application, consider the requirements of data localization to store sensitive data within national borders when complying with local privacy laws and regulations.
- User Empowerment and Control: In addition to the clear alternatives to transparency about privacy choices, such as opt-out, data deletion, and AI-based decision-making processes, the importance of controlling citizens through confidentiality features, such as text data portability, access controls, and consent management equipment.
- Multi-layered Security Measures: Use multi-layered security measures, including strong authentication, access restrictions, and encryption protocols to protect AI systems and data from both internal and external threats. To find possible safety errors and fix them, run weakness assessments, penetration tests, and security on a regular basis. Work together with industry partners, regulatory agencies, and cybersecurity specialists to keep in mind new risks and best practices.
- Public Awareness and Education: Through education campaigns, community access programs, and counseling, people try to raise awareness about the risks of data privacy and security associated with the AI-powered Smart City initiative. It also hopes to develop digital literacy and responsible data in individuals, companies, and government institutions.

## High Initial Investment Costs

### Challenges:

- Capital-Intensive Nature: Implementation of AI in smart cities requires significant initial costs in hardware, software, infrastructure, and human resources. As a result, due to high initial costs, limited financial resources, resource-limited areas, or AI may be a barrier to the adoption of AI for municipalities in developing countries.
- ROI (return on investment) uncertainty: For this reason, it is difficult for the decisions to justify the up-front costs and get lending to AI investments in smart cities due to unexpected long-term economic benefits and ROIs. Decisions on investments and risk assessments are made more difficult through the absence of a defined step and benchmark.

*Figure 3. Challenges and solutions: High initial investment costs for AI in smart cities*

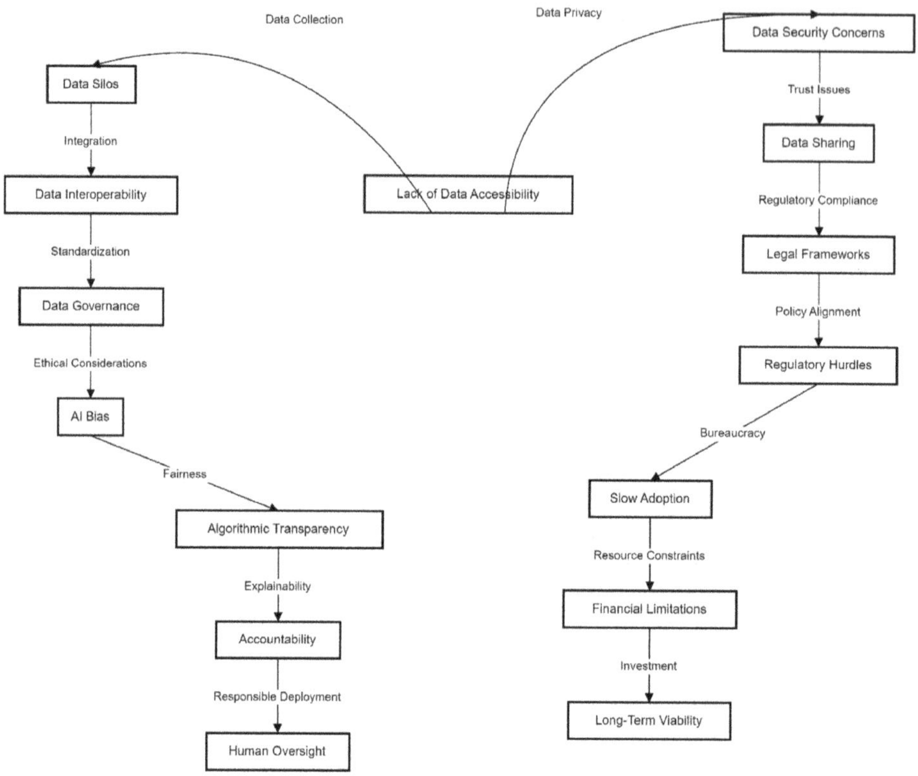


Implementation of sustainable professional models in smart cities using AI, access to data, security concerns, trust issues, data governance, legal framework, AI bias, regulatory barriers, resource limitations, financial limitations, liability, and long-term. Challengers face numerous challenges, such as regulation and oversizing, as shown in Figure 3. Obstacles, addressing AI bias, securing investment, confirming responsibility and transparency in AI-powered decision-making processes, incorporating human observation, and durability and scalability of AI-powered business models (Sundar et al., 2024).

## Solutions

- Public-Private Partnerships (PPPs): This article encourages AI investment in smart cities between the public and the private sectors to work together to share the costs, risks, and benefits of AI investments. For co-finance and development of the AI initiative, it is suggested to create a public-private partnership (PPP), which will ease the burden on public budgets and speed up the implementation. In addition, it will emphasize the interests of all parties involved in contracts, income-collection plans, and exhibition-based rewards.

- Grant Funding and Incentives: The scheme suggests the AI-powered Smart City initiative, especially in the disadvantaged or economically marginalized areas. It suggests tax benefits, incentives, and low-interest loans for new and small companies as well as social industries. In order to promote competition and cooperation among stakeholders, it also recommends organizing innovation funds, challenges, and prize competitions.
- Phased Implementation and Pilot Projects: It is recommended to implement AI in phases, starting with proof-of-concept F-Concept trials and pilot projects to show the viability and value of AI technologies in solving urban problems. The purpose is to mimic the best efforts in sections and scales successful pilot projects to ROI to pt over Optim and reduce the risks of implementation.
- Performance-Based Procurement: These methods encourage suppliers to provide innovative, reasonably priced solutions that meet municipal goals and produce wholesale results from traditional cost-based standards by giving the results, creativity, and value creation priority.

## Proposed Solutions

### Public-Private Partnerships (PPPs)

The public-private partnership can reduce the high early investment costs associated with AI-powered smart city initiatives by combining both industry resources, knowledge, and creative ability.

- Co-Financing and Co-Development: This concept creates cooperative funding methods for the development of AI projects in smart cities and promotes cooperation between public and private partners to share the financial risks and rewards associated with AI investments.
- Resource Sharing and Expertise Exchange: By combining resources, skills, and technical structures, the partnership between public agencies and commercial partners can improve efficiency and cost-efficiency.
- Outcome-Based Contracts: To ensure that interests and responsibilities are aligned, the PPP contract should be designed around the outcome-based matrix. In order to encourage private partners, financial incentives and penalties must be linked to certain goals.

## Supportive Policies

By placing supporting policies to resolve regulatory barriers, promote investment, and reduce investment risks, governments can promote the use of AI in smart cities.

- Regulatory Frameworks: Provide standards, rules, and certification programs for AI technology. Ensure privacy, security, and moral concerns in the establishment of a clear, transparent, and predictable regulatory structure for AI deployment.
- Incentive Mechanisms: In order to stimulate the private sector investment in the AI-operated Smart City initiative, the scheme suggests paying tax exemptions, grants, venture capital credit, and low-interest loans.
- Procurement Guidelines: In order to recruit various suppliers and promote competition in the AI market, it is recommended to improve the procurement process to promote innovation, quality, and value construction. Clever techniques such as challenge-based competitions or innovative partnerships can also be adopted.
- Data Governance and Sharing: Create a framework for data sharing that strikes a balance between security, privacy, and creativity; Support open data projects; and create a contract between public and commercial organizations to distribute data related to AI research and development.

## Ethical AI Deployment Frameworks

For the development of responsible and incorporated AI technology in smart cities, a moral AI deployment framework is required. They provide the best efforts, standards, and principles to consider moral issues and social reactions, including important elements, as shown in Figure 4.

*Figure 4. Ethical AI deployment for smart city*

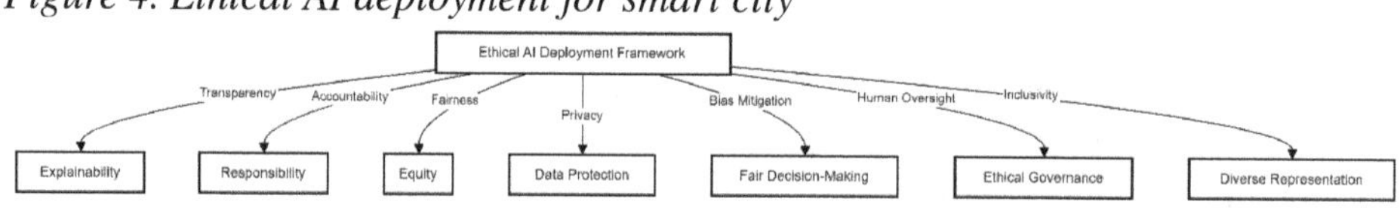


Smart cities include transparency, liability, less pain, privacy, reducing prejudice, human observation, and incorporation in the ethical AI deployment structure. Fair addresses partial parties, while privacy protects sensitive information. Bias Shaman measures identify and reduce bias in AI algorithms, while human inspection monitors and interferes with AI systems (Das et al., 2024; Kumar et al., 2023; Prasad et al., 2024).

- Justice and Equity: To guarantee justice and equity in AI algorithms and decision-making processes, eliminate prejudice, discrimination, and unjust treatment of people or groups, and provide algorithmic transparency, explanation, and liability processes.
- Privacy and Data Protection: In AI applications, respect users' privacy and data protection rights, including privacy, data anonymity strategy, and improvement technologies. Reduces the amount of data collected, stored, and shared to protect the user's privacy and maintain trust.
- Accountability and Transparency: Promote responsibility and transparency in AI's development and execution processes by recording decision criteria, datasets, and algorithms. To ensure that legal and moral criteria are met, provide tools for the effectiveness, results, and effects of AI systems, reporting, dating, and tracking.
- Human-Centered Design: AI technologies give top priority to user interaction techniques and man-centered design concepts during the AI development process, to ensure that the user's demand, values, and preferences are consistent. To promote incorporation and user acceptance, include various stakeholders in co-forming and assessing AI solutions, such as individuals, communities, and civil society groups (Revathi et al., 2024).

The establishment of a culture of innovation, integrity, and responsibility within the enterprise and in the AI ecosystem is a way to show moral leadership and governance. Create interdisciplinary moral review panels, advisory boards, or committees to direct and monitor moral AI practices and judgment. Smart cities can reduce high initial investment costs and guarantee responsible and sustainable deployment of AI technology for all residents by placing a supporting law, promoting public-private cooperation, and complying with moral AI deployment guidelines.

## FUTURE TRENDS AND OPPORTUNITIES

### Renewable Energy Management

Due to the AI application in renewable energy, the production, distribution, and consumption of energy in cities are changing. The main development and probability in this field is represented by machine learning, predictive analysis, and optimization algorithms, which facilitate better decision-making and effective use of renewable energy resources (Nishanth et al., 2023). Smart Grid Optimization: AI-powered smart grid optimization approaches improve stability, reliability, and elasticity of the AI-powered smart grid optimization approaches by integrating renewable energy sources, dynamically adjusting supply and demand, and improving the grid performance in real-time.

*Figure 5. Sustainable business models for smart cities using AI*

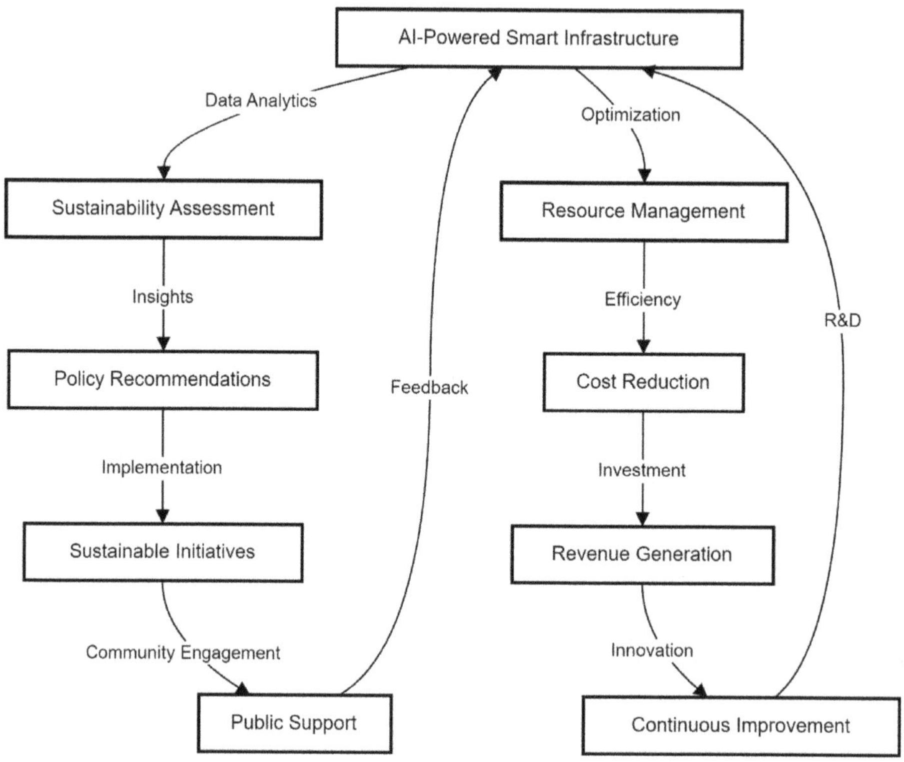


An AI-operated durable economic strategy for smart cities is shown in Figure 5. AI applications for sustainable management, resource management, policy instructions, durability evaluation, cost-cutting, generation, sustainable initiatives, community partnership, and continuous improvement are all covered. These components try to promote the resolution of economic expansion, innovation, and social and environmental issues in smart cities. Graph publishes how crucial AI is to reduce costs, make money from creative sustainable projects, and to include people in sustainable efforts (Nishanth et al., 2023).

- Energy forecasting: Artificial intelligence (AI)-Driving models increase the accuracy of the forecast for renewable energy zones, allowing utilities to change the supply and demand and reduce their dependence on fossil fuels.
- Management of Distributed Energy Resources (DERs): Artificial intelligence (AI) ENERGY makes it easier to integrate and operate energy resources distributed in the grid, including storage devices, wind turbines, and solar panels. AI systems maximize energy production, reduce grid congestion and cost, and ease the optimization of the installation and maintenance of delivered energy resources.
- Demand Response Programs: AI-run demand feedback programs encourage consumers to change their habits of using grid issues, market signals, and the availability of renewable energy sources. Estimates of energy usage, to improve load shading tactics and save energy, are provided by Artificial Intelligence (AI) algorithms, smart meters, Internet of Things (IoT) devices, and weather forecasts.

## Smart Buildings

AI-powered smart building techniques are transforming buildings, construction, and operations to increase stability, comfort, and energy efficiency. New possibilities for improving efficiency and reducing environmental impact are represented by the development of sensors, IoT devices, and building management systems (Sharma et al., 2024).

- Energy Management Systems: AI-powered energy management systems optimize lighting, HVAC, heating, and other building systems to reduce the use of energy and improve internal comfort and air quality.
- AI algorithms are used in maintenance to evaluate the influence indicators of sensor data and devices to plan for abnormalities, breakdown of prediction devices, and plan for maintenance functions. Forecast maintenance strategies reduce downtime, increase building asset longevity, and avoid expensive repairs.
- Occupant Behavior Analysis: To maximize building operations and scope usage, AI-operated business behavior analysis technologies try to track the level of business activities, preferences, and comfort. Building managers can improve user experience and productivity by customizing environmental conditions and services based on their understanding of professional requirements and preferences.
- Sustainable Design and Construction: To reduce environmental impact and enhance energy efficiency, AI-based design and construction techniques im-

prove building layouts, material selection, and energy-efficient features. AI systems direct design options, model performance indicators, and economically sensitive stability plans.

## Adaptive Urban Planning

Adaptive urban planning is undergoing a revolution because AI technologies, which allow cities to better allocate resources, make decisions, and enhance the quality of life for citizens, are able to collect, evaluate, and work with large amounts of data. Important development and trends (Boopathi, 2024a).

- Data-driven Decision-Making: To find trends, patterns, and insights that guide urban planning decisions, AI-powered data analytics systems collect and test various datasets, including demographic, mobility, environmental, and economic data.
- Urban organizers can predict the effects of intervention on various development scenes, laws, and urban systems and infrastructure using AI-powered simulation and modeling tools. Cities can evaluate the risks, try tricks, and make the best investment decisions through the modeling of potential futures.
- AI-based traffic management systems integrate real-time data from AI-based traffic management systems sensors, cameras, and mobile devices to reduce traffic flow, reduce congestion, and increase road safety. To reduce traffic jams and increase mobility, artificial intelligence (AI) systems examine traffic patterns, predict travel time, and suggest adaptive traffic control techniques.
- It makes it easier for the AI community to be involved in urban planning processes by providing insurable platforms, virtual reality simulation, and participatory decision-making tools. Cities can ensure that development plans reflect local needs, interests, and values by including locals in the planning process.

AI-based solutions for smart buildings, adaptive urban planning, and renewable energy are a huge possibility of realizing urban issues for smart cities and realizing the objectives of sustainable development. Cities can create a more integrated, ecologically durable environment by increasing urban elasticity, maximizing resource use, and improving energy efficiency (Naveeenkumar et al., 2024).

## CONCLUSION

In this chapter, the possibility of AI integration in smart city programs is investigated, in which special attention is paid to the rule, public-private partnerships, moral issues, and emerging trends. It is noted that AI has the ability to overcome urban problems, enhance the quality of life, and support sustainable development. To ensure privacy, security, and moral consideration in the proper deployment of AI Technol .G, governance and policy support. Government agencies, corporations, and other interested parties can work together on AI-operated Smart City initiatives through public-private partnerships. The framework for AI's moral deployment is crucial for AI's responsible, incorporated development and application when supporting privacy rights, human rights, and social values. Communitics, companics, and individuals gain confidence when justice, responsibility, and openness are given the first priority in AI systems.

Smart cities can increase their elasticity, durability, and efficiency by using AI in smart buildings, renewable energy zeal management, and adaptive urban design. Cities can create an ecologically durable environment by improving urban mobility, maximizing resource use, and increasing energy efficiency. For successful implementation, a comprehensive strategy associated with regime, policy, ethics, and technical innovation is required. Cities should use the revolutionary possibility of AI to create smart, elastic, and durable urban futures by accepting innovation, cooperation, and responsible stewards.

## REFERENCES


Ali, M. N., Senthil, T., Ilakkiya, T., Hasan, D. S., Ganapathy, N. B. S., & Boopathi, S. (2024). IoT's Role in Smart Manufacturing Transformation for Enhanced Household Product Quality. In *Advanced Applications in Osmotic Computing* (pp. 252–289). IGI Global.

Boopathi, S. (2024a). Advancements in Machine Learning and AI for Intelligent Systems in Drone Applications for Smart City Developments. In *Futuristic e-Governance Security With Deep Learning Applications* (pp. 15–45). IGI Global.

Boopathi, S. (2024b). Sustainable Development Using IoT and AI Techniques for Water Utilization in Agriculture. In *Sustainable Development in AI, Blockchain, and E-Governance Applications* (pp. 204–228). IGI Global.

Boopathi, S., & Khang, A. (2023). AI-Integrated Technology for a Secure and Ethical Healthcare Ecosystem. In *AI and IoT-Based Technologies for Precision Medicine* (pp. 36–59). IGI Global.

Das, P., Ramapraba, P., Seethalakshmi, K., Mary, M. A., Karthick, S., & Sampath, B. (2024). Sustainable Advanced Techniques for Enhancing the Image Process. In *Fostering Cross-Industry Sustainability With Intelligent Technologies* (pp. 350–374). IGI Global.

Dhanalakshmi, M., Tamilarasi, K., Saravanan, S., Sujatha, G., Boopathi, S., & Associates. (2024). Fog Computing-Based Framework and Solutions for Intelligent Systems: Enabling Autonomy in Vehicles. In *Computational Intelligence for Green Cloud Computing and Digital Waste Management* (pp. 330–356). IGI Global.

Dhanya, D., Kumar, S. S., Thilagavathy, A., Prasad, D., & Boopathi, S. (2023). Data Analytics and Artificial Intelligence in the Circular Economy: Case Studies. In *Intelligent Engineering Applications and Applied Sciences for Sustainability* (pp. 40–58). IGI Global.

Durairaj, M., Jayakumar, S., Karpagavalli, V., Maheswari, B. U., & Boopathi, S. (2023). Utilization of Digital Tools in the Indian Higher Education System During Health Crises. In *Multidisciplinary Approaches to Organizational Governance During Health Crises* (pp. 1–21). IGI Global.

Gopal, M., Lurdhumary, J., Bathrinath, S., Priya, A. P., Sarojwal, A., & Boopathi, S. (2024). Energy Harvesting and Smart Highways for Sustainable Transportation Infrastructure: Revolutionizing Roads Using Nanotechnology. In *Principles and Applications in Speed Sensing and Energy Harvesting for Smart Roads* (pp. 136–165). IGI Global. DOI: 10.4018/978-1-6684-9214-7.ch005

Hanumanthakari, S., Gift, M. M., Kanimozhi, K., Bhavani, M. D., Bamane, K. D., & Boopathi, S. (2023). Biomining Method to Extract Metal Components Using Computer-Printed Circuit Board E-Waste. In *Handbook of Research on Safe Disposal Methods of Municipal Solid Wastes for a Sustainable Environment* (pp. 123–141). IGI Global.

Hussain, Z., Babe, M., Saravanan, S., Srimathy, G., Roopa, H., & Boopathi, S. (2023). Optimizing Biomass-to-Biofuel Conversion: IoT and AI Integration for Enhanced Efficiency and Sustainability. In *Circular Economy Implementation for Sustainability in the Built Environment* (pp. 191–214). IGI Global.

Ingle, R. B., Swathi, S., Mahendran, G., Senthil, T., Muralidharan, N., & Boopathi, S. (2023). Sustainability and Optimization of Green and Lean Manufacturing Processes Using Machine Learning Techniques. In *Circular Economy Implementation for Sustainability in the Built Environment* (pp. 261–285). IGI Global.

Jebbar, W. A., Razzaq, R. H., & Tahayur, D. H. (2024). Blockchain and cryptography framework of e-apps with big data. *Journal of Education for Pure Science, 14*(3).

Koshariya, A. K., Kalaiyarasi, D., Jovith, A. A., Sivakami, T., Hasan, D. S., & Boopathi, S. (2023). AI-Enabled IoT and WSN-Integrated Smart Agriculture System. In *Artificial Intelligence Tools and Technologies for Smart Farming and Agriculture Practices* (pp. 200–218). IGI Global.

Koshariya, A. K., Khatoon, S., Marathe, A. M., Suba, G. M., Baral, D., & Boopathi, S. (2023). Agricultural Waste Management Systems Using Artificial Intelligence Techniques. In *AI-Enabled Social Robotics in Human Care Services* (pp. 236–258). IGI Global.

Kumar, M., Kumar, K., Sasikala, P., Sampath, B., Gopi, B., & Sundaram, S. (2023). Sustainable Green Energy Generation From Waste Water: IoT and ML Integration. In *Sustainable Science and Intelligent Technologies for Societal Development* (pp. 440–463). IGI Global.

Maguluri, L. P., Ananth, J., Hariram, S., Geetha, C., Bhaskar, A., & Boopathi, S. (2023). Smart Vehicle-Emissions Monitoring System Using Internet of Things (IoT). In *Handbook of Research on Safe Disposal Methods of Municipal Solid Wastes for a Sustainable Environment* (pp. 191–211). IGI Global.

Maguluri, L. P., Arularasan, A., & Boopathi, S. (2023). Assessing Security Concerns for AI-Based Drones in Smart Cities. In *Effective AI, Blockchain, and E-Governance Applications for Knowledge Discovery and Management* (pp. 27–47). IGI Global.

Malathi, J., Kusha, K., Isaac, S., Ramesh, A., Rajendiran, M., & Boopathi, S. (2024). IoT-Enabled Remote Patient Monitoring for Chronic Disease Management and Cost Savings: Transforming Healthcare. In *Advances in Explainable AI Applications for Smart Cities* (pp. 371–388). IGI Global.

Naveeenkumar, N., Rallapalli, S., Sasikala, K., Priya, P. V., Husain, J., & Boopathi, S. (2024). Enhancing Consumer Behavior and Experience Through AI-Driven Insights Optimization. In *AI Impacts in Digital Consumer Behavior* (pp. 1–35). IGI Global.

Nishanth, J., Deshmukh, M. A., Kushwah, R., Kushwaha, K. K., Balaji, S., & Sampath, B. (2023). Particle Swarm Optimization of Hybrid Renewable Energy Systems. In *Intelligent Engineering Applications and Applied Sciences for Sustainability* (pp. 291–308). IGI Global.

Pachiappan, K., Anitha, K., Pitchai, R., Sangeetha, S., Satyanarayana, T., & Boopathi, S. (2024). Intelligent Machines, IoT, and AI in Revolutionizing Agriculture for Water Processing. In *Handbook of Research on AI and ML for Intelligent Machines and Systems* (pp. 374–399). IGI Global.

Periasamy, J. K., Subhashini, S., Mutharasu, M., Revathi, M., Ajitha, P., & Boopathi, S. (2024). Synergizing Federated Learning and In-Memory Computing: An Experimental Approach for Drone Integration. In *Developments Towards Next Generation Intelligent Systems for Sustainable Development* (pp. 89–123). IGI Global. DOI: 10.4018/979-8-3693-5643-2.ch004

Prasad, M. S. C., Dhanalakshmi, M., Mohan, M., Somasundaram, B., Valarmathi, R., & Boopathi, S. (2024). Machine Learning-Integrated Sustainable Engineering and Energy Systems: Innovations at the Nexus. In *Harnessing High-Performance Computing and AI for Environmental Sustainability* (pp. 74–98). IGI Global. DOI: 10.4018/979-8-3693-1794-5.ch004

Rahamathunnisa, U., Sudhakar, K., Padhi, S., Bhattacharya, S., Shashibhushan, G., & Boopathi, S. (2024). Sustainable Energy Generation From Waste Water: IoT Integrated Technologies. In *Adoption and Use of Technology Tools and Services by Economically Disadvantaged Communities: Implications for Growth and Sustainability* (pp. 225–256). IGI Global.

Rebecca, B., Kumar, K. P. M., Padmini, S., Srivastava, B. K., Halder, S., & Boopathi, S. (2024). Convergence of Data Science-AI-Green Chemistry-Affordable Medicine: Transforming Drug Discovery. In *Handbook of Research on AI and ML for Intelligent Machines and Systems* (pp. 348–373). IGI Global.

Revathi, S., Babu, M., Rajkumar, N., Meti, V. K. V., Kandavalli, S. R., & Boopathi, S. (2024). Unleashing the Future Potential of 4D Printing: Exploring Applications in Wearable Technology, Robotics, Energy, Transportation, and Fashion. In *Human-Centered Approaches in Industry 5.0: Human-Machine Interaction, Virtual Reality Training, and Customer Sentiment Analysis* (pp. 131–153). IGI Global.

S., B. (2024). Advancements in Optimizing Smart Energy Systems Through Smart Grid Integration, Machine Learning, and IoT. In *Advances in Environmental Engineering and Green Technologies* (pp. 33–61). IGI Global. DOI: 10.4018/979-8-3693-0492-1.ch002

Sengeni, D., Padmapriya, G., Imambi, S. S., Suganthi, D., Suri, A., & Boopathi, S. (2023). Biomedical waste handling method using artificial intelligence techniques. In *Handbook of Research on Safe Disposal Methods of Municipal Solid Wastes for a Sustainable Environment* (pp. 306–323). IGI Global.

Sharma, M., Sharma, M., Sharma, N., & Boopathi, S. (2024). Building Sustainable Smart Cities Through Cloud and Intelligent Parking System. In *Handbook of Research on AI and ML for Intelligent Machines and Systems* (pp. 195–222). IGI Global.

Sonia, R., Gupta, N., Manikandan, K., Hemalatha, R., Kumar, M. J., & Boopathi, S. (2024). Strengthening Security, Privacy, and Trust in Artificial Intelligence Drones for Smart Cities. In *Analyzing and Mitigating Security Risks in Cloud Computing* (pp. 214–242). IGI Global.

Sundar, R., Srikaanth, P. B., Naik, D. A., Murugan, V. P., Karumudi, M., & Boopathi, S. (2024). Achieving Balance Between Innovation and Security in the Cloud With Artificial Intelligence of Things: Semantic Web Control Models. In *Advances in Web Technologies and Engineering* (pp. 1–26). IGI Global. DOI: 10.4018/979-8-3693-1487-6.ch001

Sundaramoorthy, K., Singh, A., Sumathy, G., Maheshwari, A., Arunarani, A., & Boopathi, S. (2024). A Study on AI and Blockchain-Powered Smart Parking Models for Urban Mobility. In *Handbook of Research on AI and ML for Intelligent Machines and Systems* (pp. 223–250). IGI Global.

Tahayur, D. H., Jebbar, W. A., & Razzaq, R. H. (2024). Dependable Concealing Algorithm of E-apps Repositories Combined with a Robust Blockchain Approach. *Advanced Research on Information Systems Security*, *4*(2), 32–56.

Tirlangi, S., Teotia, S., Padmapriya, G., Senthil Kumar, S., Dhotre, S., & Boopathi, S. (2024). Cloud Computing and Machine Learning in the Green Power Sector: Data Management and Analysis for Sustainable Energy. In *Developments Towards Next Generation Intelligent Systems for Sustainable Development* (pp. 148–179). IGI Global. DOI: 10.4018/979-8-3693-5643-2.ch006

Upadhyaya, A. N., Saqib, A., Devi, J. V., Rallapalli, S., Sudha, S., & Boopathi, S. (2024). Implementation of the Internet of Things (IoT) in Remote Healthcare. In *Advances in Medical Technologies and Clinical Practice* (pp. 104–124). IGI Global. DOI: 10.4018/979-8-3693-1934-5.ch006

Venkateswaran, N., Kiran Kumar, K., Maheswari, K., Kumar Reddy, R. V., & Boopathi, S. (2024). Optimizing IoT Data Aggregation: Hybrid Firefly-Artificial Bee Colony Algorithm for Enhanced Efficiency in Agriculture. *AGRIS On-Line Papers in Economics and Informatics*, *16*(1), 117–130. DOI: 10.7160/aol.2024.160110

Vijaya Lakshmi, V., Mishra, M., Kushwah, J. S., Shajahan, U. S., Mohanasundari, M., & Boopathi, S. (2024). Circular Economy Digital Practices for Ethical Dimensions and Policies for Digital Waste Management. In *Harnessing High-Performance Computing and AI for Environmental Sustainability* (pp. 166–193). IGI Global., DOI: 10.4018/979-8-3693-1794-5.ch008

Zekrifa, D. M. S., Kulkarni, M., Bhagyalakshmi, A., Devireddy, N., Gupta, S., & Boopathi, S. (2023). Integrating Machine Learning and AI for Improved Hydrological Modeling and Water Resource Management. In *Artificial Intelligence Applications in Water Treatment and Water Resource Management* (pp. 46–70). IGI Global.

Chapter 3

# Monitoring Vehicle Emissions Through Intelligent Transportation Systems for Smart City Development: Emission-Aware Mobility

**Asha Bharathi S.**
https://orcid.org/0000-0002-3941-7749
*Department of Electronics and Communication Engineering, Jyothy Institute of Technology, Bengaluru, India*

**Jayantkumar A. Rathod**
*Department of Computer Science and Engineering, Vidyavardhaka College of Engineering, Mysuru, India*

**S. Thenmozhi**
https://orcid.org/0000-0001-6681-3897
*Department of Civil Engineering, KCG College of Technology, Chennai, India*

**Sachin Upadhye**
https://orcid.org/0000-0001-7255-1838
*Department of Computer Science and Applications, Ramdeobaba University, Nagpur, India*

**S. Kiruba**
*Department of Physics, St.Joseph's College of Engineering, Chennai, India*

**M. Kumar**
https://orcid.org/0009-0006-2989-9883
*SRM University, India*

## ABSTRACT

*This chapter explores the integration of vehicle emission monitoring within intelligent transport systems (ITS) to support the development of a permanent smart city.*

DOI: 10.4018/979-8-3373-8133-6.ch003

*The real-time data enables the continuous monitoring and control of vehicles by taking advantage of data analytics, IoT sensors, and advanced traffic management technologies. Systems that improve air quality, urban planning, and environmentally friendly mobility solutions have been explored in this chapter. Case studies and emerging innovations are presented to highlight practical implementation and challenges. The future urban ecosystems are emphasized as data-driven policy-making, civil engagement, cross-sector cooperation, and status-comprehensive awareness.*

## INTRODUCTION

Due to the rapid urbanization, the density of the population in the metropolitan areas, the demand for transportation, and environmental concerns have led to unprecedented growth. The most challenging issue facing modern cities is the pollution from vehicles, which contributes significantly to air quality, greenhouse gas emissions, and public health issues. In this regard, the concept of smart cities emerged as a holistic and technically advanced approach to urban planning and management. Smart cities provide digital infrastructure, data analytics, and intelligent systems to enhance urban services, improve the quality of life, and ensure environmental stability. In this composition, intelligent transport systems (ITS) play a major role in the challenges related to transportation, especially in the monitoring and prevention of vehicle emissions (Hernafi et al., 2016).

ITS refers to the integration of information and communication technologies in transportation infrastructure and vehicles, enabling the management of real-time data storage, analysis, and transportation networks. Its evolution has shifted to a dynamic, responsive, and interconnected mobility system from traditional traffic management. One of its crucial programs in the context of smart cities is monitoring the emission of vehicles, providing accurate, real-time insights into pollution levels and traffic-induced environmental influence to urban organizers, environmental agencies, and policymakers. It refers to the integration of information and communication technologies in transportation structures and vehicles, enabling real-time data storage, analysis, and transportation network management (Balasubramaniam et al., 2017). Its evolution has changed into an example of the dynamic, feedback, and interconnected mobility system from traditional traffic management. In terms of smart cities, monitoring the emissions of one of its critical programs, providing accurate, real-time insights and traffic-induced environmental influence to urban organizers, environmental agencies, and policy makers. ITS deployment for emissions monitoring contains several components: air quality sensors on the side of the road that receive pollutant concentrations; In-vehicle telematics systems that monitor engine performance and exhaust output; And the centralized traffic management platform that analyzes data and provides active insights (Turner & Uludag, 2017). Together, these components form an intelligent ecosystem that enables ITS to find high-emissions zones, identify pollutant vehicles, reduce passive time, and inform regulatory actions. Moreover, the integration of geographical information systems (GIS) allows the spatial analysis of emissions of hotspots, facilitates targeted intervention, such as re-operating traffic, applying low-emergency zones, or planning for green infrastructure.

Smart cities are increasingly adopting their solutions to emission-awareness to combine global durability goals, including the United Nations Sustainable Development Goals (SDGs) and national climate action schemes. Cities like Singapore, London, and Amsterdam have applied advanced traffic and environmental monitoring systems that use their technologies to control traffic, reduce carbon footprints, and promote transport options. These systems not only contribute to environmental objectives, but also increase urban lifestyle by reducing congestion, improving travel efficiency, and supporting active mobility modes such as cycling and walking (Meneguette et al., 2018). These components create an intelligent ecosystem that enables TI PTMA to find high-emission zones, identify pollutant vehicles, reduce passive time, and inform regulatory actions. Moreover, the integration of geographical information systems (GIS) allows the spatial analysis of the emission of hotspots, facilitating targeted intervention, such as re-operating traffic, applying low-emergency zones, or a plan for green infrastructure. Moreover, public engagement is crucial for the success of its emission control measures. Citizens should be informed about the environmental influence of their transport choices and encouraged to adopt cleaner travel modes such as electric vehicles (EVs), public transport, or carpooling (Telang et al., 2020). Despite ITS promising possibility under the emission supervision, many challenges remain unchanged. Technical challenges include the need for high-precision sensors, reliable communication networks, and scalable data infrastructure. Institutional challenges include organizing multiple stakeholders, funding for infrastructure upgrades, and establishing a regulatory framework for data privacy and moral use. In addition, in order to ensure the inclusion and durable deployment of its solutions, social-political factors such as public acceptance, equity consideration, and behavioral resistance must be considered (Chavhan et al., 2022).

Innovations in the relevant areas are ready to enhance its capabilities for its emissions monitoring. The integration of edge computing reduces the delay in data processing and can enable real-time decisions at the source. Blockchain technology offers transparent and tamper-proof data management systems that can improve trust and liability in emission reporting (Atiyah & Razzaq, 2024; Duaa, 2025). Artificial intelligence can support predictive analyses, enabling active traffic and environmental management based on historical accuracy and contextual data. Moreover, electric and autonomous vehicle techniques can pave the way for zero-emission, intelligent mobility ecosystems in smart cities of the future (Musa et al., 2023). In conclusion, monitoring the emission of a vehicle by intelligent transport systems represents a crucial step towards achieving a durable, elastic, and living urban environment. By using real-time data, digital connectivity, and the power of intelligent infrastructure, cities can move beyond reactive environmental management towards active, adaptive, and unified urban planning (Elassy et al., 2024; Sun et al., 2023). As the global focus on climate change and air quality intensifies, it will be important for the strategic implementation of emissions inspection, shaping the upcoming generation of smart cities, which prioritize both technical innovation and environmental care. Subsequent sections of this chapter will pay attention to the architecture of its emissions, review successful case studies, examine implementation challenges, and propose policy and design recommendations for future smart urban development.

### Objectives

This chapter aims to explore the role of intelligent transport systems (ITS) in the monitoring and management of vehicle emissions in the smart city framework. It tries to analyze technical components, data integration methods, and implementation strategies that enable real-time emission tracking. Objectives include evaluating its environmental and mobility benefits, identifying challenges and limits in deployment, and case teaching of successful implementation. In addition, in the chapter, strategic recommendations have been proposed to integrate them into durable urban planning and policy formation.

## BACKGROUND: INTELLIGENT TRANSPORTATION SYSTEMS

Intelligent Transportation Systems (ITS) represent the conversion of digital technology, communication infrastructure, and data-based intelligence, as shown in Figure 1. Designed to enhance the efficiency, safety, and durability of urban mobility, it is the basic component of smart cities worldwide. As cities are struggling with the inability of crowds, pollution, and mobility, the transport systems offer a strategic, system-level approach to the change of how they work and interact with widespread urban ecosystems (Lu & Wang, 2024).

*Figure 1. Principles of intelligent transportation systems*

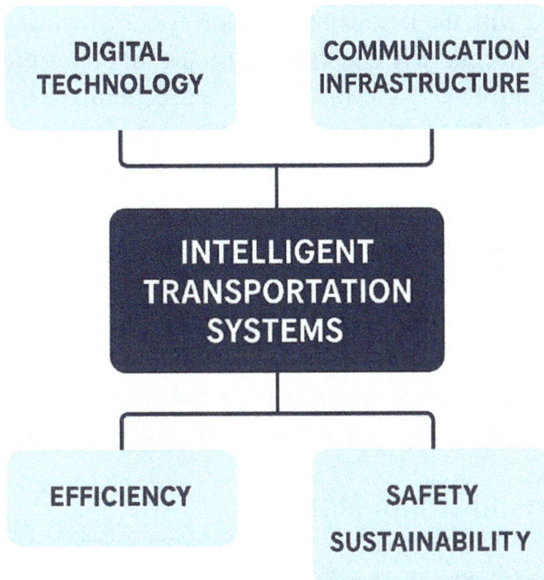


## Key Technologies Enabling ITS

ITS depends on the suite of advanced technologies that act consistently to collect, analyze, and respond to transport data in real-time (Dui et al., 2024). Key enabling technologies include:

Internet of Things (IoT) and GPS techniques are crucial for real-time data storage and management of vehicles. IoT devices collect data on vehicle speed, road status, and emissions, while GPS enables specific tracking and location-based services. Wireless communication facilitates instant data exchange between networks, such as 5G and DSRC, real-time updates, and vehicles for Automation, road infrastructure, and central control systems. AI and ML algorithms process large datasets to identify traffic patterns, to predict behavior, to plan over traffic light sequences, and to help make autonomous decisions in traffic management. GIS integrates spatial data for real-time mapping and analysis, identifying traffic hotspots and infrastructure requirements. Cloud and Edge computing enable scalable data processing and local response, creating a technical backbone of intelligent transportation systems (ITS).

## Evolution and Global Trends

It has developed with the first pay generation system, focusing on stable traffic management tools. Second pay generation systems introduced real-time monitoring and adaptive control using sensors, CCTV, and centralized traffic management centers (Almalki et al., 2023). Contemporary ITS includes integrated multi-model systems, environmental surveillance, connected and autonomous vehicles, and forecast traffic analytics. Global deployment is focusing on smart city integration, durability attention, public-private partnerships, and policy and regulation configuration. Cities are integrating ITS into smart city strategies, reducing carbon emissions, promoting electric mobility, and supporting low-emission zones. Governments are especially collaborating with technical companies to build and manage their structure in the emerging economy. The global market is expected to increase significantly due to demand for urban mobility, emission control, and digital infrastructure investments.

## ITS Applications in Urban Mobility

It is transforming urban dynamics into a wide range of spreading in private, public, and commercial transport modes (Almalki et al., 2023; Zhao et al., 2022).

ITS increases traffic management by adaptive signals, dynamic lane control, and congestion prices, improving traffic flow. It also has excellent public transport through real-time tracking, integrated ticketing systems, and schedule optimization, enabling rapid accident investigation and emergency response. Smart parking systems offer real-time information on space availability and digital payment options, reducing circling time and emissions. ITS integrates with emission sensors to track pollution levels and guide policy actions. It supports electric and autonomous vehicles, charging coordination, and vehicle-to-grid integration. By delivering data-driven insights and real-time control, ITS enhances mobility experiences while supporting goals such as reduced emissions, increased safety, and equitable transportation access. As urban challenges intensify, ITS will remain essential in enabling intelligent, resilient, and sustainable transportation systems in smart cities (Zhao et al., 2022).

Smart parking systems provide real-time information on the availability of space and digital payment options, which reduces dizziness time and emissions. It is integrated with an emission sensor to make the level of pollution track and guide policy actions. It supports electric and autonomous vehicles, charging coordination, and vehicle-to-grid integration. By delivering data-based insights and real-time control, ITS increases the experiences of mobility while reducing emissions, supporting targets such as reduced emissions, increased safety, and similar transport access. As urban challenges intensify, ITS will be necessary to enable intelligent, elastic, and durable transport systems in smart cities.

## VEHICLE EMISSIONS AND THEIR URBAN IMPACT

Urban atmosphere is experiencing the increasing pressure of the increasing number of vehicles on the roads, a trend that contributes to the quality of direct air and environmental degeneration. Vehicle emissions are one of the primary sources of urban air pollution, especially in Figure 2, according to congestion and high traffic areas. The emissions include various harmful pollutants, which are emitted from gasoline / diesel-powered internal combustion engines, which have environmental and health impacts. Effective management and reducing vehicle emissions are therefore central to the development of durable and smart cities (G. Zhang et al., 2024). To consider this issue strategically, it is important to understand the emerging requirement for real-time emission tracking through advanced systems, such as vehicle pollutants, their effects, traditional monitoring approach deficiencies, and intelligent transportation systems.

*Figure 2. Vehicle emissions and their urban impact*

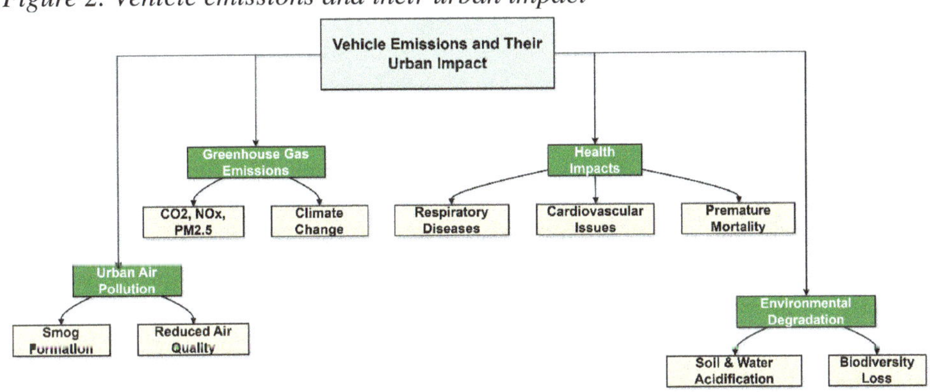


### Types of Vehicular Pollutants

Vehicle emissions are made up of many air pollutants, contributing to environmental damage and risks to human health. The most critical pollutants include carbon monoxide, nitrogen oxides (NOx), hydrocarbons, particulate meters, and carbon dioxide. Carbon monoxide is a colorless, odorless gas that is produced by the incomplete combustion of fuel and is inhaled. They contribute to ground-level ozone formation and acid rain and are harmful to respiratory systems. Hydrocarbons, including unstable organic compounds, react with nitrogen Ox butter in the presence of sunlight to form fog and ozone, which is dangerous to both the environment and public health. Particulate matter, especially PM 2.5 (smaller particles than 2.5 microns), poses a serious health risk as it can penetrate the Deep Bund in the lungs and also enter the bloodstream (Alam et al., 2024). Finally, carbon dioxide, although non-toxic at the typical atmospheric level, is a greenhouse gas that contributes significantly to global warming. Diesel engines, in particular, nitrogen emit in the form of ox butcher and particle substances, making them significant concerns in the operation of urban air quality.

## Environmental and Health Implications

The results of the vehicle emissions are extensive and tend to deeply affect both ecosystems and public health. From an environmental point of view, this emission reduces the quality of the air, contributes to the formation of fog, and accelerates climate change. As a result of sulfur dioxide emissions, the testimony of acid leads to the acidification of the soil and water bodies, damaging the life of the plant and aquatic organisms. Ground-level ozone, formed by the interaction of sunlight with NOX, damages crops and forests and is a major component of urban smoking (G. Zhang et al., 2024).

The effects of health are the same, if not more, worrying. Long-term exposure to vehicle-related pollutants is linked to respiratory diseases such as asthma, bronchitis, and chronic obstructive pulmonary disease. Fine particulate matter, especially PM 2.5, is associated with cardiovascular issues, stroke, and premature mortality. Children, the elderly, and those with pre-existing conditions are especially susceptible. The World Health Organization has shown that millions of premature deaths are attributed to air pollution globally, and urban vehicle emissions are a significant contributor. Moreover, the accumulated exposure to these pollutants, even at the lowest level, can have a long-term effect on lung development, immune function, and overall quality of life.

## Limitations of Traditional Monitoring Methods

Traditional approaches to monitoring vehicle emissions usually depend on the surrounding air quality monitoring stations and periodic vehicle inspections. While these methods provide valuable data, they suffer from many limitations that reduce their effectiveness in the operation of urban emissions. The quality of the air is fixed at the location of the monitoring stations and often at a distance, leading to a limited spatial resolution. As a result, they will not be able to get local pollution incidents due to traffic congestion, lazy vehicles, or road work. Moreover, these stations usually measure the level of overall pollution, attributing specific sources of emissions, such as high-emitting vehicles or crowded intersections (Bakirci, 2024).

Vehicle Inspector Programs, which involve testing emissions at service centers or government facilities, are conditioned infrequently and provide only a snapshot of a vehicle's email profile. These programs may miss the state of real-world driving and fail to identify the deterioration between observations. In addition, due to the limits, corruption, or lack of public compliance, the implementation of emission standards in low and middle-income countries is often limited. As urbanization continues and traffic volume increases, these traditional monitoring systems are unable to provide granular, real-time data needed for targeted interventions and policy decisions.

## The Need for Real-Time Monitoring

Given the dynamic and complex nature of urban traffic and emissions, there is a crucial need for real-time emissions monitoring systems that can provide continuous, specific, and source-specific data. Real-time monitoring allows immediate emission spikes, identification of high-emission vehicles, and assessment of traffic rules and the effectiveness of environmental policies. Intelligent Transportation Systems (ITS) give a comprehensive solution to this requirement by integrating IoT sensors, in-vehicle diagnostics, GPS tracking, and wireless communications into a unified monitoring network (G. Zhang et al., 2024). Through ITS, cities can deploy air quality sensors and traffic cameras on the side of the road that feed real-time data to the central analytics platform. These systems can identify emissions hotspots, predict pollution trends on the basis of traffic flow, and warn both officials and the public. In addition, ITS enables dynamic traffic management strategies such as adaptive signal control, congestion pricing, and rearranging vehicles to help reduce emissions from all idling and stop-start driving behavior. Moreover, the integration of emission data with GIS platforms allows spatial analysis and visualization, facilitating more informed urban planning and resource allocation.

Real-time monitoring also supports behavioral change by increasing awareness and responsibility. When passengers receive feedback about their driving behavior or the influence of a vehicle, they are likely to adopt environmental systems such as idling, regular vehicle maintenance, or migrating to cleaner modes of transportation. At the policy level, real-time data is empowered to respond to regulatory agencies, and the creation of incentives for evidence-based steps, such as low-emitting zones, high-pollution days, and the adoption of electric vehicles. Hence, Vehicle emissions are an important challenge for urban durability and public health, which requires advanced and active monitoring solutions. Traditional methods are limited in addressing the spatial and temporal change of emissions in a complex urban environment. The integration of real-time emissions monitoring by intelligent transport systems presents a transformative step in manifesting urban air quality, reducing environmental risks, and enhancing the overall well-being of the city residents. As cities develop in smart ecosystems, emission-intensive mobility will be the main pillar of sustainable development strategies.

*Figure 3. Integrating emission monitoring into ITS frameworks*

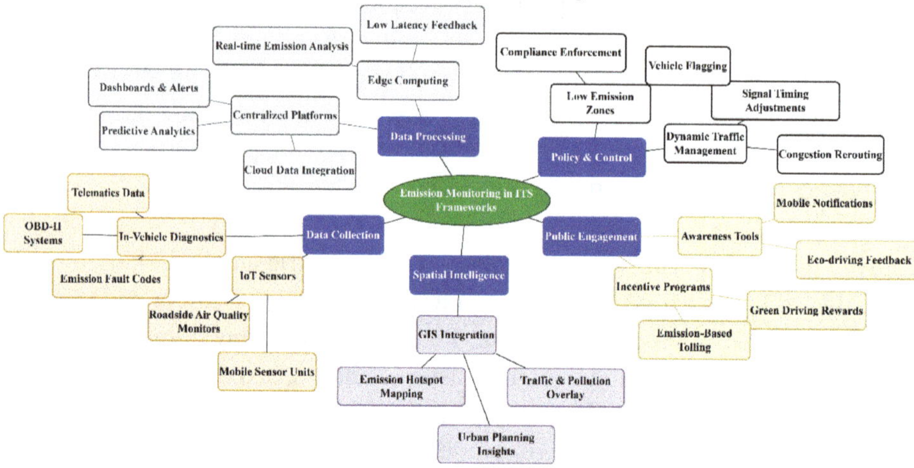


## INTEGRATING EMISSION MONITORING INTO ITS FRAMEWORKS

Integration of emission inspection in intelligent transport systems (ITS) framework, as shown in Figure 3, cities represent significant progress in how cities can manage environmental stability through data-based mobility solutions. Traditional air quality monitoring systems lack the necessary granularity and response needed to effectively address the dynamic nature of urban traffic emissions. By embedding emission monitoring capabilities directly in the ITS architecture, cities can develop real-time, scalable, and intelligent infrastructure to identify, analyze, and reduce vehicle pollution. This integration depends on the suite of mutually relevant technologies and methods, including IoT sensors, in-vehicle diagnostics, GIS, and centrally-based data analytics platforms operating to create a response and predictive emission management ecosystem (Hernafi et al., 2016; G. Zhang et al., 2024).

## IoT Sensors and Data Collection

At the root of real-time emissions monitoring is the IoT, which enables the deployment of sensors connected to each other in the urban landscape. This sensor is capable of obtaining pollutants such as carbon monoxide (CO), nitrogen oxide (NOX), sulfur dioxide (SO2), and particulate matter (PM 2.5 and PM10), embedded in urban structures, and units on the side of the road, traffic lights. Advanced multi-parameter air quality sensors use electrochemical, optical, and laser-based investigation methods to ensure high accuracy and response (Aderibigbe & Gumbo, 2024; G. Zhang et al., 2024).

Beyond stable sensors, mobile sensors mounted on public transport, municipal fleet, or drones provide extensive spatial coverage and enable dynamic monitoring in various traffic corridors and emission zones. These sensors communicate with central control units through wireless protocols such as LTE, 5G, ensuring close-to-embrace of environmental data. The real-time nature of the IoT-based monitoring allows city officials to find pollution spikes, evaluate the influence of traffic congestion, and adjust the traffic signal or re-operate vehicles away from critical areas.

## In-Vehicle Diagnostics and Telematics

Another important component of the emission-awareness is the integration of the carrying diagnostics and telematics systems. Modern vehicles, especially OBD-II (on-board diagnostics), are equipped with sensors, compatible with standards that monitor engine performance, fuel efficiency, and emission levels. These systems can detect faulty emissions control components - such as catalyst converters or exhaust gas recirculation valves - and transmit fault codes to central monitoring systems (Bakirci, 2024; Louati et al., 2024). The combination of telematics units, GPS, cellular connectivity, and onboard computing enables real-time tracking of individual vehicles and their environmental influence. Through the telematics platform, fleet tors can be successful. This granular layer of monitoring allows the identification of high-pollutant vehicles, the execution of emission standards, and the implementation of preventive maintenance programs. Moreover, vessels with excessive emissions can be automatically flagged, enabling targets in targeted observations or low-emission zones. The integration of in-vehicle diagnostics promotes eco-driving behaviors not only through regulatory compliance but also through feedback methods and incentive programs in private and commercial drivers.

## GIS and Spatial Emission Mapping

Geographical information systems (GIS) play a crucial role in translating raw emission data into enabling spatial intelligence. By combining IoT sensors and vehicle location-GED pollution data, GIS enhances widespread emission hotspot mapping, connecting geographical facilities such as road networks, land use patterns, and population density. Through spatial analyzes, city organizers and environmental officials can imagine the distribution of emissions at various urban areas and time intervals. For example, GIS mapping may announce that the experience of a particular intersection increases the repetitive NOX during the peak hours, or that the nearest bus depot is affected by excessive PM levels in nearby areas. These insights are important for establishing green buffers, presenting traffic quiet measures, or applying any thought policies (Aderibigbe & Gumbo, 2024). GIS also supports scenario modeling, allowing organizers to imitate the environmental influence of future structural development, policy changes, or changes in traffic patterns. When real-time is integrated with its platforms, GIS can trigger adaptive reactions such as algorithms that reduce emissions in sensitive areas, thus organizing transportation operations with urban stability targets.

## Centralized Data Management and Analytics

All data collected by IoT sensors, vehicle diagnostics, and GIS tools must be efficiently administered and analyzed to achieve meaningful insights. The Centralized Data Management Platform, often hosted in a cloud environment, provides the calculation power and scalability required to handle the wider, racial datasets produced in the transport network. Advanced analytics techniques, including machine learning, pattern validation, and forecast modeling, are used to process these data and highlight trends, inconsistencies, and correlations. For example, predictive models can estimate the level of future emissions based on weather forecasts, traffic density, and historical data, enabling active decision-making. Incompatible spikes in pollutant layers, implementation teams to remove congestion, or automatic adjustments in signal time can stimulate real-time alerts (Aderibigbe & Gumbo, 2024; Bakirci, 2024).

Moreover, this platform supports dashboards and visualization tools for policymakers and the people. Decisions can use these insights to evaluate the effectiveness of the rules, such as the impact of the newly introduced congestion pricing plan on emissions. Public-facing portals and mobile applications can increase transparency and engagement by providing instructions for real-time air quality updates, emission scores for specialized routes, or environmental travel options. The integration of emissions monitoring in it also paves the way for a data-based regime.

By combining emission data with traffic, meteorological, and socio-economic data, cities can formulate widespread mobility and climate action plans that are based on response and evidence. Hence, Integration of emissions in intelligent transport systems addresses environmental stability and public health. By combining IoT sensors, in-vehicle diagnostics, GIS-based mapping, and centralized analytics, it provides tools for monitoring, operating, and reducing vehicle emissions in real time. This layered approach not only improves air quality and transport efficiency but also emphasizes the cooperation of city administrators, urban organizers, and citizens to achieve a cleaner and smarter urban future. As it continues, its role in the environmental regime will become increasingly important, especially in achieving long-term goals related to climate elasticity and living.

## CASE STUDIES AND GLOBAL BEST PRACTICES

The successful integration of intelligent transport systems (ITSs) for vehicle emissions monitoring and durable urban mobility can be seen in some global cities that have initiated an innovative strategy in line with their unique challenges. This case study explains that smart mobility and emission control can be combined to enhance urban lifestyle, reduce environmental impact, and increase data-based regimes. By examining cities such as Singapore, London, Amsterdam, and India's emerging smart cities, we can identify the scalable models, critical success factors, and policy insights applicable to urban centers around the world (Sun et al., 2023; S. Zhang et al., 2018).

Singapore is a global benchmark for smart mobility and air quality management through its effective deployment. With limited land space and high vehicle population density, Singapore has strategically applied an integrated transport management ecosystem that emphasizes real-time data, congestion control, and environmental monitoring. In order to manipulate traffic current and discourage vehicle consumption during peak hours, the advanced electronic road pricing (ERP) system uses a network of gantries equipped with city-state sensors and wireless communication technologies. The ERP rate is adjusted in real-time depending on the layers of the crowd, encouraging the drivers to change the way, to switch to a different travel time or public transport. In addition, Singapore's Green Men+ System and Intelligent Traffic Signal Control increase mobility for pedestrians and reduce the sluggishness of unnecessary vehicles, which contributes to lower emissions. The Land Transport Authority (LTA) also arranges a fleet management system for public buses, enabling the optimization, thereby reducing fuel efficiency and emissions. To monitor air quality, the National Environment Agency (NEA) integrates data from the air quality sensor into the centralized platform, enabling response policy measures such as emission-based vehicle taxes and retirement of high-pollutant vehicles. Singapore's success lies in its integrated policy structure, strong public transport infrastructure, and technical innovation in the regime.

London presents an attractive case for congestion management and its use for the implementation of low-emission zones. The charge of the London crowd presented was one of the first large-scale urban pricing plans designed to reduce traffic volume and pollution in the city center. The system, automatic number plate recognition (ANPR), is monitored by the camera, charging vehicles entering the designated zone during peak hours. In recent years, this has evolved in the Ultra Low Emission Zone (ULEZ) and Low Emission Zone (LEZ) policies, where vehicles should meet strict emission standards or pay daily charges (Aderibigbe & Gumbo, 2024). These steps are made by its competent implementation structure, including a vehicle database attached to the air quality sensor and emission compliance records on the side of the road. Transport for London (TFL) also benefits from real-time traffic monitoring, smart traffic lights, and predictive analytics to manage traffic flow and reduce environmental impact. TFL Accordingly, the introduction of ULEZ was reduced by 44% at the end of the road. London's integrated platform supports data sharing in departments and promotes behavioral shifts through digital tools that inform citizens about air quality, transportation options, and environmental influence, making it a strong example of emission-vigilant urban regime.

Amsterdam, known for its progressive durability agenda, effectively uses to promote green mobility. By combining smart transportation systems with active and shared mobility strategies, the city emphasizes multi-model integration. Amsterdam has deployed its operated traffic management systems that prefer bicycles and public transportation, automatically adjusting signal time to reduce the congestion of vehicles and prefer trams and buses. The city also uses real-time parking guidance systems, which steer the drivers towards parking spaces and discourage unnecessary cruising, which often contributes to urban emissions. The air quality sensor is strategically placed on the high-traffic corridor and is integrated with GIS-based dashboards to visualize the level of pollution and support targeted interventions. In addition, Amsterdam's public transport fleet uses more and more electric and hybrid buses, coordinating the fleet telematics for road efficiency and tracking of energy consumption. The city's smart mobility program, cooperation between municipalities, private tech companies, and research institutes, continues to pilot innovations such as app-based incentives for geofencing for emissions-sensitive zones, and application-based incentives for low-carbon travel behavior. Amsterdam's success is in line with its people-centered planning approach, effective use of real-time data, and its wide climate goals.

In India, many cities are emerging as smart mobility leaders by adopting their structure to face two challenges of traffic congestion and air pollution. For example, a consolidated traffic management system (ITMS) depicting adaptive traffic signals, CCTV surveillance, and automatic number plate recognition (ANPR) to manage and enhance the implementation of Pune traffic flows. In addition, the city uses real-time pollution monitoring stations to inform policy decisions, such as Track Vehicles Emissions and Vehicle Restrictions on High-pollution days. Bhubaneswar, known as one of the top smart cities in India, has developed a smart traffic management platform that integrates traffic data, vehicle flow analytics, and emission reports for dynamic signal control and environmental management. Delhi, which faces some of the highest pollution levels globally, has run GPS-based tracking and telematics in public transport to reduce idling and increase route planning. In India, its applications are increasingly linked to electric dynamics initiatives, such as electric bus fleets in Bangalore and Ahmedabad, powered by telematics systems to monitor battery consumption, emission savings, and operational efficiency. However, challenges such as infrastructure gaps, data integration limitations, and inconsistent regulatory structures still cause obstacles to full-scale implementation. Nevertheless, motion in Indian smart cities reflects the growing belief as a foundation for durable urban transformation.

In summary, this global case study shows its diversity and the possibility of reducing vehicle emissions and promoting sustainable urban mobility. Through crowd prices in London, ERP systems in Singapore, active mobility in Amsterdam, or emerging data-centered systems in Indian cities, integration with emission monitoring offers a powerful toolkit to meet environmental, economic, and public health objectives. These examples offer valuable lessons of governance, technical deployment, and citizen engagement that can inform the initiative of future emission-awareness smart cities around the world.

*Figure 4. Challenges of monitoring vehicle emissions through ITS for smart city developments*

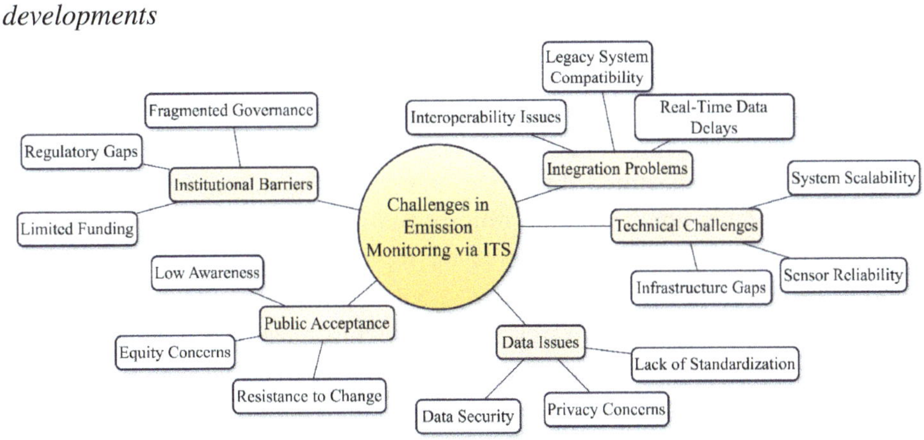

## CHALLENGES AND LIMITATIONS

Despite the transformative possibility of intelligent transport systems (ITSs) in enabling real-time vehicle emission inspection and durable urban mobility, many challenges and limitations are widespread in the widespread adoption and effectiveness. These challenges are spreading across technical, regulatory, institutional, and social dimensions. In smart cities, emissions-awareness needs to address them for the successful implementation of its framework. Key barriers include technical and structural limitations, data privacy and interoperability concerns, institutional and regulatory barriers, and issues related to public awareness and behavioral transformation (Bakirci, 2024; Elassy et al., 2024; G. Zhang et al., 2024). The challenges of monitoring vehicle emissions through ITS for smart city developments are shown in Figure 4.

### Technical and Infrastructure Barriers

Its framework includes one of the most notable challenges in integrating emissions monitoring and structural features. Real-time emissions monitoring depends on the network of air quality sensors, in-vehicle diagnostic systems, GPS, and wireless communication infrastructure, all of which must be operated together to provide accurate and reliable data. However, there is a need to bring the digital infrastructure needed to support such systems, especially in many urban areas in developing countries. Points such as poor internet connectivity, unreliable power supply, and insufficient sensor calibration capabilities weaken the influence of its technologies (Alam et al., 2024).

Furthermore, deploying and maintaining a large-scale network of IoT sensors and telematics devices is capital-intensive and requires constant investment. Sensors can be affected by environmental conditions, wear and tear, or vandalism, leading to data gaps or inaccuracies. The challenge is enhanced when cities try to rearrange existing infrastructure, which often lacks the flexibility to update its components. Additionally, unifying various data sources, from on-traffic cameras and weather stations to vehicle systems-united platforms, requires significant technical skills and strong system architecture, which many municipalities may not have internally. Scalability is another concern. Pilot projects and local implementation can work effectively, but scaling them in the entire metropolitan field creates new demand on hardware, bandwidth, system synchronization, and analytics capabilities. These technical challenges can result in fragmented systems, delayed deployment or use of their equipment, eventually limiting their effectiveness in emission inspection.

## Data Privacy and Interoperability Issues

The effectiveness of the emission vigilance depends greatly on the collection and processing of its large amount of real-time data, most of which is sensitive or individually recognizable. This data is a serious concern related to privacy and security. Collect information about in-vehicle telematics systems, for example, driver behavior, vehicle location, fuel consumption, and engine performance (Hammed & Jebbar, 2025). Without proper safety, these data can be abused for surveillance, profiling, or commercial exploitation. Data collections surrounding public mistrust can lead to resistance to its adoption, especially if there is a lack of transparency or the privacy policies are unclear (S. Zhang et al., 2018).

In addition to privacy, interoperability is a constant issue. Its framework often includes hardware and software systems from multiple vendors, with each vendor having its own ownership protocol, data formats, and integration standards. This creates silence that hinders seamless communication between devices and platforms. Lack of interoperability system upgrades and expansion is expensive and time-consuming, as new components may require custom integration or seller-specific solutions. Standardization efforts continue globally - for example, it's directing the European Union and ISO standards for it - but the implementation regions and jurisdictions are inconsistent. In the absence of universal standards, cities face challenges to integrate their components, distribute data to agencies, and ensure long-term system compatibility. This interoperability limits the feeling of an integrated, scalable, and efficient ecosystem for garbage emissions monitoring.

## Institutional and Regulatory Constraints

Organizational coordination is crucial for its success, although it is often a major barrier. Its emissions intersect with many areas, including transportation, environment, health, urban planning, and ICT for monitoring. These domains require clear command, arranged objectives, and shared responsibilities for effective collaboration. However, government agencies often work in Silos with overlapping jurisdiction, fragmented budgets, and contradictory priorities. Due to this lack of institutional harmony, there are vain efforts, policy gaps, and delayed project execution.

Moreover, many cities lack the necessary regulatory structures to support their deployment. Points such as sensor placement permits, data-sharing agreements, vehicle emission compliance standards, and electronic implementation methods require strong law and implementation capacity. In many countries, especially in the global south, regulatory bodies are under-resourced or prohibited by old policies that are not responsible for digital innovation (Dui et al., 2024; Lu & Wang, 2024). The fund is another institutional challenge. ITS projects require long-term financial commitments, but the government's funding cycles are often short-term and politically influenced. Security for public-private partnership (PPP) can provide financial relief, but these arrangements should be carefully managed to avoid the provision of monopoly or uneven service. Without a supporting institutional structure, its projects risk instability, poor coordination, or unhealthy consequences.

## Public Awareness and Behavioral Factors

The technical vehicle alone cannot solve the problem of emissions. Equally important is public awareness and behavioral change in transit-emission-intensive mobility. However, many cities face significant challenges in incorporating people and promoting travel behaviors that are environmentally friendly. For example, passengers may be unaware of the environmental influence of their driving habits or suspect the accuracy of emission monitoring data. Others are not willing to relocate to public or non-motorized transportation options from private vehicles due to facilities, security concerns, or social vision.

The resistance to the change is especially strong in regions where driving is culturally imposed or where public transport is structured. Policies such as congestion prices, low-emitting zones, or vehicle restrictions are environmentally beneficial, but often face public reactions unless widespread access, education, and incentives do not come. Moreover, its capable systems, such as dynamic traffic routing or eco-driving response methods, need to be effective in the user's engagement. If users ignore the notifications or do not understand how to interpret data, the effect of the system is reduced (Almalki et al., 2023; Zhao et al., 2022). Equity concerns also come up. Its deployment often benefits high-income users of new vehicles equipped with tech-savvy, digital tools and diagnostic systems. Meanwhile, a low-income population, the elderly, can operate more polluting vehicles, and cannot withstand disproportionate penalties without sufficient support for parking upgrades or public transportation options. Addressing these behavioral and equity factors requires extensive policy design, user-friendly technologies, and durable public engagement campaigns.

*Figure 5. Core innovations and future directions in emission monitoring through ITS*

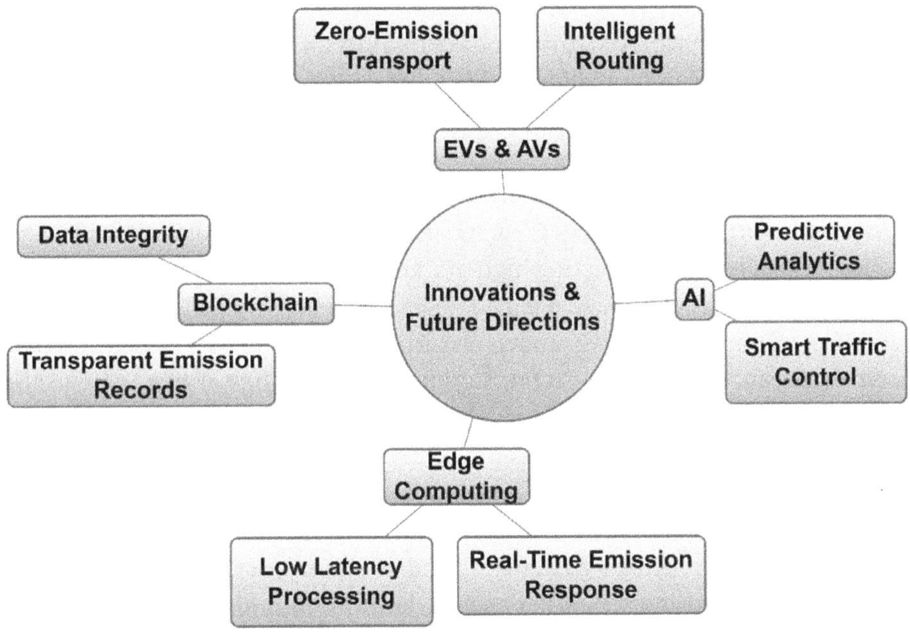


## INNOVATIONS AND FUTURE DIRECTIONS

Integration of Intelligent Transportation Systems (ITS) with advanced digital techniques is unlaying the new frontiers in vehicle emission monitoring and management, leading smart cities to achieve their durability targets. As the urban environment becomes more and more complex and data-rich, the demand for smart, faster, and more reliable decisions is increasing. Emerging technologies such as artificial intelligence (AI), edge computing, blockchain, and the growing adoption of electric and autonomous vehicles (EV and AVS) reshape how their framework works and develops. These innovations not only increase the accuracy and response of emission monitoring systems but also promote more transparency, efficiency, and environmental liability in transport ecosystems (Almalki et al., 2023; Zhao et al., 2022). Core innovations and future directions in emission monitoring through ITS are illustrated in Figure 5.

## AI and Predictive Emission Analytics

Artificial intelligence (AI) is playing a key role in transforming its reactive systems into predictive and adaptive platforms. Traditional traffic and emissions monitoring methods are often descriptive, focused on analyzing what has already happened. On the contrary, AI enables cities to predict future traffic and pollution levels, allowing for leading actions that can reduce them before adverse environmental effects occur.

Machine Learning (ML) models, an AI subset, identifying emission trends, finding inconsistencies, and predicting high-emitting events can be trained on sensors, GPS, weather forecasts, vehicle telemetry, and urban activity patterns collected in history. For example, predictive models can estimate NOx or PM 2.5 concentrations in certain places based on the next traffic pattern, meteorological changes, and special events such as a parade or road closure. Officials can then deploy a strategy to reduce temporary emissions, such as traffic diversion, public transport frequency, or implementation of low-emission zones (Aderibigbe & Gumbo, 2024). In addition, AI-propelled analytics can predict the traffic signal time in real time to reduce the sluggish and stop-and-go movement, which is a major contributor to elevated emissions in crowded areas. Reinforcement education algorithms can continuously learn from traffic answers to maximize flow, reduce pollution, and improve signal coordination. Moreover, AI can facilitate the profiling of vehicle-level emissions by analyzing driving behaviors, engine loads, and fuel consumption to assign real-time emissions scores. These scores can provide information on the implementation of eco-driving feedback systems or emission compliance rules.

## Edge Computing and Real-Time Control

While AI models require large datasets and calculations, their real-time effectiveness is often limited by network latency and centralized processing bottlenecks. Edge computing data addresses this challenge by bringing data near the source, whether it is a sensor, an in-vehicle device, or a traffic camera on the side of the road. By processing the data locally on the "edge" of the network, cities can receive lower latency in the examination and response of emissions (Aderibigbe & Gumbo, 2024; Sun et al., 2023).

For example, an edge-capable road unit can immediately analyze air quality readings and traffic density to trigger adaptive signal changes without waiting for the central server's instructions. Similarly, in-vehicle systems equipped with edge computing capabilities can analyze emission output, engine diagnostics, and driving behavior in real time, provide immediate response to the driver, or flag the issues for fleet operators and regulators. Edge computing also increases system elasticity by reducing the dependence on cloud connectivity. Incidentally, where the communication network is disrupted - disasters, cyberattacks, or infrastructure limitations - local edge tumors can continue to operate autonomously. This capability is especially important in managing time-sensitive excretion control functions, such as rebuilding vehicles during high pollution episodes or activating the geofenced low-enemy zone. Moreover, before sending the same device data to the Centralized Analytics platform, the bandwidth consumption is reduced, and it can be pre-processed before improving data storage and recovery efficiency. This makes the large-scale deployment of IoT-based emissions monitoring systems more practical, especially in bandwidth-constrained or resource-limited environments.

## Blockchain for Transparent Emission Reporting

Transparency and trust in emission data are essential for policy implementation, public responsibility, and stakeholder cooperation. Blockchain technology, known for its decentralized and tamper-proof ledger system, provides a promising settlement for safe and transparent emissions reporting in its framework. By recording emissions data, cities can ensure data integrity and traceability - on blockchain, from vehicles, sensors, or traffic systems. Each data point is time-stemmed, cryptographically secure, and unchanged, which prevents manipulation or unauthorized access. This is especially valuable in this regard, where the regulatory implementation is weak or where there is a doubt about the reliability of the emission figures (Bakirci, 2024).

Blockchain emissions can also facilitate trading plans or promotion-based programs by automating transactions and compliance investigations through a smart agreement. For example, vehicles that maintain low emission levels can get carbon credits or financial incentives, which are transparently tracked on the blockchain. On the contrary, high-emission vehicles may face automatic penalties or be flagged for compulsory inspection. Multi-Stakes Atmosphere-Governments, private transport tors patterns, environmental agencies, and citizens interact-Opp ensures that all parties have equal, verified data, promoting cooperation and reducing disputes. It also enhances public engagement by allowing individuals to access their own emissions records or by user-friendly dashboards connected with blockchain, tracking the environmental impact of their transport choices.

## Synergies with EVs and Autonomous Vehicles

The transition into electric vehicles (EVs) and autonomous vehicles (AVs) represents the basic shift in urban mobility, providing new opportunities to reduce emissions and excellent transportation efficiency. When integrated with ITS, these vehicles can serve as dynamic elements in the emission management ecosystem (Chavhan et al., 2022; Musa et al., 2023).

EVS contributes to the targets of reducing emissions by eliminating the tailpipe pollutants. It can facilitate their integration by providing real-time data on the availability of a charging station to avoid overloading during the peak charging time, route planning, and real-time data on grid coordination depending on the battery level. Vehicle-to-infrastructure (V2I) communications can also support intelligent ENERGY management, where EV charges during a low-demand period or use renewable energy from zero sources, reducing their environmental impact. Autonomous vehicles, with their ability to adhere to optimized driving algorithms, can maintain constant motion and communicate with infrastructure and other vehicles (V2X), significantly reducing emissions associated with improper driving behavior. Integrated A.V. with its platform. Can coordinate with traffic signals, adjust routes to avoid congestion, and participate in the vehicle overturn, all of which increase fuel efficiency and reduce emissions.

Moreover, the combination of EVs creates a powerful harmony for emission-free, intelligent urban transport. Shared autonomous electric fleets-Jen's smart dynamics operate as part of the infrastructure, providing low-emission options, low-cost, at a cost-expense for owning a minor car ownership. It can replace these fleets by using real-time demand data, optimizing routes, and reducing empty vehicle trips. The future of emission-intensive mobility in smart cities lies at the intersection of digital innovation and urban stability. By accepting AI for predictive analyzes, deploying edge computing for real-time response, the benefit of blockchain for transparency, and unifying AVs into the ITS framework, cities can transform their approach to vehicle emission management. These technologies not only increase the efficiency and reliability of emission monitoring systems but also empower stakeholders with equipment to make knowledgeable, sustainable decisions. As the global urban population grows, it will be necessary to adopt these forward-looking solutions to create cleaner, smarter, and more elastic cities.

## POLICY RECOMMENDATIONS AND STRATEGIC FRAMEWORKS

The successful deployment of intelligent transport systems (ITSs) for vehicle emissions inspection in smart cities demands a strategic policy structure that organizes technical innovation with a durable urban regime. The central focus of this structure is the integration of emission-awareness in its urban planning processes. To reduce the dependence of overall vehicles in urban development, it is important to prefer a transport-oriented design, mixed land-use plan, and non-motorized transport infrastructure. By embedding emissions monitoring data in urban planning equipment such as geographical information systems (GIS) and transport simulation models, the organizers can make data-jaws related to road network design, zoning, traffic flow management, and infrastructure placement. Such integration ensures that the reduction in emissions becomes a basic criterion in the city's expansion, redevelopment, and transportation strategy (Gautam et al., 2024).

It is equally important that the establishment of strong multi-stakeholder co-operation models that unite public agencies, private sector institutions, academia, and civil society in a shared mission. Its projects are required for multiple domains-transportation, environment, information technology, and public health-cross-sectoral coordination. Governments must develop institutional structures that promote collaboration through international functional groups, joint funding methods, and open data policies. Public-private partnerships (PPPs) can accelerate their structural deployment, while educational and research institutes can contribute skills to system modeling, data analytics, and policy evaluation. It is also important to prioritize the participation of the citizens to ensure transparency, guardian behavioral transformation, and increase confidence in emission monitoring techniques. Strategic communications, community response loops, and participating planning methods can help set its goals with local needs and expectations (Zhan et al., 2024). Promoting clean transport is another crucial pillar of a policy structure. Financial incentives can promote electric vehicles (EVs), promote eco-driving behaviors, and shift travel patterns toward low-emission modes. These may include tax benefits, subsidies for EV purchases, reduced tolls or parking fees for green vehicles, and funding support to recycle old vehicles with emissions-molten techniques. In addition, IT-generated data can be used to personalize incentives based on driver behavior and emission profiles. For example, passengers who follow consistent eco-driving practices or use clean mobility options can receive digital rewards through smart mobility applications (L. Zhang et al., 2024).

Finally, a Strong monitoring and evaluation (M&E) matrix must be embedded in all its based emission management programs. This matrix should not only do the technical operation tasks - such as sensor accuracy or data transmission rate - but also environmental influence indicators such as NOx, PM2.5, and $CO_2$ levels over time. M&E systems should include baseline data, periodic assessments, and adaptive response methods that enable constant policy purification. The use of dynamic dashboards, performance scorecards, and public reporting tools can ensure responsibility-based decisions. A structured, matrix-based approach will enhance its implementation-awareness transparency, measurement, and long-term durability.

## CONCLUSION

The integration of intelligent transportation systems (ITS) with real-time vehicle emissions monitoring represents major progress in the search for durable and elastic smart cities. In urban areas, such as air pollution, traffic congestion, and climate change, it provides a dynamic, data-based structure to manage mobility while reducing environmental effects. By providing benefits to technologies such as IoT sensors, in-vehicle diagnostics, GIS mapping, AI analytics, and blockchain, cities can achieve precise, active insights into the pattern of emissions, enable timely interventions, and long-term policy planning. From the Global Case Studies-Singapore's ERP and London's ULEZ to Amsterdam's Green Mobility and the emerging smart cities of India, it is not only technically possible, but also supported by sound policy and institutional cooperation. However, to realize its full potential, serious barriers to infrastructure, data privacy, public behavior, and regulatory configuration need to be removed.

Consolidation with urban planning, multi-stakeholder governance, incentives for clean transport, and strong monitoring metrics must be preferred within the structure of strategic policy. As cities move to electric and autonomous mobility, the conversion of their emissions and emissions control will help to shape a healthy urban future. This chapter reflects the importance of active, technical-enabled solutions for emission-vigilant mobility as the foundation of smart city development.

## REFERENCES


Aderibigbe, O.-O., & Gumbo, T. (2024). Smart cities and their impact on urban transportation systems and development. In *Emerging technologies for smart cities: Sustainable transport planning in the Global North and Global South* (pp. 105–129). Springer.

Alam, T., Gupta, R., Nasurudeen Ahamed, N., Ullah, A., & Almaghthwi, A. (2024). Smart mobility adoption in sustainable smart cities to establish a growing ecosystem: Challenges and opportunities. *MRS Energy & Sustainability : a Review Journal*, *11*(2), 304–316.

Almalki, F. A., Alsamhi, S. H., Sahal, R., Hassan, J., Hawbani, A., Rajput, N., Saif, A., Morgan, J., & Breslin, J. (2023). Green IoT for eco-friendly and sustainable smart cities: Future directions and opportunities. *Mobile Networks and Applications*, *28*(1), 178–202.

Atiyah, R. G., & Razzaq, R. H. (2024). Intermediary decentralized computing and private blockchain mechanisms for privacy preservation in the Internet of medical things. *Mesopotamian Journal of CyberSecurity*, *4*(3), 152–165.

Bakirci, M. (2024). Smart city air quality management through leveraging drones for precision monitoring. *Sustainable Cities and Society*, *106*, 105390.

Balasubramaniam, A., Paul, A., Hong, W.-H., Seo, H., & Kim, J. H. (2017). Comparative analysis of intelligent transportation systems for sustainable environment in smart cities. *Sustainability*, *9*(7), 1120.

Chavhan, S., Gupta, D., & Gochhayat, S. P., N, C. B., Khanna, A., Shankar, K., & Rodrigues, J. J. (2022). Edge computing AI-IoT integrated energy-efficient intelligent transportation system for smart cities. *ACM Transactions on Internet Technology*, *22*(4), 1–18.

Duaa, T. (2025). Security Cooperation in the Protection Concerns of Agriculture Data Using Efficient Signatures and Artificial Bee Colony Manner. In *Sustainable Information Security in the Age of AI and Green Computing* (pp. 439–460). IGI Global Scientific Publishing.

Dui, H., Zhang, S., Liu, M., Dong, X., & Bai, G. (2024). IoT-enabled real-time traffic monitoring and control management for intelligent transportation systems. *IEEE Internet of Things Journal*.

Elassy, M., Al-Hattab, M., Takruri, M., & Badawi, S. (2024). Intelligent transportation systems for sustainable smart cities. *Transportation Engineering*, *16*, 100252.

Gautam, S., Gautam, A. S., Awasthi, A., & N, R. (2024). Regulatory Frameworks and Policies. In *Sustainable Air: Strategies for Cleaner Atmosphere and Healthier Communities* (pp. 49–52). Springer.

Hammed, M., & Jebbar, W. A. (2025). Blockchain-Powered Dynamic Segmentation in Personal Health Record. *Mesopotamian Journal of CyberSecurity*, *5*(3), 953–976.

Hernafi, Y., Ahmed, M. B., & Bouhorma, M. (2016). An approaches' based on intelligent transportation systems to dissect driver behavior and smart mobility in smart city. *2016 4th IEEE International Colloquium on Information Science and Technology (CiSt)*, 886–895.

Louati, A., Louati, H., Kariri, E., Neifar, W., Hassan, M. K., Khairi, M. H., Farahat, M. A., & El-Hoseny, H. M. (2024). Sustainable smart cities through multi-agent reinforcement learning-based cooperative autonomous vehicles. *Sustainability*, *16*(5), 1779.

Lu, C., & Wang, F. (2024). Towards Secure Internet of Things-Enabled Intelligent Transportation Systems: A Comprehensive Review. *International Journal of Advanced Computer Science and Applications*, *15*(7).

Meneguette, R. I., De Grande, R., & Loureiro, A. (2018). Intelligent transport system in smart cities. *Cham: Springer International Publishing*, *1*, 182.

Musa, A. A., Malami, S. I., Alanazi, F., Ounaies, W., Alshammari, M., & Haruna, S. I. (2023). Sustainable traffic management for smart cities using internet-of-things-oriented intelligent transportation systems (ITS): Challenges and recommendations. *Sustainability*, *15*(13), 9859.

Sun, Y., Hu, Y., Zhang, H., Chen, H., & Wang, F.-Y. (2023). A parallel emission regulatory framework for intelligent transportation systems and smart cities. *IEEE Transactions on Intelligent Vehicles*, *8*(2), 1017–1020.

Telang, S., Chel, A., Nemade, A., & Kaushik, G. (2020). Intelligent transport system for a smart city. In *Security and privacy applications for smart city development* (pp. 171–187). Springer.

Turner, S. W., & Uludag, S. (2017). Toward Smart Cities via the Smart Grid and Intelligent Transportation Systems. *Smart Grid*, •••, 117–166.

Zhan, W., Wang, Z., Deng, J., Liu, P., & Cui, D. (2024). Integrating system dynamics and agent-based modeling: A data-driven framework for predicting electric vehicle market penetration and GHG emissions reduction under various incentives scenarios. *Applied Energy*, *372*, 123749.

Zhang, G., Sun, X., & Zhong, S. (2024). The impact of smart city construction (SCC) on pollution emissions (PE): Evidence from China. *Scientific Reports*, *14*(1), 6633. PMID: 38503860

Zhang, L., Wei, J., & Tu, R. (2024). Temporal-spatial analysis of transportation CO2 emissions in China: Clustering and policy recommendations. *Heliyon*, *10*(2). PMID: 38312644

Zhang, S., Niu, T., Wu, Y., Zhang, K. M., Wallington, T. J., Xie, Q., Wu, X., & Xu, H. (2018). Fine-grained vehicle emission management using intelligent transportation system data. *Environmental Pollution*, *241*, 1027–1037. PMID: 30029310

Zhao, C., Wang, K., Dong, X., & Dong, K. (2022). Is smart transportation associated with reduced carbon emissions? The case of China. *Energy Economics*, *105*, 105715.

# Chapter 4
# Mitigating Cybersecurity Challenges in Smart City Development:
## Threats, Risks, and Strategic Solutions

**M. Vijayalakshmi**
*SRM Institute of Science and Technology, India*

**L. A. Anto Gracious**
https://orcid.org/0000-0003-2386-9182
*R.M.K. College of Engineering and Technology, India*

**P. Girija**
https://orcid.org/0009-0000-1691-8180
*Panimalar Engineering College, India*

## ABSTRACT

*Smart cities are the result of significant innovations like IoT, AI, and 5G, and new forms of cyber threats have appeared. This chapter aims to identify and discuss the major cybersecurity threats, risks, and challenges in smart cities, such as IoT-based threats, privacy and data protection issues, and network-level threats. It also assesses the solutions that have been adopted at the strategic level with a view to managing these risks, including encryption, the use of artificial intelligence in threat detection, and blockchain in matters concerning data authenticity. The study focuses on the need to have policy structures in place, international cooperation, and constant development to meet emerging threats in the field of cybersecurity. As more and*

DOI: 10.4018/979-8-3373-8133-6.ch004

*more smart cities are being developed, it will become paramount to ensure that there are adequate security measures put in place to safeguard the infrastructure that will be in place as well as the citizens.*

## INTRODUCTION

### Overview of Smart Cities

Smart cities are defined as cities that connect physical with digital technologies particularly IoT, Data and advanced infrastructure systems for the betterment of the people living in the cities (Bahl et al 2024; Ponmalar, A et al., 2025). These cities use various smart technologies to make every facet of city living as a system where transport, health, power, security, and other aspects are linked through the processing and analyzing of data in real-time. The idea of smart cities has developed over the past decade due to the improvement in technology and the need for cities to seek solutions to some of the challenges that come with growth of population, management of resources, environment, and traffic jam among others. The key elements are an IoT infrastructure that is made up of smart devices and sensors that gather data on resources in a city (Gómez et al 2017). For instance, smart traffic signals can detect traffic patterns and adapt the signals accordingly to minimize traffic build up, smart meters can also detect energy usage patterns of homes and businesses to optimize energy consumption. Also, data analytics platforms are important in a smart city, as they are used to consolidate and analyze the large amount of data from various sources to identify patterns and trends, and identify problems. Such information has its usage in decision making and long term planning. Smart cities also depend on advanced communication technologies, cloud technologies, as well as big data patterns. Such systems are effective in the interconnection of services and quick decision-making to improve the reaction of municipalities to challenges. For example, in case of leakage in a water pipe, a smart city system can identify the problem promptly and determine the extent of the damage and at the same time send repairmen, without inconvenience to the users (Pattani et al 2024).

### Importance of Cybersecurity in Smart Cities

More and more cities are incorporating technology in the lives of their inhabitants and this leads to higher rates of integration of digital and interdependent systems. As much as the usage of IoT devices and smart systems in the infrastructure holds a lot of advantages, it also creates a number of cybersecurity risks. Every object or piece of technology that is connected to the smart city framework can be a target for cybercriminals. In the current world where almost everything is being connected to the internet especially in the city this is a very risky step. Starting from surveillance cameras to traffic lights all these are a potential target which makes security issues a major challenge for the successful implementation of smart cities. The effects that come as a result of cyber security attacks in critical city facilities are dire. Whereas stealing a precious item or vandalism are remedies to theft in a traditional city, the threats posed by smart city security can be far more detrimental. Indicatively, an attacker can possibly gain control of the transport system in a city, cause traffic jams or steal electricity distribution systems, and make an entire city black. The technology applied in the healthcare sector in managing patient records can be breached and numerous lives could be lost. Even the most insignificant ones like smart waste management or water treatment could be attacked and led to the environmental pollution or health risks to the inhabitants. All these systems are interconnected, which means that the issue in one of them can easily cause multiple other problems related to different spheres of city life. Moreover, as cities are the repositories of an enormous data sets of individuals and organizations of various types, the safety of such information is essential. The threats posed by data breaches in smart cities include lack of trust in government systems, identity theft, loss of money, and violation of rights to privacy. Thus, the protection of data in a smart city for confidentiality, integrity, and availability is crucial for citizens to trust such technologies and have their lives improved without endangering them.

## Objective of the Chapter

This chapter seeks to discuss the emerging issues of cybersecurity as the world advances in smart cities development. As these cities integrate and develop, the threats in the cybersecurity level also increase, and it is important to know about the smart city threats. In this chapter, the following objectives will be achieved: The first objective is to identify the various cybersecurity threats that affect smart cities, the threat brought by IoT devices, threats to public facilities, and the challenges of data sharing across the various platforms. The survey will also look into threats that cities will face in future with advancement in technology like the deepening of cyber threats through artificial intelligence and machine learning (Yavanoglu, O., & Aydos, M. 2017). In addition, it is the intention of the chapter to also examine the current measures and interventions being proposed and adopted to tackle these risks. This will involve looking at the IT solutions like encryption, AI, and the use of blockchain in the protection of data and infrastructure of cities. It also looks at legal and political factors that relate to protection of cyberspace, for example national cyber security policies, data protection legislation and cooperation between governments, business entities and global organizations at the local level. Specifically, the survey will establish the level of awareness of the current strategies and practices in place to prevent and counteract cyber threats and make recommendations on the optimal ways to enhance the readiness and response to such threats by cities. It is the aim of this survey to offer a broad view of cybersecurity in smart cities as well as present detailed information about threats and countermeasures that define the protection of digital systems in urban environment. As the deployment of smart cities is set to progress and advance further, cybersecurity will always play a significant role in the success and longevity of smart cities. Thus, the knowledge of threats and application of countermeasures will be crucial for the successful implementation of smart cities' concept and for the protection of the residents' interests.

## CYBERSECURITY THREATS IN SMART CITIES

### Overview of Cybersecurity Threat Landscape

The prospects of smart cities have made it possible to have the integration of technology in every aspect of living through the use of digital infrastructure, IoT devices, data analytics, and integrated systems. But these advancements also brought new levels of complication and frequency of the threats in the sphere of cybersecurity (Azizi, N., & Haass, O. 2023). Smart cities are built on the basis of interconnected technologies and this is why even the smallest of the weaknesses can lead to different types of cyber threats. The main problem of cybersecurity in smart cities is the large number of threats that are associated with those intelligent systems. In this area, every connected device, sensor or an object is an endpoint and bad actors in town got ways of penetrating through the city's essential systems. The first danger of smart cities is associated with the penetration by external cybercriminals who can hack into systems to gain access to data or control over infrastructure. These are attacks that can be in the form of hacking, phishing, ransomware, and data breaches, among others. Cyber criminals are especially lethal since they are capable of attacking various sectors in the society such as transport systems and surveillance systems. Data breaches are also another threat that poses a serious threat since it compromises citizens' personal and financial details thus violating their privacy, impersonation, and loss of confidence in the city's administration. The implications of such breaches can be dire including loss of money, loss of public confidence in the government's capacity to protect the people of the city. Such risks are magnified when considering that smart cities are built with higher interconnected systems. With the increased use of devices in networks and the sharing of data across different systems and applications, the chances of getting entry points for hackers also increase dramatically. Unlike other urban systems where security was applied on single entities, smart cities make it possible for a breach in one system to affect other systems. For example, an attack on traffic management system of a city will result in traffic jams, while an attack on database of a public health facility will compromise patients' information and the services. There is a high probability that the various devices, networks, and platforms used in smart city systems can be subjected to inadequate security (Nalini et al., 2025).

## Specific Threats

There are several specific types of threats that are of particular concern for the development and functioning of smart cities. These include isolated attacks on single IoT devices all the way up to coordinated attacks on systems that control the functions of an entire city. These are the particular threats that should be understood so that it is possible to take appropriate countermeasures and to ensure that smart cities can safely grow.

Smart City Concerns: IoT forms the web of most paths of smart city developments. The sphere of waste management, energy, transportation, public safety and others are the areas where smart devices, sensors, and actuators are implemented. The disadvantage of these devices is that they are largely employable without being very expensive but the drawback is that it lacks or has minimal security. The majority of IoT devices are resource constrained and hence the software is likely to be affected by a number of software defects such as insecure communication, weak encryption, or weak authentication.

With such loopholes, hackers can assume control of the devices, do with them or use them to carry out other heinous activities such as the use of the devices in a DDoS attack. The threats posed by the IoT devices are even greater due to the fact that they have been implemented in cities. Due to the ever rising number of devices within a smart city, monitoring and regulating the devices becomes difficult. This can result in the fact that infected devices or networks may be lurking in the shadows for a long time, and cybercriminals can take control over important systems like traffic signals, water supply systems, or energy supply systems. For instance, an attacker can take control of the streetlights that are connected to the IoT to spy on people or even cause traffic jams that result in accidents or traffic congestion.

*Figure 1.* **Cybersecurity Threats**

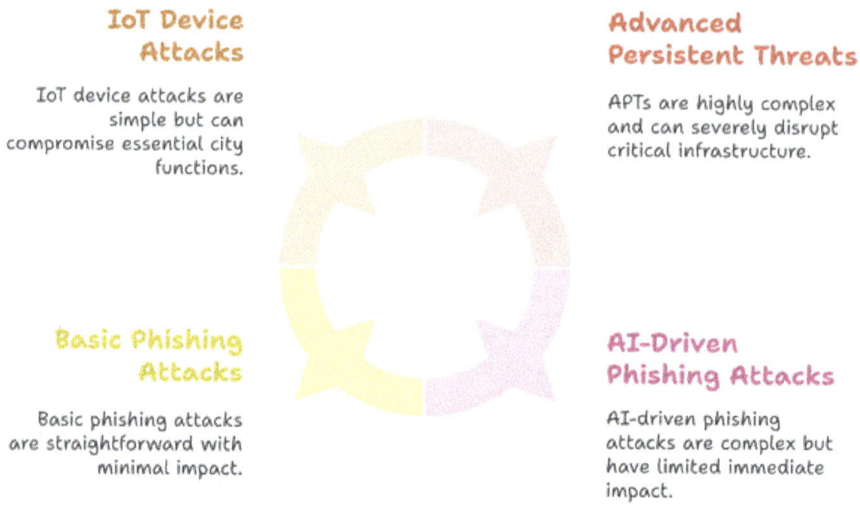


Network Attacks: Smart cities make use of various communication networks through which the various components and devices are connected. Despite the fact that these networks are used for data sharing and real-time monitoring, they are also very vulnerable to cyber threats. The most important of them are DDoS attacks, MITM attacks, and data interception. In DDoS the attacker sends a large number of requests to a network or a server to overload the system and make it unavailable. In view of smart city, such attacks can be directed to key infrastructures like the emergency services, traffic signals, and utilities. MITM attacks are a type of attack where the attacker intercepts the communication between two other parties with a view of altering or capturing the information being exchanged. For instance, in the smart city, the hacker can intercept the signal between the traffic lights and cars leading to traffic jams or accidents. These networks are very sensitive as any intrusion can lead to disastrous consequences in the interest of the public and the city. Furthermore, many smart city systems are based on the use of cloud computing and third-party data sources that make the smart city more vulnerable to attacks on third-party infrastructure.

Security Threats: This is in relation to the fact that much of smart city functions entail the use of data, and such data may contain private information. Smart cities gather information from the interaction of individuals with the services they receive, traffic, the environment, and health care facilities. It is therefore useful for such purposes as city planning, organizing resources and the delivery of services. However, it also brings a big threat to privacy and security.

Municipal data privacy risks are when hackers compromise the data that is collected and stored in municipal databases including name, address, health records and financial information. As a result, the information may be used for identity theft, fraud, blackmail, and other unlawful activities. But besides stealing personal data, there is a possibility of data manipulation. Hackers may manipulate or contaminate the data to cause denial of services or provide wrong information to the decision makers. For instance, interfering with the traffic data would lead to traffic jam, while manipulating public health data would lead to wrong treatment advice or diagnosis. These risks can only be minimized if the integrity and confidentiality of the data being used is maintained.

Advanced Persistent Threats (APTs): These are a type of advanced cyber threat that is usually elaborate and usually involves an ongoing and covert attempt to gain unauthorized access into a system. These attacks are normally executed by professional attackers with adequate financial and technical resources like state sponsored hackers or cybercriminal organizations. In the context of smart cities, APTs can attack the infrastructure such as water treatment plants, electrical power stations, or emergency services networks. APTs are typically performed to maintain persistent unauthorized access in such systems, steal information, or disrupt the systems. APT's characteristics make them especially threatening in smart cities since the infrastructure of such cities is closely intertwined. APT cyber-attack may take several weeks or even months in order to accomplish all these things because the attack is not easily detected. Due to the high consequences of APT, such as compromising the safety of the public, the defense against them involves the use of more enhanced security systems and consistent monitoring.

## Emerging Threats

Smart cities are still in their development stage, and there is a constant emergence of more intelligent methods to improve the use of modern technologies and the occurrence of new threats. Especial attention should be paid to those ones that use artificial intelligence (AI) and machine learning (ML) as such technologies are revolutionizing the approaches to cyberattacks (Iyer, S. S., & Rajagopal, S. (2020). AI and Machine Learning threats: These are relatively new threats in the field of cyber security since the use of AI and ML in cyberattacks is becoming more and more popular. AI is actually very dangerous in the hands of hackers since it can be used to launch attacks, process big data to find out weaknesses, and even create self-evolving malware (Ganapathi, P., & Shanmugapriya, D 2019). The AI-driven attacks in a smart city can affect the traffic control systems, security surveillance systems, and even others. They are equally a challenge to counter because AI-based attacks are capable of adapting to the context of the environment in use. For instance, it is possible to hack the city by learning or understanding how the traffic flow or communication networks work in the city. Secondly, AI can orchestrate more advanced phishing attacks since it can now observe patterns of communications and design attacks to target certain person or system. Cyber-Physical Attacks: There is a rising concern in the possibility of cyber-physical attacks in smart cities as the physical and cyber systems are linked hence the physical harm can be caused by a cyber-attack. These kinds of attacks involve attacking the physical aspects of a city, including transport means, energy supply, and water supply facilities and the hacking of the computer systems that regulate them. For example, an attacker might disrupt a city's electricity supply or he can attack the water supply system and this will lead to contamination or disruption of the supply. Cyber-physical attacks are more dangerous than the others, as they may lead not only to the economic and operational losses but also to the threats to human lives. This is especially true in inter-linking of the physical and digital systems within smart cities as the probability of such risks is higher hence the need for the planner and the cybersecurity personnel to collaborate and design safe and secure structures (Prabhu, D et al., 2025).

## CYBERSECURITY RISKS IN SMART CITY DEVELOPMENT

### Physical Infrastructure Risks

Another potential cybersecurity threat in smart cities relates to the defense of smart structures including power structure, water, structures and transport structures. These systems can be regarded as the core of any urban environment and are rather critical for the functioning of cities. However, as the cities get interconnected through these physical structures by the use of digital technologies, the physical structures become exposed to cyberattacks. For instance, the electric power distribution networks are operated by complex digital devices and these devices are sometimes linked to the outer networks for monitoring. Despite these benefits, this connectivity enhances efficiency and enables a more dynamic energy management, it poses severe risks. A cyberattack on a power grid can cause blackouts in homes as well as other essential facilities such as hospitals, emergency services, communication networks among others. In the same way, water supply systems in smart cities are integrating information technologies for control and management. It is possible to monitor the water usage, the water quality, and water leakage through sensors and IoT devices and the systems they employ are interconnected with other smart city services such as waste management or environment tracking (Sandhu, K 2021).

*Figure 2. Cybersecurity risks in Smart city development*

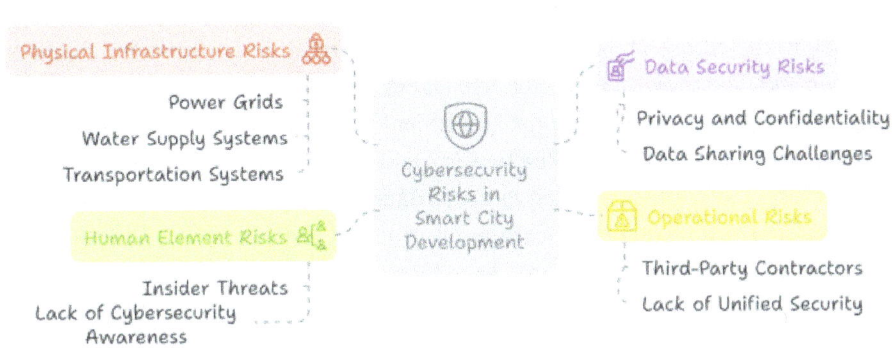


However, there is one disadvantage in the complexity of these interrelated systems and that is the security risks. An attack on a water treatment plant may lead to contamination of water or even its safety, which is a threat to the society. Another type is the attacks on transportation systems, which are also very dangerous in a way that they can cause traffic jam, accidents or even breakdown of public transport systems which are used daily for transport and this may lead to loss of lives. First of all, the integration of new technologies to the organizational system which may be older, isolated or less secure opens up another frontier of risk. One common issue that many smart cities experience is how to integrate the old infrastructure with the new smart systems since the former may be outdated in some ways. It is not easy to reconcile old systems with new technologies since the former may not have the same levels of security as the latter. These are old systems that may lack the adequate security attributes to counter this new breed of hackers who are more improved and sophisticated in their tactics hence leaving the system insecure in some ways. This is due to the fact that the process of integrating these systems can be very complex, and the risk of disrupting services can lead to some vulnerabilities being overlooked, which can be exploited by attackers.

## Data Security Risks

Under cyber threats, a smart city is faced with the problem of handling a large amount of data generated and processed in the area. Smart cities are based on solution of big data coming from various sources such as IoT devices, sensors, public utilities, and citizens. This data contains easily identifiable information about individuals, including personally identifiable information such as health records, location, and finances; business-related information such as traffic, energy use, and environmental feedback in the cities. The reason is that such information is enormous in quantity and type, and it becomes a welcome to hackers who would want to exploit it to their benefit. Therefore, one of the most significant concerns of security is the security of information in smart cities. The privacy and confidentiality of city and personal data is another one of the largest risks of data security in smart cities. It is quite important to avoid instances where the information is accessed, modified or stolen inappropriately given that many cities are turning to become information hubs. This is particularly because personal information can be accessed resulting to identity theft, frauds and invasion of privacy. Also, with the distributed data storage of the smart cities such as the cloud storage, on-site data center and third party service, it becomes difficult to ensure data safety in these areas. Any of the above mentioned platforms may not be adequately secured hence creating a weak point which can be used. One of the problems is the challenge of data sharing between various parties, for example the government, private entities as well as the service providers. The need to share information is fundamental to smart city infrastructures, yet when there are no established guidelines on the proper handling of data then there remains a major risk of hacking or misuse of the data. There are instances where citizens would be willing to share their personal data for services like health care or transport, but if the information is shared inappropriately it may infringe on their freedom or go against the law. Security in such a diverse setting essentially involves linking and implementing; data encryption; ability to regulate, limit, and control access to data; as well as adherence with data security policies and other legal requirements (Yamini B et al., 2024).

## Operational Risks

Therefore, it can be concluded that operational risks are also a major threat to the development of secure smart cities, along with physical and data security risks. These risks are associated with third party contractors and service providers in the development, management and operation of smart city systems. Third-party vendors in the project can be useful from the point of view of expertise and cost relatively to the company, but they might also pose a security threat. A vendor may not conform to the security standards of the city; the absence of an effective management of third-party relationships may lead to severe security issues. For instance, a vendor in the traffic management software or energy distribution software, may not apply the necessary security measures to protect the system. Thirdly, the involvement of third-party vendors implies that cities provide such parties with their data and do not always have full transparency of their security measures. The consequences may go as far as the whole city as the vendor's breach may affect key services and compromise the security of the city. Another operational risk is that there is no unified system of security and security standards in smart city projects. Smart cities are initiated and implemented through collaborations of both public and private organisations and each smart city project may employ different technologies, systems and security measures. This can cause some gaps that may make it difficult to achieve proper coverage of cybersecurity. For example, one segment of the city's structure may employ very strong encryption, while another segment may be using weak encryption. This makes it very challenging to evaluate the general state of security of the city's systems and guarantee that each segment has been secured to the maximum. This leads to the creation of what can be referred to as a 'patchwork of vulnerabilities' where it is challenging to address all the problems that the city may face due to its growth and development.

## Human Element Risks

Undoubtedly, one of the biggest challenges that cities face today is the human factor that is often underestimated in the development of smart cities. Insider threats with or without malicious intent can pose a serious cybersecurity threat to smart city infrastructures. Any malicious use of this system can be by any individual who has access to the critical systems or data and may use it either to obtain something or to inflict damage considering that they are an employee of the city or a contractor that has access to the critical systems or data. As an example, the employee in charge of control of the traffic control systems in the city might alter the traffic signal to create traffic jam or accidents. Similarly, the contractors working on the power grid of a city may introduce vulnerabilities themselves, such as an insecure password or outdated software. Less desirable yet not the least problematic is that city staff lacks adequate amounts of cybersecurity awareness and readiness. The technological system of smart cities is growing larger and bigger as these cities are becoming more developed, thus the employees of the smart cities should be aware of how to recognize the dangers of cyber-attacks. Regrettably, a plethora of urban employees might be less conversant with the most prevalent cybersecurity standards, and they will be vulnerable to social engineering, phishing, and other such fraudsters. This is particularly true in cases where no regular trainings and awareness programs are in place to reduce the chances of human error or recklessness. As an example, an innocent city worker can download an email attachment that contains the virus or city worker can ignore proper access controls that result in the compromise of networks within the city. Thirdly, the use of third-party contractors to carry out certain duties in the smart city projects increases the chances of human element risks as well. The independent contractors that are not fully assimilated into the security culture and practices of the city may pose risks because of bad screening, bad security measures and bad knowledge of the risks that the city may encounter. All the people who are concerned with the activities of the smart city need to be trained and follow the cybersecurity to minimize such risks.

## STRATEGIC SOLUTIONS FOR MITIGATION CYBERSECURITY RISKS

### Policy and Governance Approaches

Strong policy frameworks and governance structures play key roles as far as cybersecurity threats in smart cities are concerned. The national and local governments must have candy-cyber policies necessary, which should be formulated to deal with the problem of smart city organizations. Such policies must consider the fact that the urban systems are growing more complex and there are many threats to consider regarding the different sectors, including transportation, energy, and health care. Authorities must acknowledge that the process of smart cities is not only about the technology but the necessity of having a coherent system of control in relation to the physical and digital infrastructures of a city. This needs the establishment of new laws or the amendment of the current ones to include new threats which are expected to emerge with the advancement of technology.

There is also the need to set the policies and regulations to be followed in protecting the critical infrastructure and sensitive information. These regulations should set the required level of cybersecurity that needs to be implemented by organizations that are involved in designing, implementing, and managing the smart city systems. For instance, adherence to secure coding standards, requirement for data encryption both at rest and when in transit, as well as strict access control measures are basic requirements of securing sensitive infrastructure. Furthermore, there is a need to establish policies that check the use of data that belongs to individuals and other sensitive information with an aim of protecting the rights of citizens. Furthermore, the local and national government agencies' participation in the decision-making process of cybersecurity contributes to the formation of a joint approach to managing risks, where the responsibility is divided between all the sectors. Besides regulative measures, governance strategies have to focus on the issues of monitoring and reporting. This entails defining structures of authority in both the public and private domain in regard to following the security measures put in place and also in the event of a violation. Finally, it is recommended that governments encourage multidisciplinary stakeholders' engagement of urban planners, IT security professionals, and legal systems to ensure that IT security is considered right from the design and development of smart city systems.

## Technology-driven Solutions

It is true that policy and governance are vital however, technology solutions should also be employed to counter smart city threats. Such urban environments are vast and complex hence the need to adopt sophisticated technological solutions to protect systems and information. The most crucial technological details relate to encryption, artificial intelligence and machine learning, decentralized processing via the blockchain technology, and point specific IoT security.

Advanced Encryption Methods: Encryption is among the oldest and the fundamental security schemes that are implemented to secure the data in smart cities. Due to the huge amounts of sensitive data that are transmitted between the IoT devices, sensors and the central city management systems, encryption assists in rendering the data inaccessible to other parties other than the people with whom they are intended to be directed. Strong protocols and end-to-end encryption are relevant and both should be involved to improve the security state and to prevent leaks. As an example, one can safeguard the connection between traffic management systems and vehicles to eliminate the probability of the attacker taking control of the traffic lights signals or gaining access to data of the passengers. This is one of the aspects that smart cities must have as it must ensure that they embrace the best encryption standards in the market because of the dynamic nature of technology. Moreover, the data must be encrypted in every form of media storage so that even when physical storage systems are stolen, the city data such as health records or financial data will not be left in the wrong hands.

AI and Machine Learning for Threat Detection: The volume and the speed of the information provided by the smart city setting are so immense and huge that it is nearly unfeasible to control the possible threats manually. This is where application of artificial intelligence and learning can come into play. Machine learning algorithms can be used to detect such patterns in the traffic, behavior, and use of the network in smart cities. Since AI can process large volumes of data in real time, such systems can easily identify any irregularities that may indicate an attack. For instance, AI can alert in cases of anomalies in public service, for instance, an increase in traffic data or if there is unusual communication from IoT devices. Furthermore, it is easier to prevent a threat with machine learning since the models can learn from previous events to reduce the number of incidents. This technology can also be used to detect areas that may be exploited by criminals hence making the city stronger.

Blockchain for Data Integrity: After it was initially conceptualized for the purpose of creating Bitcoin, the technology of blockchain is beneficial in the field of ensuring the security of data transactions in smart cities. The very architecture of blockchain, where data is distributed across nodes and linked by cryptography, is very secure against alterations and frauds. This is especially good for the protection of sensitive data that is transmitted between city services and other organizations. For example, in a smart city, smart contract could be applied to protect the transactions in energy distribution or water supply to ensure that no one tampers with records.

In addition, it is possible to increase the transparency and credibility of the interaction since all changes in the process can be checked at any time. This is particularly relevant in handling personal information or public funds as it increases the confidence of the citizens and other stakeholders in the government's handling of the data. IoT Security Solutions: Since IoT devices are the fundamental to smart city systems, it is crucial to protect it. Smart devices and sensors including different types of cameras and smart meters are widely used and the numbers of these are often huge thus making them lucrative targets. The main problem in protecting IoT devices is that they are diverse and may have restricted security features. To reduce such risks, cities have to put in place multiple layers of security that can protect IoT devices and their networks, including secure booting, device identification and end-to-end encryption. In addition, smart cities should ensure that IoT devices are placed in a separate network from other systems; this is because if one IoT device is infected, it should not be able to compromise the whole network. Keeping IoT devices up to date is also important in avoiding use of vulnerabilities that are already known by attackers. At times it might be possible that the standard for IoT device manufacturers is to be set higher in order to make sure that all the devices are secure before they are deployed in the city.

## Collaboration and Information Sharing

It is necessary for different stakeholders in smart cities to appreciate the fact that cybersecurity cannot be solved in isolation of the other; there is the need to share information in order to effectively protect the smart cities. There must be collaboration with the governments, private companies, and international organizations especially to share information on the best practices, intelligence and technicalities. In this way, by developing partnerships between public and private sectors, smart cities can use the knowledge and technology from both spheres in order to respond to new threats in the field of cybersecurity. It also applies to the international level as many threats are worldwide in their scope and impact. Working with other cities and countries is useful because the current threats and the defense measures are also changing all the time. Moreover, the readiness of information exchange in real-time to enhance threat intelligence can also be a way to enhance the reaction to the attacks. These platforms facilitate sharing of cybersecurity intelligence, trends and information among different towns, departments or nations. It also helps cities to share the experiences of each other and prevent any incidence of attack by putting measures in place. These platforms also provide a cooperative problem-solving environment in which cities can collaborate on coming up with effective solutions to numerous cybersecurity issues.

## Incident Response and Recovery

In realtime to say that there is no prevention that can be applied in cyberspace and that is why a good response is essential. One of the important aspects that must be factored in the general development of smart cities is implementation of sound incident handling measures and recovery history that will ensure such facilities are not so vulnerable to cyber-attacks. A perfect incident response plan ought to entail specifications on how an incident can be recognized, examined, and subsequent actions of the people involved in incident response. Additionally, the response plan must involve the analysis of the attack and the application of forensic tools to identify the particular vulnerabilities which are to be reduced. Testing and simulation subjects are essential in career readiness to a cyber event. Learner to intelligent cities, it is necessary to determine an action plan to prepare against terrorist sea threats through cyber security drills and pen testing. These tests simulate real-life situations in that the city authorities and the responders are allowed to practice their roles and identify the possible weaknesses. Those can be further implemented to improve the general strategy of managing incidents and support successful recovery.

## Public Awareness

Finally, there should be awareness and capacity building to ensure cyber security threats in smart cities are effectively addressed. Individuals should be educated about the dangers that could most probably be committed against them in a globalized world, and empower them to protect themselves. The increase of awareness among the residents on how to defend against cyber threats such as the use of password and phishing email could be effective. In the same breath, there is a necessity to hire a talented cybersecurity staff, which can potentially address the problem of smart city security. This involves coming up with curricula that will generate the right knowledge required to design, install and manage cybersecurity of large metropolitan buildings. Universities, technical institutes and governments should develop programs that will help in filling training needs of smart cities.

## FUTURE DIRECTIONS IN SMART CITY CYBERSECURITY

### Emerging Technologies and Cybersecurity

Thus, as intelligent cities develop further maturity, some new technologies like 5G, edge, and quantum computing will significantly transform cybersecurity (Ravindran et al., 2025). These technologies are beneficial in terms of connectivity, computing, and data processing but have drawbacks that need to be met in order to save cities (Jha, A., & Jha, A. 2024). The future of the fifth generation of telecommunication networks or 5G technology is expected to enhance internet speed, reduce latency and connect more devices. In the smart cities context, it will improve the functionality of the IoT devices, increase the rate of data processing in real-time and support the increasing number of connected systems. But, this connectivity increases the exposure of the network because more devices and services are connected to it. The key benefit of having a low latency of 5G results in more responsive service, however the negative of having low latency is that in the same manner cyber-attacks can be initiated and spread out rapidly and with a higher level of effectiveness. This speed of communication could be an advantage and a disadvantage because the hackers may use the speed to launch attacks to the critical infrastructures faster. In addition, the network structures of 5G networks are more complex and these structures can pose new threats in case the networks are not implemented properly. Therefore, since 5G will become a significant element of the smart city development, the effective security measures in the process of 5G implementation will play a crucial role in sustaining the general cybersecurity of the cities. Another technology that will define the future of smart cities is the edge computing which involves processing of data at the point where it is generated for example by the IoT devices. Edge computing minimizes latency and bandwidth requirements since the data processing is done locally which makes it suitable for applications such as traffic control or service of emergency calls. However, the decentralization of the data processing brings about new security challenges (Virmani, C et al 2020).

*Figure 3. Future directions in smart city cybersecurity*

As most of the data is set to be processed at the edges, protecting the edges and devices become paramount. Hacking can take place in the edge nodes and this can cause leakage of information, introduction of malware, or manipulation of the city systems. The issue for smart cities will be to provide better security at the edge, so that devices as well as the communications between them are secure from attacks and yet the performance of these technologies is not compromised. Last but not least, quantum computing is now possible, and it may bring a change to a number of aspects of cybersecurity. On the one hand, quantum computers are capable of cracking the current encryption techniques as they can solve these problems in a shorter time than classical computers. Quantum cryptography for instance, is an exciting field that aims at offering encryption that cannot be cracked easily due to use of quantum mechanics principles. In the context of smart cities, quantum technologies could result in the creation of new security measures that are significantly less vulnerable to cyber threats compared to the current ones (Almeida, F. 2023).

However, as the quantum computing technology is developed, cities will have to be ready to invest in quantum-safe encryption and be prepared to a situation in which quantum-powered attacks might become a real threat to the city's infrastructure. The introduction of quantum computing will definitely bring a change in how smart cities adapt to cybersecurity and the need to come up with security measures that will be strong enough to combat the effects of quantum computing. Political, economic, social, technological, legal and environmental factors of smart cities Increasingly globalization and integration of smart devices will produce new collar threats. As the number of smart devices tech grows, the kinds of attacks increase, and the technologies continue to advance, existing security paradigms will be inadequate. Challenges may increase for attackers and include concentrating on certain aspects of smart city systems, on interfaces between the systems, or on edge computing networks or on the 5G network on which smart city actions are based. Further, as cities pay more dependence on the advanced mechanisms of automation and AI to regulate urban services, there will be a high risk of adversaries' interference or tampering with those systems. It is expected that APTs will increase in the future and focus on attacking critical systems of a city as the attackers seek to infiltrate restricted sectors and stay unnoticed for a long time.

## Policy and Standardization Trends

With more and more smart cities being developed and implemented there is a realization that there is a need to have international strategies to put in place to enhance security of cities. These are crucial as they help in maintaining the standard, guidelines, and responsibility of the numerous systems and technology being used in smart cities. With the advancement of cities integrated with AI, IoT, and autonomous systems, it will be crucial to develop a set of guidelines that will help to avoid the situation when cities have different or overlapping security solutions and protocols. The most significant trend observed in the policies is the emergence of cybersecurity measures for smart cities. These are designed to offer a framework for the planning, deployment, and operation of smart city systems where security is considered at the strategic and technical level throughout the design of cities and their technologies. There are already certain global organizations, which are engaged in the creation of cybersecurity guidelines in smart cities. Such standards can be communication standards, data privacy, device security, and procedures to follow should the cyber-attack occur. In this manner, cities will be confident that they are indeed doing everything within their means to address any of the cybersecurity threats and risks that are likely to happen in the future. Moreover, these standards can enable the smart city projects of other countries to be more compatible and this will provide a foundation to collaborate in solving cybersecurity threat in the globe. These standards also play a vital role in the establishment of progressive regulations and collaboration of the international community in the area of cybersecurity in smart cities. The governments in most countries are beginning to formulate policies that regulate the minimum degree of security required to be installed in the smart city requires data security, software security, and vulnerability regulation. As an illustration, there are some provisions concerning the processing of personal data provided in the General Data Protection Regulation of the European Union, and such guidelines can be established throughout the entire world to address the problem of cyber security in smart urban environment. These legislations help in protecting the confidentiality of the information of the citizens and their privacy besides instilling confidence among the governments, service providers and the people. As the cities of the world become smart and become a part of the global systems and networks, collaboration between countries in cybersecurity and cybersecurity standards will become unavoidable. The local and central governments must note that they must collaborate and integrate their practices to structure and design an approach of cooperation with other cities in the world on cybersecurity incidents. The information sharing and mutual defense mechanisms are also regarded as a part of the collaboration. Analyzing the problems of cyber threats, it is possible to say that no city can act independently in terms of dealing with these issues. Partnership with international organizations is one of the ways through which cities can have access to such information and knowledge as this gives reports on threats, new attacks and emerging weaknesses. By sharing this information, the cities are able to stay abreast of the threats and eliminate the occurrence of risks. Moreover, defense such as cyber defense collaboration and joint response to cyber-attack and security will also lead to a well-built intelligent city network in the entire world. It does not just improve the individual area compliance but also assists in developing an ecosystem of effective security in the world so as to handle the dynamic new challenges faced to the cyber world. To sum up, with the development and the sophistication of smart cities, technologies and the emergence of new policy demands will play the successor in the creation of cybersecurity. Therefore, 5G, edge computing and quantum technologies are great opportunities for further development, but at the same time, it is necessary to open new security approaches and global cooperation. In the same respect, the development of the international standards and the future regulations will help to mitigate the risks of cyber threats and maintain the smart cities' effectiveness and safety for the population. Thus, by keeping up with the progress, cities create the necessary conditions for the formation of a secure digital environment in which, technologies act for the benefit of society, not vice versa.

## CONCLUSION

Smart cities are known to be cities that are full of systems and devices that are in a network with one another. However, this interconnection increases the vulnerability of the cities to various cyber threats and risks. The issues are the weak IoT protection, data protection and confidentiality, network threats, and potential

APTs for critical infrastructures. Such consequences as lack of services, financial losses, and personal data leakage of the citizens can be the results of such risks. The constantly changing more advanced technologies such as 5G, the edge computing, and AI only worsen the situation by offering new avenues of attack that must be recognized and countered before they are utilized. The strategies implemented to address such risks include the formation of a robust cybersecurity policy, encryption, artificial intelligence, and the blockchain. These solutions have proved to possess a tremendous potential in securing the smart city systems, improving response time to the threat, and securing personal information. Nevertheless, the effectiveness of these solutions strongly relies on how they are introduced into the city operation and how they can be changed according to the threats that can emerge. The engagement with other governments, business, and organizations is also essential because it is considered to be the source of information, creation of norms, and creative stimulation. Therefore, the issue of cybersecurity will be constantly evolving and changing as intelligent cities will continue to evolve. The necessity to constantly be on the alert, creative, and cooperative to maintain a movement could not have been over-emphasized. The government, technologists, and information security experts should be able to anticipate the threats that might occur in the future, enhance the existing strategies, and implement the most recent technologies that will lead to the security of the city. Infrastructure of smart cities may be safeguarded by addressing the concept of cybersecurity and creating a culture of continual improvement and, therefore, contributing to the security of the people.

## REFERENCES


Almeida, F. (2023). Prospects of cybersecurity in smart cities. *Future Internet*, *15*(9), 285.

Azizi, N., & Haass, O. (2023). Cybersecurity issues and challenges. In *Handbook of research on cybersecurity issues and challenges for business and FinTech applications* (pp. 21–48). IGI Global.

Bahl, A., Kandpal, S., & Rajendran, R. K. (2024). Innovative Strategies for Urban Construction Optimization in the IoT Era. In *The Climate Change Crisis and Its Impact on Mental Health* (pp. 213–226). IGI Global.

Gómez, J. E., Marcillo, F. R., Triana, F. L., Gallo, V. T., Oviedo, B. W., & Hernández, V. L. (2017). IoT for environmental variables in urban areas. *Procedia Computer Science*, *109*, 67–74.

Iyer, S. S., & Rajagopal, S. (2020). Applications of machine learning in cyber security domain. In *Handbook of research on machine and deep learning applications for cyber security* (pp. 64–82). IGI Global.

Jha, A., & Jha, A. (2024). Securing tomorrow's urban frontiers: A holistic approach to cybersecurity in smart cities. Information System and Smart City, 3(1).

Ganapathi, P., & Shanmugapriya, D. (Eds.). (2019). *Handbook of research on machine and deep learning applications for cyber security*. IGI Global.

Pattani, Nalini, M., Yamini, B., Ambhika, C., & Siva Subramanian, R. (2025). Enhancing early attack detection. Novel hybrid density-based isolation forest for improved anomaly detection. *International Journal of Machine Learning and Cybernetics*, *16*(5), 3429–3447.

Ponmalar, A., Muthuram, A., Therasa, M., Priya, V., Sathya, V., Subha, S., & Subramanian, R. S. (2025). Convergence of Advanced Technologies for Sustainable Development and Smart Cities. In *AI and Green Technology Applications in Society* (pp. 189–218). IGI Global Scientific Publishing.

Prabhu, D., & Sudha, L. MR, P. K., Adaikkammai, A., Aparna, P., & Sathya, V. (2025). Machine Learning in Cybersecurity: Challenges, Applications, and Future Directions. *Exploiting Machine Learning for Robust Security,* 25-48.

Ravindran, D., Revathi, S., Sowndharya, V., Farzhana, I., Sathya, V., Girija, P., & Subramanian, S. (2025). Unraveling the Quantum Computing Frontier: Advancements, Challenges, and Future Prospects. *Integration of AI, Quantum Computing, and Semiconductor Technology*, 139-158.

Sandhu, K. (Ed.). (2021). *Handbook of research on advancing cybersecurity for digital transformation*. IGI Global.

Virmani, C., Choudhary, T., Pillai, A., & Rani, M. (2020). Applications of machine learning in cyber security. In *Handbook of research on machine and deep learning applications for cyber security* (pp. 83–103). IGI Global.

Yamini, B. MAY, P. M. A., Shobana, R., TP, A., & Nalini, M. (2024, December). Cybersecurity: Strategies, Sector-Specific Challenges, and Future Prospects. *In 2024 4th International Conference on Ubiquitous Computing and Intelligent Information Systems* (ICUIS) (pp. 1338-1345). IEEE.

Yavanoglu, O., & Aydos, M. (2017, December). A review on cyber security datasets for machine learning algorithms. *In 2017 IEEE international conference on big data (big data) (pp. 2186-2193)*. IEEE.

Chapter 5
# Privacy and Data Protection in Smart City Agricultural Markets

**Harshit Mishra**
https://orcid.org/0009-0000-1951-7278
*Acharya Narendra Deva University of Agriculture and Technology, Kumarganj, India*

## ABSTRACT

*Data protection in smart agricultural markets remains a critical area of inquiry amid escalating digital transformations. This chapter examines the challenges and solutions surrounding privacy in agricultural data ecosystems, with particular attention to encryption, blockchain, and federated learning technologies. It also evaluates global legal, ethical, and regulatory frameworks such as the GDPR and CCPA that influence data governance in digital agriculture. As of 2023, over 75% of large-scale farms in developed nations employ IoT and AI-driven tools for data collection, yet only 38% have robust data protection measures in place, exposing vulnerabilities in ownership, consent, and access control. The integration of privacy-preserving mechanisms such as homomorphic encryption, zero-knowledge proofs, and secure multi-party computation is discussed as a pathway to sustainable data security. The findings emphasize the urgent need for interoperable standards and policy-driven frameworks to protect stakeholders, particularly smallholder farmers, within smart agricultural marketplaces.*

DOI: 10.4018/979-8-3373-8133-6.ch005

## INTRODUCTION

Smart agricultural market systems have ushered in a new era of digital transformation in agriculture, revolutionizing farming practices, market linkages, and supply chain efficiency. These systems leverage a wide range of digital tools and technologies, including Internet of Things (IoT) devices, satellite imaging, artificial intelligence (AI), and cloud-based platforms, to collect, process, and analyse real-time data (Yang *et al.,* 2021). With the global smart agriculture market valued at approximately USD 15.1 billion in 2021 and projected to reach USD 33.0 billion by 2027, the scale and complexity of data-driven agricultural ecosystems continue to expand (Borrero and Mariscal, 2022). This digital transformation, while promising enhanced productivity, efficiency, and decision-making, raises significant concerns regarding data privacy, ownership, and protection—especially for smallholder farmers and stakeholders operating in vulnerable digital environments (Amiri-Zarandi *et al.,* 2022). The increasing deployment of IoT-enabled sensors, drones, AI-driven analytics, and GPS-enabled machinery contributes to the massive generation of granular agricultural data. This includes data related to environmental conditions, crop health, soil characteristics, pest and disease incidence, and market trends. According to the Food and Agriculture Organization (FAO), such data has the potential to improve yields by up to 25% while reducing input costs by nearly 15% (Prasad *et al.,* 2022). However, this digital footprint exposes sensitive information that, if mishandled, can lead to unauthorized access, surveillance, or exploitation of farmer data by third parties, including agribusiness firms and digital platform providers. The lack of standardized protocols and clarity regarding data ownership further complicates the ethical and legal management of agricultural data (Gyamfi *et al.,* 2024).

Privacy issues in smart agricultural markets manifest in various forms, such as unauthorized access to farm-level data, the use of surveillance technologies without explicit consent, and the opaque data-sharing practices of cloud-based service providers. Notably, a 2022 study by the International Institute for Sustainable Development (IISD) highlighted that over 60% of farmers in developing countries were unaware of how their data was collected or shared by agri-tech platforms (Gupta *et al.,* 2020; Sudaryanto *et al.,* 2022). This asymmetry of information not only undermines farmers' rights but also challenges the ethical basis for data-driven agriculture (Duaa and Hammed, 2025). The problem is exacerbated in regions with weak or non-existent data protection frameworks, leaving stakeholders susceptible to exploitation and market manipulation. In response to these challenges, various global and regional regulatory frameworks have emerged governance (Mishra *et al.,* 2024). The European Union's General Data Protection Regulation (GDPR) and the California Consumer Privacy Act (CCPA) provide comprehensive mechanisms to ensure data transparency, user consent, and accountability in digital services, including agriculture. However, their implementation in agriculture remains limited due to the unique characteristics of the sector, such as seasonal data cycles, fragmented ownership, and localized data needs (Karunathilake *et al.*, 2023). Many agri-tech companies face compliance challenges, particularly in aligning their data practices with evolving legal norms. Furthermore, developing nations often lack robust legal infrastructure and institutional capacity to enforce such frameworks, leading to an uneven landscape of agricultural data governance (Ferris, 2017; Saeed El Etaiby, 2023).

Cryptographic technologies have emerged as a vital component of safeguarding agricultural data. Encryption mechanisms, both symmetric and asymmetric, along with advanced techniques such as homomorphic encryption and secure multi-party computation, offer promising avenues for secure data sharing and analysis. Blockchain technology, too, presents opportunities for creating transparent and tamper-proof records of agricultural transactions, enhancing trust and accountability in digital marketplaces (Kaur *et al.*, 2022). These technologies, when integrated with AI-based solutions, such as federated learning and privacy-preserving analytics, can enable data processing at the edge while maintaining confidentiality. Innovations like anomaly detection and AI-assisted access control systems further strengthen the defense against cybersecurity threats in agricultural IoT environments (Le *et al.*, 2023). Despite technological advances, securing agricultural data demands a multifaceted strategy involving technical safeguards, ethical practices, and robust institutional frameworks. Future innovations, such as zero-knowledge proofs and decentralized finance (DeFi) mechanisms, hold potential to redefine privacy standards in agricultural markets (Kaur and Dara, 2023; Singh, 2022). At the same time, governments and policy-makers must play a proactive role in ensuring that legal protections evolve in tandem with technological changes. Integrating data privacy considerations into national digital agriculture strategies, fostering participatory governance models, and enhancing farmer awareness are essential steps toward equitable and sustainable smart agricultural markets (Regan, 2019). The primary objective of this chapter is:

- To critically examine the challenges and solutions surrounding data privacy and protection in smart agricultural market systems;
- to analyse technological innovations such as encryption, blockchain, and federated learning in securing agricultural data ecosystems; and
- to evaluate legal, ethical, and regulatory frameworks influencing data governance in digital agriculture.

## DATA COLLECTION AND PROCESSING IN SMART AGRICULTURAL MARKETS

Smart agricultural markets rely extensively on data-driven technologies to enhance productivity, optimize resource utilization, and improve decision-making. The integration of digital tools such as the IoT, AI, and remote sensing technologies has transformed the agricultural sector into a highly interconnected ecosystem. However, with the rapid advancement in data collection and processing, concerns regarding data privacy, security, and ownership have become significant challenges. Understanding the sources, types, and processing methods of agricultural data is crucial in addressing the associated risks and ensuring robust data protection mechanisms (López *et al.,* 2023).

### Sources of Data in Smart Agriculture

The data-driven transformation of agriculture is facilitated by various technological sources that continuously collect, process, and analyse vast amounts of information. These sources primarily include IoT sensors, drones, satellite imaging, and AI-driven farm management systems, each playing a unique role in enhancing agricultural efficiency.

#### IoT Sensors and Smart Farming Devices

IoT-enabled sensors and smart farming devices have revolutionized data collection in agriculture by enabling real-time monitoring of critical farm parameters. These sensors are embedded in farm equipment, irrigation systems, and weather stations to collect data on soil moisture, temperature, humidity, and crop health. For instance, soil moisture sensors help farmers optimize irrigation schedules, thereby reducing water wastage and improving crop yield. Similarly, livestock monitoring systems equipped with IoT sensors track animal movement, health conditions, and feeding patterns, aiding in efficient herd management. One of the major concerns associated with IoT-based data collection is data security. As these sensors continuously transmit data to cloud storage platforms, they become vulnerable to cyber threats such as unauthorized access, data breaches, and manipulation. Ensuring end-to-end encryption and secure data transmission protocols is essential to mitigate such risks.

#### Drones and Satellite Imaging

Drones and satellite imaging provide high-resolution aerial data, enabling precision farming and large-scale monitoring of agricultural fields. Drones equipped with multispectral and thermal cameras capture detailed images of crop health, pest infestations, and nutrient deficiencies. Satellite imaging, on the other hand, facilitates large-scale monitoring of climate conditions, vegetation indices, and soil degradation patterns. The integration of remote sensing technology with AI enables predictive analytics for better decision-making. For example, AI-powered image recognition algorithms can analyse drone-captured images to detect early signs of crop diseases, allowing farmers to take timely preventive measures. However, the use of drones and satellites raises concerns regarding data ownership and surveillance. Farmers may lack control over how their farm data is utilized, leading to potential misuse by third parties, including agribusiness corporations and government agencies.

### AI-Driven Farm Management Systems

AI-driven farm management systems integrate data from various sources, including IoT devices, drones, and market intelligence platforms, to provide real-time insights and predictive analytics. These systems use machine learning algorithms to optimize planting schedules, recommend precise fertilizer applications, and forecast market demand for agricultural produce. For instance, AI-powered decision support systems analyse historical climate data and current weather conditions to suggest the most suitable crop varieties for a particular region. Additionally, AI-based chatbots assist farmers by providing instant recommendations on pest control measures and soil nutrient management. Despite their advantages, AI-driven farm management systems pose significant privacy risks (Ali *et al.*, 2024). The collection and processing of large datasets raise concerns about data sovereignty, as farmers often lack control over their own data. Moreover, the reliance on proprietary AI algorithms developed by tech companies creates power imbalances, where small-scale farmers may be at a disadvantage due to restricted access to data-driven insights.

## Types of Agricultural Data Collected

The data collected in smart agricultural markets can be broadly categorized into environmental and climate data, soil and crop health data, market and supply chain data, and personal farmer data. These data types play a crucial role in enhancing productivity, forecasting risks, and ensuring sustainable agricultural practices. However, each category also entails specific privacy and security risks (Table 1).

### Environmental and Climate Data

Environmental and climate data are critical for monitoring weather patterns, predicting climate change impacts, and optimizing farming operations. This category includes data on temperature, precipitation, humidity, solar radiation, and wind speed. Advanced meteorological stations and climate models leverage historical data to forecast droughts, floods, and extreme weather events, enabling farmers to make informed decisions. However, collecting climate data raises challenges related to data accuracy and reliability. Variability in climate models and sensor calibration errors can lead to inaccurate predictions, affecting agricultural planning. Furthermore, access to real-time climate data is often controlled by government agencies and private corporations, limiting its availability to small-scale farmers.

### Soil and Crop Health Data

Soil and crop health data provide insights into soil fertility, nutrient levels, pest infestations, and crop growth patterns. IoT-based soil sensors measure parameters such as pH levels, organic matter content, and electrical conductivity to assess soil quality. Additionally, drone-mounted hyperspectral sensors detect early symptoms of plant diseases and nutrient deficiencies, allowing farmers to implement targeted interventions (Wiseman *et al.,* 2019). One of the key challenges in soil and crop data collection is data standardization. Different sensor manufacturers use varying data formats, making it difficult to integrate and analyse information across multiple platforms. Moreover, concerns regarding data privacy arise when agribusiness firms collect and analyse soil data without farmers' consent, potentially influencing market prices and agricultural policies.

### Market and Supply Chain Data

Market and supply chain data include information on commodity prices, demand fluctuations, logistics, and trade policies. Digital platforms use AI-powered algorithms to analyse historical market trends and forecast future price movements, helping farmers make better selling decisions. Additionally, blockchain technology is increasingly being utilized to enhance supply chain transparency and traceability (Hammed and Jebbar, 2025). However, market data collection involves risks related to data manipulation and unfair trade practices. Large agribusiness corporations and e-commerce platforms may exploit market data to gain a competitive advantage, potentially marginalizing small-scale farmers. Therefore, regulatory frameworks are necessary to ensure fair access to market intelligence (Wolfert *et al.,* 2017).

### Personal Farmer Data

Personal Farmer Data, such as landholding information, income levels, Aadhaar details, and geolocation, are frequently collected through mobile applications and digital platforms. These datasets are often linked to subsidy programs, insurance, or credit access. However, they also pose serious privacy risks. Unauthorized access can lead to identity theft, surveillance, or discriminatory practices based on profiling.

*Table 1. Types of data collected in smart agriculture and associated privacy risks*

| S. No. | Type of Data | Source | Examples | Privacy Risks |
|---|---|---|---|---|
| 1. | Environmental and Climate Data | IoT sensors, weather stations | Rainfall, temperature, humidity | Misuse for unauthorized prediction models |
| 2. | Soil and Crop Health Data | Drones, soil sensors, satellite imaging | Nutrient levels, pest infestation, yield | Exposure of competitive insights and proprietary methods |
| 3. | Market and Supply Chain Data | ERP systems, digital trading platforms | Pricing trends, logistics, buyer info | Market manipulation, data theft, and price discrimination |
| 4. | Personal Farmer Data | Mobile apps, digital ID systems | Land ownership, income, Aadhaar, geolocation | Identity theft, unauthorized surveillance |

Source: Author's compilation

## Processing and Storage of Agricultural Data

The processing and storage of agricultural data involve multiple stages, including data collection, cleaning, integration, analysis, and storage in cloud or decentralized databases. Modern agricultural data platforms employ big data analytics and AI-driven algorithms to extract meaningful insights from raw data. Cloud-based storage solutions offer scalability and accessibility, enabling real-time data sharing among stakeholders (Choudhary *et al.,* 2024). However, cloud storage raises concerns regarding data breaches, unauthorized access, and third-party control over agricultural data. To mitigate these risks, decentralized storage solutions such as blockchain-based ledgers are being explored to enhance data security and transparency. Additionally, data anonymization techniques are essential to protect farmers' privacy. Personal identifiers should be removed or encrypted before data is shared with research institutions, government agencies, or agribusiness firms. Implementing robust cybersecurity measures, including multi-factor authentication and secure access controls, is crucial to safeguarding sensitive agricultural information.

## Risks Associated with Data Collection in Agriculture

While smart agricultural markets offer numerous benefits, they also introduce significant risks related to data privacy, security, and ethical concerns. Some of the key risks include:

- **Unauthorized Data Access:** Cyber threats such as hacking, phishing, and ransomware attacks pose significant risks to agricultural data security. Unauthorized access to farm data can result in financial losses and operational disruptions.
- **Data Ownership and Control:** Farmers often lack clarity on who owns the data collected from their farms. Tech companies and agribusiness corporations may use farm data for commercial gains without adequately compensating farmers.
- **Surveillance and Privacy Concerns:** The use of drones and satellite imaging raises concerns about constant surveillance, leading to ethical dilemmas regarding data privacy.
- **Algorithmic Bias and Discrimination:** AI-driven farm management systems may exhibit biases in data analysis, favouring large-scale commercial farms over smallholder farmers. This can create disparities in resource allocation and market access.

To address these risks, regulatory measures such as data protection policies, ethical AI frameworks, and farmer-centric data governance models must be implemented. Ensuring that farmers have control over their data and are adequately informed about data usage policies is essential in promoting ethical and sustainable data practices in smart agricultural markets.

## PRIVACY CONCERNS IN SMART AGRICULTURAL MARKETS

The integration of smart technologies in agriculture has led to a significant increase in data generation, collection, and processing. While these advancements enhance productivity, efficiency, and sustainability, they also introduce critical privacy concerns. Farmers, agribusinesses, and stakeholders are increasingly relying on digital tools, sensors, and cloud-based platforms to manage farm operations, optimize supply chains, and make data-driven decisions (Farroq *et al.*, 2019). However, issues related to data ownership, unauthorized access, surveillance, cloud security, and transparency in data sharing remain crucial areas of concern. Addressing these privacy challenges is essential to ensuring trust, regulatory compliance, and the ethical use of agricultural data in the digital era.

## Data Ownership and Farmers' Rights

One of the most pressing privacy concerns in smart agricultural markets is the issue of data ownership. With the proliferation of precision agriculture, IoT devices, and satellite-based farm monitoring, large volumes of data are generated daily. The key question that arises is: who owns this data? Farmers, as the primary data generators, often assume they own the data collected from their land, machinery, and livestock. However, in many cases, agribusiness corporations, technology providers, and third-party vendors claim ownership rights through contractual agreements embedded in digital service platforms. The ambiguity surrounding data ownership poses risks to farmers' autonomy and decision-making capabilities. Without clear regulations, agricultural data may be used, stored, or shared without the explicit knowledge or consent of the farmers (Kethineni and Gera, 2023). To safeguard farmers' rights, there is a growing demand for legal frameworks that define data ownership, ensuring that farmers have control over how their data is used, who can access it, and under what conditions. Policies such as the GDPR in Europe set precedents by granting data subjects ownership and access rights. However, similar comprehensive policies specific to agriculture are still lacking in many countries.

## Risks of Unauthorized Data Access

Unauthorized access to agricultural data poses significant risks to privacy, farm security, and competitive advantage. Smart agricultural systems, which rely on wireless sensors, automated machinery, and cloud storage, are vulnerable to cyber threats such as hacking, data breaches, and industrial espionage. Cybercriminals may exploit weaknesses in farm management software, IoT networks, or unsecured cloud platforms to gain unauthorized access to sensitive information, including soil data, yield forecasts, market transactions, and farm financial records. The consequences of such breaches can be severe. Unauthorized access to farm data may lead to price manipulation, unfair competition, or even targeted cyber-attacks on critical infrastructure such as irrigation systems and autonomous machinery. Farmers and agribusinesses must implement robust cybersecurity measures, including data encryption, multi-factor authentication, and firewall protections, to prevent unauthorized intrusions. Additionally, regulatory bodies should establish data protection standards and conduct regular security audits to ensure compliance with best practices.

## Surveillance and Tracking in Digital Agriculture

The increasing use of GPS-enabled devices, drones, and real-time monitoring systems has raised concerns regarding surveillance and tracking in digital agriculture. While these technologies are beneficial for precision farming, supply chain optimization, and pest monitoring, they also introduce risks of excessive data collection, profiling, and surveillance of farming activities. In some cases, agribusiness corporations, government agencies, or financial institutions use farm-level data to monitor compliance with sustainability standards, assess creditworthiness, or influence policy decisions. While such practices may have legitimate applications, they can also lead to unintended consequences such as loss of farmers' privacy, algorithmic discrimination, and exploitation by larger market players. Moreover, the continuous tracking of farm activities raises ethical concerns about data-driven decision-making that may disadvantage smallholder farmers (Tiwari *et al.,* 2023). For instance, insurance companies may use surveillance data to adjust premiums based on farming practices, potentially penalizing farmers without their explicit knowledge. To mitigate these risks, regulations should ensure transparency in data collection, limits on data retention, and explicit consent mechanisms before implementing surveillance technologies in agriculture.

## Privacy Issues in Cloud-Based Agricultural Platforms

Cloud computing has become an integral part of smart agriculture, enabling remote data storage, real-time analytics, and collaboration among stakeholders. However, cloud-based agricultural platforms also pose significant privacy risks, including data security breaches, third-party access, and jurisdictional conflicts regarding data storage and processing. One of the primary concerns is the lack of control over data localization (Cyriac and Thomas, 2024). Many cloud service providers store agricultural data across multiple servers located in different countries, leading to uncertainties regarding data sovereignty and compliance with national privacy laws. For instance, a farmer in India using a cloud-based farm management platform hosted in the United States may face challenges in asserting their data protection rights under domestic regulations. Additionally, cloud storage increases the risk of data misuse by third-party entities. In some cases, platform providers may share agricultural data with commercial enterprises for targeted marketing, pricing strategies, or financial speculation without obtaining explicit farmer consent. Ensuring end-to-end encryption, strict access controls, and legal protections for farmers' data is crucial in addressing these privacy concerns (de Araujo Zanella *et al.,* 2020).

## The Role of Consent and Transparency in Data Sharing

Consent and transparency are fundamental principles of ethical data management in smart agricultural markets. Farmers and agribusinesses must have clear and informed choices regarding how their data is collected, stored, processed, and shared. However, in many digital agriculture platforms, terms and conditions related to data usage are often complex, vague, or buried in lengthy agreements, making it difficult for farmers to fully understand their rights (Sharma *et al.,* 2022). The lack of transparent data governance increases the risk of coerced consent, where farmers are compelled to agree to data-sharing policies in order to access essential services. In some cases, farmers may unknowingly grant broad permissions, allowing agribusiness corporations to use their data for commercial or research purposes without any direct benefits in return. To enhance fair and transparent data-sharing practices, the following measures should be implemented:

1. **Simplified and Accessible Data Policies** – Contracts should be written in clear, easy-to-understand language, ensuring farmers can make informed decisions.
2. **Granular Consent Mechanisms** – Instead of blanket approvals, farmers should have options to selectively permit data sharing for specific purposes.
3. **Audit Trails and Data Portability** – Farmers should have access to records of how their data has been used and the ability to transfer their data between platforms.
4. **Ethical Data Partnerships** – Agreements between farmers, agribusinesses, and technology providers should include fair compensation mechanisms when farm data contributes to commercial benefits.

## DATA PROTECTION FRAMEWORKS AND REGULATIONS

The rise of smart agricultural markets, driven by digital transformation, IoT, and AI-driven analytics, has necessitated robust data protection measures. These technologies collect vast amounts of agricultural data, including farm operations, soil conditions, weather patterns, and market transactions. However, without proper data protection frameworks, these innovations could lead to privacy risks, data breaches, and misuse of sensitive information. Various global and regional regulations provide guidelines on handling agricultural data, ensuring compliance, and protecting stakeholders' rights (Roopaei *et al.,* 2017).

## Global Data Protection Laws Relevant to Agriculture

As agricultural data becomes digitized, several global and regional data protection laws have emerged to regulate its collection, processing, and storage. These laws aim to balance technological advancements with privacy rights, ensuring that farmers, agribusinesses, and consumers have control over their data.

### General Data Protection Regulation (GDPR)

GDPR, implemented by the European Union (EU) in 2018, is one of the most comprehensive data protection laws. While initially designed for personal data, its principles are increasingly relevant in smart agricultural markets where digital platforms collect and analyse farmer and consumer information.

Some principles of GDPR include:

- **Lawful processing:** Data collection must have a legal basis, such as consent or contractual necessity.
- **Data minimization:** Only necessary data should be collected and stored.
- **Right to access and rectification:** Farmers and agribusinesses have the right to access their data and request corrections.
- **Right to erasure (Right to be forgotten):** Individuals can request deletion of their personal data.
- **Data portability:** Stakeholders must be able to transfer their data to other service providers.

In agricultural settings, GDPR impacts data-sharing agreements between farmers, agritech firms, and supply chain actors. Compliance requires clear data governance policies, secure storage mechanisms, and transparency in data transactions (Ellis and Paustian, 2024).

### California Consumer Privacy Act (CCPA)

CCPA, enacted in 2020, is a leading data privacy law in the United States. It applies to businesses that collect data from California residents, including agricultural technology companies operating within the state. The CCPA grants consumers several rights, as shown in Figure 1.

*Figure 1. Consumers' rights under CCPA*

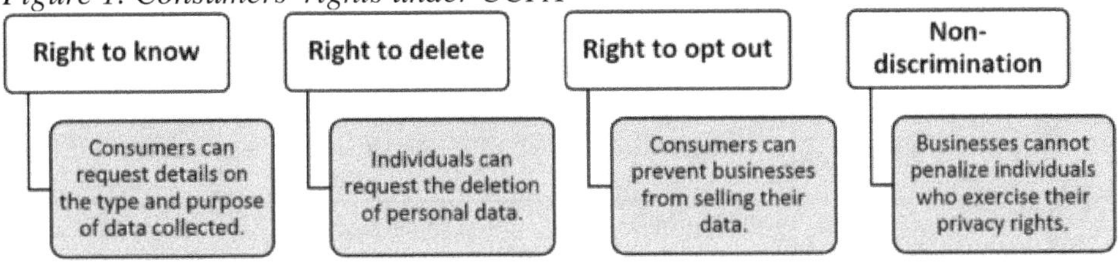


In agricultural markets, the CCPA affects data collected from farmers, agricultural suppliers, and digital platforms that facilitate market transactions. Agri-tech companies must ensure transparent data policies, provide opt-out mechanisms, and implement secure data storage to comply with the law.

## Other Regional Data Protection Frameworks

Beyond GDPR and CCPA, several regional data protection laws influence agricultural data management. These include:

- **India's Personal Data Protection Bill (PDPB)**: India's evolving data protection framework emphasizes data localization and explicit user consent, impacting foreign agritech firms.
- **Brazil's General Data Protection Law (LGPD)**: Similar to GDPR, it mandates clear data governance and consumer rights for agricultural enterprises.
- **China's Personal Information Protection Law (PIPL)**: Enforces strict regulations on data processing and cross-border transfers, affecting agritech firms operating in China.

Each framework poses unique challenges and opportunities for global agricultural markets, requiring companies to adapt their data management strategies accordingly (Ahmed *et al.*, 2024). A comparative analysis of these data protection laws relevant to agriculture is presented in Table 2.

*Table 2. Comparative overview of international data protection laws and their relevance to smart agriculture*

| S. No. | Aspect | GDPR (EU) | CCPA (California, USA) | India's DPDP Act (2023) |
|---|---|---|---|---|
| 1. | Scope | Personal data of EU citizens | Personal data of California residents | Personal data of Indian citizens |
| 2. | Consent Requirement | Explicit and informed | Opt-out model | Notice and consent-based |
| 3. | Applicability to Agri-Tech | Yes, if dealing with personal/farm data | Yes, includes farm-related platforms | Yes, for all entities handling farm data |
| 4. | Right to be Forgotten | Yes | Limited | Yes |
| 5. | Penalties for Non-compliance | Up to €20 million or 4% of global turnover | Up to $7,500 per violation | Up to 250 crore |
| 6. | Impact on Data Sharing in Agriculture | Restricts unauthorized sharing | Allows sharing with opt-out | Requires strict compliance |

Source: Author's compilation

## Compliance Challenges for Agri-Tech Companies

Adhering to multiple data protection laws presents significant challenges for agritech companies. Some of the key compliance difficulties include:

- **Diverse regulatory landscapes:** Companies operating in multiple regions must navigate varying laws, leading to complex compliance requirements.
- **Data ownership issues:** Determining whether data belongs to farmers, agri-businesses, or technology providers remains ambiguous.
- **Cross-border data transfers:** Many agricultural platforms operate globally, requiring compliance with regulations that restrict data movement across borders.
- **Security vulnerabilities:** Cyberattacks, data breaches, and inadequate encryption pose threats to agricultural data security.
- **Farmer awareness and consent:** Many small-scale farmers lack awareness of their data rights, making informed consent a challenge.

To address these issues, agritech firms must develop robust data governance policies, invest in cybersecurity infrastructure, and implement clear consent mechanisms for data collection and sharing.

## The Role of Governments in Ensuring Data Security in Agriculture

Governments play a critical role in safeguarding agricultural data by implementing policies, regulatory frameworks, and technological interventions. Key government actions include:

- **Developing national data protection laws** tailored to agricultural data while aligning with international best practices.
- **Enforcing compliance** through monitoring, audits, and penalties for non-compliant entities.
- **Promoting secure digital infrastructure**, such as blockchain based data authentication and encrypted storage.
- **Funding research and awareness programs** to educate farmers and agri-businesses on data privacy rights.
- **Encouraging public-private partnerships** to create secure and interoperable agricultural data platforms.

By adopting a multi-stakeholder approach, governments can ensure that agricultural data contributes to efficiency and innovation while maintaining privacy and security (Ferrag *et al.,* 2020).

## Ethical and Legal Considerations in Agricultural Data Handling

The collection and processing of agricultural data raise significant ethical and legal concerns, particularly in terms of data ownership, consent, and equitable data access.

### Ethical Considerations

- **Farmer autonomy:** Farmers should have control over their data and be able to decide how it is used.
- **Transparency:** Agri-tech firms must clearly communicate data collection, processing, and sharing practices.
- **Fair data-sharing models:** Companies should ensure that farmers benefit from data-driven insights rather than being exploited.
- **Bias and discrimination:** AI models using agricultural data must be free from biases that disadvantage certain regions or farmer groups (Raja *et al.,* 2024).

## Legal Considerations

- **Data breach liability:** Who is responsible in the event of data leaks—agritech firms, governments, or third-party service providers?
- **Intellectual property rights:** If AI-driven analytics generate new insights from farm data, who owns these innovations?
- **Contractual agreements:** Clear contracts should outline data rights, access permissions, and revenue-sharing terms.

Addressing these issues requires a legal and ethical framework that balances innovation, data security, and farmer rights. Below (Figure 2) is a conceptual flow-chart illustrating the steps agri-tech firms must take to ensure compliance with data protection regulations.

*Figure 2. Steps in data protection compliance for agri-tech companies (Source: Author's compilation)*

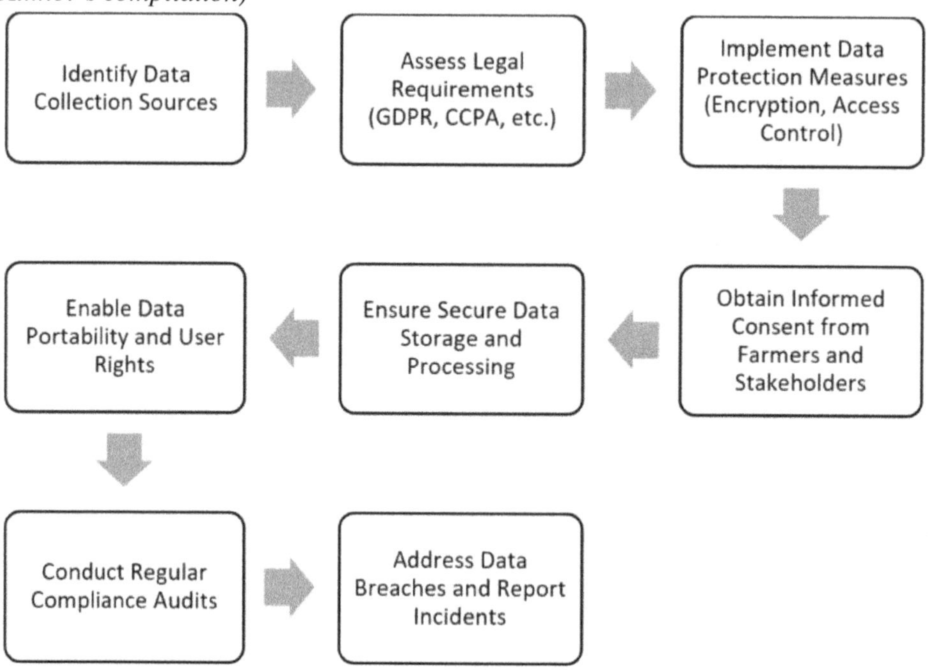

# CRYPTOGRAPHIC TECHNIQUES FOR DATA SECURITY IN AGRICULTURE

## Role of Cryptography in Protecting Agricultural Data

With the increasing digitization of agricultural systems, vast amounts of data are generated daily from smart farming devices, sensors, and automated machinery. This data is crucial for optimizing agricultural productivity, improving supply chain efficiency, and facilitating precision farming techniques (NC, 2020). However, it is also highly sensitive, encompassing information related to soil health, crop yields, weather patterns, and even proprietary farming techniques. Cryptography plays a pivotal role in ensuring the confidentiality, integrity, and authenticity of agricultural data, thereby preventing unauthorized access, tampering, or theft. In smart agricultural markets, cryptographic methods safeguard the transmission and storage of data collected from IoT devices, cloud-based platforms, and decentralized marketplaces. Cryptographic protocols enable authentication mechanisms that ensure only authorized users can access critical agricultural datasets (Yazdinejad *et al.*, 2021). Additionally, cryptographic techniques contribute to building trust among stakeholders, including farmers, agribusinesses, financial institutions, and policymakers, by ensuring the integrity and verifiability of transactions and data exchanges. To better understand the range of cryptographic approaches used in agricultural data security, Table 3 provides a comparative summary of key techniques, their applications, benefits, and associated challenges.

## Encryption Techniques for Smart Farming Systems

Encryption is one of the most fundamental cryptographic techniques employed to secure agricultural data. It involves the transformation of readable data (plaintext) into an unreadable format (ciphertext) using an encryption algorithm and a cryptographic key. The encrypted data can only be converted back into its original form by authorized users who possess the decryption key. Various encryption techniques have been developed to address different security challenges in smart agricultural markets (Figure 3).

### Symmetric and Asymmetric Encryption

Encryption techniques are broadly categorized into symmetric and asymmetric encryption.

*Figure 3. Symmetric and asymmetric encryption*

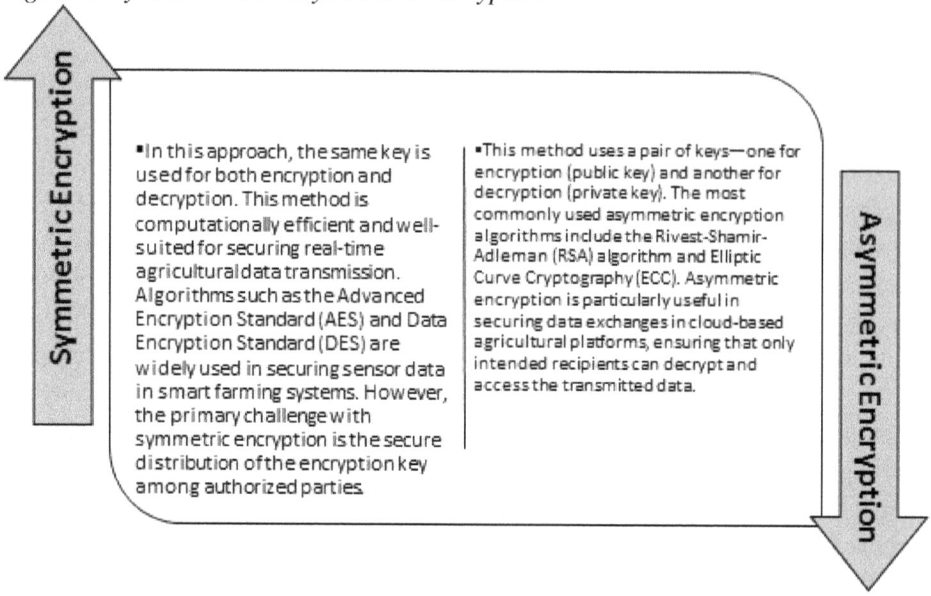


The following equation represents the basic operation of RSA encryption:

$$C = M^e \, mod \, n \tag{1}$$

where:
C is the ciphertext,
M is the plaintext message,
e is the public key exponent, and
n is the product of two large prime numbers.
Decryption is performed using the private key exponent d, following the equation:

$$M = C^d \, mod \, n \tag{2}$$

## Homomorphic Encryption for Secure Computation

Homomorphic encryption (HE) is an advanced cryptographic technique that allows computations to be performed on encrypted data without requiring decryption. This is particularly beneficial in smart agricultural markets where sensitive data needs to be analysed by external entities, such as agritech companies, financial institutions, or government agencies, without exposing the raw data. Fully homomorphic encryption (FHE) schemes enable complex computations, such as machine learning-based yield predictions or precision agriculture analytics, while preserving data privacy (Mayakannan *et al.,* 2023). The mathematical foundation of homomorphic encryption ensures that operations performed on encrypted data yield results identical to those obtained from operations on plaintext data. The basic operation of an additive homomorphic encryption scheme, such as the Paillier cryptosystem, can be expressed as follows:

$$E(M_1) \times E(M_2) = E(M_1 + M_2) \quad (3)$$

where E(M) represents the encryption function and $M_1$, $M_2$ are plaintext values. This property is useful in privacy-preserving computations, such as collaborative yield forecasting in smart agriculture.

## Secure Data Transmission and Storage

Ensuring the secure transmission and storage of agricultural data is critical in preventing data breaches, cyberattacks, and unauthorized access. Secure communication protocols and data storage mechanisms play a crucial role in achieving this objective (Kuntke, 2024).

### Secure Data Transmission:

- **Transport Layer Security (TLS):** TLS ensures secure communication between IoT devices, cloud platforms, and mobile applications used in smart farming. It encrypts data during transmission to prevent interception by attackers.
- **Virtual Private Networks (VPNs):** VPNs establish secure encrypted tunnels for data exchange between different agricultural entities, ensuring data privacy and preventing unauthorized network access.
- **Secure Multi-Party Computation (SMPC):** This cryptographic technique allows multiple parties to jointly compute a function over their inputs while keeping their individual inputs private. It is particularly useful for sharing sensitive agricultural data among different stakeholders without exposing proprietary information (Zampati, 2023).

### Secure Data Storage:

- **End-to-End Encryption (E2EE):** In this approach, data is encrypted before being transmitted and remains encrypted while stored in cloud or local databases. Only authorized users with decryption keys can access the data.

- **Decentralized Storage Systems:** Distributed ledger technologies, such as blockchain-based storage, offer enhanced security by preventing single points of failure and unauthorized data modifications.

## Blockchain for Secure and Transparent Agricultural Transactions

Blockchain technology provides a decentralized and tamper-resistant framework for securing agricultural transactions and data exchanges. In smart agricultural markets, blockchain can enhance transparency, traceability, and trust among stakeholders by creating immutable records of transactions.

### Features of Blockchain for Agriculture:

- **Data Integrity:** Blockchain ensures that once data is recorded, it cannot be altered or deleted, preventing fraudulent activities in supply chains and smart contracts.
- **Decentralization:** Unlike traditional centralized databases, blockchain eliminates the need for intermediaries, reducing costs and enhancing security.
- **Smart Contracts:** These self-executing contracts automate transactions based on predefined conditions. For example, a smart contract can automatically release payments to farmers upon verification of crop delivery.
- **Supply Chain Traceability:** Blockchain enables real-time tracking of agricultural products from farm to market, ensuring food safety and reducing fraudulent labelling.

### Mathematical Representation of Blockchain Hashing:

Blockchain security relies on cryptographic hash functions, such as the SHA-256 algorithm, which converts input data into a fixed-size hash value:

$$H = SHA - 256(D) \tag{4}$$

where:
H is the hash output,
D is the input data.

The immutability of blockchain records ensures that any modification to agricultural transactions alters the hash value, immediately detecting unauthorized changes (Bronson, 2018).

*Table 3. Cryptographic techniques and their applications in agricultural data security*

| S. No. | Technique | Application | Benefits | Challenges |
|---|---|---|---|---|
| 1. | Symmetric Encryption | Data transmission in IoT networks | Fast and efficient | Key distribution complexity |
| 2. | Asymmetric Encryption | Secure cloud data access | Public-private key model for safe sharing | Slower processing |
| 3. | Homomorphic Encryption | Computation on encrypted farm data | Privacy-preserving analytics | High computational overhead |
| 4. | Blockchain | Transparent supply chain records and smart contracts | Tamper-proof, decentralized, auditable | Scalability, regulatory uncertainty |
| 5. | Federated Learning | AI model training across distributed farm data | Local data remains private, reduced risk | Requires robust infrastructure and bandwidth |

Source: Author's compilation

## AI AND MACHINE LEARNING IN DATA PRIVACY FOR SMART AGRICULTURE

The integration of AI and ML in smart agriculture has revolutionized data collection, analysis, and decision-making processes. However, as agricultural systems become increasingly digitalized, concerns regarding data privacy and security have emerged. AI and ML offer advanced mechanisms to safeguard sensitive agricultural data, ensuring compliance with regulatory standards and protecting farmers' proprietary information. This section explores AI-driven solutions for privacy-preserving data analytics, federated learning, anomaly detection, and identity management in smart agricultural markets.

### AI-Driven Privacy-Preserving Data Analytics

The large-scale adoption of smart agricultural technologies generates vast amounts of data related to soil health, crop yields, weather patterns, and market prices. While this data is invaluable for improving productivity, sharing it without proper privacy measures can expose farmers and agribusinesses to security risks. AI-driven privacy-preserving data analytics ensure that insights can be extracted from agricultural data without compromising confidentiality (Johnraja *et al.,* 2024). Techniques such as differential privacy, homomorphic encryption, and secure multiparty computation enable data analysis without direct access to raw information. Differential privacy adds statistical noise to datasets, preventing the identification of specific farms or individuals while maintaining overall analytical accuracy. Homomorphic encryption allows computations to be performed on encrypted data, ensuring that sensitive agricultural records remain secure even during processing. These AI-enabled techniques enhance data privacy, allowing stakeholders to leverage agricultural insights without violating confidentiality agreements. An effective implementation of such AI technologies requires a structured risk management framework to ensure data protection, model transparency, and threat mitigation. A comprehensive process for managing AI-related risks is presented in Figure 4, highlighting stages such as scope definition, risk identification, security protocols, and continuous improvement.

*Figure 4. Flowchart of AI risk management framework for privacy-preserving agricultural data systems (adopted from Villegas et al., 2023).*

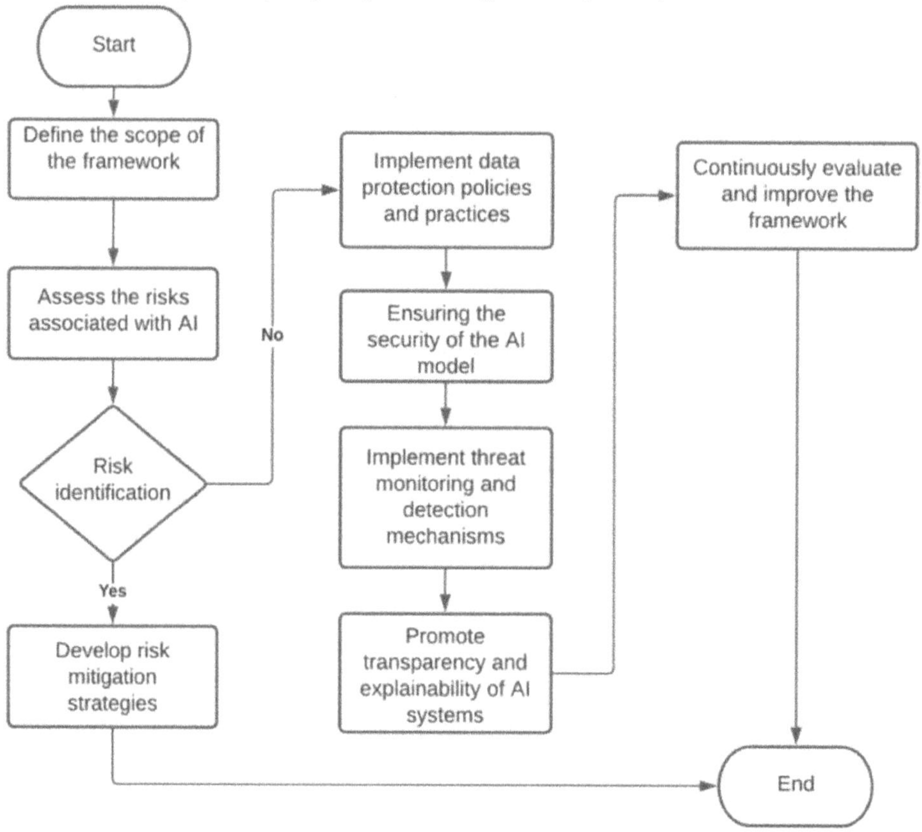

## Federated Learning for Decentralized Data Processing

Federated learning (FL) is an emerging AI approach that enables collaborative model training across multiple decentralized devices without exchanging raw data. This is particularly beneficial in smart agriculture, where various stakeholders, including farmers, agribusinesses, and researchers, generate valuable data. Instead of transferring sensitive agricultural data to a central server, FL trains machine learning models locally on edge devices such as IoT sensors, drones, and farm management systems (Alahe *et al.,* 2024). The decentralized nature of FL enhances data privacy by keeping data within the local environment, reducing the risk of unauthorized access or breaches. Moreover, FL minimizes bandwidth consumption and computational overhead, making it suitable for rural agricultural regions with limited internet connectivity. In smart agricultural markets, federated learning facilitates secure collaboration while ensuring that individual farms retain ownership and control over their data (Mishra and Mishra, 2024).

## Anomaly Detection for Cybersecurity in Smart Farming

AI-based anomaly detection plays a crucial role in safeguarding agricultural networks from cyber threats. Smart farms rely on IoT sensors, autonomous machinery, and cloud-based platforms, which are vulnerable to cyberattacks such as data breaches, malware, and unauthorized access. AI-driven anomaly detection systems continuously monitor agricultural networks, identifying irregular patterns that may indicate security breaches. By leveraging ML algorithms such as unsupervised learning, neural networks, and statistical modelling, anomaly detection systems can recognize deviations from normal operations. For example, an unexpected spike in data transmission from a farm's IoT network may indicate a cyber intrusion. AI-driven security mechanisms can trigger alerts and initiate automated responses, such as isolating compromised devices, restricting access, or deploying security patches. These proactive measures protect agricultural data integrity and ensure the resilience of smart farming infrastructure.

## AI in Access Control and Identity Management

Access control and identity management are fundamental aspects of data privacy in smart agricultural markets. AI enhances these mechanisms by implementing adaptive authentication and biometric verification techniques. Traditional username-password authentication methods are often insufficient in protecting sensitive agricultural data, especially in cloud-based systems accessed by multiple stakeholders. AI-powered identity management systems utilize behavioural biometrics, facial recognition, and voice authentication to verify users' identities securely (Sullivan *et al.,* 2024). Machine learning algorithms analyse login patterns, device usage, and user behaviour to detect anomalies and prevent unauthorized access. Furthermore, AI-based role-based access control (RBAC) ensures that different users—such as farmers, agronomists, and policymakers—have appropriate data access privileges. These AI-driven access control mechanisms mitigate the risks of data breaches and unauthorized data modifications in agricultural markets (Jouanjean *et al.,* 2020).

## SECURING AGRICULTURAL IOT AND CLOUD-BASED PLATFORMS

Smart agriculture heavily relies on IoT-enabled devices and cloud-based platforms for real-time monitoring, data storage, and automated decision-making. However, these technological advancements introduce cybersecurity risks that must be addressed to ensure the confidentiality, integrity, and availability of agricultural data. This section examines the cybersecurity challenges in agricultural IoT networks, secure data storage strategies, access control mechanisms, and multi-factor authentication solutions for smart agricultural platforms.

### Cybersecurity Challenges in Agricultural IoT Networks

Agricultural IoT (Agri-IoT) networks connect a diverse range of devices, including soil moisture sensors, weather stations, drones, and automated irrigation systems. These interconnected devices improve agricultural efficiency but also present cybersecurity vulnerabilities. Common threats include unauthorized access, data interception, malware attacks, and device spoofing. One of the primary challenges in securing Agri-IoT networks is the lack of standardized security protocols (Ofori and El-Gayar, 2019). Many IoT devices used in agriculture operate on limited computational resources, making it difficult to implement robust encryption and authentication mechanisms. Additionally, the distributed nature of smart farms increases the attack surface, making them attractive targets for cybercriminals. Addressing these challenges requires AI-driven intrusion detection systems, strong encryption protocols, and regular security updates to prevent exploitation.

### Secure Data Storage in Cloud-Based Agricultural Systems

Cloud computing provides scalable storage solutions for agricultural data, enabling remote access and real-time decision-making. However, cloud-based systems also introduce data privacy risks, including unauthorized data access, leakage, and loss due to cyberattacks or system failures. Secure data storage mechanisms are essential to protect agricultural data from potential threats. Techniques such as encryption-at-rest and encryption-in-transit ensure that stored data remains protected from unauthorized access (Kumar *et al.,* 2024). Advanced encryption standards (AES) and secure hash algorithms (SHA) prevent data tampering and maintain data integrity (Shen, 2023). Moreover, distributed ledger technologies (DLTs), such as blockchain, provide an additional layer of security by ensuring transparent and immutable data storage. Implementing these security measures enhances trust in cloud-based agricultural systems and ensures compliance with data protection regulations.

## Access Control Mechanisms for Agricultural Databases

Smart agricultural platforms manage vast datasets related to crop health, market prices, weather forecasts, and supply chain logistics. Unauthorized access to these databases can lead to data manipulation, financial losses, and market disruptions. Implementing robust access control mechanisms is crucial to maintaining data confidentiality and integrity. Role-based access control (RBAC) and attribute-based access control (ABAC) frameworks define user permissions based on roles, responsibilities, and contextual factors (Gyamfi *et al.,* 2024). For instance, farm owners may have full access to all agricultural data, while external researchers may have restricted access to specific datasets. AI-driven access control mechanisms can dynamically adjust permissions based on user behaviour, device security status, and environmental conditions, reducing the risk of unauthorized data breaches (Relf-Eckstein *et al.,* 2019).

## Multi-Factor Authentication for Smart Agricultural Platforms

Multi-factor authentication (MFA) enhances security by requiring multiple forms of verification before granting access to smart agricultural platforms. Traditional password-based authentication is vulnerable to phishing attacks and password breaches. MFA mitigates these risks by combining two or more authentication factors, as shown in Figure 5.

*Figure 5. Flowchart of AI risk management framework for privacy-preserving*

| Something You Know | Something You Have | Something You Are |
|---|---|---|
| • Passwords or security questions. | • Mobile authentication apps, security tokens, or smart cards. | • Biometric verification, such as fingerprint scans or facial recognition. |

Implementing MFA ensures that only authorized users can access critical agricultural data and management systems. AI-powered authentication methods, such as adaptive authentication, further enhance security by analysing contextual factors like device usage patterns, geolocation, and network behaviour. If an anomaly is detected—such as an unusual login attempt from an unfamiliar location—the system may prompt additional authentication steps or restrict access (Jakku *et al.,* 2019).

## PRIVACY-PRESERVING MARKET MECHANISMS AND SMART CONTRACTS

With the increasing adoption of digital technologies in agriculture, concerns regarding data privacy and security have gained significant attention. Traditional market mechanisms often expose sensitive agricultural data, leading to risks of exploitation, unfair market practices, and breaches of confidentiality (Atik, 2022). Privacy-preserving market mechanisms leverage cryptographic techniques and decentralized frameworks to ensure secure transactions, equitable participation, and data protection. Smart contracts, privacy-enhanced marketplaces, and DeFi solutions play a crucial role in safeguarding data while facilitating seamless trade in agricultural markets (Sarhya *et al.,* 2024).

### Role of Smart Contracts in Secure Agricultural Transactions

Smart contracts, which are self-executing digital agreements embedded in blockchain networks, provide a secure and automated way to conduct agricultural transactions. These contracts eliminate intermediaries, reduce transaction costs, and enhance trust between buyers and sellers by ensuring predefined conditions are met before executing a trade. Mathematically, a smart contract can be represented as follows:

$$SC = \{T, C, A\} \tag{5}$$

Where:

SC the smart contract,

T is the set of transaction rules,

C denotes the conditions that must be fulfilled,

A refers to the automated actions executed once conditions are met.

For instance, in a contract between a farmer and a retailer, the agreement may state that payment will be automatically released only when the IoT sensors confirm the delivery of fresh produce at the designated warehouse. The integration of blockchain ensures that transaction data is immutable and transparent while maintaining the confidentiality of sensitive information (Meziani *et al.,* 2024).

## Privacy-Preserving Marketplaces for Agricultural Products

Traditional agricultural markets often involve intermediaries who collect and analyse farmers' production data, leading to concerns regarding data misuse. Privacy-preserving marketplaces utilize advanced cryptographic protocols, such as homomorphic encryption and differential privacy, to allow farmers to participate in digital markets without compromising their sensitive information (Lipper *et al.,* 2014).

These marketplaces employ techniques such as:

- **Differential privacy:** Ensuring individual data points remain undisclosed while still allowing meaningful market analytics.
- **Zero-knowledge proofs (ZKPs):** Enabling farmers to prove their eligibility for market access without revealing personal or farm-specific data.
- **Decentralized identity verification:** Allowing farmers to trade using anonymous credentials while ensuring compliance with regulatory standards.

By implementing these privacy-enhancing techniques, digital agricultural markets can maintain trust, ensure data security, and empower smallholder farmers with equitable access to fair pricing.

## Decentralized Finance (DeFi) for Agricultural Trade

DeFi introduces blockchain-based financial solutions that eliminate the reliance on traditional banks and financial intermediaries. In the agricultural sector, DeFi facilitates direct farmer-to-consumer transactions, micro-loans, and secure payments through cryptocurrency and stablecoins (Kumari *et al.,* 2024).

The DeFi ecosystem enables:

- **Peer-to-peer lending platforms:** Farmers can obtain credit based on their past transaction history without requiring extensive collateral.
- **Decentralized insurance mechanisms:** Smart contracts automatically compensate farmers for crop failures based on predefined weather and yield conditions.
- **Automated liquidity pools:** Ensuring farmers receive fair market prices by enabling decentralized commodity trading.

$$Y = f(X) + \epsilon \tag{6}$$

Where:
Y represents the financial outcome for a farmer,
X includes factors such as creditworthiness and yield projections,
$\epsilon$ accounts for market volatility and uncertainties.

By leveraging DeFi solutions, agricultural trade becomes more accessible, transparent, and resilient to economic fluctuations (Demestichas *et al.,* 2020).

## Ensuring Fair and Transparent Market Access

One of the critical challenges in agricultural trade is ensuring that small-scale farmers and marginalized communities have equal access to markets. Privacy-preserving technologies contribute to fair and transparent market participation by preventing price discrimination and data monopolization.

Strategies to achieve this include:

- **Decentralized market platforms:** Eliminating the dominance of large corporations by enabling peer-to-peer trading.
- **Encrypted price discovery mechanisms:** Preventing market manipulation and ensuring fair pricing through secure bidding processes.
- **Smart subsidies and incentive programs:** Governments and cooperatives can provide targeted financial support while maintaining privacy through cryptographic token systems.

By integrating these solutions, digital agricultural markets can foster inclusivity, protect sensitive data, and promote economic sustainability (Schönfeld *et al.,* 2018).

## FUTURE DIRECTIONS AND INNOVATIONS IN AGRICULTURAL DATA PRIVACY

As the digital transformation of agriculture accelerates, the need for robust data privacy solutions continues to grow. Emerging privacy-enhancing technologies offer new ways to safeguard agricultural data while enabling valuable insights for market participants. Innovations such as zero-knowledge proofs, secure multi-party computation, and privacy-preserving AI models are poised to redefine data security in smart agricultural markets.

### Emerging Trends in Privacy-Preserving Technologies

The future of agricultural data privacy relies on advanced cryptographic techniques and distributed computing frameworks. Some emerging trends include:

- **Federated learning:** A machine learning approach where data remains decentralized, allowing predictive models to be trained without exposing sensitive information.
- **Secure data enclaves:** Hardware-based secure zones that ensure confidential data processing without external access.
- **Post-quantum cryptography:** Developing encryption methods resilient to quantum computing threats, ensuring long-term data security.

By integrating these technologies, agricultural stakeholders can leverage big data insights while maintaining strict privacy controls.

### The Potential of Zero-Knowledge Proofs in Agricultural Data Protection

Zero-knowledge proofs (ZKPs) enable one party to prove the validity of a statement without revealing the underlying data. This cryptographic technique is highly beneficial for agricultural markets, allowing farmers to verify information without exposing sensitive production details (Parashar *et al.*, 2024). A ZKP-based market authentication can be formulated as:

$P \rightarrow V$: Proof that $x \in L$ without revealing x

Where:

P is the prover (e.g., a farmer),

V is the verifier (e.g., a buyer or regulatory body),

x represents sensitive agricultural data,

L denotes a set of valid statements that can be verified without revealing x.

By applying ZKPs, farmers can prove their produce meets organic certification standards or quality benchmarks without exposing trade secrets.

## Advancements in Secure Multi-Party Computation for Agriculture

Secure Multi-Party Computation (SMPC) enables multiple parties to collaboratively compute functions over their inputs while keeping those inputs private (Marcu *et al.,* 2020). This technique is particularly useful in agricultural data sharing and market analysis. Some applications of SMPC in agriculture include:

- **Privacy-preserving yield forecasting:** Multiple farms can collectively analyse yield predictions without exposing individual data.
- **Confidential market trend analysis:** Agricultural cooperatives can derive price trends without revealing proprietary sales data.
- **Regulatory compliance monitoring:** Ensuring adherence to safety and environmental standards without direct data access (Amiri-Zarandi *et al.,* 2022).

The mathematical representation of an SMPC function can be given as:

$$F(x_1, x_2, \ldots, x_n) = y \qquad (7)$$

Where:
$x_1, x_2, \ldots, x_n$ are private inputs from different participants,
y is the final computed output,
The computation ensures that $x_i$ values remain undisclosed to other participants.

SMPC enables data-driven decision-making while ensuring confidentiality and compliance.

## Policy Recommendations for Strengthening Agricultural Data Security

To establish a secure and privacy-conscious agricultural data ecosystem, policymakers must implement stringent regulations and incentivize the adoption of privacy-enhancing technologies. Some recommendations include:

- **Developing standardized privacy frameworks:** Establishing guidelines for data-sharing agreements and ethical AI usage in agriculture.

- **Encouraging the adoption of privacy-preserving tools:** Providing financial support for blockchain integration, federated learning, and cryptographic data protection.
- **Ensuring transparency in digital agricultural platforms:** Mandating open-access policies while safeguarding sensitive market data.
- **Promoting cross-sector collaborations:** Encouraging partnerships between governments, research institutions, and private sectors to advance data security solutions.

By implementing these policy measures, smart agricultural markets can achieve a balance between data-driven innovation and privacy preservation, fostering sustainable and equitable trade ecosystems (Kosior, 2019).

## CONCLUSION

Privacy and data protection in smart agricultural markets have become crucial in the era of digital farming, where vast amounts of data are generated, processed, and shared across multiple platforms. The integration of IoT sensors, AI-driven farm management systems, and satellite imaging has significantly enhanced agricultural productivity but has also introduced risks related to data ownership, unauthorized access, and cybersecurity threats. A report by Markets and Markets (2023) estimated that the global agricultural IoT market would reach USD 30.8 billion by 2026, underscoring the scale of data-driven farming and the pressing need for stringent data protection measures. Farmers, as primary data contributors, often face challenges in maintaining control over their data, with concerns arising over surveillance, unauthorized tracking, and the potential misuse of sensitive agricultural insights by third parties. Ensuring compliance with global data protection laws, such as the GDPR and CCPA, remains a challenge for agri-tech companies, especially in developing nations where regulatory frameworks are still evolving. Cryptographic techniques, including homomorphic encryption and blockchain, offer promising solutions for securing agricultural data while maintaining transparency in transactions. AI-driven privacy-preserving analytics and federated learning further enhance data security by enabling decentralized processing without compromising privacy. Despite these advancements, cybersecurity risks persist, with a report by Cybersecurity Ventures predicting that cybercrime damages could reach USD 10.5 trillion annually by 2025, emphasizing the urgency of securing agricultural IoT and cloud-based platforms. As smart agricultural markets continue to expand, a collaborative approach involving governments, industry stakeholders, and researchers is essential to develop robust, ethical, and legally sound data protection strategies that balance innovation with farmers' rights and data sovereignty.

## REFERENCES


Ahmed, B., Shabbir, H., Naqvi, S. R., & Peng, L. (2024). *Smart Agriculture: Current State, Opportunities and Challenges*. IEEE., DOI: 10.1109/ACCESS.2024.3471647

Alahe, M. A., Wei, L., Chang, Y., Gummi, S. R., Kemeshi, J., Yang, X., & Sher, M. (2024). Cyber security in smart agriculture: Threat types, current status, and future trends. *Computers and Electronics in Agriculture, 226*, 109401. DOI: 10.1016/j.compag.2024.109401

Ali, I. A., Bukhari, W. A., Adnan, M., Kashif, M. I., Danish, A., & Sikander, A. (2024). Security and privacy in IoT-based Smart Farming: A review. *Multimedia Tools and Applications*, •••, 1–61. DOI: 10.1007/s11042-024-19653-3

Amiri-Zarandi, M., Dara, R. A., Duncan, E., & Fraser, E. D. (2022). Big data privacy in smart farming: A review. *Sustainability, 14*(15), 9120. DOI: 10.3390/su14159120

Amiri-Zarandi, M., Hazrati Fard, M., Yousefinaghani, S., Kaviani, M., & Dara, R. (2022). A platform approach to smart farm information processing. *Agriculture, 12*(6), 838. DOI: 10.3390/agriculture12060838

Atik, C. (2022). Towards comprehensive European agricultural data governance: Moving beyond the "data ownership" debate. *IIC-International Review of Intellectual Property and Competition Law, 53*(5), 701–742. DOI: 10.1007/s40319-022-01191-w

Borrero, J. D., & Mariscal, J. (2022). A case study of a digital data platform for the agricultural sector: A valuable decision support system for small farmers. *Agriculture, 12*(6), 767. DOI: 10.3390/agriculture12060767

Bronson, K. (2018). Smart farming: Including rights holders for responsible agricultural innovation. *Technology Innovation Management Review, 8*(2), 7–14.

Choudhary, R., Mantri, S. P., Barse, M. V. A., & Chitnis, S. (2024). Leveraging AI in Smart Agro-Informatics: A Review of Data Science Applications. [IRJAEM]. *International Research Journal on Advanced Engineering and Management, 2*(06), 1964–1975.

Cyriac, R., & Thomas, J. (2024). Smart Farming with Cloud Supported Data Management Enabling Real-Time Monitoring and Prediction for Better Yield. In *Intelligent Robots and Drones for Precision Agriculture* (pp. 283–306). Springer Nature Switzerland., DOI: 10.1007/978-3-031-51195-0_14 de Araujo Zanella, A. R., Da Silva, E., & Albini, L. C. P. (2020). Security challenges to smart agriculture: Current state, key issues, and future directions. *Array (New York, N.Y.)*, *8*, 100048.

Demestichas, K., Peppes, N., & Alexakis, T. (2020). Survey on security threats in agricultural IoT and smart farming. *sensors, 20*(22), 6458, DOI: .DOI: 10.3390/s20226458

Duaa, T., & Hammed, A. (2025). Security Cooperation in the Protection Concerns of Agriculture Data Using Efficient Signatures and Artificial Bee Colony Manner. In *Sustainable Information Security in the Age of AI and Green Computing* (pp. 439–460). IGI Global Scientific Publishing.

Ellis, E., & Paustian, K. (2024). Importance of on-farm research for validating process-based models of climate-smart agriculture. *Carbon Balance and Management*, *19*(1), 16. DOI: 10.1186/s13021-024-00260-6

Ferrag, M. A., Shu, L., Yang, X., Derhab, A., & Maglaras, L. (2020). Security and privacy for green IoT-based agriculture: Review, blockchain solutions, and challenges. *IEEE Access : Practical Innovations, Open Solutions*, *8*, 32031–32053. DOI: 10.1109/ACCESS.2020.2973178

Ferris, J. L. (2017). Data privacy and protection in the agriculture industry: Is federal regulation necessary? *Minnesota Journal of Law, Science & Technology*, *18*, 309.

Gupta, M., Abdelsalam, M., Khorsandroo, S., & Mittal, S. (2020). Security and privacy in smart farming: Challenges and opportunities. *IEEE Access : Practical Innovations, Open Solutions*, *8*, 34564–34584. DOI: 10.1109/ACCESS.2020.2975142

Gyamfi, E. K., ElSayed, Z., Kropczynski, J., Yakubu, M. A., & Elsayed, N. (2024, April). Agricultural 4.0 leveraging on technological solutions: Study for smart farming sector *2024*. In *IEEE 3rd International Conference on Computing and Machine Intelligence (ICMI)* (pp. 1-9). IEEE, DOI: DOI: 10.1109/ICMI60790.2024.10585910

Gyamfi, E. K., Kropczynski, J., Johnson, J. S., & Yakubu, M. A. (2024, May). Internet of Things Security and Data Privacy Concerns in Smart Farming *2024*. In *IEEE World AI IoT Congress (AIIoT)* (pp. 0575-0583). IEEE, DOI: DOI: 10.1109/AIIoT61789.2024.10578972

Hammed, M., & Jebbar, W. A. (2025). Blockchain-Powered Dynamic Segmentation in Personal Health Record. *Mesopotamian Journal of CyberSecurity*, *5*(3), 953–976.

Jakku, E., Taylor, B., Fleming, A., Mason, C., Fielke, S., Sounness, C., & Thorburn, P. (2019). "If they don't tell us what they do with it, why would we trust them?" Trust, transparency and benefit-sharing in Smart Farming. *NJAS Wageningen Journal of Life Sciences*, *90*, 100285.

Johnraja, J. I., Leelipushpam, P. G. J., Shirley, C. P., & Princess, P. J. B. (2024). Impact of cloud computing on the future of smart farming. In *Intelligent Robots and Drones for Precision Agriculture* (pp. 391–420). Springer Nature Switzerland., DOI: 10.1007/978-3-031-51195-0_18

Jouanjean, M. A., Casalini, F., Wiseman, L., & Gray, E. (2020). Issues around data governance in the digital transformation of agriculture: The farmers' perspective.

Karunathilake, E. M. B. M., Le, A. T., Heo, S., Chung, Y. S., & Mansoor, S. (2023). The path to smart farming: Innovations and opportunities in precision agriculture. *Agriculture, 13*(8), 1593. DOI: 10.3390/agriculture13081593

Kaur, J., & Dara, R. (2023). Ensuring Privacy in Smart Farming: Review of Regulations, Codes of Conduct, and Best Practices. *Encyclopedia of Digital Agricultural Technologies*, 480-495, DOI: DOI: 10.1007/978-3-031-24861-0_272

Kaur, J., Hazrati Fard, S. M., Amiri-Zarandi, M., & Dara, R. (2022). Protecting farmers' data privacy and confidentiality: Recommendations and considerations. *Frontiers in Sustainable Food Systems*, *6*, 903230. DOI: 10.3389/fsufs.2022.903230

Kethineni, K., & Gera, P. (2023). IoT-based privacy-preserving anomaly detection model for smart agriculture. *Systems*, *11*(6), 304.

Kosior, K. (2019). Towards a new data economy for EU agriculture. *Studia Europejskie*, *23*(4), 91–107. DOI: 10.33067/SE.4.2019.6

Kumar, V., Sharma, K. V., Kedam, N., Patel, A., Kate, T. R., & Rathnayake, U. (2024). A comprehensive review on smart and sustainable agriculture using IoT technologies. *Smart Agricultural Technology, 100487*. Advance online publication. DOI: 10.1016/j.atech.2024.100487

Kumari, S., Tiwari, S., Naithani, K., & Subbiah, P. (2024). Internet of things for smart agriculture: a survey. In *AI Applications for Business, Medical, and Agricultural Sustainability* (pp. 100-121). IGI Global, DOI: DOI: 10.4018/979-8-3693-5266-3.ch005

Kuntke, F. (2024). The Role of Privacy in Digitalization—Analyzing Perspectives of German Farmers. In *Resilient Smart Farming: Crisis-Capable Information and Communication Technologies for Agriculture* (pp. 81–107). Springer Fachmedien Wiesbaden.

Le, D. D., Dao, M. S., Tran, A. K., Nguyen, T. B., & Le-Thi, H. G. (2023, October). Federated learning in smart agriculture: an overview *2023*. In *15th International Conference on Knowledge and Systems Engineering (KSE)* (pp. 1-4). IEEE, DOI: DOI: 10.1109/KSE59128.2023.10299497

Lipper, L., Thornton, P., Campbell, B. M., Baedeker, T., Braimoh, A., Bwalya, M., & Torquebiau, E. F. (2014). Climate-smart agriculture for food security. *Nature Climate Change*, *4*(12), 1068–1072. DOI: 10.1038/nclimate2437

López, I. D., Grass, J. F., Figueroa, A., & Corrales, J. C. (2023). A proposal for a multi-domain data fusion strategy in a climate-smart agriculture context. *International Transactions in Operational Research*, *30*(4), 2049–2070. DOI: 10.1111/itor.12899

Marcu, I., Suciu, G., Bălăceanu, C., Vulpe, A., & Drăgulinescu, A. M. (2020). Arrowhead technology for digitalization and automation solution: Smart cities and smart agriculture. *Sensors (Basel)*, *20*(5), 1464. DOI: 10.3390/s20051464

Mayakannan, S., Saravanan, M., Arunbharathi, R., Srinivasan, V. P., Prabhu, S. V., & Maurya, R. K. (2023). Navigating Ethical and Legal Challenges in Smart Agriculture: Insights from Farmers. In *Predictive Analytics in Smart Agriculture* (pp. 175-190). CRC Press.

Meziani, L., Radjef, M. S., Perito, M. A., & Hammoudi, A. (2024). Will the development of smart agriculture improve food safety in international markets? A theoretical approach. *Frontiers in Sustainable Food Systems*, *8*, 1440006. DOI: 10.3389/fsufs.2024.1440006

Mishra, A., Alzoubi, Y. I., & Gavrilovic, N. (2024). Quality attributes of software architecture in IoT-based agricultural systems. *Smart Agricultural Technology*, *8*, 100523. DOI: 10.1016/j.atech.2024.100523

Mishra, H., & Mishra, D. (2024). Sustainable Smart Agriculture to Ensure Zero Hunger. In *Sustainable Development Goals* (pp. 16–37). CRC Press., DOI: 10.1201/9781003468257-2

NP, C. (2020). Challenges of Security and Privacy with Internet of Things in Smart Agriculture. *Akwapoly Journal of Communication & Scientific Research, 5*(1).

Ofori, M., & El-Gayar, O. (2019, December). The State and Future of Smart Agriculture: Insights from mining social media *2019*. In *IEEE International Conference on Big Data (Big Data)* (pp. 5152-5161). IEEE, DOI: DOI: 10.1109/BigData47090.2019.9006587

Parashar, A., Mabrouki, J., & Sharma, J. (2024). AI and Smart Technologies for Smart Agriculture Environment. In *Advanced Systems for Environmental Monitoring, IoT and the application of Artificial Intelligence* (pp. 95–107). Springer Nature Switzerland., DOI: 10.1007/978-3-031-50860-8_6

Prasad, C. G. V. N., Mallareddy, A., Pounambal, M., & Velayutham, V. (2022). Edge Computing and Blockchain in Smart Agriculture Systems. *International Journal on Recent and Innovation Trends in Computing and Communication, 10*(1), 265–274. DOI: 10.17762/ijritcc.v10i1s.5848

Raja, S. R., Subashini, B., & Prabu, R. S. (2024). 5G Technology in Smart Farming and Its Applications. In *Intelligent Robots and Drones for Precision Agriculture* (pp. 241–264). Springer Nature Switzerland., DOI: 10.1007/978-3-031-51195-0_12

Regan, Á. (2019). 'Smart farming'in Ireland: A risk perception study with key governance actors. *NJAS Wageningen Journal of Life Sciences*, *90*, 100292.

Relf-Eckstein, J. E., Ballantyne, A. T., & Phillips, P. W. (2019). Farming Reimagined: A case study of autonomous farm equipment and creating an innovation opportunity space for broadacre smart farming. *NJAS Wageningen Journal of Life Sciences*, *90*, 100307.

Roopaei, M., Rad, P., & Choo, K. K. R. (2017). Cloud of things in smart agriculture: Intelligent irrigation monitoring by thermal imaging. *IEEE Cloud Computing*, *4*(1), 10–15. DOI: 10.1109/MCC.2017.5

Saeed El Etaiby, Y. (2023). Smart agriculture and future technologies for achieving food security. *International Journal of Family Studies. Food Science and Nutrition Health*, *4*(1), 56–71. DOI: 10.21608/ijfsnh.2024.293384.1006

Schönfeld, M. V., Heil, R., & Bittner, L. (2018). Big data on a farm—Smart farming. *Big data in context*, 109-120, DOI: .DOI: 10.1007/978-3-319-62461-7_12

Sharma, V., Tripathi, A. K., & Mittal, H. (2022). Technological revolutions in smart farming: Current trends, challenges & future directions. *Computers and Electronics in Agriculture*, *201*, 107217. DOI: 10.1016/j.compag.2022.107217

Shen, M. (2023, October). Privacy Protection Smart Agriculture Based on Functional Encryption. In *2023 International Symposium on Networks, Computers and Communications (ISNCC)* (pp. 1-5). IEEE.

Singh, A. K. (2022). Smart farming: Applications of IoT in agriculture. In *Handbook of Smart Materials, Technologies, and Devices: Applications of Industry 4.0* (pp. 1655–1687). Springer International Publishing., DOI: 10.1007/978-3-030-84205-5_114

Sudaryanto, T., Wahida, H. J., Rafani, I., & Andoko, E. (2022). *Promoting Smart Farming based-Digital Business Technology in the Context of Agricultural Transformation in Indonesia*. FFTC J Agric Policy.

Sullivan, C. S., Gemtou, M., Anastasiou, E., & Fountas, S. (2024). Building trust: A systematic review of the drivers and barriers of agricultural data sharing. *Smart Agricultural Technology, 100477*. Advance online publication. DOI: 10.1016/j.atech.2024.100477

Tiwari, A. K., Mishra, H., Nishad, D. C., & Pandey, A. (2023). Sustainable water management in agriculture: irrigation techniques and water conservation. *Dr. Ajay B. Jadhao, 53*.

Villegas-Ch, W., & García-Ortiz, J. (2023). Toward a comprehensive framework for ensuring security and privacy in artificial intelligence. *Electronics (Basel), 12*(18), 3786. DOI: 10.3390/electronics12183786

Wiseman, L., Sanderson, J., Zhang, A., & Jakku, E. (2019). Farmers and their data: An examination of farmers' reluctance to share their data through the lens of the laws impacting smart farming. *NJAS Wageningen Journal of Life Sciences, 90*, 100301.

Wolfert, S., Ge, L., Verdouw, C., & Bogaardt, M. J. (2017). Big data in smart farming–a review. *Agricultural Systems, 153*, 69–80. DOI: 10.1016/j.agsy.2017.01.023

Yang, X., Shu, L., Chen, J., Ferrag, M. A., Wu, J., Nurellari, E., & Huang, K. (2021). A survey on smart agriculture: Development modes, technologies, and security and privacy challenges. *IEEE/CAA Journal of Automatica Sinica, 8*(2), 273-302, DOI: .DOI: 10.1109/JAS.2020.1003536

Yazdinejad, A., Zolfaghari, B., Azmoodeh, A., Dehghantanha, A., Karimipour, H., Fraser, E., & Duncan, E. (2021). A review on security of smart farming and precision agriculture: Security aspects, attacks, threats and countermeasures. *Applied Sciences (Basel, Switzerland), 11*(16), 7518. DOI: 10.3390/app11167518

Zampati, F. (2023). Ethical and legal considerations in smart farming: A farmer's perspective. *Towards Responsible Plant Data Linkage: Data Challenges for Agricultural Research and Development, 257*.

## KEY TERMS AND DEFINITIONS

**Access Control:** Mechanisms and policies that restrict data access to authorized users only, crucial for maintaining the security of agricultural information systems.

**AI-Driven Farm Management Systems:** Artificial intelligence-based platforms that analyse agricultural data to support decision-making in areas such as planting schedules, irrigation, pest control, and yield prediction.

**Anomaly Detection:** The use of AI algorithms to identify unusual patterns or behaviours that may indicate cybersecurity threats or system failures in smart farming networks.

**Asymmetric Encryption:** A cryptographic technique using a pair of keys (public and private) for secure data exchange, especially useful for ensuring secure communications in agriculture.

**Blockchain:** A decentralized and tamper-proof digital ledger used to record agricultural transactions securely and transparently, supporting traceability and trust.

**California Consumer Privacy Act (CCPA):** A state-level data privacy law in the United States that gives California residents greater control over their personal information and imposes obligations on data processors.

**Cloud-Based Agricultural Platforms:** Online platforms that store, process, and provide access to agricultural data and services via the internet, often involving third-party cloud providers.

**Cryptography:** The science of encoding information to protect it from unauthorized access, widely used in agricultural data systems to ensure confidentiality and integrity.

**Cybersecurity:** The practice of protecting systems, networks, and data from digital attacks, crucial in securing agricultural IoT infrastructure and cloud-based services.

**Data Breach:** An incident in which sensitive, protected, or confidential agricultural data is accessed or disclosed without authorization, leading to potential harm.

**Data Consent:** The informed, voluntary agreement by data subjects (e.g., farmers) to allow the collection, use, or sharing of their personal or farm-related data.

**Data Ownership:** Legal and ethical concept defining who holds the rights and control over the data generated on farms, often contested between farmers and agri-tech companies.

**Decentralized Finance (DeFi):** A blockchain-based financial system that allows peer-to-peer trading and lending, increasingly applied in agriculture to enable inclusive financial access.

**Drones and Satellite Imaging:** Aerial tools used to monitor agricultural fields, assess crop health, map farmland, and gather high-resolution imagery for precision agriculture.

**Environmental and Climate Data:** Information related to weather conditions, temperature patterns, rainfall, wind, and other climatic factors that influence agricultural outcomes.

**Ethical Data Handling:** Adherence to moral principles in the collection, storage, and use of agricultural data, ensuring respect for privacy, fairness, and accountability.

**Federated Learning:** A machine learning approach that trains algorithms across decentralized devices or servers holding local data samples, enhancing privacy by not sharing raw data.

**General Data Protection Regulation (GDPR):** A comprehensive data protection law enacted in the European Union that governs the collection, processing, and storage of personal data, with extraterritorial implications.

**Homomorphic Encryption:** A form of encryption that allows computations on encrypted data without needing to decrypt it first, supporting privacy-preserving data analysis in agriculture.

**IoT (Internet of Things) Sensors:** Devices embedded with sensors and connectivity that collect and transmit real-time data from agricultural environments, including soil moisture, temperature, humidity, and crop growth metrics.

**Market and Supply Chain Data:** Economic and logistical information related to the production, pricing, distribution, and sale of agricultural goods within the supply chain.

**Multi-Factor Authentication (MFA):** A security process that requires users to verify their identity using multiple methods (e.g., password and mobile device) before accessing agricultural data systems.

**Privacy-Preserving Marketplaces:** Digital platforms that enable the exchange of agricultural products or data with built-in privacy safeguards to protect participants' sensitive information.

**Secure Multi-Party Computation (SMPC):** A cryptographic method allowing multiple parties to jointly compute a function over their inputs while keeping those inputs private from each other.

**Smart Agriculture:** The application of advanced technologies such as IoT, AI, big data, and cloud computing to optimize farming practices, increase productivity, and ensure sustainability in agricultural operations.

**Smart Contracts:** Self-executing contracts with predefined rules encoded on a blockchain, facilitating automated, secure, and transparent agricultural transactions.

**Soil and Crop Health Data:** Data concerning soil composition, nutrient levels, crop diseases, and plant vitality, collected through sensors or imaging technologies.

**Symmetric Encryption:** An encryption method where the same key is used for both encrypting and decrypting data, typically faster but requires secure key distribution.

**Transparency:** The practice of openly communicating how data is collected, processed, and shared, allowing stakeholders to make informed decisions and build trust.

**Zero-Knowledge Proofs (ZKPs):** Cryptographic protocols that enable one party to prove to another that a statement is true without revealing any additional information, ensuring data privacy.

# Chapter 6
# Integrating Circular Aviation Systems for Smart City Infrastructure Developments:
## Security in Drone and Small Aircraft Services

**Suresh Bysani Venkata Naga**
https://orcid.org/0009-0006-5764-1660
*AI Infrastructure, Eightfold.ai, San Francisco, USA*

**Krishnaiah Narukulla**
https://orcid.org/0009-0006-5602-1021
*Distributed Systems, Roku, USA & Cohesity, San Francisco, USA*

**Santhosh Kumar Kuchoor**
https://orcid.org/0009-0006-5503-3258
*AI Infrastructure, Palo Alto Networks, San Francisco, USA*

## ABSTRACT

*This chapter explores the integration of smart city infrastructure with innovative drones and small aircraft services operated by Circular Professional Models. Smart cities benefit from advanced technologies to enhance urban efficiency, durability, and quality of life. Drones and small aircraft play major roles in this atmosphere, optimizing logistics, public services, and transportation, and providing solutions. A circular professional model approach guarantees resource efficiency and reduces waste, and this promotes sustainable practices in interconnected systems. It discusses*

DOI: 10.4018/979-8-3373-8133-6.ch006

*case studies and emerging trends where these technologies are integrated, showing their transformative effect on urban mobility, logistics, and service distribution. By accepting the circular in business strategies, cities can achieve elasticity, economic benefits, and environmental conditions for future smart city developments.*

## INTRODUCTION

The concept of smart cities represents an example in urban development, using advanced technologies to improve efficiency, durability, and overall quality of life for residents. The center of this evolution has innovations such as drone technology and small aircraft services, which provide unique solutions for long-lasting urban challenges (Rai et al., 2016). The goal is to integrate intelligent systems and infrastructure, reduce environmental influence, and increase citizens' engagement. The drone has emerged as a versatile tool in this regard, which is capable of revolutionizing logistics, emergency response, and structural inspection. Their skills and ability to navigate urban landscapes make them invaluable assets in smart city operations. The integration of these techniques is not only additive but transformative, providing holistic solutions that increase urban elasticity and durability (Canca et al., 2022).

The central circle of this integration is professional models, emphasizing regenerative methods and closed-loop systems. Circular economy promotes the principles of the economy, recycling, renewal, and resources, reducing waste and maximizing value in the production life cycle. In terms of smart cities, circular professional models ensure that technical innovations contribute to long-term environmental and economic stability. The synergy between smart city infrastructure, drones, and small aircraft services is an example of the possibility of disruptive innovation in the urban environment. By adopting circular professional models, cities can achieve multiple objectives: reduction in operational costs, increase service distribution, and reduce environmental impact. These models promote cooperation in areas and stakeholders promoting innovation and scalability in urban development initiatives (Canca Ortiz et al., 2022).

Looking forward, the integration of drones and small aircraft services in smart cities promises to address urban issues such as traffic congestion, pollution, and emergency response. With developed regulatory landscapes and public acceptance, the technology is paving the way for widespread adoption. As cities continue to develop, accepting innovation and durability will be key to creating an elastic and resilient urban environment for future generations (Moshref-Javadi & Winkenbach, 2021). Therefore, the integration of smart cities, drones, and small aircraft services through circular professional models presents a transformative approach to urban development. By giving the benefit of these techniques in a sustainable structure, cities can achieve economic prosperity, environmental stewardship, and quality of life for residents (Beigi et al., 2022).

This chapter detects the possibility of unified technologies to reshape urban landscapes and presents the challenges and opportunities to realize this vision. In the fast-growing landscape of urban development, the integration of advanced technologies is deeply important to enhance the efficiency, durability, and overall quality of life in cities around the world. These technologies, artificial intelligence (AI) and Internet of Things (IoT) devices, from drones and autonomous vehicles, offer a transformative possibility in various aspects of urban life (Al-Dhaqm et al., 2021).

Predictive analytics can optimize waste management schedules, reduce costs and environmental impact, and promote sustainable urban development. Smart grid techniques optimize energy distribution, including renewable sources, and increase grid stability. IoT-enabled systems monitor air and water quality, eliminating pollution. Advanced transport systems, including electric vehicles and autonomous fleets, reduce emissions and traffic congestion, promoting cleaner urban mobility. These technologies also increase urban elasticity and disaster preparedness. AI Algorithms analyze data from different sources and improve the time of the initial warning systems and crisis, to predict and react to natural disasters such as floods or earthquakes (Al-Dhaqm et al., 2021). In addition, smart buildings with IoT-enabled infrastructure, such as automatic emergency protocols, increase safety and reduce weaknesses during an emergency. Socially, integrating advanced technologies improves the quality of life for residents by increasing inclusion (Moshref-Javadi et al., 2021).

Smart City Initiatives, such as digital inclusion programs and accessible transportation systems, bridge the digital split and improve mobility for the elderly and disabled population. AI-powered healthcare systems enable remote diagnostics and personal treatment, enhancing healthcare access and results. However, the integration of advanced technologies in urban development is not without challenges. Concerns regarding data collection and cyber safety risks require strong regime structures and transparent policies to protect civil rights. In addition, digital literacy and equal access to all residents are required to enhance existing social inequalities and benefit from technological advancement for all residents (Tezza & Andujar, 2019).

Hence, the importance of integrating advanced technologies in urban development lies in their possibility of transforming cities into a more durable, elastic, and incorporated environment. By providing AI, IoT, drone, and autonomous techniques in a consistent urban strategy, cities can focus on resource management, reduce environmental impact, increase public safety, stimulate economic development, and improve the quality of life for all residents. As cities continue to grow and develop, it would be crucial to accept digital innovation to eliminate complex urban challenges and create rich communities for future generations.

## Background

The integration of drones and small aircraft services in smart city design is an increasing area powered by technical, urbanization, and the progress of the need for efficient city management. Smart cities offer the benefit of IoT, AI, and data analytics for their inhabitants to improve the quality of life, increase durability, and provide optimum services to urban residents. Drone and small aircraft provide unique capabilities that complement these goals, providing innovative solutions for transportation, logistics, surveillance, and emergency response.

## Scope

The scope of integrating drones and small aircraft services in smart cities contains many major areas. It includes urban air mobility for transporting passengers and cargo, which reduces traffic congestion and emissions. The last-mile delivery logistics using a drone increase efficiency. The drone helps with constant surveillance and security, providing real-time monitoring and fast emergency response. They support infrastructure inspection and maintenance, ensure safety, and reduce downtime. Environmental inspection benefits from the ability of a drone to collect data on air quality, noise, and weather. This integration also involves developing regulatory structures, public acceptance, and ensuring data protection and privacy.

## Chapter Objectives

The objectives of integrating advanced technologies in urban development are multifaceted. First, these techniques aim to increase operational efficiency by optimizing resource management, reducing costs, and improving service distribution through real-time data analytics and Auto Tomatoes. Second, they try to promote durability by reducing environmental influence, enhancing energy efficiency, and adopting renewable energy sources. Third, advanced technologies aim to increase urban elasticity by improving disaster preparedness, increasing public safety measures, and promoting infrastructure against natural and man-made threats. In addition, this initiative aims to stimulate economic development by attracting investment, promoting innovation, and creating job opportunities in the digital sectors. Socially, the objectives include improvement in the quality of life by increasing accessibility, inclusion, and healthcare services through technological advancement. Ultimately, to integrate advanced technologies in urban development, there are smart cities that balance economic prosperity with environmental stability and social equality.

## ROLE OF DRONE TECHNOLOGY

*Figure 1. Drone technology in logistics and public services*

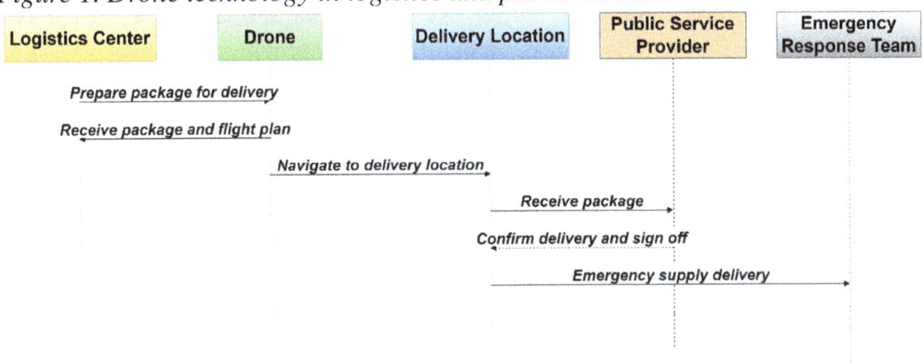


In urban environments, drones have emerged as transformative equipment, offering a wide range of efficiency, safety, and durability in different fields. The ability to access their versatility and hard-to-reach areas accentuates their invaluable wealth in the planning and management of a modern city. One of the primary applications of the drone in the urban environment is in structural inspection and maintenance. Traditional methods of monitoring bridges, roads, and buildings often cause time-consuming, expensive, and security risks to employees. A drone equipped with high-resolution cameras and sensors can make detailed observations more effectively and safely (Beard & McLain, 2012). Figure 1 explains the use of drone technology in logistics and public services, depicting the flow and interactions of various processes.

In the field of public safety and law enforcement, drones have become important tools for raising awareness and improving response capabilities. They can be quickly deployed to observe large crowds during public events, evaluate disaster-stricken areas for search and rescue missions, and survey the scenes of crime without disturbing critical evidence. Equipped with thermal imaging and infrared cameras, drones can detect heat signatures and help in the location of missing individuals or suspects. This technical integration significantly improves operational efficiency while reducing the time of response in critical conditions (Boopathi et al., 2022; Boopathi, 2024b).

Moreover, the drone is revolutionizing urban logistics and delivery services. With the rise of Mars and delivery expectations of the same day, the drone offers a solution for faster and more cost-effective delivery of goods. Companies like Amazon and UPS are looking for drone delivery systems that can transfer packages directly to customers' doors, bypass traffic congestion, and reduce carbon emissions associated with traditional delivery methods. In urban planning and development, the drone provides valuable insights through air surveys and mapping. They produce high-resolution 3D models of cities, seizing detailed topographical data and urban landscapes. This data helps city organizers, architects, and developers to make informed decisions about land use, structural development, and environmental protection (Gift et al., 2024; Senthil et al., 2023).

Furthermore, drone contributes to environmental surveillance and defense efforts in urban areas. They monitor the quality of air and water, detect pollution sources, and evaluate the environmental effects of urban development projects. Collects real-time data on drone pollutants equipped with special sensors, enabling officials to take active steps to reduce environmental degradation and improve public health results (Puranik et al., 2024; Sonia et al., 2024). Therefore, the role of drone technology in the urban environment is a major and multifaceted one. From infrastructure inspection and public safety to logistics, urban planning, environmental monitoring, and emergency response, drone provides innovative solutions that increase efficiency, safety, and durability in modern cities. As advances in technology and regulatory structures develop, the drone will play an incredible role in shaping smarter, more elastic urban landscapes worldwide (Riboldi & Gualdoni, 2016).

## Benefits of Drone Technology in Logistics and Public Services

- Efficiency in Delivery: Drone traffic congestion by bypassing traffic congestion and delivering packages directly to customers' places, significantly reducing delivery time.
- Cost Savings: Automatic delivery routes reduce operational costs and labor requirements, contributing to lower fuel consumption, cost savings, and environmental stability than traditional vehicles.
- Accessibility and Reach: The ability to cause remote or hard-to-reach areas to be accessible where traditional logistics infrastructure does not limit or exist, facilitating delivery services in rural or disaster-affected regions. Accessibility increases for Customers in urban areas with traffic or restricted delivery zones, ensuring timely and efficient service.
- Enhanced Safety and Security: Drone improves safety by reducing accidents and injuries to employees, reducing the risks associated with manual handling and delivery operations.
- Environmental Impact: Low carbon footprint and decrease in emissions compared to traditional delivery vehicles contribute to environmental stability.
- Public Services and Emergency Response: Providing air surveillance and monitoring capabilities, supporting public services such as fire extinguishers by increasing conditions awareness and response efficiency.

- Data Collection and Analysis: Data-based decisions for urban planning and public safety strategy collect drone real-time data on traffic patterns, congestion management, and environmental conditions. Enables infrastructure inspection and maintenance with high-resolution imaging and sensor techniques, actively identifying maintenance requirements and potential risks.
- Innovation and Future Potential: Stimulates innovation in logistics and public service fields, promoting the research and development of advanced drone techniques for extended abilities. Future prospects include integration with autonomous drone fleets and smart city infrastructures, and public service distribution.

Hence, drone technology offers many benefits, including an increase in logistics efficiency, improving public service distribution, and supporting emergency response efforts. As technological advances continue, the drone will play an important role in shaping smart, more elastic cities and communities worldwide.

## SMALL AIRCRAFT SERVICES IN URBAN CONTEXTS

Small aircraft services represent a promising border in urban transport, which offers unique benefits that consider the increasing challenges of congestion, efficiency, and durability in modern cities. This aircraft, including electric vertical takeoff and landing vehicles and drones designed for human transport, complements the existing urban transport system and redefines the possibilities of air mobility (Köhler & Jeschke, 2021). Figure 2 illustrates the concept of small aircraft services in urban transportation.

*Figure 2. Concept of small aircraft services in urban transportation*

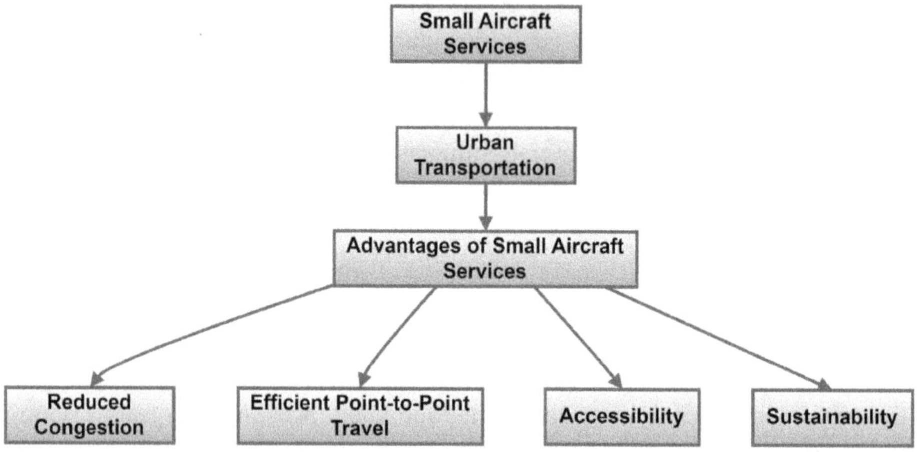


- Reduced Congestion and Faster Commutes: Small aircraft can bypass land crowds by flying straight places, significantly reducing travel time. This capacity is especially beneficial in densely populated cities where traffic congestion is a big issue. For travelers, this means faster and more reliable transportation options, improving overall productivity and quality of life.
- Scalability and Flexibility: Modular design of a small aircraft allows for scalability to meet the demand for various passengers. Used for short intra-City hops or long regional flights, this aircraft relieves root planning and can adapt to the requirements of dynamic urban mobility. This scalability also supports the efficient use of airspace and infrastructure resources.
- Environmental Benefits: Electric operated small aircraft contribute to emission and noise pollution compared to traditional aircraft and land transport. They operate on clean energy sources, such as batteries or hydrogen fuel cells, adjust with stability goals and improve air quality in urban areas. This environmental benefit is crucial to reduce the influence of transportation on weather change and urban air quality.
- Enhanced Connectivity and Accessibility: Small aircraft services improve the connection between urban centers and surrounding regions, increasing the reach of residents and businesses. They can provide direct connections to airports, professional districts and remote communities that are underprice by traditional transportation options. This connectivity is especially beneficial for promoting economic development and regional integration.

- Emergency Response and Disaster Relief: Rapid deployment capabilities make small aircraft invaluable for emergency response and disaster relief efforts. They can quickly transport medical employees, supplies and equipment to disaster areas, eliminate land barriers, and improve response time in critical conditions. This capacity increases the possibility of natural disasters or crisis in urban environments.
- Technological Innovation and Safety Features: Technical renovation in aviation is ahead of a small aircraft, including advanced safety features and autonomous flight capabilities. These features include real-time data connectivity for collision avoidance systems, redundant power systems and enhanced operational safety. Autonomous flight technologies promise to improve reliability and safety, reducing human error in the urban airstrip.
- Economic Opportunities and Job Creation: Development and deployment of small aircraft services stimulates economic development by creating new industries and job opportunities in the sectors, production and service sectors. They contribute to local and regional economic elasticity, attracting investment in the structural development, research and training of skilled employees.
- Public Acceptance and Regulatory Considerations: It is crucial to create public confidence for the successful integration of small aircraft services in the urban environment and ensure regulatory compliance. Transparent communications about safety, noise level and privacy concerns are required to obtain public acceptance. Meanwhile, regulatory structures must be considered in the air sector management, certification standards and integration with existing air traffic control systems to ensure safe and efficient operation.

Thus, small aircraft services provide significant benefits for urban transport, ranging from congestion and environmental benefits to increased connectivity and emergency response capabilities (Maguluri et al., 2023; Periasamy et al., 2024; Sonia et al., 2024). As the technological advances continue and the regulatory structure develops, the aircraft is likely to revolutionize urban mobility, making cities more accessible, durable, and elastic in the face of future challenges.

## CIRCULAR BUSINESS MODELS

### Circular Economy Principles

Circular economy is a systemic approach to economic development designed to benefit businesses, societies, and environments. Unlike the traditional linear model of " tech, mac, disposal", the circular economy emphasizes the continued use of resources through principles such as reuse, repair, renovation, recycle, and resurrection. This model tries to design waste, use products and materials, and reproduce natural systems (Min et al., 2015). Circular economy focuses on the design for life, resource efficiency, product-as-a-service (PAAS), closed-loop systems, and ecosystem thinking. It is to promote cooperation in the fields to create products with extended life cycles, reduce inputs, optimize output to the optimum, open access to the models, rearrange the products of life, and reduce the negative externality. These principles support environmental stability, reduce costs, and promote innovation by challenging traditional production and consumption patterns.

## Application of Circular Business Models in Smart Cities

Smart cities-urban areas that use digital techniques to enhance the influence and well-being of fertile land for the implementation of circular professional models. By integrating technology, data, and circular principles, smart cities can create more durable and elastic urban systems (Min et al., 2015).

*Figure 3. Application of Circular Business Models in Smart Cities*

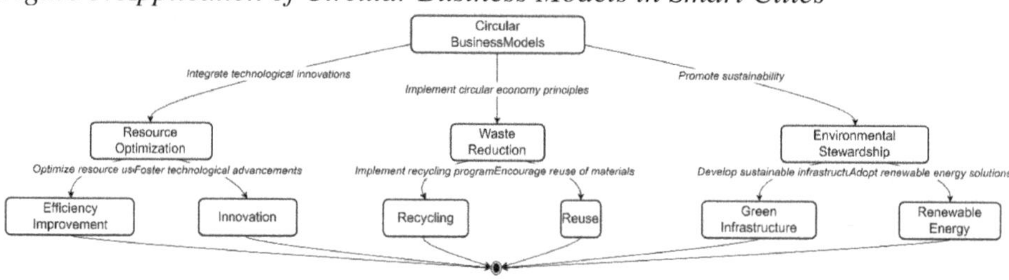


Figure 3 illustrates the application of circular business models in smart cities and transitions between different phases of the business models. Smart cities offer the benefit of IoT-enabled sensors and data analytics for garbage collection and recycling processes. Circular professional models promote waste on recycling initiatives and sources, promote the re-recovery procurement of valuable materials, and reduce landfill waste. Technologies such as AI-propelled Sena Rating systems and blockchain-enabled trace book increase the transparency and efficiency in the recycling supply chain (Harikaran et al., 2023; Janardhana et al., 2023; Koshariya et al., 2023; Selvakumar et al., 2023). CBM applications in Smart Cities include waste-to-resource platforms, shared mobility services, smart buildings with modular components, digital product passports, and urban farming and regenerative systems (Duaa & Hammed, 2024). Digital product passports track product materials and life cycles, optimizing end-of-life processes for electronics, appliances, and construction materials. Urban farming and regenerative systems use organic waste for compost, water recycling, and closed-loop nutrient cycles for sustainable food production.

Water management is important for sustainable urban development. Circular professional models integrate IoT sensors and smart water meters to monitor water consumption, search for leaks, and control the irrigation system OPTIM. Water recycling and reusing technologies, such as gravatar recycling systems and rainwater harvesting, conserve fresh water resources and reduce drought and water scarcity in urban areas (Gunasekaran & Boopathi, 2023; Jeya et al., 2023; Zekrifa et al., 2023). Thus, Circular professional models are important for advancing sustainable practices in smart cities, organizing economic prosperity with environmental stewardship and social equality. By accepting the principles of the circular economy and benefiting from technical innovations, smart cities can promote resource efficiency, reduce environmental impact, and increase elasticity by facing global challenges. These models not only support economic development and innovation but also enable future generations to create a living, inclusive, and sustainable urban environment.

## INTEGRATION OF TECHNOLOGIES

In the evolution towards a smart and more durable urban environment, the integration of advanced technologies such as drones and small aircraft plays a major role in increasing efficiency, safety, and elasticity. These air technologies provide unique capabilities that complement the existing smart city infrastructure, eliminating various challenges from crowd operating to emergency response and environmental monitoring (Grauer & Morelli, 2015; Riboldi, 2018). Figure 4 illustrates the integration of advanced technologies like drones and small aircraft.

*Figure 4. Integration of advanced technologies (drones and small aircraft for circular economy principles)*

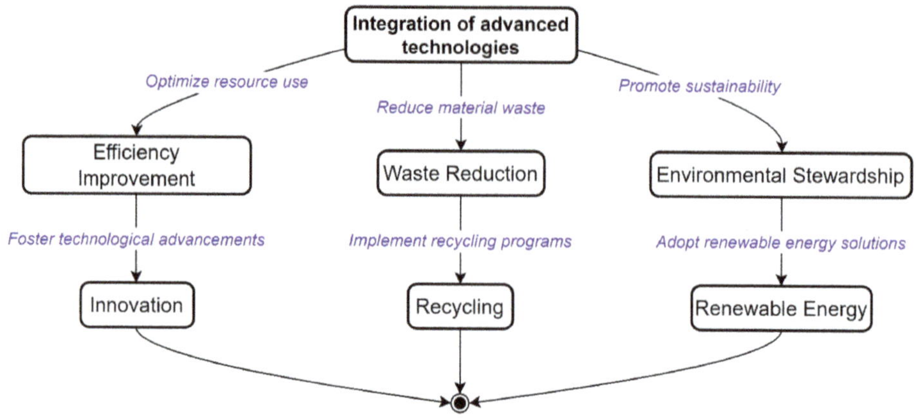


Small aircraft, including electric vertical takeoff and landing vehicles, support intercity transit quickly and increase connection between urban centers and surrounding regions, supporting regional integration and economic development. Aerial technologies in infrastructure inspection and maintenance provide cost-effective and non-violent methods for the monitoring of critical assets such as bridges, roads, and utilities. A drone equipped with high-resolution cameras and sensors can regularly observe, identifying maintenance requirements and structural defects as soon as possible. This active approach improves infrastructure elasticity, reduces downtime, and increases public safety by reducing the risks associated with aging infrastructure. Drone and small aircraft increase emergency response capabilities in smart cities by providing rapid air surveillance and search and rescue operations. During natural disasters or public safety events, these technologies enable real-time saturation awareness, assessing damage to officials, deploying resources, and more effectively coordinating evacuation efforts. Equipped with thermal imaging and infrared sensors, the drone can detect people left in disaster areas, and can deliver the necessary supplies such as medical kits or communication appliances, eliminate ground-level barriers, and respond in a timely manner (Kuṃara et al., 2023).

Aerial technologies increase public safety and safety in smart cities through advanced surveillance capabilities and crime redressal measures. AI-driven analytics and facial validation drones equipped with software can monitor the crowd during large-scale incidents, detect suspicious activities, and support law enforcement agencies in maintaining public order. Small aircraft CCTV networks complement Aerial petrol and perimeter surveillance; ground-based surveillance extends coverage in inaccessible or remote areas where ground-based surveillance is limited. Thus, the integration of drones and small aircraft in smart city infrastructure increases mobility, safety, and stability while optimizing resource use and improving the quality of life for urban residents. These technologies represent innovative solutions that complement the existing urban structure, moving towards a more elastic, connected, and living future.

## INTEGRATION OF TECHNOLOGIES: CHALLENGES AND OPPORTUNITIES

The integration of emerging technologies such as AI, IoT, blockchain, Big Data Analytics, and cloud computing is transforming industries, public services, and social functions (Razzaq & Hammed, 2025). While the conversion of these technologies creates a powerful harmony, it also represents complex challenges. A strategic approach is required to explore both the opportunities and risks associated with this integration (Moshref-Javadi et al., 2021; Tezza & Andujar, 2019; Zhang et al., 2021).

### Opportunities for Efficiency and Innovation

In manufacturing, the Industrial Internet provides a forecast for main maintenance, reducing downtime and operational costs. Similarly, the AI-integrated platform in healthcare improves diagnostic accuracy and enables individual treatment plans based on wide datasets. In the urban environment, smart infrastructure systems integrating IoT and AI can predict traffic flows, monitor the level of pollution, and manage utilities. This integration not only trimmed the workflows but also opens up a new way for production and service innovation in the fields.

### Improved Customer Experience and Personalization

Technical integration also changes the customer's engagement. By combining AI, machine learning, and customer data analytics, companies can have very personal experiences. Chatbots, recommended engines, and automatic support systems are now normal, providing 24/7 interaction and personal service. The integration of the CRM platform with social media analytics enables businesses to achieve customer insights, promote loyalty, and increase user satisfaction. This convergence of tools also allows the omnichannel strategy, ensuring consistency in physical and digital touchpoints.

## Challenges in Interoperability and Legacy Systems

Despite these advantages, one of the main challenges is interoperability - the ability to operate in the United Way of various systems and technologies. Organizations often struggle to integrate modern platforms with inheritance systems that lack consistency. This creates obstacles to data flow, increases complexity, and increases integration costs. Problems are especially serious in public sector institutions and traditional industries where older structural digital changes are taking place. The solutions require not only technical upgrades but also regeneration and stockholder configuration.

## Data Security and Privacy Concerns

As the technologies combine, the volume and sensitivity of the data shared on the platform increase rapidly. This raises significant data protection and privacy challenges. Integrated systems often have multiple points, increasing cyberattacks. Ensuring end-to-end encryption, adopting a secure API, and compliance with data protection rules like GDPR and the DPDP Act of India becomes crucial.

## Skill Gaps and Organizational Readiness

Architecture, cyber safety, and process automation demands cross-functional skills. Many organizations face talent shortages or lack internal capabilities to manage complex integration. In addition, the resistance to the change in staff and inadequate leadership support can be delayed or from the bandage. Investing in training, promoting the culture of innovation, and appointing dedicated change leaders is the essential strategy to eliminate this challenge.

## Cost and Scalability Considerations

In addition to obtaining costs related to customization, maintenance, and training, the economic burden. Moreover, it is a crucial concern to ensure that integrated solutions are scalable and acceptable to future needs. Cloud-based platforms and modular architectures provide a more flexible and cost-effective integration route, allowing bodies to expand on an additional basis as they develop their needs.

## Strategic Alignment and Governance

Successful integration requires a strategic arrangement of professional goals, technical architecture, and regime policies. Integrated implementation without an integrated vision often leads to redundant and suboptimal results. The establishment of a clear governance framework, adjusting it with professional objectives, and adopting crisp methods can significantly increase the success rate of the initiative of integration.

While the integration of techniques offers transformative benefits - from operational excellence and innovative experience - it also presents multidimensional challenges. Organizations must adopt a strategic, security-conscious, and focused approach to exploring these complications. Addressing interoperability, data governance, skills development, and scalability, stakeholders can unlike the full potential of durable and elastically integrated digital ecosystems.

## CASE STUDIES AND BEST PRACTICES

The case studies and best practices illustrate successful approaches in various industries (Moshref-Javadi & Winkenbach, 2021). A few examples are listed here.

- Smart City Initiatives - Barcelona, Spain: Barcelona has utilized IoT, data analytics, and sustainability to advance urban services. Their implementation includes improving transportation methods through efficient public transport and smart parking, Waste management optimization, and providing real-time data using a sensor network. This has enabled better management of the city, a decrease in traffic and congestion, and civic satisfaction (Boopathi, 2024a).
- Healthcare - Mayo Clinic, USA: Mayo Clinic uses AI, machine learning, and IoT to provide better patient care and operate more efficiently at lower costs. They have integrated electronic health records (EHRs) with predictive analysis, individual treatment plans, and recommend using AI algorithms to supervise remote patients. As a result of this integration, the Mayo Clinic has decreased hospital readmission, improved treatment outcomes, and advanced in healthcare delivery (Boopathi et al., 2023).
- Manufacturing - Siemens Digital Factory: The Siemens industry employs 4.0 principles, integrated automation, robotics, and IoT in its production facilities worldwide. They use digital twins for virtual simulation, forecast maintenance, and quality control. This integration has increased the efficiency of the product, and downtime has been reduced, resulting in a crisp response to the demand for the market.
- Retail - Amazon Go: Amazon Go employs computer vision, sensor fusion, and deep learning algorithms to create cashier-less stores. Their combination of these three technologies provides a shopper experience by allowing consumers to choose things and walk out of the store without a physical checkout

process. Such integration has improved operational effectiveness, reduced labour expense, and improved shopping satisfaction.

- Transportation - Uber integrates GPS navigation, mobile application technology, and AI algorithms to provide ride-sharing services worldwide. Their technology platform fuses drivers and passengers, calculates routes in real-time, and provides AI-based dynamic pricing and forecasts of demand. As a result of the integration, Uber has lessened urban mobility, reduced traffic congestion, and created flexible income-generating opportunities for drivers (Gopal et al., 2024).

### Best Practices

This technology emphasizes the importance of clear vision and strategy for integration, promoting cooperation between IT, operations, and business units. It emphasizes data-based decisions, scalability and flexibility, user-centered design, security and compliance, and constant evaluation and improvement. It emphasizes the need for a flexible system that can adapt to technological advances and accommodate growth. Organizations can guide organizations in using the full potential of integrated technology ecosystems by adopting a strategic approach and learning from successful implementations.

## IMPACT ON URBAN MOBILITY AND SUSTAINABILITY

Integrated technologies are reforming urban mobility and durability by removing major challenges such as traffic congestion, environmental influence, and resource efficiency (Maguluri et al., 2023; Malathi et al., 2024; Sharma et al., 2024; Sonia et al., 2024; Sundaramoorthy et al., 2024). Figure 5 illustrates the significant impact of integrated technologies.

*Figure 5. Impact of integrated technologies on urban mobility and sustainability*

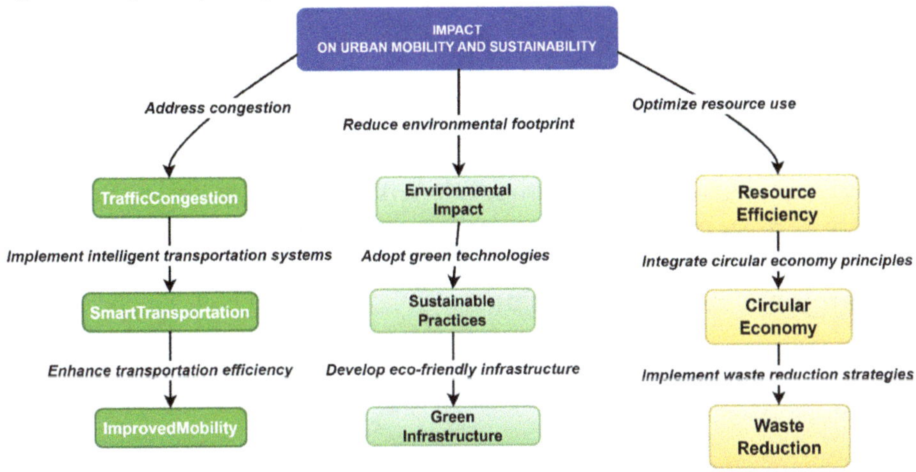


## Enhanced Traffic Management

Integrated technologies improve traffic management by using data analytics, predictive modelling, and intelligent infrastructure, allowing for near real-time traffic management (Boopathi, 2024a). Multi-Modal Transportation Integration: Interconnected platforms like these via mobile applications will aid urban mobility by incorporating connections to grow modes of transport, including all buses, trains, bikes, and virtually every ride-sharing service. Travel that begins cycling to mobility spaces will receive real-time information (via mobile app) about location, transport schedules, route options, and shared mobility options. These mobility integrations will support sustainable travel behaviors that will reduce reliance on the private vehicle, in addition to enhancing the available transport options for all residents (Sharma et al., 2024; Sundaramoorthy et al., 2024).

## Environmental Sustainability

Through slashing carbon emissions, maximizing resource efficiencies and increasing urban resiliency, integrated technologies are linked to environmental sustainability: Following up on electric and autonomous vehicles: Smart cities endorse electric vehicles (EV) and the infrastructure to charge these vehicles - Autonomous Vehicle (AV) Trials and Pilot Projects A.I. Include the associated carbon footprints also from the combined integration of sensor technologies, and reducing car accidents, etc.

Energy-Efficient Buildings and Smart Grids: IoT sensors and smart meters monitor energy zeal consumption in buildings, optimizing HVAC systems, lighting, and device consumption. Smart grids effectively govern the distribution of energy by integrating renewable energy sources such as solar and wind. This initiative reduces the emissions of greenhouse gas, lowers the cost of energy, and enhances the elasticity of energy during peak demand periods (Sundaramoorthy et al., 2024).

## Challenges and Considerations

Despite their benefits, integrating technologies for urban mobility and sustainability poses several challenges:

- Digital Divide and Equity Issues: Ensuring the same access to technical benefits in different socio-economic groups is a challenge. Planning, community engagement, digital infrastructure, and affordable access to services are needed to complete the digital split.
- Data Privacy and Security: Managing a large amount of sensitive data involves being concerned about the risks of privacy breaches and cyber safety. Cities must apply strong data protection measures, follow the rules, and educate residents about data usage and consent.
- Infrastructure Investment and Funding: Infrastructure upgrades, technology adoption, and maintenance require significant investments to deploy unified technologies. Protecting funds through public-private partnerships, grants, and sustainable lending methods for long-term project viability.

Consolidated technologies are aimed at urban mobility and durability, efficiency of driving, reducing environmental effects, and enhancing the quality of life in cities around the world. By providing data-based insights and innovative solutions, cities can reduce traffic congestion, promote sustainable transportation options, and promote elastic urban ecosystems. Strategic planning, stakeholder collaboration, and continuous innovation are essential to maximize the positive effects of integrated technologies and eliminate emerging challenges in urban development.

## Economic and Social Benefits of Integrated Technologies in Urban Environments

Integrated technologies in urban settings produce significant economic and social benefits by increasing efficiency, improving the quality of life, and promoting sustainable development (Dhanya et al., 2023; Mohanty et al., 2023; Vijaya Lakshmi et al., 2024). The integration of advanced technologies such as IoT, AI, and data analytics in the urban environment significantly increases both economic performance and social well-being. Economically, smart technologies reduce operational costs for city administration through Automation and Infrastructure Forecasts, such as Energy room grid, water systems, and transport networks. For example, smart traffic management systems reduce congestion, reduce fuel consumption, and increase productivity by reducing travel time (Babu et al., 2022; N. et al., 2024; Ravisankar et al., 2023; Vijayakumar et al., 2024).

On the social front, integrated technologies improve the accessibility and quality of public services accessibility and quality. The e-governance platform streams bureaucratic processes, increasing transparency and citizen engagement. Health and safety systems, powered by real-time data, such as air quality sensors and emergency response networks, protect the urban population and enhance public health. Conversion of technology with urban planning promotes sustainable development. Cities become more adaptable to climate challenges through data-based environmental inspection and green infrastructure features. After all, unified technologies simply do not "smart" cities; they make them more incorporated, efficient, and alive - creating a virtuous cycle of economic development and social progress that can encourage the entire urban population.

## Social Benefits

Integrated technologies increase public services, healthcare delivery, and educational opportunities, improving the overall quality of life for urban residents. Smart Healthcare Systems provides an improvement in remote patient monitoring, telemedicine, and personal care options, increased access, and improved health results of healthcare services. Smart Education Initiative gives the benefit of digital platforms and e-learning techniques to enhance the opportunities for educational access, skills development, and lifelong learning. Citizen-centered Smart City initiatives promote community engagement and a participatory regime. Enables digital platforms, mobile applications, and social media residents to respond, report issues, and participate in the decision-making process. Transparent data sharing and open government initiatives enhance civil partnerships, responsibility, and trust between residents and local officials.

Integrated technologies make digital split by ensuring the same access to services and opportunities for all inhabitants. Universal design principles in the urban planning and transportation framework improve accessibility by pushing for the inclusion of older individuals, people with disabilities, and the marginalized. Shared mobility services, affordable housing initiatives, and public spaces are incorporated to promote social inclusion and enhance social connections in different urban populations. Sustainable urban development methods supported by unified technologies reduce environmental influences and promote ecological stewards. Green building standards, energy-efficient technologies, and renewable energy integration reduce greenhouse gas emissions, improve air quality, and protect natural resources. Urban green spaces, biodiversity conservation efforts, and sustainable transportation options contribute to the resilient, living cities that prefer environmental stability for future generations.

Consolidated technologies in the urban environment provide significant economic and social benefits by increasing productivity, promoting innovation, improving the quality of life, and promoting sustainable development. As cities continue to develop as the center of innovation and economic activity, strategic investments in technological integration, structural development, and community empowerment are required to realize the full potential of smart and durable urban ecosystems. By giving priority to incorporated development, environmental stewardship, and civilian well-being, cities can increase elastic, righteous, and rich futures in a world more and more connected.

## FUTURE TRENDS AND EMERGING TECHNOLOGIES

The integration of drones, small aircraft, and circular professional models in smart city infrastructure represents a transformative trend in urban development. As cities continue to grow, the need for innovative solutions that enhance efficiency, durability, and quality of life becomes more and more serious. This chapter is looking for future trends that are expected to shape the conversion of these technologies and professional strategies. The vision of smart cities will be forward (Boopathi, 2024a; Maguluri et al., 2023; Periasamy et al., 2024; Puranik et al., 2024).

**Advanced Urban Mobility**: Drones and small aircraft will revolutionize urban mobility by offering faster, more efficient transportation options. The rise of EVTOL (electric vertical takeoff and landing) aircraft and drone delivery systems is a main component in this shift. These technologies are expected to significantly reduce traffic congestion and carbon emissions, especially in urban areas with a crowded population. Future smart cities will widely adopt air vehicles for tasks such as potential emergency response, passenger transport, and last-mile delivery, which are integrated into the existing urban structure.

**Circular Economy and Sustainability**: The Circular professional model approach, which emphasizes resource efficiency, waste reduction, and reuse of materials, will play a major role in deploying drones and small aircraft services. By adopting circular principles, smart cities can reduce the environmental impact of these technologies. For example, the use of renewable energy sources for powering drones, recycling of drone components, and re-installation of old aircraft materials are trends that will contribute to a more durable urban ecosystem. Circular professional models will also promote economic elasticity by creating new value chains and reducing dependence on limited resources.

**Smart Logistics and Public Services**: Drone and small aircraft applications are expected to expand quickly in logistics and public services. Future trends indicate the rising dependence on these technologies for the real-time delivery of goods, medical supplies, and other critical services. A drone equipped with AI and IoT capabilities will enable smart cities to monitor and react to urban challenges such as traffic management, environmental monitoring, and structural maintenance. This technology will lead to a more responsive and adaptive urban environment, which will improve overall service distribution and quality of life.

## CONCLUSION

The integration of advanced technologies represents the main shift in the urban development strategy, providing unprecedented opportunities to eliminate pressure challenges while increasing economic prosperity, environmental stability, and social well-being in cities around the world. Throughout this chapter, we have introduced the in-laws of unified technologies on various aspects of urban life, from transportation and energy management to healthcare and community engagement.

- Using data analytics, artificial intelligence, and the power of IoT, cities can optimize resource allocation, improve service distribution, and reduce operational costs in the fields. Real-time insights enable active decisions, increase urban mobility, and reduce environmental effects. The unified technologies play a crucial role in promoting environmental stewards through the renewal of renewable energy zones, smart grid implementation, and sustainable structural development. This initiative not only reduces climate change but also increases urban elasticity in environmental risks.
- From improved healthcare access and educational opportunities to engagement and enhanced public safety, unified technologies prioritize the well-being and empowerment of urban residents. Smart City initiatives, promoting inclusive growth, bridge the digital divide and promote social connection in various urban communities. Adoption of unified technologies stimulates economic development by attracting investment, promoting innovation ecosystems, and creating jobs in emerging tech sectors. Smart City initiatives promote urban competitiveness globally, placing cities at the center of innovation and economic mobility.

- While the benefits are attractive, challenges such as digital equity, data privacy, and infrastructure investment require thoughtful consideration and strategic planning. Cooperation between stakeholders, strong regime structures, and continuous evaluation are required to explore these complications and maximize the benefits of technical integration.

In conclusion, accepting integrated technologies is not only a trend, but it is necessary for cities to create durable, incorporated, and elastic urban ecosystems. Cities can move towards the future, where the technology serves as a catalyst for positive change, prosperity, and well-being for all urban residents, by benefiting from the technical innovations and promoting participation in the fields. As we look forward, the courageous vision for traveling towards smart and durable cities, adaptive strategies, and a collective commitment to shape urban landscapes requires the needs of dynamic, equal, current, and future generations.

## REFERENCES


Al-Dhaqm, A., Ikuesan, R. A., Kebande, V. R., Razak, S., & Ghabban, F. M. (2021). Research challenges and opportunities in drone forensics models. *Electronics (Basel)*, *10*(13), 1519.

Babu, B. S., Kamalakannan, J., Meenatchi, N., Karthik, S., & Boopathi, S. (2022). Economic impacts and reliability evaluation of battery by adopting Electric Vehicle. *IEEE Explore*, 1–6.

Beard, R. W., & McLain, T. W. (2012). *Small unmanned aircraft: Theory and practice*. Princeton university press.

Beigi, P., Rajabi, M. S., & Aghakhani, S. (2022). An overview of drone energy consumption factors and models. *Handbook of Smart Energy Systems*, 1–20.

Boopathi, S. (2024a). Advancements in Machine Learning and AI for Intelligent Systems in Drone Applications for Smart City Developments. In *Futuristic e-Governance Security With Deep Learning Applications* (pp. 15–45). IGI Global.

Boopathi, S. (2024b). Enabling Machine Control Through Virtual Methods: Harnessing the Power of 5G. In *Advances in Logistics, Operations, and Management Science* (pp. 50–74). IGI Global. https://doi.org/DOI: 10.4018/979-8-3693-1862-1.ch004

Boopathi, S., Arigela, S. H., Raman, R., Indhumathi, C., Kavitha, V., & Bhatt, B. C. (2022). Prominent Rule Control-based Internet of Things: Poultry Farm Management System. *IEEE Explore*, 1–6.

Boopathi, S., Siva Kumar, P. K., & Meena, R. S. J., S. I., P., S. K., & Sudhakar, M. (2023). Sustainable Developments of Modern Soil-Less Agro-Cultivation Systems: Aquaponic Culture. In *Advances in Environmental Engineering and Green Technologies* (pp. 69–87). IGI Global. https://doi.org/DOI: 10.4018/978-1-6684-4118-3.ch004

Canca, D., Navarro-Carmona, B., & Andrade-Pineda, J. L. (2022). Design and assessment of an urban circular combined truck–drone delivery system using Continuum approximation models and integer programming. *Sustainability*, *14*(20), 13459.

Canca Ortiz, J. D., Navarro Carmona, B., & Andrade Pineda, J. L. (2022). Design and Assessment of an Urban Circular Combined Truck–Drone Delivery System Using Continuum Approximation Models and Integer Programming. *Sustainability*, *14*(10), 13459.

Dhanya, D., Kumar, S. S., Thilagavathy, A., Prasad, D., & Boopathi, S. (2023). Data Analytics and Artificial Intelligence in the Circular Economy: Case Studies. In *Intelligent Engineering Applications and Applied Sciences for Sustainability* (pp. 40–58). IGI Global.

Duaa, T., & Hammed, A. (2024). Enhancing electronic agriculture data security with a blockchain-based search method and e-signatures. *Mesopotamian journal of Cybersecurity*, 4(3), 1-21.

Gift, M. D. M., Senthil, T. S., Hasan, D. S., Alagarraja, K., Jayaseelan, P., & Boopathi, S. (2024). Additive Manufacturing and 3D Printing Innovations: Revolutionizing Industry 5.0. In *Technological Advancements in Data Processing for Next Generation Intelligent Systems* (pp. 255–287). IGI Global. https://doi.org/DOI: 10.4018/979-8-3693-0968-1.ch010

Gopal, M., Lurdhumary, J., Bathrinath, S., Priya, A. P., Sarojwal, A., & Boopathi, S. (2024). Energy Harvesting and Smart Highways for Sustainable Transportation Infrastructure: Revolutionizing Roads Using Nanotechnology. In *Principles and Applications in Speed Sensing and Energy Harvesting for Smart Roads* (pp. 136–165). IGI Global. https://doi.org/DOI: 10.4018/978-1-6684-9214-7.ch005

Grauer, J. A., & Morelli, E. A. (2015). Generic global aerodynamic model for aircraft. *Journal of Aircraft*, *52*(1), 13–20.

Gunasekaran, K., & Boopathi, S. (2023). Artificial Intelligence in Water Treatments and Water Resource Assessments. In *Artificial Intelligence Applications in Water Treatment and Water Resource Management* (pp. 71–98). IGI Global.

Harikaran, M., Boopathi, S., Gokulakannan, S., & Poonguzhali, M. (2023). Study on the Source of E-Waste Management and Disposal Methods. In *Sustainable Approaches and Strategies for E-Waste Management and Utilization* (pp. 39–60). IGI Global.

Janardhana, K., Singh, V., Singh, S. N., Babu, T. R., Bano, S., & Boopathi, S. (2023). Utilization Process for Electronic Waste in Eco-Friendly Concrete: Experimental Study. In *Sustainable Approaches and Strategies for E-Waste Management and Utilization* (pp. 204–223). IGI Global.

Jeya, R., Venkatakrishnan, G. R., Rengaraj, R., Rajalakshmi, M., Pradeep Mohan Kumar, K., & Boopathi, S. (2023). Water Resource Managements in Soil and Soilless Irrigation Systems Using AI Techniques. In *Advances in Environmental Engineering and Green Technologies* (pp. 245–266). IGI Global. https://doi.org/DOI: 10.4018/979-8-3693-0338-2.ch014

Köhler, J., & Jeschke, P. (2021). Conceptual design and comparison of hybrid electric propulsion systems for small aircraft. *CEAS Aeronautical Journal, 12*(4), 907–922.

Koshariya, A. K., Khatoon, S., Marathe, A. M., Suba, G. M., Baral, D., & Boopathi, S. (2023). Agricultural Waste Management Systems Using Artificial Intelligence Techniques. In *AI-Enabled Social Robotics in Human Care Services* (pp. 236–258). IGI Global.

Kumara, V., & Sharma, M. D., Samson Isaac, J., Saravanan, S., Suganthi, D., & Boopathi, S. (2023). An AI-Integrated Green Power Monitoring System: Empowering Small and Medium Enterprises. In *Advances in Environmental Engineering and Green Technologies* (pp. 218–244). IGI Global. https://doi.org/DOI: 10.4018/979-8-3693-0338-2.ch013

Maguluri, L. P., Arularasan, A., & Boopathi, S. (2023). Assessing Security Concerns for AI-Based Drones in Smart Cities. In *Effective AI, Blockchain, and E-Governance Applications for Knowledge Discovery and Management* (pp. 27–47). IGI Global.

Malathi, J., Kusha, K., Isaac, S., Ramesh, A., Rajendiran, M., & Boopathi, S. (2024). IoT-Enabled Remote Patient Monitoring for Chronic Disease Management and Cost Savings: Transforming Healthcare. In *Advances in Explainable AI Applications for Smart Cities* (pp. 371–388). IGI Global.

Min, S., Harrison, E., Jimenez, H., & Mavris, D. N. (2015). Development of aerodynamic modeling and calibration methods for general aviation aircraft performance analysis-a survey and comparison of models. *15th AIAA Aviation Technology, Integration, and Operations Conference*, 2853.

Mohanty, A., Venkateswaran, N., Ranjit, P., Tripathi, M. A., & Boopathi, S. (2023). Innovative Strategy for Profitable Automobile Industries: Working Capital Management. In *Handbook of Research on Designing Sustainable Supply Chains to Achieve a Circular Economy* (pp. 412–428). IGI Global.

Moshref-Javadi, M., Hemmati, A., & Winkenbach, M. (2021). A comparative analysis of synchronized truck-and-drone delivery models. *Computers & Industrial Engineering, 162*, 107648.

Moshref-Javadi, M., & Winkenbach, M. (2021). Applications and Research avenues for drone-based models in logistics: A classification and review. *Expert Systems with Applications, 177*, 114854.

Periasamy, J. K., Subhashini, S., Mutharasu, M., Revathi, M., Ajitha, P., & Boopathi, S. (2024). Synergizing Federated Learning and In-Memory Computing: An Experimental Approach for Drone Integration. In *Developments Towards Next Generation Intelligent Systems for Sustainable Development* (pp. 89–123). IGI Global. https://doi.org/DOI: 10.4018/979-8-3693-5643-2.ch004

Puranik, T. A., Shaik, N., Vankudoth, R., Kolhe, M. R., Yadav, N., & Boopathi, S. (2024). Study on Harmonizing Human-Robot (Drone) Collaboration: Navigating Seamless Interactions in Collaborative Environments. In *Cybersecurity Issues and Challenges in the Drone Industry* (pp. 1–26). IGI Global.

Rai, S., Meschini, M., & Genangeli, S. (2016). *The Implementation of Drones in the Business Model of Photovoltaic Companies* [PhD Thesis]. Copenhagen Business School Frederiksberg, Denmark.

Ravisankar, A., Sampath, B., & Asif, M. M. (2023). Economic Studies on Automobile Management: Working Capital and Investment Analysis. In *Multidisciplinary Approaches to Organizational Governance During Health Crises* (pp. 169–198). IGI Global.

Razzaq, R., & Hammed, A. (2025). Combining Fog Computing and Blockchain Based on the Internet of Medical Things to Preserve Patient Information Privacy. In *Sustainable Information Security in the Age of AI and Green Computing* (pp. 525–546). IGI Global Scientific Publishing.

Riboldi, C. E. (2018). An optimal approach to the preliminary design of small hybrid-electric aircraft. *Aerospace Science and Technology*, *81*, 14–31.

Riboldi, C. E., & Gualdoni, F. (2016). An integrated approach to the preliminary weight sizing of small electric aircraft. *Aerospace Science and Technology*, *58*, 134–149.

Selvakumar, S., Adithe, S., Isaac, J. S., Pradhan, R., Venkatesh, V., & Sampath, B. (2023). A Study of the Printed Circuit Board (PCB) E-Waste Recycling Process. In *Sustainable Approaches and Strategies for E-Waste Management and Utilization* (pp. 159–184). IGI Global.

Senthil, T., Puviyarasan, M., Babu, S. R., Surakasi, R., Sampath, B., & Associates. (2023). Industrial Robot-Integrated Fused Deposition Modelling for the 3D Printing Process. In *Development, Properties, and Industrial Applications of 3D Printed Polymer Composites* (pp. 188–210). IGI Global.

Sharma, M., Sharma, M., Sharma, N., & Boopathi, S. (2024). Building Sustainable Smart Cities Through Cloud and Intelligent Parking System. In *Handbook of Research on AI and ML for Intelligent Machines and Systems* (pp. 195–222). IGI Global.

Sonia, R., Gupta, N., Manikandan, K., Hemalatha, R., Kumar, M. J., & Boopathi, S. (2024). Strengthening Security, Privacy, and Trust in Artificial Intelligence Drones for Smart Cities. In *Analyzing and Mitigating Security Risks in Cloud Computing* (pp. 214–242). IGI Global.

Sundaramoorthy, K., Singh, A., Sumathy, G., Maheshwari, A., Arunarani, A., & Boopathi, S. (2024). A Study on AI and Blockchain-Powered Smart Parking Models for Urban Mobility. In *Handbook of Research on AI and ML for Intelligent Machines and Systems* (pp. 223–250). IGI Global.

Tezza, D., & Andujar, M. (2019). The state-of-the-art of human–drone interaction: A survey. *IEEE Access : Practical Innovations, Open Solutions*, *7*, 167438–167454.

Vijaya Lakshmi, V., Mishra, M., Kushwah, J. S., Shajahan, U. S., Mohanasundari, M., & Boopathi, S. (2024). Circular Economy Digital Practices for Ethical Dimensions and Policies for Digital Waste Management. In *Harnessing High-Performance Computing and AI for Environmental Sustainability* (pp. 166–193). IGI Global., DOI: 10.4018/979-8-3693-1794-5.ch008

Vijayakumar, G. N. S., Domakonda, V. K., Farooq, S., Kumar, B. S., Pradeep, N., & Boopathi, S. (2024). Sustainable Developments in Nano-Fluid Synthesis for Various Industrial Applications. In *Adoption and Use of Technology Tools and Services by Economically Disadvantaged Communities: Implications for Growth and Sustainability* (pp. 48–81). IGI Global.

Zekrifa, D. M. S., Kulkarni, M., Bhagyalakshmi, A., Devireddy, N., Gupta, S., & Boopathi, S. (2023). Integrating Machine Learning and AI for Improved Hydrological Modeling and Water Resource Management. In *Artificial Intelligence Applications in Water Treatment and Water Resource Management* (pp. 46–70). IGI Global.

Zhang, J., Campbell, J. F., Sweeney, D. C.II, & Hupman, A. C. (2021). Energy consumption models for delivery drones: A comparison and assessment. *Transportation Research Part D, Transport and Environment*, *90*, 102668.

Chapter 7

# Securing Ovarian Cancer Detection Using Efficient Net Model and Patient Data Privacy Based on Lightweight Encryption

**R. Mohandas**
*New Horizon College of Engineering, Bengaluru, India*

**Vijilius Helena Raj**
*New Horizon College of Engineering, Bengaluru, India*

**C. Muthukumaran**
*K. Ramakrishnan College of Technology, Trichy, India*

**Arunadevi Thirumalraj**
https://orcid.org/0009-0003-5396-6810
*K. Ramakrishnan College of Technology, Trichy, India*

**Gopikha Sundaramoorthy**
*St. Joseph's College of Engineering, India*

## ABSTRACT

*This chapter suggests a Simple and Lightweight Method for Encrypting Images. This combines the Lorenz Chaotic System with DNA coding. This hiding method makes sure that private patient details are kept secret and safe during the study process. Further, it introduces optimal key selection using the Child Drawing Development*

DOI: 10.4018/979-8-3373-8133-6.ch007

*Optimization Algorithm (CDDOA). This makes the encryption key better, which helps increase the safety. Using these methods together makes a complete way to find out ovarian cancer. It is both very accurate in diagnosis and safe for patient information. The Proposed EfficientNet model achieves an exceptional ovarian cancer classification accuracy of 98.88% and outperforms other existing models also in precision, recall, specificity, and F1 score. The proposed Lightweight Encryption model excels with superior security, entropy 6.9, PSNR 40.5, and remarkable efficiency in encryption and decryption processes. This study opens the way for improvements in research on ovarian cancer and sets a model for safe and fast handling of genetic data in medical situations.*

## INTRODUCTION

In women, the fifth most frequent cause of cancer-related mortality is ovarian cancer (OC). Most of the time (75%), they happen to patients after menopause. Every year, there are 40 cases for every 100,000 people over the age of 50. Spotting sickness early on greatly increases the chance of living 5 years, from just 3% at stage 4 to 90% at stage 1 (Zamwar et al., 2022). Checking samples under a microscope is a better path to finding out if someone has ovarian cancer. It is identified into histological types. Interpretation of cellular structure helps to understand the different types of OC and directs them. Making a treatment plan (Handley et al., 2022), which is best done by skilled doctors for ovarian tumors. But some differences in how observer grades have been noticed. Different ways of reading a sample of cells under a microscope can cause wrong decisions about the future, weak treatments, and lower quality of life (Breen et al., 2023; Gajjela et al., 2023). This shows that we need to make computer ways that can accurately guess OC. To reach this goal, different OC diagnosis models were made in the past decade. They used just one kind of picture from a test called histopathology (Kodipalli et al., 2022; Köbel & Kang, 2022). This type of picture shows how a cell looks, which is very connected to the aggressiveness of OC. Also, it is known that the levels of gene expression and changes in the genes can indirectly affect the growth of cancers by speeding up how fast cells grow and changing the small surroundings of the tumor (Farahani et al., 2022). Therefore, genetic features are key indicators that guide medical testing. They include a list of gene activity marks, changes in DNA letter sequences, local differences in copy amounts of DNA parts, and how much methylation changes. This is according to research (Saida et al., 2022).

Recent changes in certain types of deep learning models, like CNNs, have a big impact on medical diagnosis. So, a big problem in the deep learning area is making models better. Right now, deep learning methods are being looked at to fix the problems of ML algorithms (Chen et al., 2022). Right now, many different ways of using deep learning are very popular. These include things like CNN, RNN, and a special type of memory called LSTM. All of them are praised for helping to classify medical pictures. DL methods can accurately guess an important collection of sample features without help from experts in the field (Gajjela et al., 2023). Deep learning (DL) and object detection algorithms both mimic the way the brain functions in humans when they recognize and pick up a wide range of concepts by seeing examples of them (Jung et al., 2022).

Encryption is very important for keeping cancer image classification data safe and private (Ahmed et al., 2023). As the medical picture field gets better, the need to keep private patient details becomes more important. Encryption is a safety shield that keeps secret cancer pictures safe and private (Jebbar, 2025). Healthcare workers and scientists can keep out unwanted access and protect patient information by using strong codes (Castro et al., 2023; Tahayur, 2025). This way, they can reduce the chance of patients' details being taken by bad people (Lata & Cenkeramaddi, 2023). This is very important in cancer picture sorting. Accurate diagnosis and treatment plans need an understanding of and reading of medical pictures (Razzaq, 2025). The use of encryption technologies makes important data more secure. It also helps patients and doctors trust that private medical information will be handled rightly and privately (Selvaraj et al., 2023).

## Motivation

These studies are mainly about changing how we find out about ovarian cancer. They really care about keeping patient information safe. The study wants to make medical testing better. It aims at setting up a model that keeps patients' private information safe and secure. The aim is to improve how we find ovarian cancer better and keep patients' secrets safe through new ways in cancer detection and data protection. This will help the health field grow, increase trust in medical work, and set new rules for handling genetic information.

## Chapter Objectives

**Hybrid Filtering Technique (MMG)**: Start with a new way to clean the TCGA-OV dataset using the Mean-Median-Gaussian hybrid filter. This method gives good results.

**Feature Extraction with Faster SqueezeNet**: Using the faster SqueezeNet model to spot important parts of DNA that help guess the correct stages of ovarian cancer.

**EfficientNet-V2 Classification**: Using the EfficientNet-V2 network helps in accurately and quickly identifying the different stages of ovarian cancer. This leads to better diagnosis.

**Secure Patient Data Encryption**: Developing a Lightweight Lorenz Chaotic System and DNA Coding Image Encryption Scheme. This guarantees strong secrecy and safety of patient information during analysis.

**Optimal Key Selection with CDDOA**: Starting the Child Drawing Development Optimization Algorithm (CDDOA) helps to pick the best keys in the secret codes. This improves the safety of patient details in studies about ovarian cancer.

## RELATED WORKS

The study by Ziyambe et al. (2023) described a new algorithm for ovarian cancer diagnosis and prediction using convolutional neural networks (CNNs) in order to address these problems. A dataset of histopathological images was used in this work to train a CNN. The dataset was pre-augmented and separated into validation and training subsets. The accuracy rate of the model was an impressive 94%, correctly classifying 93.02% of healthy cells and correctly identifying 95.12% of cancer instances. This study is important because it addresses issues like increased rates of misclassification, variability among observers, and extended periods of analysis resulting from human expert review. This work offers a more precise, effective, and trustworthy method for ovarian cancer diagnosis and prognosis.

The aim of the study by Binas et al. (2023) was to give medical professionals and biomedical engineers a tool for personalized medicine by introducing a novel technique that uses quantitative features extracted from medical images to assess intratumoral cellularity. This method is also referred to as sophisticated image processing, radiomics, and algorithms for artificial intelligence. The findings show that within the population under study (n = 22), the suggested method's average accuracy rating was above 85%.

The article by Jeya & Brintha (2023) offered the IEDL-OVD model, a clever Internet Explorer that uses deep learning to diagnose ovarian tumors. The IEDL-OVD model aims to improve the quality of the input medical image, which will lead to better diagnostic results. An IE technique based on black widow optimization is included in the recommended IEDL-OVD method. The ovarian tumor is detected using a stacked autoencoder (SAE) as a classification model and the VGG16 model as a feature extractor. Via a thorough experimentation analysis, the diagnostic result of the IEDL-OVD model is investigated, and the findings are evaluated regarding various assessment parameters. The IEDL-OVD model produced better recall and precision rates, 0.612 and 0.735, respectively, with 100 photos. With the use of quality IE, the black widow optimization algorithm (BWOA) produced results with a homogeneity of 0.94, a weighted peak signal-to-noise ratio (WPSNR) of 20.43, a high contrast of 0.97, and a contrast-to-noise ratio (CNR) of 92.74%.

In the paper by Acharya et al. (2023) on Kaggle, a deep convolutional neural network architecture was suggested for the prediction of ovarian cancer using a dataset with 349 patient instances. Subsequently, the dataset underwent a suite of feature extraction techniques and data-cleaning procedures. Additionally, the model's efficacy has been demonstrated by contrasting Using seven conventional machine learning classifiers, the proposed model, such as Linear Discriminant Analysis, Multilayer Perceptron, Random Forest, Gradient Boosting Tree, AdaBoost, XGBoost, and Decision Tree. The analysis of the results shows that the F1 score, ROC-AUC, recall, and precision are all higher for the proposed CNN architecture.

The model by Maria et al. (2023) integrated YOLO v5 detection model's effectiveness and the U-Net segmentation model's accuracy in identifying malignant ovarian tumors on a computed tomography image. Clinical data is used to validate this model's performance, and an analysis has been done on its performance metrics. Simulated results show that ovarian tumors can be treated with the suggested model with good accuracy and dice scores. The ovarian tumors were detected by the YOLO v5 model with 98% accuracy, and they were segmented by U-Net with 99.2% accuracy that have been found. Radiologists can diagnose ovarian cancer with the use of this computer-aided diagnosis system.

The Internet of Things' security for medical images (Selvaraj et al., 2023) employed optimization techniques and a novel cryptographic model. A distinct framework is required for the safe and efficient exchange of medical image data and patient data. Using the Rivest-Shamir-Adleman (RSA-AM) based Arnold map, it will select the supervisor responsible for overseeing and enhancing the security of lock and unlock processes. This will involve obstruction flower raising betterness optimization (OBBO) and hostile team direction (HO). The optimal metrics to assess the effectiveness of the proposed scheme are the peak signal-to-noise ratio (PSNR), entropy, bit error rate (BER), structural similarity index (SSI), mean square error (MSE), and correlation coefficient (CC).

Research suggests a low-cost technique for encrypting multiple images in a medical setting (Ghoniem et al., 2021) has a computational cost comparable to that of encrypting a single image and can use a single encryption operation to both encrypt and decrypt an unlimited number of medical images of various sizes. To guarantee that every plaintext image is the same size, the various-sized plaintext images are filled at the bottom and right of the image. After that, each filled image is stacked to produce a superimposed image. Using the algorithm for linear congruence, the original key is the first step in creating the encryption key sequence, produced by the SHA-256 algorithm. Next, the superimposed image is encrypted using the cipher picture using DNA encoding and the encryption key. Incorporating a method for decrypting the image independently can further strengthen the algorithm's security by lowering the possibility of data loss while decrypting.

## Research Gaps

Ziyambe et al. (2023) did not talk much about how good their ovarian cancer CNN was at handling different groups of data and working well for things other than what they trained it on. This made it hard to use. Binas et al. (2023) has says we need to look into tools for personalized medicine. It must think about how big they can be, use them in real life, and make sure they work on lots of patients to prove they are reliable (Jeya & Brintha, 2023). The IEDL-OVD model has potential, but it hasn't been checked completely on different sets of data and compared to existing ways for finding out if someone has ovarian cancer. Acharya et al. (2023) CNN for ovarian cancer doesn't understand how it works, possible unfair actions, or right and wrong issues. Resolving these would make it more trusted. Maria et al. (2023) mixed YOLO v5 and U-Net model. It seems good, but there are some problems that need to be checked in medical use, usefulness in real life, and adding such tech to their system. Selvaraj et al. (2023) said that the security model for IoT should be checked using real health data, looked at how big it can grow, and explored areas where it might be weak and how to protect against them. Wu et al. (2023) made a low-cost image scrambling answer. It needs more testing to see how fast it works, find possible weaknesses, and check how strong it is against various attacks before it can be used in real life.

## PROPOSED METHODOLOY

Figure 1 shows the workflow of the proposed model.

*Figure 1. Block diagram*

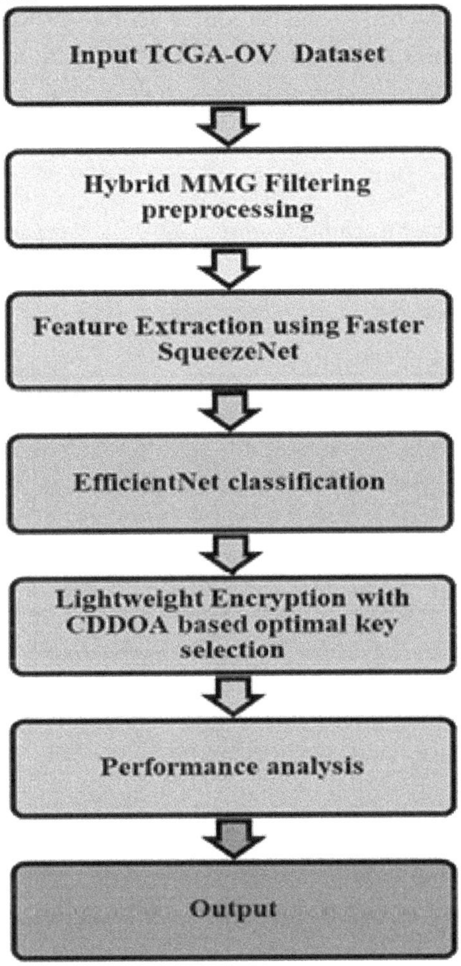


## Dataset Description

For OC stage prediction, a publicly available dataset from the Cancer Genome Atlas portal (accessed on March 2, 2021) was used. More specifically, the TCGA-OV can be found at https://portal.gdc.cancer.gov/. Data on copy number variants and gene expressions from 587 OC patients are included in the dataset. Every patient also has a large number of pathological images. One modality type is associated with the colored pathology images, whereas the gene expression and copy variant data have a single dimension. It refers to them as pathology image modal and gene modal in this work, respectively (Ghoniem et al., 2021). Table 1 lists all of the features of the multi-modal dataset of TCGA-OV. It displays how many patient samples correspond to each OC stage. About 6426 data indicators were included in the gene expression data, whereas about 24,776 data indicators were included in the copy number variants data. Additionally, for every patient, one to ten pathological images were available.

*Table 1. An explanation of the multimodal TCGA-OV dataset*

| **Clinical Characteristics** | **Number of Samples** |
|---|---|
| Patients with Serous Ovarian Carcinoma Having Clinical Data | $N = 587$ |
| Stage Not Available | 5(0.85%) |
| Stage IV | 89(15.16%) |
| Stage III | 446(75.98%) |
| Stage II | 30(5.11%) |
| Stage I | 17(2.90%) |
| **Data Category** | **Number of Attributes** |
| Gene expressions | 6426 |
| Pathology images for each sample | 1375 images |
| Copy number variants | 1 – 10 images |

## Preprocessing Using MMG Filter

First, a sample image was used to calculate the kernel matrix size. In the study's methodology section, a 3x3 kernel matrix is given as an illustration. The sample image was subjected to Gaussian filters, matrix size mean, and median using this kernel (Aksoy & Salman, 2020). One image was produced by calculating the resultant vectors of the same pixels from the images to which the mean, median, and Gaussian filters were applied. A mathematical formula was used to normalize the image that was obtained by taking the resultant vectors. The normalization was carried out by computing the resultant vector of the pixel values corresponding to the three filtering techniques using equation (1).

$$MMG_{i,j} = 255 \cdot \frac{\sqrt{\left(Mean_{i,j}\right)^2 + \left(Median_{i,j}\right)^2 + \left(Gaussian_{i,j}\right)^2}}{Max\left(MMG_{i,j}\right)} \quad (1)$$

The new image that has been softened by a filter is represented by MMG in the equation $Max(MMG_{i,j})$ represents, before normalization, the maximum pixel value that could be extracted from the resultant vector. The research findings section contains the results of testing the MMG hybrid filter's performance using a sample image.

## Extraction Using Faster SqueezeNet

A faster SqueezeNet was introduced in this study to enhance the efficiency and precision of OC feature extraction. The authors included BatchNorm and residual frameworks to prevent over-fitting. Concat was also used in tandem with DenseNet to link different layers in order to enhance the first layer's expressiveness. Fast SqueezeNet consists of three block layers: four convolution layers, a global average pooling layer, and a BatchNorm layer. The main improvements to Fast SqueezeNet are listed below.

(1) In order to further improve the data flow between the layers, the current study offers a novel connection mode while imitating the DenseNet architecture (Al Duhayyim et al., 2022). This is made up of a pooling layer and a fire module. Finally, the convolutional layer that followed was connected to the two concat layers as well.

Every feature map from the previous layer is obtained by the current layer, which then uses $x_0, \ldots, x_{l-1}$ as the input; following $x_l$ is shown as indicated by the equation (2) below.

$$x_l = H_l([x_0, x_1, \ldots, x_{l-1}]) \tag{2}$$

Where $[x_0, x_1, \ldots, x_{l-1}]$ depicts the relationship between the layer's feature graph created, $0, 1, \ldots, l-1$, and $H_l$ represents the concatenation of multiple inputs. Moreover, the maximum pooling layer can be found by $x_0$, $x_1$ denote the Fire layer, while $x_l$ stands for the Concat layer.

If there's not a significant increase in considering the number of network parameters, efficiency can still be maximized early on. Data can be simultaneously transported directly over any two-layer network.

(2) A fire module and a pooling layer were presented to distinct components after a thorough understanding of the ResNet architecture to ensure a successful network convergence. Lastly, two layers were appended and connected to the subsequent convolution layer. A common representation of the fundamental mapping is *H*(*x*). To fit alternative mappings of the stacked non-linear layer,

$F(x) := H(x) - x$. The initial mapping is arranged differently into $F(x) + x$. $F(x) + x$ is implemented as a shortcut connection structure. It makes use of ResNet's residual architecture to address problems like gradient degradation and disappearing without adding more network variables.

## Classification Using EfficientNet Framework

To achieve better classification results, a strong set of image features is necessary because it directly aids in differentiating between the various image data groups. Dense deep learning networks can be used to compute a set of more efficient features, which raises the recall rate of techniques (Nazir et al., 2023). When deep networks are used, the models' computational capabilities are limited by the memory and processing power requirements, which have a big impact on how these CNN techniques are used. As such, there are always trade-offs between the evaluation's outcomes and computing costs. Because of this, it is necessary to create an OC diagnosis system that can exhibit increased precision in classification without raising computing costs. To improve model performance, this study provides a simple and reliable computational method for the classification of different anomalies.

An enhanced version of the EfficientNetV2-B4 model, dubbed EfficientNet, is presented to detect OC. An enhanced version of EfficientNet is called EfficientNetV2. In essence, in order to maintain a high recall rate and increase the pool of resources, the improved EfficientNetV2 model is provided. A rapid and efficient composite scaling technique was used to create the improved EfficientNetV2 model, which allows a standard ConvNet that can be modified for any resource constraints without compromising the functionality of the technique. Consequently, the suggested method provides the best option for network architecture, including network layers and feature vector size, in addition to the best way to calculate costs. Using a few model parameters, the EfficientNetV2 technique performs classification operations with robustness.

To detect OC, EfficientNet-V2 with dense layers was developed because it is a lightweight, efficient method with fewer parameters and a lower training time requirement. Using neural architecture search, the EfficientNetV2 method decreases training time and feature vector size while improving classification accuracy (NAS). Furthermore, the architecture of EfficiceiNetV2 maximizes the operational power and makes effective use of mobile or server accelerators by incorporating the Fused-MBConv (FMBConv) blocks. In contrast, the primary building block of an MBConv block is used in the traditional EfficientNet approach, which solely employs depth-wise convolutions. Convolutions that are depth-wise minimise the quantity of operations required, but they don't make full use of newly created hardware accelerators. To optimise computing gains, the EfficientNetV2 technique fully utilises the MBConv and FMBConv blocks. The FMBConv substitute's standard 3*3 convolution layers for the depth-wise 3*3 convolution. The main aim is to run the method as quickly as possible while maintaining the classification results.

To complete the sorting process, it employed EfficientNetV2 with the B4 structure. The primary cause for the B4 base was chosen because it offers a better balance between the complexity of time and the model's ability to sort things out. Swish activation, MBConv blocks with 3*3 and 5*5 convolutions, and squeeze-and-excitation blocks (SEB) are used in the updated EfficientNet-V2 model, which is sophisticated. FMBConv blocks are utilised in the lower layers. MBConv blocks uphold a close relationship with the SEB and guarantee accurate classification outcomes.

ReLU activation (ReLUAF) is changed within the architecture by the Swish activation function (SAF) because ReLU eliminates negative values and discards a significant portion of the crucial ECG signal. Equation (3) can be utilized to find the SAF:

$$SAF(x) = X.Sigmoid(x) \tag{3}$$

To further reduce the input image sizes, the framework was extended with an initial batch normalisation layer. This is because only three of the many parameters available to FMBConv blocks for large values of O were used. In order to mitigate the problem of overfitting and lower the model parameters, A layer of global average pooling was added following the MBConv framework. Two additional dense inner layers were added in addition to dropout and ReLUAF layers, which help calculate the more efficient gathering of image attributes through their efficient arrangement. A 30% dropout rate was selected at random to improve the work of the model. Ultimately, a layer of softmax was used to categorise OC. A detailed view of the enhanced EfficientNetV2 method is provided in Table 2.

*Table 2. Specifics of the layers and blocks that make up the suggested model*

| SI No. | Layers |
|---|---|
| 1 | ConvL $(3 \times 3)$ |
| 2 | BatchNormalization |
| 3 | 2 × FMBConv4 Block |
| 4 | 3 × FMBConv4 Block |
| 5 | 2 × FMBConv1 Block |
| 6 | Conv2d $(1 \times 1)$ Block |
| 7 | 12 × MBConv6 Block |

continued on following page

*Table 2. Continued*

| SI No. | Layers |
|---|---|
| 8 | 7 × MBConv6 Block |
| 9 | 5 × MBConv4 Block |
| 10 | Dropout |
| 11 | Dense Layer |
| 12 | Dropout |
| 13 | Softmax Layer |
| 14 | Global average pooling |
| 15 | FC Layer |
| 16 | Dense Layer |

## Loss Function (LF)

Models use the loss function (LF) to evaluate how well they are performing. Automated learning is used by networks to discover patterns and make predictions for massive volumes of data. Determining the degree of change between the expected and real values is the main objective of the LF. To lower error, the LF is continuously changed during the model training process until a robust fitting value is reached.

In order to complete the task of categorising distorted and high-quality samples, an output neuron was used to eliminate the last layer of the EfficientNet model. Because of this, the hyperparameters of the framework were chosen empirically. In the suggested method, a learning score of 0.1 is used in conjunction with when the model is being trained. Additionally, it used twenty epochs to train the model. In tasks involving classification, the cross-entropy LF assesses the difference between the actual and calculated values using the Softmax function. In equation (4), the cross-entropy LF can be computed using the following formula:

$$LF = \frac{1}{N}\sum_{k=1}^{n} \log\left(\frac{e^{s_j}}{\text{Skipping malformed tag: msubsup}\, e^{s_k}}\right) \quad (4)$$

Here, N represents all neurons, and $s_k$ is the vector input, and $sj$ is the approximate label. Only 20% of the entire parameters of the framework can be changed by the model, leaving the other 80% unchanged. Using a validation set ensured that issues related to overfitting of the model were prevented. Estimating Adaptive Moments was used to determine the learning rate value against each parameter. Equations (5) and (6), respectively, show how the impulse approach is used in this method to keep the prior gradient's exponential decay stored.

$$M_t = b1 M_t - 1 + (1 - b1)G_t \quad (5)$$

$$V_t = b2 V_t - 1 + (1 - b2)G^2 t \quad (6)$$

Here, $b1$ and $b2$ are constants; the gradient score corresponds to 0.9 and 0.999, is shown by G, and $M_t$ and $V_t$ show the vectors at the initial and subsequent moments. Each of these factors' values shows how the updated and earlier gradient values are similar. High correlation between the old and new gradient values is indicated by greater values for these parameters. Given that the two moments' initial values are set to zero, the factors used to correct for bias, $b1$ and $b2$, are needed to keep the 0 biases away. Through the use of the formulas (7) and (8), which calculate the bias-corrected Mt, such biases can be eliminated:

$$M_t = M_t - (bt1) \quad (7)$$

$$V_t = V_t - (bt2) \quad (8)$$

Equation (9) is employed in the optimisation process of the model to bring the gradient value up to date.

$$W_{t+1} = W_t - \eta / \left(V_t + \epsilon M\right)^{0.5} t \quad (9)$$

Here, $\epsilon$ is a constant, $\eta$ is a learning rate used to prevent the denominator from going to zero, with a score of 0.00001, and $W(t + 1)$ shows the parameters of the framework at a specific moment $(t + 1)$.

## Lightweight Encryption model

### Lorenz Chaotic System

A pseudorandom source that can be generated both on the sending and receiving ends is needed for the suggested cryptography system. Euler's method (Fetteha et al., 2023) is utilized to accomplish the digitization of the chaotic system, bringing it to life in the digital realm. The Lorenz chaotic system's Eulerian solution is given by the following equations:

$$X_{n+1} = X_n + h\sigma\left(Y_n - X_n\right) \quad (10)$$

$$Y_{n+1} = Y_n + h\left(\rho X_n - Y_n - X_n Z_n\right) \quad (11)$$

$$Z_{n+1} = Z_n + h(X_n Y_n - \beta Z_n) \tag{12}$$

Wherein $h$ is the size of the step, $\sigma, \rho$, and $\beta$ are the parameters of the system, and $X_0$, $Y_0$, and $Z_0$ are the variables in the system.

## DNA Coding

The value of each pixel is concealed using the DNA encoding technique. In a DNA sequence, the four potential nucleic acid bases are adenine (A), guanine (G), thymine (T), and cytosine (C); "A" is always complementary to "T," and "C" is always complementary to "G". The connections between the binary codes and the different DNA bases that correspond to them are shown in Table 3. Considering the complementary characteristics of the binary stream and the nucleic acid bases, there are eight appropriate coding rules. Guidelines for encoding and decoding DNA are compiled for Table 3's suggested cryptography system.

*Table 3. Binary codes for DNA and the rules governing their decoding and encoding*

| DNA Base | Binary Code | | Rules | | | | | | | |
|---|---|---|---|---|---|---|---|---|---|---|
| | | | 8 | 7 | 6 | 5 | 4 | 3 | 2 | 1 |
| C | 11 | C | A | G | T | G | C | T | A | C |
| T | 10 | T | C | T | C | A | A | G | G | T |
| A | 01 | A | G | A | G | T | T | C | C | A |
| G | 00 | G | T | C | A | C | G | A | T | G |

## Cryptography Algorithm

A. Encryption

- Step 1: First, determine the total number of pixels in the picture to get $P_{Sum}$.
- Step 2: Determine P, which is equivalent to $mod(P_{Sum}, 16)$.
- Step 3: Eight keys, each with 32 bits, should be created from the input key $(Key_1 \ldots Key_8)$.
- Step 4: To create the starting circumstances surrounding the chaotic sequence, XOR the keys together.

- Step 5: After executing the Lorenz chaotic system with the starting parameters from the preceding step, eliminate the redundant outputs by discarding the first 200 generated outputs.
- Step 6: Utilise the outputs of the chaotic system to produce $X_{bin1}, X_{bin2}, X_{bin3}, X_{bin4}, Y_{bin1}, Y_{bin2}, Y_{bin3}, Y_{bin4}$ such that $Y_{bin}$ is similar to $X_{bin}$ and $Z_{bin}$.
- Step 7: In order to complete the process of pixel confusion, the value of $P$. If $P$ is even, the picture is encrypted in the typical manner; if not, it is reversed before encryption. This is an easy way to modify the locations of the pixels for each iteration.
- Step 8: Use $X_{bin1}, X_{bin2}, X_{bin3}$, and $X_{bin4}$ as each of the input image's two bits' DNA encoding rule.
- Step 9: Usc $Y_{bin1}, Y_{bin2}, Y_{bin3}$, and $Y_{bin4}$ as each of the two pieces of the previously mentioned DNA decoding rule which generated DNA encoded bits.
- Step 10: XOR the step 8's produced 8-bit output with $Z_{bin}$ and mask, where mask is initialised with zero and holds the earlier output from step 10. Following this, $P = P - 1$; repeat step 5 until you reach $P = 0$.

Algorithm 1 provides more details on the encryption algorithm. If an image with LW pixels serves as the algorithm's input, the estimated complexity of time is limited by $O(LW)$.

Algorithm 1 Encryption process Input: Input image I, and encryption key $K$

Output: Encrypted image $E$, and the 16 bit value $P$

1: $P = mod(SU(I), 16)$

$.P = P // Divide\ the\ key\ into\ four\ 32 - bit\ keys.$

3. $\{Key_1, \ldots, Key_s\} = K$

*// Set up the chaotic system's initial parameters.*

4: while $P > 0$ do

5. $x_0 = Key_1 \otimes Key_2 \otimes Key K_3 \otimes Key_4$
6. $Y_0 = Key_3 \otimes Key_4 \otimes Key/5 \otimes Key_6$ ;

or $i = 1$ o $(200 + L \times W)$ do

$X = X_0 + h\sigma(Y_0 - X_0);$

$Y = Y_0 + h(\rho X_0 - Y_0 - X_0 Z_0); Z = Z_0 + h(X_0 Y_0 - \beta Z_0); X_0 = X; Y_0 = Y_i Z_0 = Z_i$

f $i > 200$ th n$X_{bim\ 1} = mod(fix(X \times 2^{13}), 8) + 1\, X_{bin\ 2} = mod(fix(X \times 2^{16}), 8) + 1$ $X_{bin3} = mod(fix(X \times 2^{19}), 8) + 1; X_{bin4} = mod(fix(X \times 2^{22}), 8) + 1\, Y_{bin1} = mod(fix(Y \times 2^{13})$ $, 8) + 1\, Y_{bin2} = mod(fix(Y \times 2^{16}), 8) + 1; Y_{bin3} = mod(fix(Y \times 2^{19}), 8) + 1; Y_{bin4} = mod(fix$ $(Y \times 2^{22}), 8) + 1; Z_{bin} = mod(fix(Z \times 2^{22}), 8) + 1$ ;

if $mod(P, 2) = = 0$ th n

$$I = L_i$$

else $I = 1_{(L \times W) - i^*}$
n i $D = DNA_{encode}(I, X_{bin1}, X_{bin2}, X_{bin3}, X_{bin\ 4});$

$$T = DNA_{decode}(D, Y_{bin1\ 1}, Y_{bin2}, Y_{bin3}, Y_{bin4\ 4})$$

$I(i) = Z_{bin} \oplus T \oplus$ m sk;
mas = $I(i)$; $P = P - 1$
e d i
nd or I = $I$;
end while
$E = I$;
return $E, P$

B. Decryption

The process of decryption is the opposite of that of encryption. The primary distinction is that P is transmitted to the receiving side along with the key rather than being calculated.

## Optimal Key Selection Using CDDO Algorithm

In this chapter, CDDOA is utilized for optimal key selection of the encryption model. While optimization approaches seek the best scenario, which, using an evaluation function, can be used to determine the global optimum, artistic works aim to achieve the most aesthetically pleasing state, which is influenced by the artwork's use of the golden ratio. Throughout the drawing process, the artist makes a number of suggestions that determine each drawing. Here, for example, a metaheuristic algorithm was formed using the components that influence a child's drawing throughout the various stages of their artistic development. The new Human behavior inspired algorithm's mathematical equations were developed with inspiration from the behavior of the child and the previous section's solid mathematical justification for the golden ratio (Abdulhameed & Rashid, 2022). The following subsections will provide a thorough explanation of each section in relation to the golden ratio, pattern memory, mathematical equations, drawing properties (such as length and width), and group member cooperation.

1). CDDO Stages

Each step's specific explanation is provided below:

### *(A) The First Stage (The Scribble)*

Most of a child's early drawings are just random marks made during their learning process. At this age, the child is learning about hand pressure and movement by observing it. Since the child is learning that hand movements with liners create lines and any additional hand movement produces curves, random motion can be both linear and curved. It is currently too forceful when holding the hand; in the next stages, it will be adjusted by trial and error while taking into account other factors, including whether it is excessively high or low.-launch $X_{ij}$ for $i = 1$ to $N$ solution.

$X$ when a child's drawing contains several factors that can be chosen from, such as the number of parameters, the length, width, golden ratio, and hand pressure reported, the current solution is represented by $j$.

### *(B) The Second Stage (Exploitation)*

The youngster gains control over their direction and mobility to create shapes during this stage. At this point, the drawings are more uniform and replicated, and the child is defining the best sketched drawing thus far and comparing it to the best pattern they have learned. In addition, they are creating new scribbles by copying the top local artists and comparing them to the best-sketched drawing that has been produced as a group thus far.

Hand pressure is one factor that is used to categorize a child's work. The child's level is high even though the hand pressure is significant. Meanwhile, that shows that a child is proficient enough to draw a picture using the correct golden ratio and little force. First, a Random Hand Pressure (RHP) is produced. The hand pressure of a current solution is evaluated using a factor called RHP, which was developed to measure hand pressure (HP). The number that separates the problem's lower boundary (LB) from the solution's upper boundary (UP) is arbitrary. Equations (13) and (14) will be used to select HP from among when Hand pressure is represented by HP, and the parameters are gathered by $j$ for the current solution, or the set of solution parameters.

$$RHP = rand(LB, UP) \tag{13}$$

$$HP = X(i, rand(j)) \tag{14}$$

### *(C) Third Stage (Golden Ratio)*

The child is now putting the abilities they have gained from experiences to use by imitating, practicing, and being enthusiastic (with trial). They attempt to decipher the drawings by looking for patterns in the real photos based on the feedback. Prior to implementing these behaviors, measure the child's hand pressure HP to gauge their level of proficiency. When evaluating the relationship between the RHP and the present hand pressure, using equation (15), if it is less than the RHP will be updated to account for the child's arbitrary level rate (LR) and skill rate (SR), that start at 0 and go up to 1, as well as whether the child displays relevant hand pressure, between 0.6 and 1. The child's knowledge and skill rate is accurate when SR and LR are set to high (0.6–1), even though it can be improved by accounting for the GR factor. The Golden Ratio (GR) is an additional element that is utilized to improve the performance and update the solution. GR represents the proportion of the two factors chosen for the solution, the child's drawing's width and length in equation (16). Equation (17) is utilised from all the components of the problem, to randomly select each of these two factors.

$$X_{i+1} = GR + SR \cdot *(X_{ilbest} - X_i) + LR \cdot *\left(X_{igbest} - X_i\right) \tag{15}$$

$$X_{iGR} = \frac{X_{iL} + X_{iW}}{X_{iL}} \tag{16}$$

$$L, W = rand(0, j) \tag{17}$$

$X_{ilbest}$ is the young artist's finest drawing to date, and it represents the best option in the area. And $X_{igbest}$ is that the kids see the world's best solution in their surroundings. In addition, the child's drawing's length (L) and width (W) ratio are known as the Golden Ratio (GR).

### *(D) Fourth Stage (Creativity)*

Every child possesses the creativity and abilities they have acquired via experience and observation of their surroundings. The quality of creativity adds to the visual appeal of any work of art. At this point, the child is updating the golden ratio-containing solutions or is very close to it by combining information. The answer, however, does not have the appropriate hand pressure to indicate that a child's abilities are still developing and should be improved by utilizing both the golden ratio and the creative factor. Furthermore, a child will attempt to replicate the most effective learning strategies in order to improve their performance. To do this, for every algorithmic solution, a Pattern Memory (PM) is generated; the size of the pattern varies depending on the issues. But one way to speed up the rate of convergence of the algorithm and, in practice, help kids learn more quickly is to choose a randomly selected PM array solution to update the underperforming solutions. Equation (18), which updates the present solution and converges towards the ideal solution, applies both CR and PM. The creativity factor is added, adding to the improvement. After much trial and error, CR=0.1 was established as a fixed value. At a later time, when both SR and LR are low (0-0.5), the child's rate of knowledge and skill acquisition is demonstrated to be inaccurate, although it can be improved by taking their creativity and pattern memory into account.

$$X_{i+1} = X_{iMP} + CR*\left(X_{igbest}\right) \tag{18}$$

*(E) Fifth Stage (Pattern Memory)*

Employing past knowledge and experience, supplementing with additional details, increasing precision, and cross-referencing with all of the best drawings. Using a random selection from the top ten child drawings, the algorithm updates the existing illustration, which disregards hand pressure while keeping an exact golden ratio. The stage mainly focuses on the minute details in inches of the drawings. Given that the behavior is displayed by the most effective updating system on the agent, it is applied in the algorithm. If a better solution becomes available, that is when the solution will be updated. This also applies to updating the population's best solution in the world. This conduct will likewise be valid when each iteration's pattern memory is updated with the best global solution currently found.

2). The steps of CDDOA

The steps and procedure of the following are the recently suggested algorithms:

1. Set up the drawing population for a child.
2. Assess drawings and select the best individual and collective drawings.
3. Determine each drawing's golden ratio.
4. Select the best drawing to use as the starting point for initial pattern memory when making changes to the current drawing.

5. Update the drawings based on the child's hand pressure, using either pattern memory or the golden ratio.
6. Update the child's level and skill rates.
7. Assess the cost values and make updates to the individual, collective, and pattern memory.

# RESULTS AND DISCUSSIONS

## Experimental Setup

A PC equipped with an Intel(R) Core (TM) i7-10700KF @ 3.80 GHz CPU, 32.0 GB RAM, six CPUs, and one NVIDIA GeForce RTX 3060 GPU is used to conduct the experimental study.

## Classification Analysis

The efficacy of the suggested pipeline is evaluated using a number of criteria, including the following: precision, Mathew correlation coefficient (MCC), sensitivity, F1-score, specificity, and accuracy. These metrics are computed using the following formulas (19)–(23). Additionally, the receiving operating characteristic (ROC) and the confusion matrix are computed.

$$Accuracy = \frac{TP + TN}{TN + FP + FN + TP} \tag{19}$$

$$Sensitivity = \frac{TP}{TP + FN} \tag{20}$$

$$Precision = \frac{TP}{TP + FP} \tag{21}$$

$$F1 - Score = \frac{2*Precision*Recall}{Precision + Recall} \tag{22}$$

$$Specificity = \frac{TN}{TN + FP} \tag{23}$$

The percentage of samples that are accurately identified as negative is known as the true positive (TP), the false negative (FN), the true negative (TN), the proportion of samples misclassified as positive, and the proportion of samples wrongly classified as positive is known as the false positive (FP).

*Table 4. Classification Analysis of the proposed EfficientNet model*

| Models | ACC | PR | RC | SPEC | F1 |
|---|---|---|---|---|---|
| ANN | 91.61 | 92.14 | 93.15 | 91.33 | 92.23 |
| AlexNet | 94.53 | 93.25 | 95.47 | 93.55 | 93.34 |
| VGG16 | 96.34 | 94.58 | 96.33 | 95.62 | 95.26 |
| ResNet | 97.65 | 96. 67 | 97.65 | 97.56 | 97.61 |
| Proposed EfficientNet model | 98.88 | 98.87 | 98.23 | 98.55 | 98.56 |

In comparing different models for classifying OC tasks from Table 4, measurements of how well they work were taken. Included were accuracy (ACC), precision (PR), recall (RC), specificity (SPEC), and F1 score. The Artificial Neural Network (ANN) worked well, being 91.61% accurate. Its scores for precision, recall, specificity, and F1 were 92.14%, 93.15%, 91.33% and 92.23% respectively. The AlexNet network worked better. It got 94.53% correct answers. Its precision, recall, specificity, and F1 score were 93.25%, 95.47%, 93.55% and 93.34% respectively. VGG16 scored better than earlier models with an accuracy of 96.34%. It had strong results for precision, recall, specificity, and F1 score with values of 94.58%, 96.33%, 95.62% and 95.26% respectively. The ResNet model made the performance even better. It got 97.65% right, with 96.67% precision, 97.65% recall, 97.56% specificity, and a score of 97.61% for F1. Lastly, the suggested EfficientNet model did very well. It was better than all other models with an accurate rate of 98.88%. These numbers for the model were equally good at 98.87%, 98.23%, 98.55%, and 98.56%of precision, recall, specificity, and F1-score, respectively.

## Privacy Validation

**Entropy Analysis:** Entropy measures the level of uncertainty or randomness in the hidden image from the encrypted picture. More mixing and puzzling during the locking process is shown by a bigger entropy.

$$H(X) = -\sum_{i=1}^{N} P(x_i) \cdot \log_2(P(x_i)) \tag{24}$$

**Peak Signal-to-Noise Ratio (PSNR):** When comparing the encrypted picture with the real one, PSNR measures how good the encrypted image is. Higher PSNR values show better preservation of image quality.

$$PSNR = 10 \cdot log_{10}\left(\frac{Max^2}{MSE}\right) \tag{25}$$

**Correlation Coefficient:** A match score is used to see how much like each other the first and coded pictures are. A lower correlation number means stronger encryption.

Correlation Coefficient

$$= \frac{\sum_{i=1}^{N}(X_i - X^{-})(Y_i - Y^{-})}{\sqrt{\sum_{i=1}^{N}(X_i - X^{-})^2 \cdot \sum_{i=1}^{N}(Y_i - Y^{-})^2}} \tag{26}$$

**Number of Pixels Change Rate (NPCR):** The difference between the original and hidden images is measured by how many pixels are different. This is called NPCR. A higher NPCR means better spreading of pixel values.

$$NPCR = \frac{1}{N \times M} \sum_{i=1}^{N} \sum_{j=1}^{M} \delta_{i,j} \tag{27}$$

Where $\delta_{i,j}$ is 0 if the original and encrypted images' corresponding pixels match, and 1 if not.

**Unified Average Changing Intensity (UACI):** The difference in brightness between matching pixels in the hidden and original photos is measured by using UACI. A smaller UACI means that the encryption is working better.

$$UACI = \frac{1}{N \times M} \sum_{i=1}^{N} \sum_{j=1}^{M} \frac{\lfloor I_{i,j} - E_{i,j} \rfloor}{255} \tag{28}$$

*Table 5. Encryption validation analysis of the proposed lightweight model*

| Models | Entropy | PSNR | | CC | NPCR (%) | UACI |
|---|---|---|---|---|---|---|
| AES | 6.2 | 35.4 | | 0.92 | 95.2 | 0.012 |
| RSA | 6.6 | 35.8 | | 0.93 | 96.5 | 0.009 |
| Blowfish | 6.7 | 36.3 | | 0.95 | 97.2 | 0.008 |
| Twofish | 6.7 | 38.6 | | 0.96 | 98.4 | 0.006 |
| Proposed Lightweight Encryption model | 6.9 | 40.5 | | 0.98 | 99.6 | 0.001 |

In the analysis of different encryption types using important measures from Table 5 and Figure 2, natural cryptography methods were tested. The Advanced Encryption Standard (AES) had an entropy of 6.2, a PSNR of 35.4, CC of 0.92, NPCR of 95.2%, and UACI of 0.012. The RSA encryption model showed a slightly higher number with an entropy of 6.6, PSNR of 35.8, CC of 0.93, NPCR of 96.5% and

UACI of 0.009. Blowfish made more improvements. It reached an entropy of 6.7, PSNR of 36.3, CC of 0.95, NPCR of 97.2% and UACI of 0.008. Twofish followed this pattern with an entropy of 6.7, PSNR of 38.6, CC of 0.96, NPCR of 98.4% and UACI of 0.006. Importantly, the suggested Lightweight Encryption model was the best. It had an entropy of 6.9, PSNR of 40.5, CC of 0.98, NPCR of 99.6% and UACI of 0.001. This shows that the proposed Lightweight encryption method works much better than others. It has better security, is harder to crack, and keeps images looking good. This makes it an excellent choice for simple encryption situations.

*Figure 2. Entropy analysis*

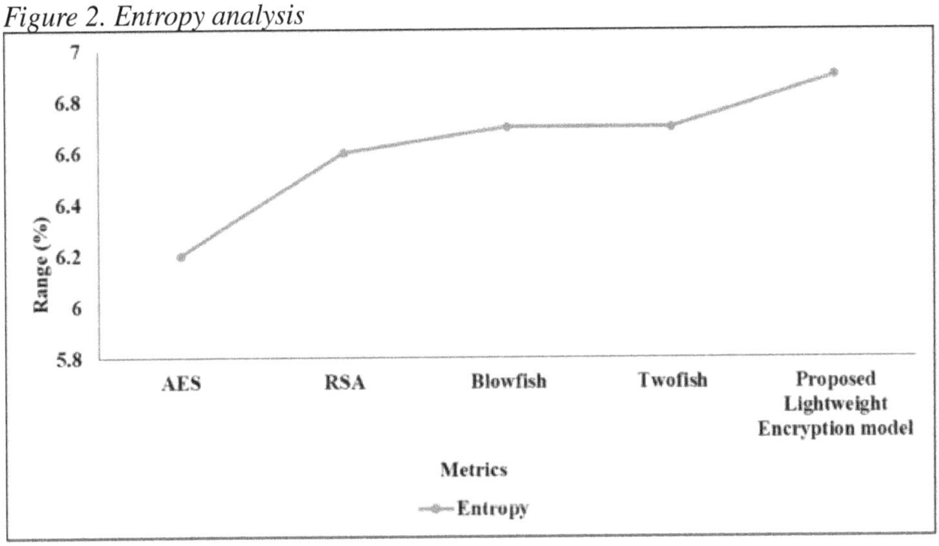


*Table 6. Computation time analysis of the proposed lightweight encryption model*

| Models | Average Encryption time (ms) | Average Decryption time (ms) |
|---|---|---|
| AES | 2.45 | 2.12 |
| RSA | 2.36 | 2.05 |
| Blowfish | 2.21 | 1.58 |
| Twofish | 1.85 | 1.46 |
| Proposed Lightweight Encryption model | 1.21 | 1.08 |

When it looked at how well different encryption models worked from Table 6 and Figure 3, it found out how long it took on average to encrypt and decrypt the information. This was measured in a tiny part of a second, called milliseconds. The

AES (Advanced Encryption Standard) showed that it takes about 2.45 milliseconds to encrypt information and 2.12 milliseconds to decrypt it. Likewise, the RSA code showed times of 2.36 milliseconds for encoding and 2.05 milliseconds for decoding. Blowfish showed better speed. It had an average time to make messages secret (encryption) of 2.21 milliseconds, and an average time to make them normal again (decryption) of 1.58 milliseconds. Twofish made these performance measures even better. On average, it took 1.85 seconds for encryption and 1.46 seconds less for decryption. The Lightweight Encryption model that was suggested worked better than all others. This was because it took a very small amount of time to encrypt, with an average of 1.21 milliseconds. It also took the smallest amount of time to decrypt, which was just 1.08 milliseconds. These results show that the light encryption model is very fast and good at solving problems. This makes it the best choice when you need to encrypt or decode things quickly.

*Figure 3. Computation time analysis*

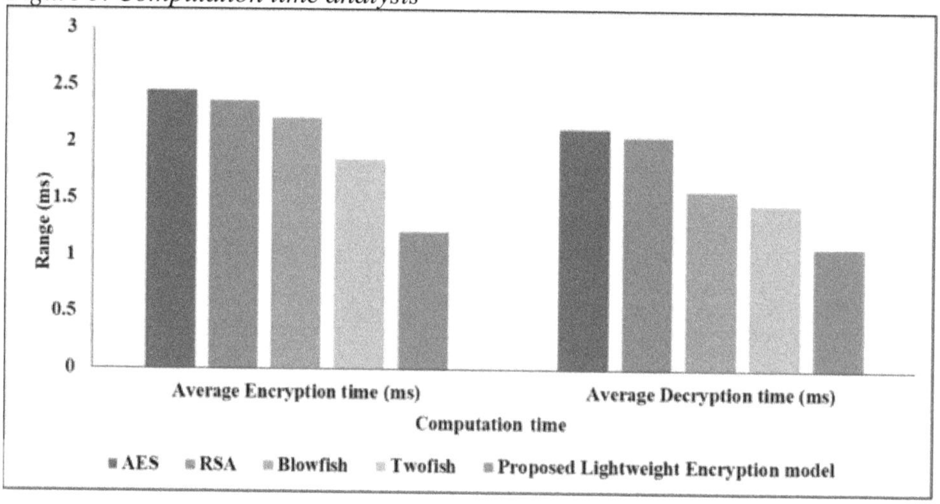


## CONCLUSION

In the end, this research has come up with a way to find ovarian cancer by using the TCGA-OV data and introducing a new method called Mean-Median-Gaussian (MMG) filtering technique. It uses the Faster SqueezeNet model to get features and then the EfficientNet network to classify them. This shows that it makes diagnosing better. The commitment to protecting patient information can be seen in the new Lightweight Image Encryption Scheme. It uses DNA coding and the

Lorenz Chaotic System to keep data safe. Using the Child Drawing Development Optimization Algorithm (CDDOA) for optimal key selection makes this encryption method stronger. All these efforts show a big step forward in being accurate and safe in ovarian cancer research. They set an example for combining new technology in medical gene studies. This big plan helps us learn more about ovarian cancer. It also makes a guide for proper and safe data handling in medical studies. The proposed EfficientNet model attains outstanding ovarian cancer classification metrics with an accuracy of 98.88%, precision of 98.87%, recall of 98.23%, specificity of 98.55%, and F1 score of 98.56%. Additionally, the proposed Lightweight Encryption model demonstrates superior security with entropy 6.9, PSNR 40.5, and remarkable efficiency, with an average encryption time of 1.21 milliseconds and an average decryption time of 1.08 milliseconds. More work in the future might look at making the Mean-Median-Gaussian hybrid filtering better, adjusting model settings, and adding to the suggested protection plan. Using new technologies and bigger data sets can help us make improvements.

## REFERENCES


Abdulhameed, S., & Rashid, T. A. (2022). Child drawing development optimization algorithm based on child's cognitive development. *Arabian Journal for Science and Engineering*, *47*(2), 1337–1351.

Acharya, S., Ghosh, D., Swapnarekha, H., Mishra, M., & Nayak, S. (2023). Integrative data analysis and automated deep learning technique for ovary cancer detection. In *Computational Intelligence in Cancer Diagnosis* (pp. 43–65). Academic Press.

Ahmed, S. T., Hammood, D. A., Chisab, R. F., Al-Naji, A., & Chahl, J. (2023). Medical Image Encryption: A Comprehensive Review. *Computers*, *12*(8), 160.

Aksoy, B., & Salman, O. K. M. (2020). A New Hybrid Filter Approach for Image Processing. *Sakarya University Journal of Computer and Information Sciences*, *3*(3), 334–342.

Al Duhayyim, M., & Mohamed, G., H., S. Alzahrani, J., Alabdan, R., Aziz, A. S. A., Zamani, A. S., ... & Alsaid, M. I. (2022). Sandpiper Optimization with a Deep Learning Enabled Fault Diagnosis Model for Complex Industrial Systems. *Electronics (Basel)*, *11*(24), 4190.

Binas, D. A., Tzanakakis, P., Economopoulos, T. L., Konidari, M., Bourgioti, C., Moulopoulos, L. A., & Matsopoulos, G. K. (2023). A Novel Approach for Estimating Ovarian Cancer Tissue Heterogeneity through the Application of Image Processing Techniques and Artificial Intelligence. *Cancers (Basel)*, *15*(4), 1058. PMID: 36831401

Breen, J., Allen, K., Zucker, K., Adusumilli, P., Scarsbrook, A., Hall, G., & Ravikumar, N. (2023). Artificial intelligence in ovarian cancer histopathology: A systematic review. *NPJ Precision Oncology*, *7*(1), 83. PMID: 37653025

Castro, F., Impedovo, D., & Pirlo, G. (2023). A Medical Image Encryption Scheme for Secure Fingerprint-Based Authenticated Transmission. *Applied Sciences (Basel, Switzerland)*, *13*(10), 6099.

Chen, H., Yang, B. W., Qian, L., Meng, Y. S., Bai, X. H., Hong, X. W., & Feng, W. W. (2022). Deep learning prediction of ovarian malignancy at US compared with O-RADS and expert assessment. *Radiology*, *304*(1), 106–113. PMID: 35412367

Farahani, H., Boschman, J., Farnell, D., Darbandsari, A., Zhang, A., Ahmadvand, P., & Bashashati, A. (2022). Deep learning-based histotype diagnosis of ovarian carcinoma whole-slide pathology images. *Modern Pathology*, *35*(12), 1983–1990. PMID: 36065012

Fetteha, M. A., Sayed, W. S., & Said, L. A. (2023). A lightweight image encryption scheme using dna coding and chaos. *Electronics (Basel), 12*(24), 4895.

Gajjela, C. C., Brun, M., Mankar, R., Corvigno, S., Kennedy, N., Zhong, Y., & Reddy, R. (2023). Leveraging mid-infrared spectroscopic imaging and deep learning for tissue subtype classification in ovarian cancer. *Analyst, 148*(12), 2699–2708. PMID: 37218522

Ghoniem, R. M., Algarni, A. D., Refky, B., & Ewees, A. A. (2021). Multi-modal evolutionary deep learning model for ovarian cancer diagnosis. *Symmetry, 13*(4), 643.

Handley, K. F., Sims, T. T., Bateman, N. W., Glassman, D., Foster, K. I., Lee, S., & Sood, A. K. (2022). Classification of high-grade serous ovarian cancer using tumor morphologic characteristics. *JAMA Network Open, 5*(10), e2236626–e2236626. PMID: 36239936

Jebbar, W. A. (2025). Optimization Solution Proposal for Smart Transaction Security of Smart Blockchain Contracts in E-Banking Applications. In *Sustainable Information Security in the Age of AI and Green Computing* (pp. 295–320). IGI Global Scientific Publishing.

Jeya Sundari, M., & Brintha, N. C. (2023). An Intelligent Black Widow Optimization on Image Enhancement with Deep Learning Based Ovarian Tumor Diagnosis model. *Computer Methods in Biomechanics and Biomedical Engineering. Imaging & Visualization, 11*(3), 598–605.

Jung, Y., Kim, T., Han, M. R., Kim, S., Kim, G., Lee, S., & Choi, Y. J. (2022). Ovarian tumor diagnosis using deep convolutional neural networks and a denoising convolutional autoencoder. *Scientific Reports, 12*(1), 17024. PMID: 36220853

Köbel, M., & Kang, E. Y. (2022). The evolution of ovarian carcinoma subclassification. *Cancers (Basel), 14*(2), 416. PMID: 35053578

Kodipalli, A., Devi, S., Dasar, S., & Ismail, T. (2022). Segmentation and classification of ovarian cancer based on conditional adversarial image to image translation approach. *Expert Systems: International Journal of Knowledge Engineering and Neural Networks*, •••, 13193.

Lata, K., & Cenkeramaddi, L. R. (2023). Deep learning for medical image cryptography: A comprehensive review. *Applied Sciences (Basel, Switzerland), 13*(14), 8295.

Maria, H. H., Jossy, A. M., & Malarvizhi, S. (2023). A hybrid deep learning approach for detection and segmentation of ovarian tumours. *Neural Computing & Applications, 35*(21), 15805–15819.

Nazir, T., Iqbal, M. M., Jabbar, S., Hussain, A., & Albathan, M. (2023). EfficientPNet—An Optimized and Efficient Deep Learning Approach for Classifying Disease of Potato Plant Leaves. *Agriculture*, *13*(4), 841.

Razzaq, R. (2025). Combining Fog Computing and Blockchain Based on the Internet of Medical Things to Preserve Patient Information Privacy. In *Sustainable Information Security in the Age of AI and Green Computing* (pp. 525–546). IGI Global Scientific Publishing.

Saida, T., Mori, K., Hoshiai, S., Sakai, M., Urushibara, A., Ishiguro, T., & Nakajima, T. (2022). Diagnosing ovarian cancer on MRI: A preliminary study comparing deep learning and radiologist assessments. *Cancers (Basel)*, *14*(4), 987. PMID: 35205735

Selvaraj, J., Lai, W. C., Kavin, B. P., & Seng, G. H. (2023). Cryptographic Encryption and Optimization for Internet of Things Based Medical Image Security. *Electronics (Basel)*, *12*(7), 1636.

Tahayur, D. H. (2025). Security Cooperation in the Protection Concerns of Agriculture Data Using Efficient Signatures and Artificial Bee Colony Manner. In *Sustainable Information Security in the Age of AI and Green Computing* (pp. 439–460). IGI Global Scientific Publishing.

Wu, J., Zhang, J., Liu, D., & Wang, X. (2023). A Multiple-Medical-Image Encryption Method Based on SHA-256 and DNA Encoding. *Entropy (Basel, Switzerland)*, *25*(6), 898. PMID: 37372242

Zamwar, U. M., Anjankar, A. P., & Anjankar, A. (2022). Aetiology, Epidemiology, Histopathology, Classification, Detailed Evaluation, and Treatment of Ovarian Cancer. *Cureus*, *14*(10). PMID: 36415372

Ziyambe, B., Yahya, A., Mushiri, T., Tariq, M. U., Abbas, Q., Babar, M., & Jabbar, S. (2023). A Deep Learning Framework for the Prediction and Diagnosis of Ovarian Cancer in Pre-and Post-Menopausal Women. *Diagnostics (Basel)*, *13*(10), 1703. PMID: 37238188

Chapter 8

# Securing Smart Cities Data Using Quantum Techniques and Preventing the Alteration of Citizens' Information

**Mishall Hammed Al-Zubaidie**
https://orcid.org/0000-0002-3149-9129
*University of Thi-Qar, Iraq*

**Tuqa Ghani Tregi**
https://orcid.org/0009-0003-4513-9751
*University of Thi-Qar, Iraq*

## ABSTRACT

*This chapter attempts to present a Post-Quantum Secure Smart City Electricity Data (PQSED) system, which generates a quantum key via the BB84 protocol and digitally signs the data using FALCON, and uses pseudonym technology to add more security and protection to the data and digital signature, and also uses Walrus Optimization Algorithm (WOA) technology to the data to detect any abnormal behavior. The proposed system has been tested against several recently known attacks, such as replay attacks, Sybil attacks, eavesdropping, advanced ransomware attacks, social engineering attacks, and critical infrastructure attacks, and it has been proven to overcome them. In terms of performance evaluation, we obtained an average signature time of about 0.004 MS, an average signature verification time of about 0.006 MS,*

DOI: 10.4018/979-8-3373-8133-6.ch008

*an average execution time of 0.66 MS, a precision of 96%, a recall of 95%, and an F1-score of 96%, which are good compared to the state-of-the-art research. Thus, our proposed system is highly acceptable for power plant applications.*

## INTRODUCTION

In developing regions of Asia and Africa, rapid urbanization of the global population has resulted in substantial transformations in social, economic, and environmental domains. By 2025, it is anticipated that 66% of the world population will reside in urban regions, resulting in the emergence of megacities and increased pressure on public infrastructure (De Guimarães et al., 2020; Li, 2020). As metropolitan regions grow, smart cities have evolved in response to the demand for better services, sustainable growth, and higher quality of living. To effectively control urban resources and improve daily life, smart cities combine digital technology and Internet of Things (IoT) systems (Al-Zubaidie et al., 2024). Among other modern infrastructure projects, they use smart electrical grids, linked healthcare systems, and automated transportation to simplify processes. But as these cities rely more on linked technology, they expose complex cybersecurity flaws (Akinade et al., 2024). The growing volume of data transmitted across networks necessitates robust security mechanisms to ensure service continuity and safeguard private information. As megacities expand, both the volume and sensitivity of collected data increase, hence heightening the risk of privacy infringements and unauthorized access (Jebbar & Al-Zubaidie, 2024). Smart city models are anticipated to progressively incorporate security and privacy by design, utilizing advanced cryptographic approaches and distributed mechanisms to ensure data integrity and confidentiality against emerging cyber threats (Gharavi et al., 2024).

## Security Challenges in Smart Cities

*Figure 1. Security challenges and solutions in smart cities*

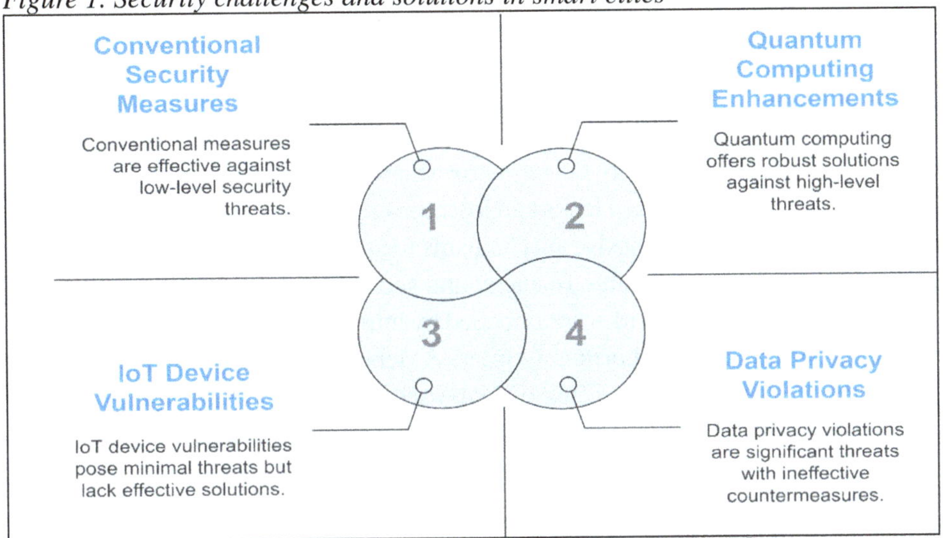


*Figure 1. Security Challenges and Solutions in Smart Cities*

Smart cities are vulnerable to a wide range of threats that could disrupt essential services, including energy, transportation, and healthcare, posing a number of complex security challenges due to their increasing reliance on digital technologies and the proliferation of smart, networked devices (Falcon & Mordant, 2022). Figure 1 depicts security challenges and solutions in smart cities. The emergence of smart, connected devices creates more potential entry points for hackers, thus compromising network security. Smart cities handle large amounts of personal data.

Information about individuals (such as energy usage, daily living habits, geographic locations) raises the possibility of unlawful data use (Fabrègue & Bogoni, 2023). For instance, power plants and critical infrastructure are possible targets for assaults that can cause the suspension or disturbance of essential services, therefore challenging the management and verification of thousands of devices and users (Razzaq & Al-Zubaidie, 2024a). Large volumes of data kept in databases also run the danger of illegal access (Al-Zubaidie & Shyaa, 2023).

The development of quantum computing has changed the rules of the game in the field of cybersecurity with relative ease and has exacerbated these difficulties even more. For instance, quantum computers can use Shor's Algorithm to rapidly break conventional encryption systems (such as RSA and ECC) in a very short time compared to classical computers (Tahayur & Al-Zubaidie, 2024), rendering smart cities that depend on these conventional systems highly susceptible to the hazards of hacking and data manipulation, especially vulnerable (Chatterjee et al., 2022). In spite of these obstacles, the evident advantages of digital technology necessitate a delicate equilibrium between the resolution of its associated issues and the utilisation of its advantages. As such, even while digital technologies offer many benefits, they also raise privacy and security issues (Al-Zubaidie & Muhajjar, 2024). Data manipulation and information security defects in data collecting, transport, and storage of data provide major security concerns for smart cities (Awaad & Jebbar, 2014). These hazards can lead to data leaks and losses resulting from inadequate protection policies and the lack of cohesive mechanisms to stop exploitation (Akinade et al., 2024). They are of considerable financial and social significance.

The activities of smart cities are impeded by intrusions, which generate mistrust between residents and authorities (Awaad & Jebbar, 2015). Consequently, data protection is essential for any effective cybersecurity strategy, as it identifies vulnerable areas. Quantum computers are a technological revolution because they are capable of solving complex problems at a quicker pace than classical computers, which has a substantial impact on traditional cryptographic methods. The security of conventional systems can be compromised by the rapid compromise of existing cryptography by quantum computing devices (Canto et al., 2023). Furthermore, endangering data privacy and integrity are the development of new quantum attacks as Quantum Key Analysis and Grover's Algorithm (Razzaq & Al-Zubaidie, 2024b). These realities compel smart cities to adopt post-quantum cryptography (PQC) and quantum key distribution (QKD) technologies in addition to safe post-quantum digital signatures (such as FALCON and Dilithium) as efficient security solutions to fight these sophisticated threats. Thus, creating security systems based on cryptography technologies immune to quantum assaults is not only a necessary need to guarantee the continuation of digital services but also a non-option now (Sahu & Mazumdar, 2024).

The central research questions guiding this chapter are as follows:

> RQ1: In what ways can the integration of quantum-resistant methods, specifically BB84 and FALCON, ensure authenticity, confidentiality, and tamper-resistance in smart electricity infrastructures?
>
> RQ2: How does tokenization-based pseudonymization contribute to regulatory compliance (GDPR) while preserving data utility in smart grid environments?

This chapter offers a smart city security architecture that uses quantum cryptography and post-quantum digital signatures to solve present and future issues. The BB84 quantum key distribution protocol, the FALCON algorithm for digital signatures, tokenization-based pseudonymization, and the WOA for anomaly detection are all integrated into the suggested multi-tiered approach for smart city data security.

## Chapter Objectives

The following is an outline of our main objectives:

- To enhance data security and authentication by utilizing BB84 to generate secure quantum keys. In smart city environments, these keys are the foundational elements for FALCON digital signatures.
- Integrating FALCON ensures tamper-proof verification of transmitted data, hence guaranteeing integrity and non-repudiation.
- Employing tokenization-based pseudonymization techniques mitigates the risk of illegal data access while safeguarding sensitive information during transmission and storage.
- Employing WOA to analyze data patterns and detect deviations from anticipated behavior, facilitating the identification of abnormalities and hostile activities in smart grid communication.
- To evaluate the robustness against prevalent threats by demonstrating its security efficacy via simulation-based examination utilizing Java and the Scyther protocol verification tool.

# RELATED WORK

This section reviews studies dealing with the security of smart cities and the Internet of Things (IoT) related to the research topic. It reviews what researchers have proposed in the field of smart city security and what technologies are used in their proposals. This section provides a critical analysis of all the included research to identify the research gap in smart city security. It will be divided into two subsections: Previous studies to protect urban application infrastructures and anomaly detection with nature-inspired and hybrid optimization.

## Previous Studies to Protect Urban Application Infrastructures

This subsection discusses the literature survey related to the proposed work. Table 1 illustrates different approaches from previous studies to protect smart cities and urban application infrastructures.

The Internet of Smart City Things (IoSCT) has been the subject of several research papers that have examined literature surveys. These surveys have identified a variety of security and privacy concerns, such as authentication, integrity, centralization, latency, and others, and have also considered potential solutions for SC applications. Chen et al. (2020) showed decentralized safe data storage via SC blockchain-based proof of data possession. Data and device authentication problems are not discussed in this chapter. Ismagilova et al. (2022) concentrated on several research studies on hazards in smart cities, stressing information security issues and difficulties with smart city infrastructure handling and processing personal data. Their research examined several of these difficulties, offered a summary of numerous important problems, and gave direction for further research. Conversely, this study lacked any practical relevance or particular solutions for the issues that were underlined. Ahmad et al. (2022) investigated algorithmic difficulties like security, resilience, and interpretability to properly apply AI in human-centric applications inside smart cities, therefore providing answers. Still, these technologies are sufficient to guarantee security in systems oriented to humans. While addressing security and privacy problems and assessing current solutions. Gupta et al. (2023) pointed out the proposals of researchers in graph-based machine learning techniques to identify malicious users in an ITS environment, through which it is easy to analyze the network traffic and detect malicious devices. Therefore, graph-based machine learning techniques can be a technique to efficiently detect malicious nodes in an ITS environment. However, these proposals have been tested in simulations and have not been used in real smart cities.

Vladislav et al. (2024) introduced the IEEE 802.11 technology to locate a wireless client. The technology uses captured frames in the wireless network. These frames are intercepted by passive scanners in the form of small computers to ensure information security. The method relies heavily on the IEEE 802.11 protocols, which may make it inapplicable to other technologies such as 5G or LPWAN. Tatipatri & Arun (2024) have extensively investigated possible ways to address cybersecurity challenges, such as smart meter security, end-user privacy, and cyber theft attacks using blockchain technology and encryption against communication attacks in the smart grid. However, deep learning algorithms require large computational resources. Achaal et al. (2024) presented an architectural diagram that included the main smart grid components and communication links. In addition, they proposed a classification of different types of cyber-attacks based on their targets and methods. However, they focused only on some common attacks and did not address more complex attacks. Khalaf et al. (2024) put forward challenges and requirements for associated communication protocols and standards are presented. The cybersecurity of ADN devices and sensors, including Phasor Measurement Units (PMUs), smart meters, advanced metering infrastructure, and protection relays, is discussed in detail. Furthermore, a comprehensive study of ADN application drivers and enablers, including microgrids, electric vehicles (EVs), Internet of Things (IoT), and smart homes, is conducted. However, the study does not mention how to integrate the new encryption with legacy electrical systems. Das et al. (2025) suggested a safe, privacy-sensitive system for data flow between customers and smart electric cars in smart cities. To show its advantage or improvement, the research did not, however, compare the suggested approach with any other one. Elmisery et al. (2025) investigated artificial intelligence and quantum risks to financial systems, suggesting adaptive security models, but the context is limited to banking and lacks testing under limited, controlled contexts like smart cities.

*Table 1. Comparison of previous studies about smart city data protection*

| Author's Name | Algorithms Used | Study Proposal | Study limitations |
|---|---|---|---|
| (Chen et al., 2020) | Blockchain-based dynamic provable data possession | Enhancing data possession security in smart cities with blockchain | Real-world implementation and efficiency evaluation |
| (Ismagilova et al., 2022) | Smart city interaction framework, security, privacy risks analysis | Development of a framework for security and privacy risk mitigation | Scalability and adaptability of security framework |
| (Ahmad et al., 2022) | Critical analysis of smart city security, data management, ethical challenges | Human-centered approach to smart city security and data management | Ethical concerns in AI-driven smart cities |
| (Gupta et al., 2023) | Graph-based Machine Learning for Malicious Node Detection | Detecting malicious users in Intelligent Transport Systems (ITS) via graph-based ML. | Lack of real-world implementation in smart cities; tested only in simulations. |
| (Vladislav et al., 2024) | IEEE 802.11 Technology for Wireless Client Localization | Using IEEE 802.11 network frame interception to improve wireless network security. | Limited applicability to non-IEEE 802.11 networks (e.g., 5G, LPWAN). |
| (Tatipatri & Arun, 2024) | Blockchain & Encryption for Smart Grid Security | Addressing cybersecurity in smart grids through encryption and blockchain. | High computational requirements for deep learning in smart grids. |
| (Achaal et al., 2024) | Cyber-Attack Classification in Smart Grids | Developing an architectural model and cyber-attack classification for smart grids. | Focuses only on common attacks, ignoring more complex cyber threats. |
| (Khalaf et al., 2024) | Cybersecurity of ADN Devices & Sensors, including PMUs & IoT | Exploring cybersecurity challenges and communication protocols in ADN and IoT. | No mention of how to integrate encryption with legacy electrical systems. |
| (Das et al., 2025) | Privacy-aware data sharing for smart electric vehicles | Securing data sharing for electric vehicles in smart environments | Regulatory and interoperability challenges |
| (Elmisery et al., 2025) | Quantum-resilient encryption, AI-based threat modeling | Assess dual threats of AI and quantum computing on financial systems | Focused on finance only; lacks real-time validation in smart cities |

## Anomaly Detection with Nature-Inspired and Hybrid Optimization

In cybersecurity systems, swarm intelligence methodologies, including particle swarm optimization (PSO), ant colony optimization (ACO), and grey wolf optimization (GWO), have demonstrated significant efficacy in enhancing selection and detection tasks. Khan & Goodridge (2024) examined the incorporation of GWO, PSO, and ACO in federated learning environments, revealing their efficacy in secure client selection amidst hostile limitations. Likewise, Karim (2022) employed GWO to enhance the training of sparse autoencoders, hence increasing the classification accuracy of intrusion detection systems. Simultaneous investigations of hybrid models and extensive comparative assessments of optimization methodologies have been undertaken. In intricate engineering and security contexts, Mohammed & Rashid (2020) introduced a hybrid GWO-WOA model that enhances convergence velocity and solution quality. Naser & Naser (2024) presented a comprehensive performance benchmark that compares PSO, ACO, GA, GWO, WOA, and ABC against the Firefighter Algorithm, offering insights into the trade-offs between efficiency and stability across many intelligent computation tasks. This research demonstrates the efficacy of swarm and hybrid optimization in enhancing performance at the algorithmic level. Nevertheless, they do not include such methodologies in comprehensive, quantum-secure systems for energy usage in smart cities. The proposed chapter addresses this gap by integrating WOA within a secure cryptographic framework that includes BB84-based key generation, FALCON digital signatures, and tokenization-based pseudonymization. Table 2 illustrates the different approaches to anomaly detection with nature-inspired and hybrid optimization.

*Table 2. Anomaly detection with nature-inspired and hybrid optimization*

| Author's Name | Algorithms Used | Study Proposal | Study Limitations |
|---|---|---|---|
| (Karim, 2022) | GWO | Sparse autoencoder training enhanced with GWO for intrusion detection classification | Did not incorporate cryptographic or privacy-preserving layers |
| (Mohammed & Rashid, 2020) | Hybrid GWO-WOA | Improved convergence for complex engineering and security optimization problems | Simulation-based; lacks integration with cryptographic systems in smart environments |
| (Khan & Goodridge, 2024) | GWO, PSO, ACO | Swarm intelligence for federated client selection under security constraints | Focused on algorithm-level optimization without integration into secure smart grid systems |
| (Naser & Naser, 2024) | PSO, ACO, GA, GWO, WOA, ABC, Firefighter Algorithm | Comparative performance benchmark across multiple swarm intelligence algorithms | No contextual application in privacy-aware or quantum-secure urban systems |

## BACKGROUND

This section describes the latest algorithms and methods used in the field of smart city security in IoT. It provides essential scientific background on the technologies adopted in this chapter. This section presents fundamental concepts and detailed algorithms for the technologies selected for this study. It includes the following subsections: Quantum Computing, Quantum Key Generation via BB84 Protocol, FALCON Digital Signature, Pseudonym, and Walrus Optimization Algorithm (WOA).

## Quantum Computing

The fundamental concepts of quantum mechanics, including superposition, entanglement, interference, and measurement, are essential for the development of quantum computers (Khrennikov, 2021). The basic feature of superposition defines quantum systems and allows them to persist in many states concurrently. Unlike traditional bits, which have just 0 or 1, a qubit may represent both. Superposition yields the simultaneous existence of 0 and 1. A crucial phenomenon known as quantum entanglement is the connection between two or more quantum particles even at physical distance (Herman et al., 2023). Even in cases when two entangled qubits are not explicitly tested, the measurement of one qubit as zero instantly signals that the second qubit is in state one. Quantum interference, resulting from overlapping wave functions and changing measurement probability, influences qubit states (Yang et al., 2023). While constructive interference improves certain results, destructive interference cancels others; this helps to explain several quantum algorithms (Tregi & Al-Zubaidie, 2025). Quantum measurement is the process by which a superposition of states collapses into a single, definite classical state, either 0 or 1, by use of measurement. During this breakdown, the quantum features of the system are lost (Ollitrault et al., 2021).

## Quantum Key Generation via BB84 Protocol

Aiming to offer a shared secret key for encrypting secure communications, BB84 is a quantum mechanical method applied to the process of secret key exchange between a sender and a receiver (Sahu & Mazumdar, 2024). The non-cloning theorem states that an unknown quantum state cannot be completely copied; the uncertainty principle states that some properties of a quantum particle cannot be accurately observed simultaneously. This is a key element in post-quantum cryptography research (Kumar & Mondal, 2025). It is required to reach ultimate security in communications. Starting from prior ideas by Wiesner (Wiesner, 1983), the first complete operation (Bennett and Brassard, 1984) emphasized development. From the two's complement bases of a two-level system, Alice generates bits in the BB84 protocol for Bob (Lu et al., 2022). Stated especially as a security justification, the non-cloning theory, the sender generates a random key, codes it into qubits, which are sent to the receiver across a quantum channel. After the result analysis, Bob counts the qubits and generates a shared secret key. Should a spy agent attempt to intercept the qubits, he may utilize sorting to find and delete the compromised qubits, therefore preserving the integrity of the key. Through error correction and privacy-enhancing methods, the sender and receiver might enhance the key creation so preserving its security and secrecy. Introduced in 1984 by Charles Bennett and Alain Brassard, BB84 and E91 are QKD systems using four distinct polarization states of photons (Abushgra, 2022).

*ALGORITHM 1: BB84 protocol*

```
Input: Seed
Output: Secret Key
1. Begin
2. B_Sender  {Bi | Bi  {0, 1}}, θ _Sender  {θi | θi  {R, D}}
3. P_Encoded  {Pi | Pi = F (Bi, θi)}
4. Receiver Generates Bases and Measures: θ _Receiver  {θ'i| θ'i  {R, D}}, B_Measured  {Mi | Mi = G (Pi, θ'i)}
5. Filter Matching Bases: θ _Shared  {i | θi = θ'i}, B_Filtered  {Bi | i  θ _Shared}
6. Verify Errors: E_Error  (Mismatched Bits) / (Total Bits In B_Filtered)
7. Abort If E_Error > E_Threshold.
8. Amplify Privacy: Secret Key  H(B_Filtered)
9. End
```

Algorithm 1 shows the Quantum key generation by BB84. At the beginning, the sender generates random bits and bases B_Sender, θ_Sender a series of random binary values (0,1). Each bit (Bi) is encoded into a photon polarization state (Pi) based on the base (θi). If Bi = 0, then θi =*R*→ Horizontal polarization, If Bi =1, then θi =D→ 45° polarization. Then the receiver generates random bases (θ _Receiver). Each photon is measured using a random base. If the base (θi) matches the base used in the measurement (θ'i), then the measured bits (Mi) match the original bits (Bi). Then, the bases of the transmitter and receiver are compared θ_Shared ← {i | θi = θ'i}. The photons measured using identical bases are kept B_Filtered ← {Bi | i ∈θ _Shared}. When the error rate is calculated, if E_Error > E_Threshold, the protocol is stopped. Privacy amplification technique is applied to the raw key to reduce the eavesdropper's potential knowledge Secret Key ← H(B_Filtered).

## FALCON Digital Signature

Designed to withstand attacks by quantum computers that can easily compromise classical systems, FALCON is a digital signature algorithm associated with post-quantum cryptography (PQC). It generates secure digital signatures using lattice cryptography, leveraging the NTRU network architecture (Gharavi et al., 2024). It is based on a difficult mathematical problem known as the short integer solution (SIS), which has not been solved instantly even with quantum computers. NIST has selected it as one of the standard digital signature algorithms for post-quantum cryptography. High performance with small signature size, FALCON is suitable for resource-constrained devices in IoSCT, unlike other PQC algorithms, has a very small signature size with good performance. It is based on the Fast Fourier Transform (FFT) (Canto et al., 2023). Computations are accelerated, and performance is improved using the Fast Fourier Transform and the Intermediate Fourier Transform (IFFT).

| *ALGORITHM 2: FALCON key generation* |
|---|
| ***Input: CSPRNG***<br>***Output: pk, sk***<br>***1. Start***<br>***2. Generate (f, g, F, G)  Random Lattice-Based Values***<br>***3. Compute h  $f^{-1} * g \pmod q$***<br>***4. Store sk  (f, g, F, G)***<br>***5. Return (pk = h, sk)***<br>***6. End*** |

Algorithm 2 explains how FALCON works to generate public key pk and secret key sk based on the Cryptographic Random Number Generator (CSPRNG) and generate random vectors (f, g, F, G) to make the keys secure and non-repeated.

| *ALGORITHM 3: FALCON signature Generation* |
|---|
| ***Input: m, sk***<br>***Output: signature***<br>*1. Start*<br>*2. r  Random bits*<br>*3. c  HashToPoint(m ‖ r, q, n)*<br>*4. t0  - (1/q) * FFT(c)  FFT(F)*<br>*5. t1  (1/q) * FFT(c)  FFT(f)*<br>*6. Repeat:*<br>*a. z  ffSampling_dyntree((t0, t1), Gram_Matrix(G))*<br>*b. s  (t - z)  FFT(B)*<br>*c. Until ‖s‖² ≤ β²*<br>*7. s  Compress(invFFT(s))*<br>*8. Return signature = (r, s)*<br>*9. End* |

Algorithm 3 generates a digital signature with *sk* and m (Lee et al., 2024). First, it generates a random integer r, then uses FFT to compute the hash point. Using a fast Fourier sampling advanced technique, ffSampling effectively generates short vectors from a Gaussian distribution in network-based encryption. It is based on the FFT, which lets calculations be quicker and lower of complexity. Data signing is much aided by ffSampling. The process is continued until a signature s satisfies the security condition $\beta^2$; after that, the signature (r, s) is restored following data compression.

| *ALGORITHM 4: FALCON signature verification* |
|---|
| ***Input: m, Signature (r, s), pk***<br>***Output: Valid, Invalid***<br>*1. Start*<br>*2. c  HashToPoint (m ‖ r, q, n)*<br>*3. s'  Decompress(s)*<br>*4. If ‖s'‖² > β² Then Return False*<br>*5. v  FFT(s') - FFT(c)  FFT(h)*<br>*6. If ‖v‖² ≤ β² Then Return True*<br>*7. Else Return False*<br>*8. End* |

Algorithm 4 authenticates the digital signature by computing the hash point $c$, then using the FFT, and comparing the length of the resultant vector $s'$ with the security criterion $\beta^2$ (Lee et al., 2024). Should the criterion be met, the signature is accepted; if not, it is denied.

## Pseudonym

The pseudonym is a method of data security whereby sensitive data, such as personal identification, is replaced with synthetic or alternate aliases. This method guarantees that the original data cannot be exactly linked to a particular person without the use of extra information, which is kept apart and safe (Nguyen et al., 2025). Tokenizing replaces sensitive data exposure with pseudo, thereby lowering the risk. This method is reversible; therefore, authorized organizations can re-identify the original data using the pertinent key or mapping. Data protection laws mandate it, particularly the general GDPR of the European Union, which aims to safeguard personal data (Zafar, 2025). This privacy-enhancing technique used in federated recommender systems replaces some attributes with pseudonyms, therefore augmenting user secrecy. This method protects users' credentials, therefore reducing the possibility of personal data leaks. While protecting their identities, the system creates pertinent recommendations depending on user preferences. Tokenized data helps to handle large data collections by separating them into smaller pieces, hence improving scalability (Upadrista et al., 2023).

## Walrus Optimization Algorithm (WOA)

It is a population-based heuristic in which the population members are represented as walruses. In the walrus optimization method, the walruses symbolize alternative solutions to the optimization issue, with their placements defining the specifications of the problem variables inside the search space (Uppalaiah et al., 2024). Consequently, each walrus is seen as a vector, and the complete walrus population is mathematically depicted as a population matrix. Initially, walrus populations are formed randomly during the introduction of the walrus optimization method.

WOA is inspired by the innate behavior of walruses in their native habitat (Geng et al., 2024). This is achieved through mathematical procedures that mimic the foraging behavior of walruses, which has two main phases: Exploration and exploitation. These behaviors are mathematically represented as follows:

$$X_{t+1} = X_t + A \cdot (X_{best} - X_t) + B \cdot (rand - 0.5) \qquad (1)$$

Where: $X_t$ is the location of the current solution, $X_{best}$ is the best solution found so far, $A$ and $B$ are control parameters that determine the exploration and exploitation ratio, while *rand* is a random number to induce variability in the search.

## SECURITY SYSTEM CONFRONTS QUANTUM COMPUTING

In this section, we present an improved PQSED system that analyzes and protects large electricity data after collecting it from SC using BB84, FALCON, Pseudonym (tokenization), and WAO techniques.

Figure 2 describes the proposed methodology in this study. The server generates a random quantum key QK via the BB84 protocol, and QK is considered as a seed in the stage of generating FALCON for the public and secret keys *PK, and SK*. After generating the keys, the stage of generating the digital signature of the data begins, then performing the pseudonym process on the data and signature. Then the signed data and the signature hidden by the pseudonym are sent to the smart meter, which in turn reverses the pseudonym process and verifies the digital signature. If it is valid, the WOA technology will be applied to the data to detect any abnormal behavior. If the data is valid, it will execute the commands issued by the server. However, if the signature or data is invalid, a security alert will be issued.

*Figure 2. General proposed methodology for proposed system*

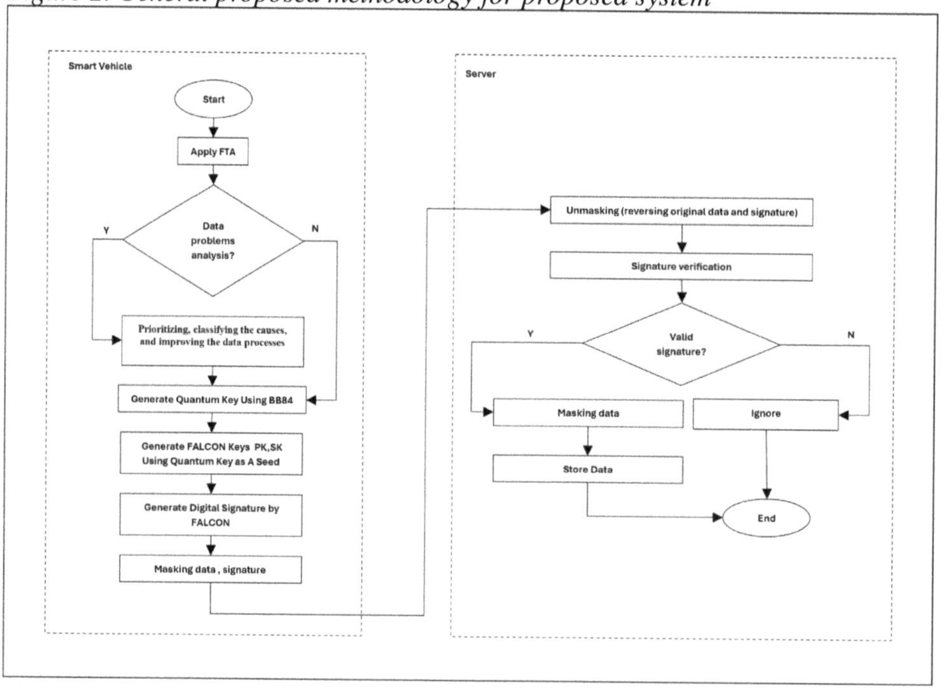

## Quantum Key Generation

The primary goal of BB84 in the proposed system is to facilitate the exchange of secret keys used in digital data signing in a secure manner. The protocol enhances security by generating and distributing quantum keys between connected nodes, leveraging quantum entanglement and the no-cloning theorem. The central computer and the distributed sensors work together to produce a quantum key that is later used to sign the data using FALCON, thus ensuring its confidentiality during transmission. The BB84 protocol guarantees a high level of security by assisting in the identification of any malicious attempts or surveillance during the key exchange process. In this widely recognized protocol, binary values (0, 1) are represented by polarized photons in discrete quantum states.

Eavesdropping is a phenomenon that arises when the state of a particle undergoes a change according to the principles of quantum physics, especially the challenge of measuring without changing the state. Although the file system for digital signatures is designed to create a strong security system that protects the transmitted data, it has also been used for key exchange. The security of the PQSED system has been enhanced by BB84 in response to cryptographic attacks and advances in quantum technology. It integrates with digital signatures and provides a new approach to protect large amounts of sensitive information stored in SCs.

## Ensuring Data Integrity with FALCON

FALCON is a key component of our methodology. Data Verification. It is the ideal choice for SC Big Data security due to its use of lattice-based encryption, making it resistant to quantum attacks. This algorithm generates a public and secret key based on the BB84 protocol. This ensures the verification of the transmitted data without revealing the secret key. These two keys ensure the authenticity of the source and the integrity of the data. FALCON signs the hidden and plain sensitive data to verify that the signature accurately represents the identity of the source and detects any changes to the data, using the secret key and complex mathematical operations. The signature will be inconsistent if any changes are made to the data, and the complex approach ensures that it has not been changed. The authenticity of the digital signature is confirmed by verifying the public key. The public key is used to verify the obtained signature, thus ensuring that the security criterion $\beta^2$ is met. The signature verifies that the data has not been changed during transmission. Mathematical networks provide strong security against both conventional and quantum attacks, as well as reliability. Algorithm 5 shows that instead of using CSPRNG to generate keys, quantum keys generated via the BB84 protocol are used as seeds to generate FALCON keys. Figure 3 also illustrates how to leverage the quantum key generated via the BB84 protocol and use it as a quantum seed to generate FALCON keys.

| *ALGORITHM 5: Quantum keys generation* |
| --- |
| ***Input:** QK key*<br>***Output:** FALCON_pk, FALCON_sk*<br>*1. Start*<br>*2. FALCON_Seed DeriveSeed(QKD Key)*<br>*3. (FALCON_pk, FALCON_sk) FALCON_GenerateKeys(FALCON.Seed)*<br>*4. return FALCON_pk, FALCON_sk*<br>*5. End* |

*Figure 3. BB84 harmony with the FALCON*

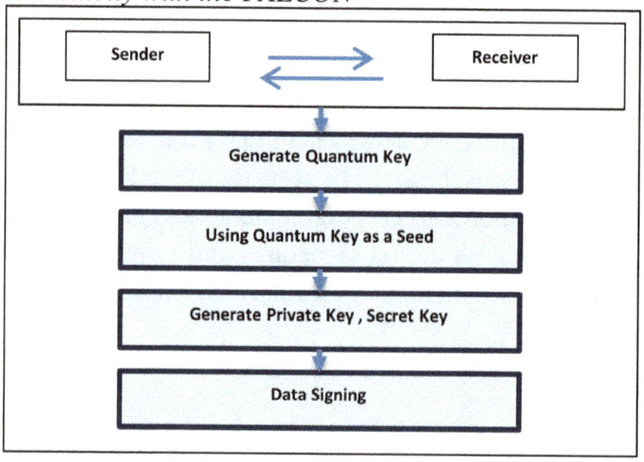


## Apply Pseudonym Using Tokenization

Tokenization is a sophisticated technology used in smart city security systems to guard digital signatures and sensitive data, whereby the original data is replaced with tokens acting as references to the real data without exposing it. Particularly in smart cities where data is shared between smart meter devices, servers, this phase is crucial to guarantee improved data security during transportation and storage. The importance of this stage is that the real data is not sent, which reduces the risk of leakage and prevents any unauthorized party from accessing the data signature, meaning that even if the system is hacked, the real data remains undetectable.

```
ALGORITHM 6: Tokenization

Input: Data, Signature, Token_Key
Output: T_data, T_sig
    1. Start
    2. T_data  []
    3. FOR each (key, value) IN data:
    4. token  Generate.Token(value, token_key)
    5. Store.Token(token, value)
    6.  T_data [key]  token
    7. T_sig  Generate.Token(signature, token_key)
    8.  RETURN (T_data, T_sig)
    9. End
```

Algorithm 6 represents the process of tokenization of data and digital signature, where each sensitive data value is replaced with a token identifier *T_data* that is stored in a secure database, and also the signature is converted to a token identifier *T_sig* to prevent its exploitation during transmission. Finally, the relationship between the original values, and tokens is stored in the token database. This relationship is used only when decoding is needed by authorized parties. Algorithm 7 explains how to recover the real data and signature (*R_data*, *R_sign*) at the smart meter.

```
ALGORITHM 7: Retrieve original data

Input: T_data, T_sig, token_key
Output: R_data, R_sign
    1. Start
    2. R_data  []
    3. FOR each (key, token) in T_data:
    4. Real_value  Retrieve_Token(token, token_key)
    5. R_data[key]  Real_value
    6. R_sig  Retrieve_Token(T_sig, token_key)
    7. RETURN (R_data, R_sig)
    8. End
```

## Data Behavior Analysis by WOA

After the tokenized data is transferred to the smart meter, which in turn retrieves the original data and verifies the validity of the digital signature via the public key, comes the role of WOA. This analyzes the retrieved data and detects any anomalies that may be caused by transmission errors or pseudonymization. This stage ensures that the data used in the PQSED system is free from noise. It is used to analyze the behavior of data, messages, and commands coming from the server. If the behavior of the data and signatures is normal and the number of invalid signatures is normal, the meter will execute the server commands, such as cutting off the power or sending information and data about the building's electricity usage. However, if the signatures are invalid or the data behavior is abnormal, the smart meter will issue a security threat alert.

A variety of nature-inspired metaheuristic algorithms inspired by nature strategies have been widely utilized in smart environments for anomaly detection tasks. This encompasses genetic algorithms (GA), ACO, PSO, and GWO. Artificial Bee Colony (ABC) offers flexible search and adaptability, though it may converge slowly. Each of these strategies possesses a unique capability to address complex nonlinear problems. The WOA method is particularly suitable for anomaly identification in smart grid data sources, demonstrating excellent accuracy, rapid convergence, and robust performance in the analysis of high-dimensional data. This study selected it due to its efficacy in detecting minor anomalies and reducing false positives. Table 3 shows the most prominent algorithms inspired by nature and also presents the advantages and disadvantages of each one of them.

*Table 3. Comparison of Nature-Inspired Optimization Algorithms*

| Study | Algorithm | Bio-Inspiration | Strengths | Weaknesses | Smart environment Applications |
|---|---|---|---|---|---|
| (Zhang, 2024) | PSO | Flocking behavior of birds or fish | Fast convergence, easy to implement | Prone to local optima, sensitive to parameter settings | Parameter tuning for neural networks in anomaly detection |
| (Miao et al., 2024) | ACO | Foraging behavior of ants using pheromones | Good for combinatorial problems, adaptive to dynamic changes | Slow convergence, parameter-sensitive | Path planning and security strategies in smart networks |
| (Sadr et al., 2023) | GA | Natural selection and genetic inheritance | High exploratory power, effective for complex optimization | Risk of premature convergence, sensitive to crossover/mutation rates | Feature selection in smart grid networks |
| (Aala Kalananda & Komanapalli, 2023) | GWO | Hunting and social hierarchy of grey wolves | Balanced exploration and exploitation, effective in non-linear problems | Degrades in high-dimensional spaces, parameter-sensitive | Intrusion detection and feature selection in smart city security systems |

continued on following page

*Table 3. Continued*

| Study | Algorithm | Bio-Inspiration | Strengths | Weaknesses | Smart environment Applications |
|---|---|---|---|---|---|
| (Tahayur & Al-Zubaidie, 2024) | ABC | Foraging behavior of honey bees | Good global search ability, simple implementation, adaptable | May suffer from slow convergence and premature stagnation | Securing electronic agriculture data using blockchain and e-signatures. |
| (Zou et al., 2023) | WOA | Social behavior and migration of walruses | Excellent exploration-exploitation balance, avoids local optima | Relatively new, less field validation | Cyber-threat detection in smart grid communications |

# ANALYSIS OF PROTECTION PROCEDURES

In this part, we test the Scyther verification tool and analyze attacks to illustrate security analysis. This section includes two subsections for analyzing security features against attacks: Analysis of threats and Scyther's analysis of security. In the first subsection, the attack landscape will be analyzed, including replay, sybil, eavesdropping, social engineering, critical infrastructure, and advanced ransomware attacks, and it will be explained how the proposed system can defend against these attacks. In the second subsection, the Scyther simulation tool is used to practically analyze the proposed system's ability to withstand these attacks.

## Analysis of Threats

1. **Replay attacks:** Replay attacks deceive legitimate participants into thinking that the protocol execution has been successfully finalized by replaying messages in a setting that is different from the original context. PQSED mitigates replay attacks by using digital signatures by FALCON that verify data integrity and ensure that only new, unspooled messages are accepted.
2. **Sybil attacks:** These are also called false-name attacks. It is commonly regarded as being among the most damaging attacks by creating a large number of pseudonymous identities to gain a disproportionately large influence. Anomaly detection using WOA and power consumption pattern analysis helps detect fake accounts.
3. **Eavesdropping:** It is a cyberattack where an unauthorized party, referred to as an eavesdropper, intercepts private data between two or more parties and

captures sensitive information. Applying pseudonymization technology to mask sensitive data renders the intercepted information meaningless, reducing the amount of information that can be accessed.

4. **Social Engineering Attacks:** Employees are tricked into handing over sensitive data, or when attackers gain privileges within the system. Tokens for digital signatures and data prevent an attacker from obtaining or modifying the real data, even if an employee is tricked into sharing data.
5. **Critical Infrastructure Attacks:** Targeting transportation networks to disrupt essential station services. The distribution of quantum keys generated via the BB84 protocol secures smart station communications and prevents any interception attempts at power stations.
6. **Advanced Ransomware Attacks:** The assailant encrypts the kept information and orders the system to pay a ransom to get it back. WOA guarantees that no suspicious modifications happen that would enable illegal encryption activities by tracking data behaviors.

## Scyther's Analysis of Security

Scyther is a powerful tool for verifying cryptographic protocols. With its advanced features, Scyther sets the standard for rapid attack detection and verification. Its users can detect attacks or perform unlimited verification. It differentiates itself from existing protocol analysis tools by integrating the benefits of abstraction-based methods (unrestricted validation) with argument proving and model checking (attack discovery and termination) (Tahayur & Al-Zubaidie, 2025). Moreover, this tool has cutting-edge functionality absent in other programs, including extensive profiling and attack selection (Al-Zubaidie & Jebbar, 2024). It may serve as a backend for analytical applications utilizing Python interface techniques, or it may function as a graphical user interface and command line interface. Scyther investigates security needs for several protocols in order to identify data leaks and confirm integrity and secrecy. This tool authenticates signatures and specific signatures using qualities that follow security standards: Weakagree, Nisynch, Alive, and Niagree (Razzaq et al., 2024).

We evaluate our proposed method with the Scyther instrument. The Security Protocols Describing Linguistics (SPDL) tool in the Scyther program helped us to get ready for our responsibilities in analysis. Here we engage the Smart Meter (SM) and Servers (S) via a set of instructions. Between the role events, we have provided simulations of our suggested protocol to allow communication between entities and validate security needs. Among the examined events are Alive, Nisynch, Niagree, and Weakagree. Using the send() and rec() functions allows us to evaluate requests and identify potential security flaws or attacks. The results show that our protocol meets security requirements. Digital signatures, which ensure information confidentiality and availability for all parties involved, are used to provide protocol security. Figures 4 and 5 show the results of the Scyther test. The tool's results showed that the PQSES protocol successfully achieves the required security properties without detecting any potential attacks.

*Figure 4. Depiction of the Scyther results*

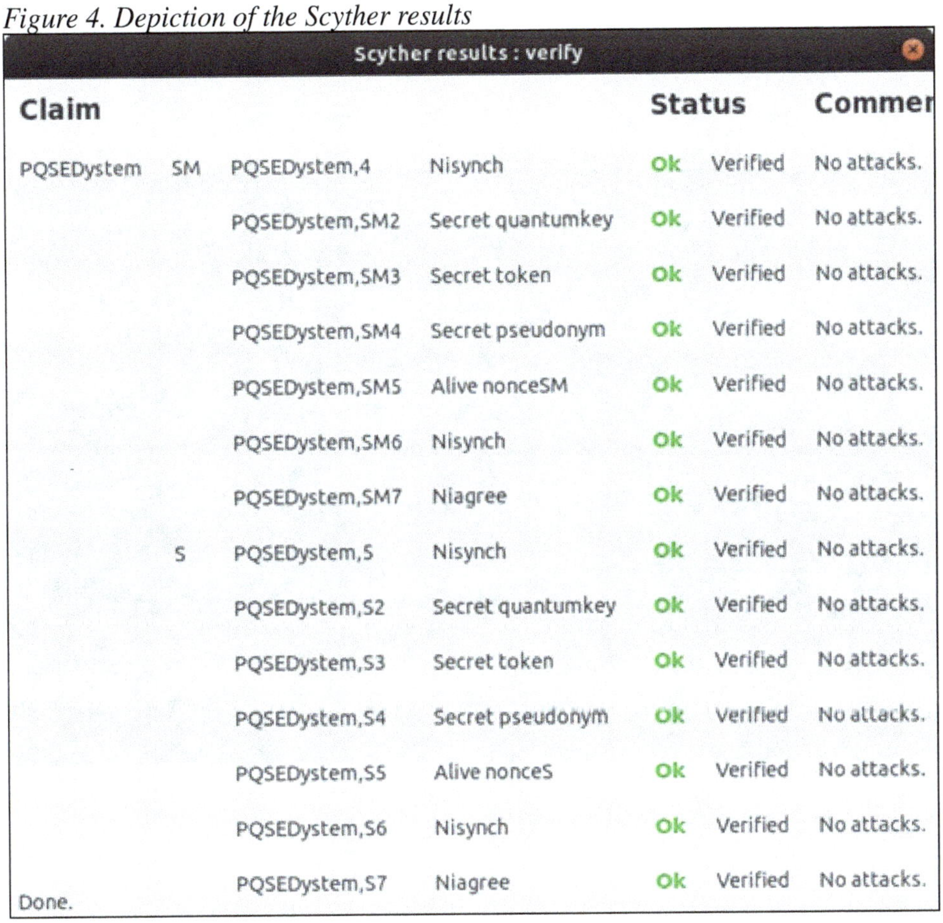
Scyther results : verify

| Claim | | | | Status | | Commer |
|---|---|---|---|---|---|---|
| PQSEDystem | SM | PQSEDystem,4 | Nisynch | Ok | Verified | No attacks. |
| | | PQSEDystem,SM2 | Secret quantumkey | Ok | Verified | No attacks. |
| | | PQSEDystem,SM3 | Secret token | Ok | Verified | No attacks. |
| | | PQSEDystem,SM4 | Secret pseudonym | Ok | Verified | No attacks. |
| | | PQSEDystem,SM5 | Alive nonceSM | Ok | Verified | No attacks. |
| | | PQSEDystem,SM6 | Nisynch | Ok | Verified | No attacks. |
| | | PQSEDystem,SM7 | Niagree | Ok | Verified | No attacks. |
| | S | PQSEDystem,5 | Nisynch | Ok | Verified | No attacks. |
| | | PQSEDystem,S2 | Secret quantumkey | Ok | Verified | No attacks. |
| | | PQSEDystem,S3 | Secret token | Ok | Verified | No attacks. |
| | | PQSEDystem,S4 | Secret pseudonym | Ok | Verified | No attacks. |
| | | PQSEDystem,S5 | Alive nonceS | Ok | Verified | No attacks. |
| | | PQSEDystem,S6 | Nisynch | Ok | Verified | No attacks. |
| | | PQSEDystem,S7 | Niagree | Ok | Verified | No attacks. |

Done.

*Figure 5. An explanation of the designated role within the suggested scheme*

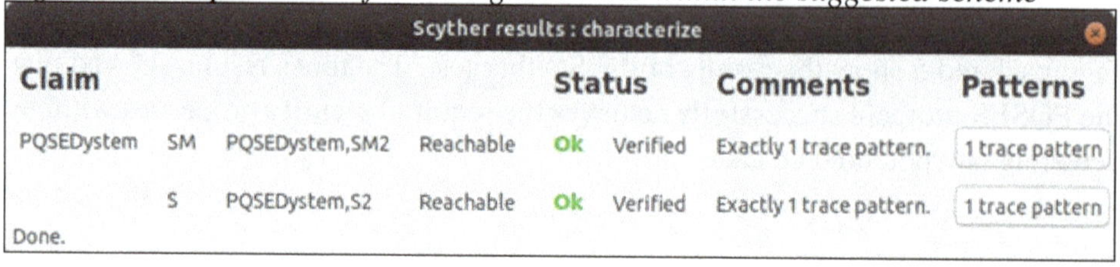


*Figure 6. Using QKD to generate quantum key*

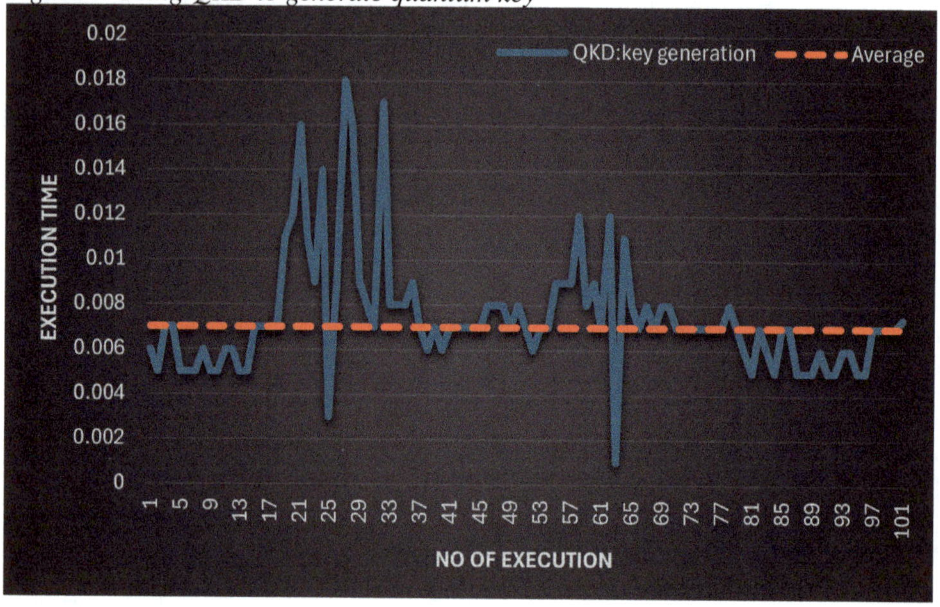


## SIMULATION SETUP AND EVALUATION CRITERIA

The PQSED system was evaluated under a Java-controlled simulation environment run on Ubuntu 18.04.6 LTS. Synthetic datasets were created to represent normal power use seen in smart city infrastructure, as access to real-world data from smart meters or utility suppliers was not accessible. These datasets were made to replicate reasonable operational circumstances while keeping test parameter uniformity. Every simulation was carried out on a personal computer running 8 GB of RAM and an Intel Core i5-1135G7 CPU (11th generation). Every test scenario was run one hundred times to guarantee statistical consistency and reduce the impact of random deviations. Stable averages and more reliable findings were produced in part by this repetition.

The study concentrated on assessing the accuracy in spotting aberrant activities, cryptographic strength, and system efficiency. From the result, we derived performance measures including execution time, memory use, entropy, accuracy, recall, and F1-score. Microsoft Excel was used to arrange and handle the gathered numerical data so that visual charts and summaries supporting the performance conversation could be produced. From a cryptography perspective, the BB84 protocol's average execution time of around 0.007 milliseconds revealed a quantum key generating value. With an average signing time of 0.006 milliseconds and a verification time of 0.004 milliseconds, the FALCON digital signature system likewise yielded encouraging results. Figures 6 and 7, respectively, help to show these outcomes.

Regarding anomaly detection, the system generated three false positives, four false negatives, and three true negatives while accurately spotting ninety real positives. These results formed the basis for computing the key assessment measures, which are covered in more detail in the comparative analysis that comes next.

*Figure 7. FALCON operations for signature and verification*

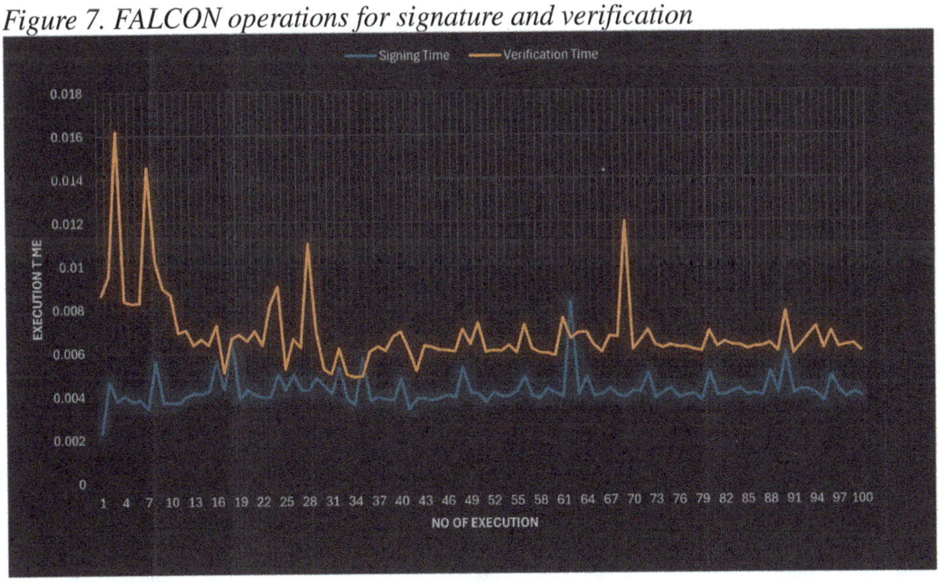


1. **Precision:** It is used to measure the accuracy of a system in identifying valid and securely verified transactions or data.

$$\text{Precision} = \frac{TP}{TP+FP} \times 100\% = \frac{90}{90+3} \times 100\% = 96\% \quad (2)$$

2. **Recall:** It plays a vital role in measuring the system's ability to identify all sensitive data that requires privacy.

$$\text{Recall} = \frac{TP}{TP+FN} \times 100\% = \frac{90}{90+4} \times 100\% = 95\% \quad (3)$$

3. **F1-score:** It is a metric used to evaluate the performance of a classification model, especially in tasks involving multi-class classification. The harmonic mean emphasizes the smaller value, making it suitable for scenarios where both precision and recall are crucial where

$$F1_{Score} = 2 \times \frac{Precision \times Recall}{Precision + Recall} \times 100\% = 96\% \quad (4)$$

4. **Execution Time:** It represents the total time it takes for data to reach from the smart devices deployed in the city at the point of origin to the main server at the power plant. This metric helps in evaluating the responsiveness and efficiency of electrical data transmission between SC equipment. The execution time rate of our system, which is 0.6 milliseconds, ensures fast and secure data transmission suitable for SC energy management. Figure 8

*Figure 8. Operations for PQSED*

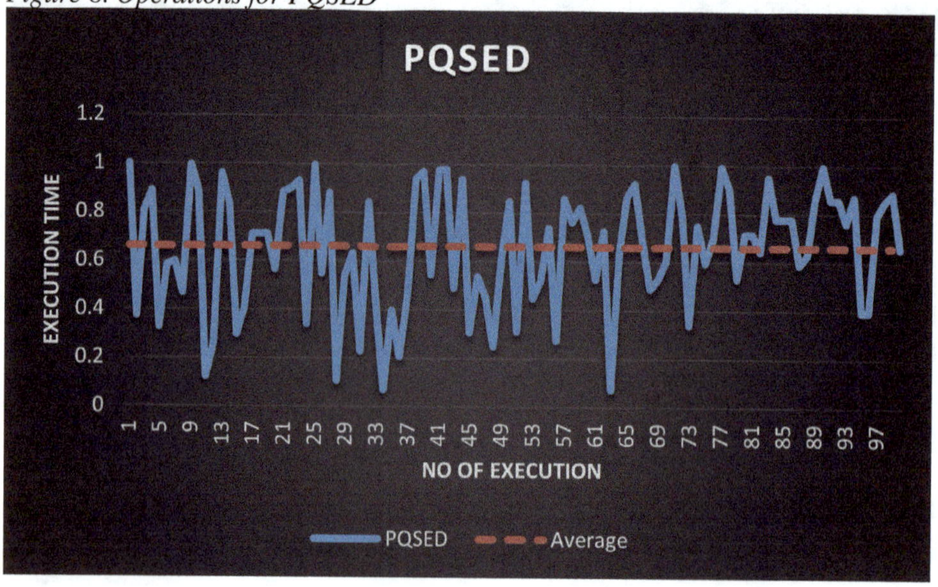

5. shows the execution time representation for 100 times.
6. **Convergence speed:** It represents how quickly the WOA algorithm reaches the optimal convergence analysis while performing data anomaly analysis operations.

$$Convergence\ Speed = \frac{1}{Iterations\ to\ reach\ the\ optimal\ solution} \tag{5}$$

Figure 9 shows the results of the convergence speed. We see a rapid improvement in the early iterations. In iteration 1, the best fit is 2.527, and by iteration 4, it drops dramatically to 0.02956. This means that the WOA is moving rapidly towards the optimal solution, and by iterations 10 to 50, it is very close to zero.

*Figure 9. Convergence speed for WOA*

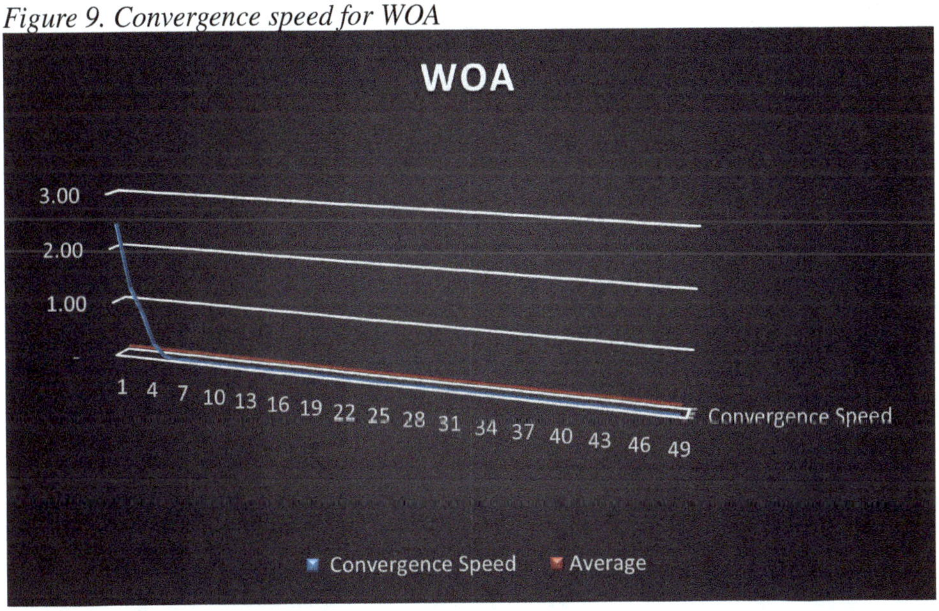

*Table 4. A comparison of execution time, precision, recall and f1-score*

| Parameters | PQSED | Previous Research |
|---|---|---|
| Precision | 96% | 92.3%, (Shahid et al., 2021)<br>91.8%, (Prasad & Srivenkatesh, 2025) |
| Recall | 95% | 91.8%, (Shahid et al., 2021)<br>90.7%,(Prasad & Srivenkatesh, 2025) |
| F1_Score | 96% | 92.0%,(Shahid et al., 2021)<br>91.2%,(Prasad & Srivenkatesh, 2025) |
| Average Execution Time | 0.66 MS | 50.6 MS, (Sharma et al., 2023) |

Table 4 and Figure 10 show a comparison between our proposed system and previous studies. Over previous research in several important evaluation measures, the suggested PQSED method showed a notable performance enhancement. All of which exceeded past benchmarks stated by Shahid et al. and Prasad & Srivenkatesh, it obtained a precision of 96%, a recall of 95%, and a F1-score of 96%. Most importantly, the average execution time dropped to 0.66 milliseconds from 50.6 milliseconds in previous models, therefore suggesting a significant improvement in real-time processing capability. These findings validate the system's exceptional capacity to

*Figure 10.* **A comparison between the proposed PQESD and previous research**

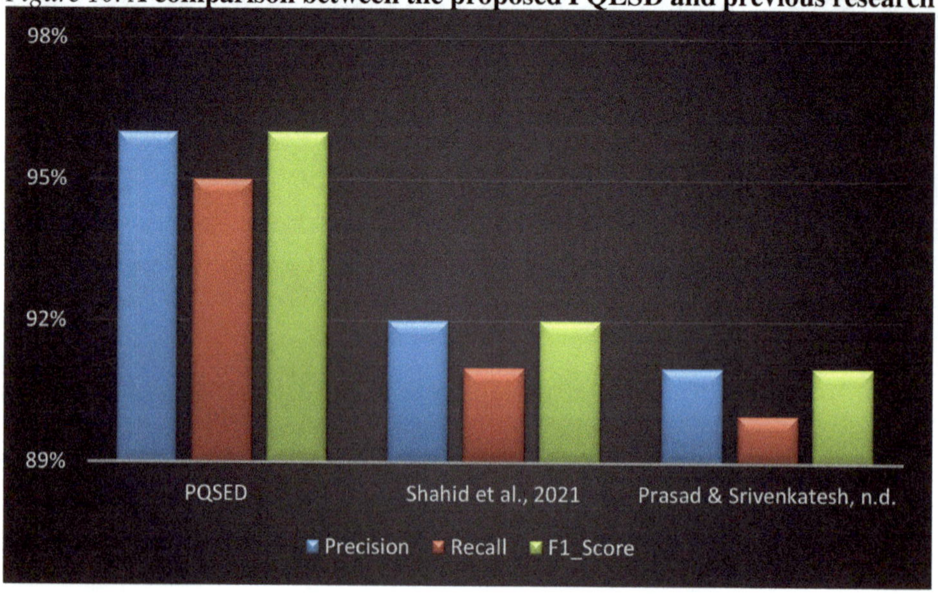


effectively and securely identify abnormalities, therefore making it quite appropriate for smart city infrastructure needing both speed and accuracy in data handling.

## PRIVACY PRESERVATION AND LEGAL COMPLIANCE

While digital signature techniques are essential for assuring data integrity, they are insufficient for guaranteeing total privacy. posing a threat to compliance with data protection requirements, particularly the GDPR (Bhatia et al., 2025). To help with this, the PQSED system includes a tokenization-based pseudonymizing layer before any processing. Context-aware, non-linkable tokens replace delicate identities like personal reference codes and meter IDs. These tokens are intrinsically temporary and unpleasant, thereby ensuring that the data used for signatures stays completely anonymous during examination. Only approved regulatory agencies with tight access control policies have access to the encrypted token map, which securely stores the original identities. This ensures that re-identification is mandated solely when essential, such as during audits or billing reconciliation, so as to uphold the principles of purpose limitation and data access minimization. This privacy-preserving design underscores the necessity for systems to implement data minimization, unlinkability, and user-governed re-identification mechanisms, in alignment with the EDPB Guidelines 05/2020 on the use of pseudonymization techniques under the GDPR (Asthana et al., 2025; Groos & Van Veen, 2020). PQSED ensures legal compliance by integrating these protections directly into the cryptographic pipeline, hence preserving the usability and auditability of power data inside smart city infrastructure.

*Table 5. PQSED System Compliance with the 7 GDPR Principles*

| GDPR Principle | Definition | How PQSED Complies | Status |
|---|---|---|---|
| Lawfulness, Fairness, and Transparency | Processing must be lawful, fair, and transparent to the data subject. | Data is pseudonymized and securely processed with informed design, though legal basis (e.g., consent) depends on deployment. | Partially Achieved |
| Purpose Limitation | Data is collected for specified, explicit, and legitimate purposes and not further processed incompatibly. | Access-Controlled Token Map ensures data is used only for authorized smart grid analytics and is not reused arbitrarily. | Achieved |
| Data Minimization | Only data that is necessary for the purpose should be collected. | Tokenization removes unnecessary identifiers from the data pipeline. | Achieved |
| Accuracy | Data must be accurate and, where necessary, kept up to date. | Not explicitly addressed in current PQSED implementation. | Not Achieved |
| Storage Limitation | Data should not be stored longer than necessary. | Data controllers should impose manual deletion procedures to avoid storing personal data longer than required. | Partially Achieved |

continued on following page

*Table 5. Continued*

| GDPR Principle | Definition | How PQSED Complies | Status |
|---|---|---|---|
| Integrity and Confidentiality (Security) | Data must be protected from unauthorized access or disclosure. | Uses BB84 for secure key distribution, FALCON for digital signatures, and encrypted token mapping. | Achieved |
| Accountability | Data controllers must demonstrate compliance with all principles. | System includes cryptographic logs, token tracking, and access control, enabling traceability and auditability. | Achieved |

Table 5 maps each of the seven core principles of the GDPR (as outlined in Article 5 of the regulation) to the corresponding design components of the PQSED system. The "Status" column reflects the extent to which each principle is fulfilled, based on current system implementation and documented control mechanisms ("Art. 5 GDPR – Principles Relating to Processing of Personal Data," n.d.).

## CONCLUSION

This chapter presents PQSED, a novel approach to address IoSCT secure data problems, especially in power plants. It is based on integrating modern technologies, including WOA analysis to improve the quality of big data, anonymization to protect privacy, quantum key generation to ensure the secure transmission of that data, and digital signatures using the FALCON algorithm to enhance integrity and reliability. Our proposal provides a comprehensive data management system that includes the stages of data collection, analysis, tokenization, signing, secure storage, and use, which enhances the efficiency of handling big data and ensures its accuracy and reliability. Future data management is supposed to be much enhanced by our solution. Integrating cutting-edge technology like anomaly detection and dynamic threat analysis would help the system to be even more able to handle the growing security concerns in the Internet of Things in service centers. Furthermore, we want to implement zero-knowledge proof in PQSED to guarantee the validity of FALCON signatures independent of validation procedures. Resistance to quantum attacks, guaranteed data integrity from source to destination, strong anonymity using tokenization, and enhanced smart performance thanks to WOA provide several major benefits over conventional systems lacking quantum protection or failing adherence to current privacy policies. An excellent fit for safe digital infrastructure for metropolitan settings, the suggested model is a security approach meant to keep pace with future breakthroughs in quantum computing and smart cities.

## LIMITATIONS AND FUTURE DEVELOPMENT

Though with a solid cryptographic basis and needing additional research, the PQSED system has numerous limitations. Particularly, it lacks techniques of confirming data accuracy or freshness before cryptographic processing, thereby guiding safe management of old or erroneous data. Moreover, missing an autonomous data retention module, the system depends on human enforcement to meet storage restriction requirements.

Future developments may include a lightweight validation layer for real-time data verification and adaptive retention rules driven by smart contracts or access control rules. Moreover, including AI-based anomaly detection and expanding interoperability with more general smart city systems would help to considcrably improve the scalability, auditability, and real-world readiness of the system.

## REFERENCES


Aala Kalananda, V. K. R., & Komanapalli, V. L. N. (2023). A competitive learning-based Grey wolf Optimizer for engineering problems and its application to multi-layer perceptron training. *Multimedia Tools and Applications*, *82*(26), 40209–40267. DOI: 10.1007/s11042-023-15146-x PMID: 37362670

Abushgra, A. A. (2022). Variations of QKD Protocols Based on Conventional System Measurements: A Literature Review. *Cryptography*, *6*(1), 1. Advance online publication. DOI: 10.3390/cryptography6010012

Achaal, B., Adda, M., Berger, M., Ibrahim, H., & Awde, A. (2024). Study of smart grid cyber-security, examining architectures, communication networks, cyber-attacks, countermeasure techniques, and challenges. *Cybersecurity*, *7*(1), 10. DOI: 10.1186/s42400-023-00200-w PMID: 38707764

Ahmad, K., Maabreh, M., Ghaly, M., Khan, K., Qadir, J., & Al-Fuqaha, A. (2022). Developing future human-centered smart cities: Critical analysis of smart city security, Data management, and Ethical challenges. *Computer Science Review*, *43*, 100452. DOI: 10.1016/j.cosrev.2021.100452

Akinade, A. O., Adepoju, P. A., Ige, A. B., & Afolabi, A. I. (2024). Cloud Security Challenges and Solutions: A Review of Current Best Practices. *International Journal of Multidisciplinary Research and Growth Evaluation*, *6*(1), 26–35. DOI: 10.54660/.IJMRGE.2025.6.1.26-35

Al-Zubaidie, M., & Jebbar, W. A. (2024). Providing security for flash loan system using cryptocurrency wallets supported by XSalsa20 in a blockchain environment. *Applied Sciences (Basel, Switzerland)*, *14*(14), 6361. DOI: 10.3390/app14146361

Al-Zubaidie, M., & Muhajjar, R. A. (2024). Integrating trustworthy mechanisms to support data and information security in health sensors. *Procedia Computer Science*, *237*, 43–52. DOI: 10.1016/j.procs.2024.05.078

Al-Zubaidie, M., Muhajjar, R. A., & Shihabe, L. A. (2024). Computer Networking and Cloud-Based Learning/Teaching Environment Using Virtual Labs Tools: A Review and Future Aspirations. *Mesopotamian Journal of Computer Science*, *2024*, 176–203. DOI: 10.58496/MJCSC/2024/015

Al-Zubaidie, M., & Shyaa, G. S. (2023). Applying detection leakage on hybrid cryptography to secure transaction information in e-commerce apps. *Future Internet*, *15*(8), 262. DOI: 10.3390/fi15080262

Art. 5 GDPR – Principles relating to processing of personal data. (n.d.). General Data Protection Regulation (GDPR). Retrieved May 25, 2025, from https://gdpr-info.eu/art-5-gdpr/

Asthana, S., Mahindru, R., Zhang, B., & Sanz, J. (2025). *Adaptive PII Mitigation Framework for Large Language Models* (No. arXiv:2501.12465; Version 1). arXiv. /arXiv.2501.12465DOI: 10.48550

Awaad, M. H., & Jebbar, W. A. (2014). Prolong the lifetime of WSN by determining a correlation nodes in the same zone and searching for the best not the closest CH. *International Journal of Modern Education and Computer Science*, *6*(11), 31. DOI: 10.5815/ijmecs.2014.11.04

Awaad, M. H., & Jebbar, W. A. (2015). Extending the WSN lifetime by Dividing the Network Area into a Specific Zones. *International Journal of Computer Network and Information Security*, *7*(2), 33–39. DOI: 10.5815/ijcnis.2015.02.04

Bhatia, A., Bitragunta, S., & Tiwari, K. (2025). Enhanced Lightweight Quantum Key Distribution Protocol for Improved Efficiency and Security. *IEEE Open Journal of the Communications Society*, *6*, 926–943. DOI: 10.1109/OJCOMS.2025.3528718

Canto, A. C., Kaur, J., Kermani, M. M., & Azarderakhsh, R. (2023). *Algorithmic Security is Insufficient: A Comprehensive Survey on Implementation Attacks Haunting Post-Quantum Security* (No. arXiv:2305.13544). arXiv. /arXiv.2305.13544. DOI: 10.48550

Chatterjee, R., Chung, K.-M., Liang, X., & Malavolta, G. (2022). A Note on the Post-quantum Security of (Ring) Signatures. In Hanaoka, G., Shikata, J., & Watanabe, Y. (Eds.), *Public-Key Cryptography – PKC 2022* (pp. 407–436). Springer International Publishing.

Chen, R., Li, Y., Yu, Y., Li, H., Chen, X., & Susilo, W. (2020). Blockchain-Based Dynamic Provable Data Possession for Smart Cities. *IEEE Internet of Things Journal*, *7*(5), 4143–4154. DOI: 10.1109/JIOT.2019.2963789

Das, D., Chaterjee, P., Ghosh, U., & Blakely, B. (2025). Secure and Privacy Aware Data Sharing Approach for Smart Electric Vehicles. *IEEE Consumer Electronics Magazine*, •••, 1–7. DOI: 10.1109/MCE.2025.3529398

De Guimarães, J. C. F., Severo, E. A., Felix Júnior, L. A., Da Costa, W. P. L. B., & Salmoria, F. T. (2020). Governance and quality of life in smart cities: Towards sustainable development goals. *Journal of Cleaner Production*, *253*, 119926. DOI: 10.1016/j.jclepro.2019.119926

Elmisery, A. M., Sertovic, M., Zayin, A., & Watson, P. (2025). *Cyber Threats in Financial Transactions—Addressing the Dual Challenge of AI and Quantum Computing* (No. arXiv:2503.15678). arXiv. /arXiv.2503.15678DOI: 10.48550

Fabrègue, B. F. G., & Bogoni, A. (2023). Privacy and Security Concerns in the Smart City. *Smart Cities*, *6*(1), 586–613. DOI: 10.3390/smartcities6010027

Falcon, E., & Mordant, N. (2022). Experiments in Surface Gravity–Capillary Wave Turbulence. *Annual Review of Fluid Mechanics*, *54*(1), 1–25. DOI: 10.1146/annurev-fluid-021021-102043

Geng, Y., Li, Y., & Deng, C. (2024). An Improved Binary Walrus Optimizer with Golden Sine Disturbance and Population Regeneration Mechanism to Solve Feature Selection Problems. *Biomimetics*, *9*(8), 501. DOI: 10.3390/biomimetics9080501 PMID: 39194480

Gharavi, H., Granjal, J., & Monteiro, E. (2024). Post-Quantum Blockchain Security for the Internet of Things: Survey and Research Directions. *IEEE Communications Surveys & Tutorials, 26*(3), 1748–1774. *IEEE Communications Surveys and Tutorials*. Advance online publication. DOI: 10.1109/COMST.2024.3355222

Groos, D., & Van Veen, E. (2020). Anonymised Data and the Rule of Law. *European Data Protection Law Review*, *6*(4), 498–508. DOI: 10.21552/edpl/2020/4/6

Gupta, B. B., Gaurav, A., Marín, E. C., & Alhalabi, W. (2023). Novel Graph-Based Machine Learning Technique to Secure Smart Vehicles in Intelligent Transportation Systems. *IEEE Transactions on Intelligent Transportation Systems*, *24*(8), 8483–8491. DOI: 10.1109/TITS.2022.3174333

Herman, D., Googin, C., Liu, X., Sun, Y., Galda, A., Safro, I., Pistoia, M., & Alexeev, Y. (2023). Quantum computing for finance. *Nature Reviews. Physics*, *5*(8), 450–465. DOI: 10.1038/s42254-023-00603-1

Ismagilova, E., Hughes, L., Rana, N. P., & Dwivedi, Y. K. (2022). Security, Privacy and Risks within Smart Cities: Literature Review and Development of a Smart City Interaction Framework. *Information Systems Frontiers*, *24*(2), 393–414. DOI: 10.1007/s10796-020-10044-1 PMID: 32837262

Jebbar, W. A., & Al-Zubaidie, M. (2024). Transaction-based blockchain systems security improvement employing micro-segmentation controlled by smart contracts and detection of saddle Goatfish. *SN Computer Science*, *5*(7), 898. DOI: 10.1007/s42979-024-03239-9

Karim, A. M. (2022). A new Sparse Auto-encoder based Framework using Grey Wolf Optimizer for Data Classification Problem (No. arXiv:2201.12493; Version 1). arXiv. /arXiv.2201.12493DOI: 10.48550

Khalaf, M., Ayad, A., Tushar, M. H. K., Kassouf, M., & Kundur, D. (2024). A Survey on Cyber-Physical Security of Active Distribution Networks in Smart Grids. *IEEE Access : Practical Innovations, Open Solutions*, *12*, 29414–29444. DOI: 10.1109/ACCESS.2024.3364362

Khan, K., & Goodridge, W. (2024). Swarm Intelligence-Driven Client Selection for Federated Learning in Cybersecurity applications (No. arXiv:2411.18877; Version 1). arXiv. /arXiv.2411.18877DOI: 10.48550

Khrennikov, A. (2021). Roots of quantum computing supremacy: Superposition, entanglement, or complementarity? *The European Physical Journal. Special Topics*, *230*(4), 1053–1057. DOI: 10.1140/epjs/s11734-021-00061-9

Kumar, M., & Mondal, B. (2025). A brief review on Quantum Key Distribution Protocols. *Multimedia Tools and Applications*. Advance online publication. DOI: 10.1007/s11042-024-20535-x

Lee, Y., Youn, J., Nam, K., Jung, H. H., Cho, M., Na, J., Park, J.-Y., Jeon, S., Kang, B. G., Oh, H., & Paek, Y. (2024). An Efficient Hardware/Software Co-Design for FALCON on Low-End Embedded Systems. *IEEE Access : Practical Innovations, Open Solutions*, *12*, 57947–57958. DOI: 10.1109/ACCESS.2024.3387489

Li, Q. (2020). Resilience Thinking as a System Approach to Promote China's Sustainability Transitions. *Sustainability*, *12*(12), 12. Advance online publication. DOI: 10.3390/su12125008

Lu, C.-Y., Cao, Y., Peng, C.-Z., & Pan, J.-W. (2022). Micius quantum experiments in space. *Reviews of Modern Physics*, *94*(3), 035001. DOI: 10.1103/RevModPhys.94.035001

Miao, W., Zhao, X., Wang, C., Chen, S., Gao, P., & Li, Q. (2024). A Gnn-Enhanced Ant Colony Optimization for Security Strategy Orchestration. *Symmetry*, *16*(9), 9. Advance online publication. DOI: 10.3390/sym16091183

Mohammed, H. M., & Rashid, T. A. (2020). A Novel Hybrid GWO with WOA for Global Numerical Optimization and Solving Pressure Vessel Design. *Neural Computing & Applications*, *32*(18), 14701–14718. DOI: 10.1007/s00521-020-04823-9

Naser, M. Z., & Naser, A. Z. (2024). The Firefighter Algorithm: A Hybrid Metaheuristic for Optimization Problems (No. arXiv:2406.00528; Version 1). arXiv. /arXiv.2406.00528DOI: 10.48550

Nguyen, T. L., Nguyen, L., Hoang, T., Bandara, D., Wang, Q., Lu, Q., Xu, X., Zhu, L., & Chen, S. (2025). Blockchain-Empowered Trustworthy Data Sharing: Fundamentals, Applications, and Challenges. *ACM Computing Surveys*. Advance online publication. DOI: 10.1145/3718082

Ollitrault, P. J., Miessen, A., & Tavernelli, I. (2021). Molecular Quantum Dynamics: A Quantum Computing Perspective. *Accounts of Chemical Research*, *54*(23), 4229–4238. DOI: 10.1021/acs.accounts.1c00514 PMID: 34787398

Prasad, R. D., & Srivenkatesh, M. (2025). A Hybrid Model Ccombining Graph Neural Networks, Reinforcement Learning, and Autoencoders for Authomated Code Refactoring and Optimization. *Journal of Theoretical and Applied Information Technology*, *103*(1).

Razzaq, R. H., & Al-Zubaidie, M. (2024b). Formulating an advanced security protocol for Internet of medical Things based on blockchain and fog computing technologies. *Iraqi Journal for Computer Science and Mathematics*, *5*(3), 723–734. DOI: 10.30880/ijcsm.2024.05.03.046

Razzaq, R. H., Al-Zubaidie, M., & Atiyah, R. G. (2024). Intermediary decentralized computing and private blockchain mechanisms for privacy preservation in the Internet of Medical Things. *Mesopotamian Journal of CyberSecurity*, *4*(3), 152–165. DOI: 10.58496/MJCS/2024/020

Razzaq, R. H., & Al-Zubaidie, M. H. (2024a). Maintaining security of patient data by employing private blockchain and fog computing technologies based on internet of medical things. *Informatica (Vilnius)*, *48*(12). Advance online publication. DOI: 10.31449/inf.v48i12.6047

Sadr, M. A. M., Zhu, Y., & Hu, P. (2023, February 10). *Satellite Anomaly Detection Using Variance Based Genetic Ensemble of Neural Networks*. arXiv.Org. https://arxiv.org/abs/2302.05525v1

Sahu, S. K., & Mazumdar, K. (2024). State-of-the-art analysis of quantum cryptography: Applications and future prospects. *Frontiers in Physics*, *12*. Advance online publication. DOI: 10.3389/fphy.2024.1456491

Shahid, H., Ashraf, H., Javed, H., Humayun, M., Jhanjhi, N., Al, A., & Zain, M. (2021). Energy Optimised Security against Wormhole Attack in IoT-Based Wireless Sensor Networks. *Computers, Materials & Continua*, *68*(2), 1967–1981. DOI: 10.32604/cmc.2021.015259

Sharma, T., Kumar, M. R., Kaushal, S., Chaudhary, D., & Saleem, K. (2023). Privacy Aware Post Quantum Secure Ant Colony Optimization Ad Hoc On-Demand Distance Vector Routing in Intent Based Internet of Vehicles for 5G Smart Cities. *IEEE Access, 11*, 110391–110399. IEEE Access. .DOI: 10.1109/ACCESS.2023.3311515

Tahayur, D. H., & Al-Zubaidie, M. (2024). Enhancing electronic agriculture data security with a blockchain-based search method and e-signatures. *Mesopotamian Journal of CyberSecurity*, *4*(3), 1–21. DOI: 10.58496/MJCS/2024/012

Tahayur, D. H., & Al-Zubaidie, M. (2025, March). Establishing an optimized searching approach with e-signatures based on blockchain for electronic agriculture applications. In AIP Conference Proceedings (Vol. 3264, No. 1). AIP Publishing. DOI: 10.1063/5.0258784

Tatipatri, N., & Arun, S. L. (2024). A Comprehensive Review on Cyber-Attacks in Power Systems: Impact Analysis, Detection, and Cyber Security. *IEEE Access : Practical Innovations, Open Solutions*, *12*, 18147–18167. DOI: 10.1109/ACCESS.2024.3361039

Tregi, T. G., & Al-Zubaidie, M. (2025). Enhancing Traffic Data Security in Smart Cities Using Optimized Quantum-Based Digital Signatures and Privacy-Preserving Techniques. *Mesopotamian Journal of CyberSecurity*, *5*(1), 256–272. DOI: 10.58496/MJCS/2025/017

Upadrista, V., Nazir, S., & Tianfield, H. (2023). Secure data sharing with blockchain for remote health monitoring applications: A review. *Journal of Reliable Intelligent Environments*, *9*(3), 349–368. DOI: 10.1007/s40860-023-00204-w PMID: 37359293

Uppalaiah, B., Reddy, D. M., Govindan, V., & Byeon, H. (2024). Optimizing quality of service forecasting in mobile networks through modified walrus optimization and multivariate approaches. *Edelweiss Applied Science and Technology*, *8*(6), 7878–7901. DOI: 10.55214/25768484.v8i6.3717

Vladislav, D., Maxim, K., Andrey, M., Viktoria, K., & Olga, K. (2024). Development of Determining a Wireless Client Location Method in the IEEE 802.11 Network to Ensure the IT Infrastructure Security. In A. A. Abd El-Latif, L. Tawalbeh, Y. Maleh, & B. B. Gupta (Eds.), *Secure Edge and Fog Computing Enabled AI for IoT and Smart Cities: Includes selected Papers from International Conference on Advanced Computing & Next-Generation Communication (ICACNGC 2022)* (pp. 241–254). Springer International Publishing. DOI: 10.1007/978-3-031-51097-7_19

Yang, Z., Zolanvari, M., & Jain, R. (2023). A Survey of Important Issues in Quantum Computing and Communications. *IEEE Communications Surveys and Tutorials*, *25*(2), 1059–1094. DOI: 10.1109/COMST.2023.3254481

Zafar, A. (2025). Reconciling blockchain technology and data protection laws: Regulatory challenges, technical solutions, and practical pathways. *Journal of Cybersecurity, 11*(1), tyaf002. Advance online publication. DOI: 10.1093/cybsec/tyaf002

Zhang, Z. (2024, August 22). *Deep Analysis of Time Series Data for Smart Grid Startup Strategies: A Transformer-LSTM-PSO Model Approach*. arXiv.Org. https://arxiv.org/abs/2408.12129v1

Zou, Y., Wu, R., Tian, X., & Li, H. (2023). Realizing the Improvement of the Reliability and Efficiency of Intelligent Electricity Inspection: IAOA-BP Algorithm for Anomaly Detection. *Energies, 16*(7), 7. Advance online publication. DOI: 10.3390/en16073021

## KEY TERMS AND DEFINITIONS

**Quantum-resistant cryptography:** cryptographic methods designed to remain secure against attacks by quantum computers and to protect sensitive data in the era of quantum computing.

**Internet of Things in a Smart City (IoSCT):** IoSCT is a dynamic and integrated system of sensors and smart devices spread over metropolitan settings. Its main goals are to simplify data collecting, communication, and real-time decision-making so boosting infrastructure efficiency and, hence, citizen quality of life.

**Quantum key distribution:** a secure communication method that uses the principles of quantum mechanics to generate cryptographic keys, providing inherent security against eavesdropping.

**FALCON digital signature:** a network-based digital signature algorithm, known for its high security and efficiency and suitable for IoSCT applications.

**Smart meters:** IoT-enabled devices installed in buildings, handling electricity usage data within smart grids.

# Chapter 9
# Blockchain Technology: Enabling Trust in Urban Systems


**Samariddin Makhmudov**
*Mamun University, Uzbekistan*

**Anorgul Atajanova**
https://orcid.org/0009-0000-5468-8187
*Urgench State Pedagogical Institute, Uzbekistan*

**Erkin Iskandarov**
*Urgench State University, Uzbekistan*

**Munir Ahmad**
https://orcid.org/0000-0003-4836-6151
*Survey of Pakistan, Pakistan*



## ABSTRACT

*This chapter explores the transformative potential of blockchain technology in reshaping urban governance. Far beyond its technical capabilities, blockchain challenges traditional, opaque models of municipal administration by offering transparency, auditability, and decentralized control. From land titling to procurement and identity management, tamper-proof records and distributed verification can help restore public trust, particularly in contexts plagued by inefficiency or corruption. Moreover, blockchain enables participatory governance through decentralized applications and smart contracts, allowing citizens to directly engage in urban planning, service oversight, and co-management of infrastructure. The chapter emphasizes the importance of incremental implementation, stakeholder coalitions, and careful integration with existing urban systems. It also calls for adaptive design, interoperability, and open-source development to ensure scalability and citizen accessibility.*



DOI: 10.4018/979-8-3373-8133-6.ch009

## INTRODUCTION

The 21st century has seen a breakneck trend in urbanization, computerization, and technology advancement, a move that has essentially redefined the way cities operate and relate to their citizens (Karger et al., 2025; Ma et al., 2024). The practice of urban governance, which was dependent on paper-based reporting and centralized decision making, is increasingly being implemented through complicated digital infrastructure and data ecosystems. City administrations have to deal with numerous participants, large volumes of data, and changeable service demands like management of the public utilities and transport systems, citizen historic records, and real-time service delivery. Nonetheless, this increased complexity has not been accompanied by a rise in equal gains in institutional efficiency, transparency, or citizen confidence in many cases. Digital transformation has revealed or even increased the traditional governance issues, such as data opacity, bureaucratic lethargy, corruption, and lack of access to marginalized population groups to the governing system in most cities (Lartey & Law, 2025; Mehmood et al., 2024; Przeybilovicz & Cunha, 2024).

Behind all these problems, there exists a chronic lack of trust. Citizens continually doubt government information, the fairness of public contracts, the integrity of urban services, and so forth (Asimakopoulos et al., 2025). The top-down model of governance faces the challenge of maintaining civic trust in a recrudescent participatory and interconnected world because the challenges of transparency and accountability are hard to achieve in top-down models of governance. Furthermore, with the increasing emphasis on the essentiality of digital systems in relationship-building acts between people and the state, i.e., digital identities, online portals, as well as e-governance platforms, systems stand to lose more confidence as a result of data manipulation, unwarranted access, and excessive institutional interference.

In that regard, blockchain is an interesting way out of the trust crisis in the cities. Blockchain promises to provide a different way of thinking about how information can be managed and action coordinated in urban environments in a trusted and transparent way, by supporting decentralized record keeping as well as cryptographically-secured transactions and immutable transaction histories (Rasha, 2025). In contrast to the traditional systems where only one authority accesses, updates data, blockchain is distributed in a network, hence the records become tamper-proof and verifiable. These characteristics are especially useful in such urban applications like the use of land registration activities, public contracts, utility billing, and managing citizens' identities, areas where precision, integrity, and transparency are most critical (Badran, 2024; Damaševičius et al., 2025; Ibrahimy et al., 2025).

It discusses how blockchain can be used in ways that would create an enabling layer of trust in urban systems. It starts with the clarification of the premises of blockchain and how they relate to modern problems of governance. The chapter also explores technical, regulatory, and institutional issues that influence the blockchain implementation in a city setting. Lastly, it speculates on the general implications of blockchain in ensuring civic legitimacy, institutional accountability, and civic action in smart city ecosystems. This chapter presents an informed critique of the promise and the constraints of blockchain technology to give a realistic view of the prospective role that it may play in redefining the future of city trust to urban planners, technologists, and policymakers.

This chapter aims to explore the transformative role of blockchain technology in enhancing urban governance processes. It examines how blockchain improves transparency, efficiency, and accountability across key sectors such as land registration, utility billing, procurement, and disaster relief. The chapter also outlines core governance principles enabled by blockchain and discusses implementation challenges and strategic opportunities for cities adopting this technology.

## BLOCKCHAIN FOUNDATIONS

Blockchain can be referred to as a disruptive technology, but fundamentally, blockchain is an infrastructure that aims to bring trust within decentralized digital infrastructure. As initially popularized by cryptocurrencies such as Bitcoin, the usefulness of blockchain has now expanded to many more than merely financial applications in the form of a wide spectrum of such applications, including governance, identity management, delivery of public services, and application to civic involvement. In order to adequately recognize the power of blockchain in urban governance, it is crucial to obtain a sense of the technical drivers that characterize blockchain first and then evaluate all the ways they can be related to issues cities have to handle in practice.

### Types of Blockchain

It is not a one-size-fits-all solution to adopt blockchain in urban systems. The governance structure, stakeholder topography, and utility scope of a given urban use case are key factors considering the type of blockchain structure to adopt, and this consideration may have a drastic impact on the performance as well as the perception of the system to the public. Broadly, the blockchain platforms can be classified into three broader sectors, namely, public, private, and consortium, each with varying degrees of decentralization, a level of control, degrees of transparency, and scale (Mlika et al., 2024; Quan et al., 2025; Šilenskytė et al., 2024). It is very important that urban decision-makers understand such fundamental differences with a view to ensuring that their solutions are not only sound on a technological level but are also socially and institutionally acceptable. Table 1 provides a comparison of the three types of blockchain.

## Public Blockchains

The public blockchain is an open network, and any participant can join it without prior authorization. Characterized by their openness and unwillingness to be censored, inclusivity, and transparency, these platforms, including Bitcoin, Ethereum, and numerous other decentralized protocols, are open and ready to accept anyone. All transactions on a public blockchain are registered publicly and cannot be removed easily because it is very hard to tamper with any data that has been confirmed by the network (Hamoud, 2025). Such an amount of openness is highly attractive in instances of city governance where there is a need to have a lot of citizen trust, like tracking campaign finance, participatory budget, or citizen voting programs. Since these platforms use a distributed consensus algorithm, such as proof of work or proof of stake, these platforms inculcate a trustless setting whereby integrity is not controlled by a central figure but rather is guarded by a network of globally distributed nodes. Nevertheless, a public blockchain is not without shortcomings. They may have low transaction performance rates and scaling capabilities (limited to a centralized design, in particular). Also, it is possible that the transparency of all data creates an issue of privacy in a scenario where sensitive data, including personal identities or administrative records, are present. Nonetheless, public blockchains have emerged as an effective alternative to situations where an application needs to be publicly verifiable and free of centralized control alternative (Barat et al., 2024; Lax et al., 2024; Takahashi et al., 2024).

## Private Blockchains

The alternative approach in private blockchains provides that only one company or affiliated institution maintains the power of a system. These blockchains do not have open participation, and no one can access the data and execute transactions by validating it. The model is ideally applicable in the internal administration of city systems whose activities involve high efficiency in processes, confidentiality of information, and regulation by standards. As an example, the city governments/ municipal departments can utilize the private blockchains to govern the verification of documents, human resource files, or municipal asset movement. Due to the fact that all participants are familiar and trusted, lighter consensus algorithms that allow transactions to process more quickly and scale better can be applied in private blockchains. Another aspect is that the network is closed, and therefore access can be strongly controlled and privacy ensured, and hence it is easier to conform to legal or institutional checks (Alaa, 2025). Nevertheless, there is also some level of centralization, which is similar to the common database systems as a result of having a private blockchain. The lower level of transparency and control in the hands of one governing body can restrict the trust of the general society and eliminate the civic goodness attributed to blockchain technology currently. However, in a setting where the sensitivity of data and speed of operation are prioritized over open verification, the picture of a reliable and efficient solution is that offered by the blockchain used privately (Ghosh et al., 2024; Oh et al., 2025; Wang et al., 2024).

## Consortium Blockchains

Consortium blockchains belong to a certain middle between the public and the secret. All these networks are controlled by a set of trusted institutions, a group that is composed of government agencies, utilities, non-governmental organizations, or academic institutions, which are all expected to share the duties of maintaining and revising the ledger. The rights and responsibilities of every participating node are clearly stated, and collaboration governance structures are used to make decisions regarding data validation and system rules. This model is quite favorable towards urban operation, where coordination among agencies is of utmost priority and where data is managed in a shared context. To take two examples, a consortium blockchain might be employed to harmonize regional transport planning across the multiple local administrations, to enable joint waste management at municipal levels, or to operate a shared system of environmental monitoring between governments and research organizations (Wid et al., 2024). Consortium blockchains represent intermediary back-office officials and decentralization. They enhance institutional accountability, data integrity while ensuring elaboration of role-based access control and performance-optimized systems. Nevertheless, it is important that protocols of governance, rules of consensus, and technical specifications should be negotiated carefully, such that long-term collaboration can be attained and system-to-system interoperability can be achieved. When done right, consortium blockchains could be used to increase the levels of coordination among stakeholders and improve the overall institutional capacity of urban institutions to handle complex issues (Chen et al., 2024; Yuan et al., 2025).

*Table 1. Comparison of blockchains*

| Feature | Public Blockchain | Private Blockchain | Consortium Blockchain |
|---|---|---|---|
| Accessibility | Open to all | Restricted access | Restricted to group members |
| Control | No central authority | Centralized | Shared control |
| Transparency | Fully transparent | Limited transparency | Partially transparent |
| Performance | Slower | Faster | Moderate |
| Consensus Mechanism | Proof of Work /Proof of Stake | Custom (PBFT, RAFT) | Group consensus', |
| Use Case Suitability | Public records, voting | Internal processes, auditing | Inter-agency data sharing |

## Core Principles of Blockchain

Blockchain technology offers a shift in the identity management paradigm of trust, data verification, and accountability of complex systems. Fundament to it are the principal principles, such as decentralization, immutability, and transparency, which meet important gaps in conventional information systems. Applied to urban governance, these principles may solve long-standing claims to fragmented ownership and access to data, the opaque nature of bureaucracy, corruption, and inefficiency (Bellaj et al., 2024; Mustafa et al., 2025; Rahman et al., 2024). This section considers all these traits and shows the practical application in learning how to manage the increasingly data-driven and multi-stakeholder environment of cities today. Core principles are summarized in Table 2.

*Table 2. Core principles of blockchain governance*

| Principle | Description |
|---|---|
| Decentralization | Control is distributed across a network of nodes, removing reliance on a single centralized authority and promoting democratic data management. |
| Transparency | Transactions are visible to all authorized participants, promoting accountability and reducing information asymmetries in governance. |
| Immutability | Once verified, records on the blockchain cannot be altered or deleted, preserving historical accuracy and enabling tamper-proof audit trails. |
| Smart Contracts | Self-executing code that automates and enforces predefined rules and agreements, increasing efficiency and reducing human error or bias. |
| Security | Advanced cryptography ensures secure, tamper-resistant records, protecting sensitive governance data from breaches and unauthorized access. |

## Decentralization

Decentralization can be defined as the spread out of data storage and verification to a network of separate nodes as opposed to having a central authority store all the information (Shamsan Saleh, 2024). In blockchain, every participant (or node) enforces and has their copy of the ledger, and any changes to the data in the ledger would have to reach consensus within the network. This removes single points of failure and subsequent unilateral manipulation.

In the urban systems, which involve municipal departments, utility providers, and private contractors, as well as citizens, decentralization presents an effective remedy to a siloed and hierarchical control over limited data. As an example, urban planning operations are usually affected by data inconsistencies that individual offices create and maintain (e.g., land use, zoning, and utility maps). A blockchain-based system may offer a common updated ledger between departments, which limits clerical redundancy, administrative delays, and decisions are made based on consistent published information. On top of that, decentralization is resilient and self-regulating. Decentralized data access helps in disaster management or maintenance of infrastructure without allowing the localized problems or the institutional constraints to derail the operational continuity. Such a distributed infrastructure is also a participant in participatory governance, whereby various interested parties, e.g., citizen watchdogs, community organizations, etc., can access and contribute to the shared decision-making platforms.

## Immutability

Immutability provides an assurance that any recorded, verified data on a block chain cannot be changed or erased unnoticed. This is done by use of cryptography, hashing, and hashing of blocks, each of which makes it computationally impossible to tamper with records retroactively without the agreement of the majority of the network (Akram et al., 2024; Curry, 2025). This attribute is especially sensitive in the urban governing system, whereby the integrity of records supports the rights to property, implementation of regulations, and the municipality's finances. One example is the land ownership wrangles, which can usually emerge because of the forged title transfer or unreported alterations to cadastral maps. A blockchain land registry would have the benefits of a secure, time-stamped registry of land ownership and history of transactions, vastly limit the possibility of fraud, and make the verification by an administration more efficient.

Internal controls and auditability are also enhanced by immutability in the public sector finance. The possibility to put all the municipal spending, payment approvals, and contractor payments on a blockchain ledger will enable cities to build end-to-end audit trails, which will deter embezzlement and make external audits significantly easier. As the strategy of digital governance is gaining traction, it is mandatory to make sure that these digital records are trustworthy and tamper-proof to establish long-term institutional credibility.

## Transparency

Transparency in blockchain systems implies that transactions in the system, according to the type of access in the system (level of permission), can be seen, tracked, and verified by network members. Whereas the transparency provided in public blockchains is complete, it is possible that even in the case of a private or a consortium blockchain, controlled visibility can be provided so that authorized parties can independently verify actions without interfering with the data privacy of the network (Burgess et al., 2024; Cui et al., 2024).

In most urban situations, a cynical outlook by people towards the government reduces due to ill transparency in the government procedures such as contract allocations, license issuance, etc. Blockchain permits such processes to be programmatically recorded and revealed in a verifiable form. For instance, the entire history of bidding, evaluation rankings, and payments on infrastructure projects can be displayed on a blockchain-based procurement platform, thereby enhancing credibility in fair competition and reducing the likelihood of collusion. Additionally, citizen engagement and civic oversight must be transparent. Cities rely more and more on the active participation of the population, be it in participatory budgeting, the feedback on services, or smart cities. Blockchain aids in the reconstitution of the social contract between states and citizens when it guarantees the transparency of those decisions and the place of people and their outcomes, so they can be recorded publicly and are accessible.

## Security

Although usually not quoted among the key principles of blockchain, security is an essential feature of blockchain systems, particularly the confidentiality of urban data in particular. Blockchain has the effect of greatly minimizing the likelihood of unauthorized usage, data manipulation, and denial-of-service attacks by using encrypted cryptography, decentralized consensus, and irrevocable, immutable recordkeeping (Rahman et al., 2024; Shamsan Saleh, 2024).

In smart cities, it is now evident that systems such as transportation, energy grids, and healthcare services are becoming increasingly digitized and interconnected, making data security a primary concern. Anti-fraud protection, Blockchain can provide a security layer that prevents vital data associated with an organization's infrastructure from being infiltrated by internal fraud or outside threats due to the log of how it was used, who it was used by, or even what service was requested. This would be especially significant in the areas where the capacity to provide institutional cybersecurity is low, where concerns related to surveillance and misuse of data by the government are increasing.

## Smart Contracts

Blockchain platforms tend to be compatible with smart contracts, which are self-executing rules scripts, and automatically enforce rules and execute actions when a set of conditions has been fulfilled. Such programmable tools eradicate intermediaries, limit the creation of errors made by human beings, and provide high output and foreseeability of administrative procedures (Curry, 2025; Rahman et al., 2024).

In the city government, smart contracts can be used to automate complicated processes like the authorization of permit applications, the granting of subsidies, or conditional payments. As one example, in public works, a smart contract might be constructed to dispense payments to a contractor only when there is verified proof of work, e.g., drone footage or data collected by Internet of Things (IoT) sensors, to demonstrate milestone achievement. On the same note, smart contracts for utility service providers will be able to automatically make the calculation and reimbursement of charges in real time, where real-time usage data will be captured, thereby doing away with the dispatch of the errors of manual billing. Smart contracts contribute to making cities pass from discretionary and paper-based processes to automated, rule-based systems because they move decision-making out of the hands of people, rendering them consistent, equitable, and harder to corrupt. Figure 1 shows the flow of a typical smart contract.

*Figure 1. Smart contract workflow*

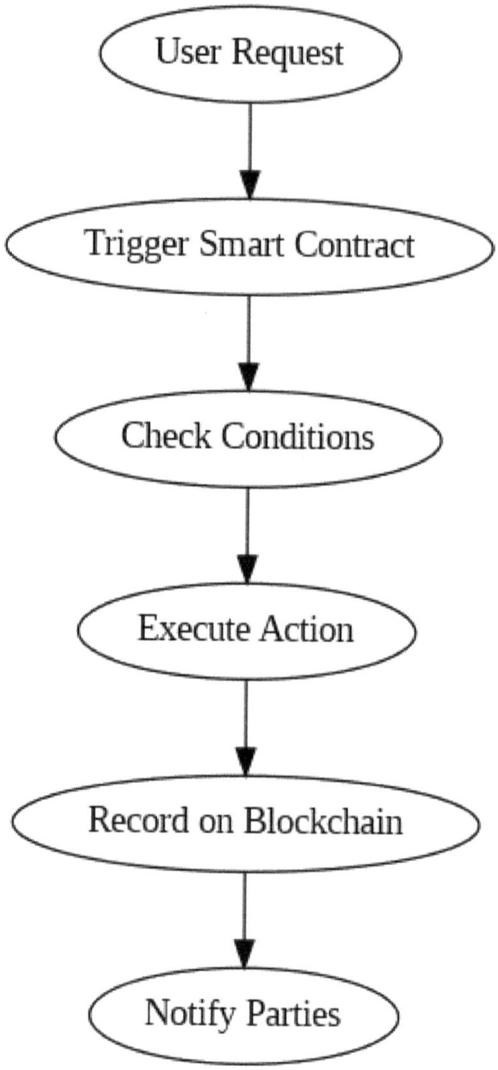


## BLOCKCHAIN IN URBAN SYSTEMS

With cities becoming more and more digital and data-driven, the amount and the complexity of information urban systems have to deal with have become exponentially larger. This situation makes the need for secure, transparent, and accountable mechanisms of managing public data and services more important than ever before.

Blockchain technology and its potential to offer a record-keeping mechanism that cannot be changed or corrupted, decentralized governance, as well as programmable automation via smart contracts, present a very interesting suite of tools to help overcome the myriad challenges that have long vexed urban management. Some of the most disruptive and pertinent blockchain use cases in a city system are examined in the sections below, showing how to use the technology to revolutionize land management, public procurement, billing utilities, and provide digital identities. Figure 2 describes some urban use cases in the context of blockchain.

*Figure 2. Blockchain characteristics and urban use cases*

## Urban Land and Property Records

Land administration is one of the areas of urban politics that is most vulnerable and thus very crucial in its management. The land and property records in most cities of various parts of the world have experienced the full might of fragmentation, inconsistency, and vulnerability to fraud or tampering. Loosely digitized systems or registries done on paper tend to create ownership disputes, loss of history, and corruption through manipulation of records. Blockchain technology provides a drastic solution by offering a tamper-evident, secure record of land transactions and deeds in the form of a ledger (Lawal & Nawari, 2024; Lee & Yang, 2025; Tang et al., 2024).

To overcome such problems, several countries have already started pilot projects that use blockchain land registry. In Sweden, the Lantmateriet (The Swedish Land Authority) has tested a blockchain platform to register real estate transactions with banks and technology companies, to shorten the time transactions take and to improve confidence in real estate transfer. The state of Andhra Pradesh in India collaborated with blockchain companies to give digitized land ownership records and minimize cases of false ownership assertions, especially in those areas where land is easily grabbed and politically interfered with. On the same note, in Georgia, the National Agency of Public Registry effectively deployed the blockchain to record more than 1.5 million land titles, providing not only effectiveness but also worldwide visibility and legal protection. Figure 3 shows the blockchain-enabled urban land registry workflow.

*Figure 3. Blockchain-enabled urban land registry workflow*

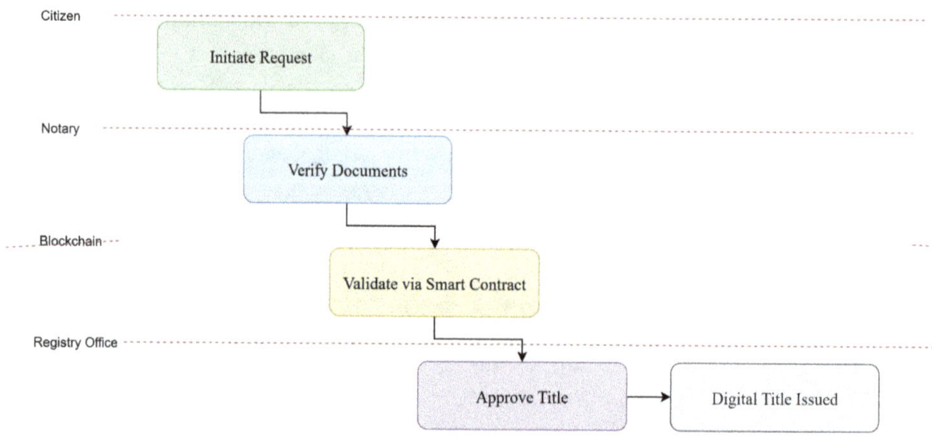


The potential of city organizations to eliminate redundant claims, streamline title verification, minimize litigation, and establish objective audit trails that foster trust in the rule of law and property rights can be achieved by incorporating blockchain into the governance systems they have in place to manage urban land.

## Public Procurement and Contracting

City, state, and municipal procurement procedures, or the process of radio construction, garbage and recycling, information technology, and school supplies, are a large part of the city's spending. Regrettably, they are also one of the most corrupt areas of government, subject to kickbacks, favoritism, bid-rigging, and closed award processes. Blockchain has the potential to boost transparency, responsibility, and efficiency in the whole procurement lifecycle (Adjorlolo et al., 2025; Alves Batista, 2024; Giamberardino et al., 2024).

With this, the tendering process can be automated in cities that use blockchain-based smart contracts so that, once certain conditions have been satisfied (e.g., the deadline on submissions or the performance goals have been met), the system will automatically pay or reward the winner without human input. All the bids, decisions, and transactions that are captured on a blockchain can be time-stamped and subjected to scrutiny by the general audience or between agencies, thus offering a verifiable chain of procurement operations. Table 3 demonstrates how blockchain improves procurement transparency, efficiency, and fairness.

*Table 3. Blockchain-enabled procurement*

| Process Stage | Traditional System | With Blockchain |
|---|---|---|
| Tender Announcement | Manual posting on fragmented platforms | Automated, decentralized ledger with public visibility |
| Bid Submission | Prone to tampering and late submissions | Immutable smart contracts ensure secure and time-stamped bids |
| Evaluation & Awarding | Time-consuming manual verification and opaque scoring | Transparent criteria embedded in smart contracts for automatic evaluation |
| Contract Execution | Delay in approvals and risk of manipulation | Real-time multi-party execution through smart contracts |
| Auditing & Compliance | Requires paper trails and prone to data loss | Tamper-proof audit trails and real-time compliance logging |

As an instance, the Colombian government experimented with a blockchain-based system of monitoring the procurement of state contracts and improving civil control. The city of Seoul in South Korea is an example since it experimented with a blockchain platform by logging all municipal contract awards so that residents could trace the expenditure of publicly owned money. In Ukraine, the ProZorro public procurement has been relying on distributed ledger technology to provide procurement data in real-time, which significantly eliminates the possibility of inside manipulation. Completing the next step and integrating blockchain in the process of procurement, city administrations will not only enhance their efficiency in everyday practice but also restore the losses in the common trust by showing transparency, honesty, and impartiality in the spending of idle funds.

## Utility Billing and Payments

Citizens experience constant contact with some of the basic utilities in the city, including electricity, water, and gas utilities, among others, which have become the lifeline of the urban space. However, utility billing processes are known to be strewn with inefficiencies, inaccurate meters and delayed billing, and non-transparent reconciliation processes. The solution is provided by blockchain, as it allows recording the usage and payments of utilities in a transparent, real-time, and tamper-proof way (Din & Su, 2024; Giri et al., 2024).

Within a blockchain billing system, smart meters may automatically record consumption data to an open ledger, with the open ledger providing billing calculations and payment trigger events using smart contracts. This minimizes the number of hands that can be involved in the process of errors, unauthorized and customer objections. Besides, with the guarantee of immutable records and automated reconciliation, it will be easier to audit consumption of energy, monitor payment compliance, among others, and even dynamic pricing schemes. Table 4 illustrates how blockchain is transforming billing and utility service accountability.

*Table 4. Blockchain in utility billing*

| Function | Traditional Issue | Blockchain Approach | Anticipated Impacts |
|---|---|---|---|
| Meter Reading | Manual data is prone to tampering and errors | IoT-integrated blockchain for real-time, immutable consumption data | Accurate, transparent usage tracking |
| Billing | Delays and opaque pricing | Smart contracts auto-generate bills based on real-time usage | Instant, verifiable billing |
| Payment | Cash-based or untraceable digital payments | Tokenized or blockchain-based payment channels | Faster, traceable payments |
| Dispute Resolution | Lengthy manual process with little audit trail | Automated logs and access to historical records | Faster resolution, less corruption |
| Subsidy Verification | Difficulty verifying eligibility | Automated eligibility rules in smart contracts | Targeted, tamper-proof subsidies |

Dubai city, under the Smart Dubai, has been examining the use of blockchain in water and electricity bills in order to simplify the process and minimize wastage and fraudulent activities. In Brooklyn, New York, the Brooklyn Microgrid pilot allowed residents to purchase and sell extra sun-produced energy using blockchain-based tokens, with each transaction registered in one blockchain distributed ledger, which eliminated central intermediaries. In developing nations where payment leakage and meter bypass are common characteristics of many utilities, blockchain-based billing systems have the potential to improve revenue collections and enforce improved consumer behavior. Additionally, blockchain may incentivize energy efficiency, re-cycling behaviors, or any other energy-policy-focused goals through digital tokens or credits given upon adherence to the usage, aligning utility policy with sustainability.

## Digital Identity and Citizen Services

Access to most of the urban public services, including healthcare and education, voting, and subsidies, is based on secure and verifiable identity. However, the identity systems across most cities are isolated, can easily be repeated, and are susceptible to data security breaches. Blockchain is also used to introduce self-sovereign identity (SSI), which implies that people maintain their digital credentials and share roles in them securely and only on a need-to-share basis, without the need to use any central registry (Bahrepour & Maleki, 2024; Hasan et al., 2024; Piccardo et al., 2024).

Under a blockchain-based identity system, e.g., gov or driving licenses as an example, credentials like birth certificates, utility accounts, or driving licenses are issued by trusted bodies and tied to a decentralized ledger. This person would own his or her identity wallet with necessary selective disclosure of his identity information to be authenticated without significant loss of privacy, risking data theft, and allowing faster access to services.

In Estonia, which pioneered digital governance, citizens can access a broad repertoire of online public services of a variety highly intimate to them (medical records) as well as to society (voting). They do so with a digital ID issued with blockchain security. In Zug, Switzerland, also known as the crypto valley, citizens can enroll their digital identities on a blockchain system and pay taxes or avail of the e-governance system, including permissions to leave the city. The Aadhaar system has also thought of incorporating some aspects of blockchain in India to enhance data privacy and the empowerment of the user.

Blockchain-based digital identity systems can also be utilized to integrate Sidelined groups, including migrants, refugees, and the unbanked, who do not have a formal identity due to a lack of identification and access to services. Municipal ID cards supported by blockchain can be issued by cities that can connect to the service entitlement without affecting the privacy of the user or causing the data to be in danger of centralization.

## Urban Mobility and Transportation Planning

The aspect of mobility is one of the most dynamic and complicated parts of urban life, and it features a continuously fluctuating ecosystem of public transit operators, ride-hailing companies, parking operators, and bicycle and pedestrian riders. Historically, the data fragmentation in the urban transport system, the absence of a coordination body among the providers, and poor transparency of fare adjustment and infrastructure design have been problems of the urban transport system. Blockchain is a chance to enhance the operational effectiveness and user confidence in mobility systems, since it will enable to incorporation of a single and tamper-proof infrastructure for the sharing and payment of data and coordination (Ali et al., 2025; Meneguzzo et al., 2024; Miron et al., 2025).

As an example, a blockchain ledger may provide a common data layer on which mobility service providers, i.e., municipal bus services, privately run ride-share services, and the metro rail network, record vehicle locations, trip data, and transactions of users in real time. This may make it possible to have integrated multi-modal ticketing systems where commuters do not pay at each mode of transportation, the booking is a single payment, and as one switches modes, the transactions are automatically reconciled and are auditable on the blockchain. This system would minimize administrative overheads and improve the convenience and integrity of data for the user. Taipei City investigated the potential of blockchain as a smart card system capable of accommodating subway, bus, and bike-sharing capabilities. In Finland, Whim has been experimenting with a blockchain as a backend to its Mobility-as-a-Service (MaaS) platform, in which the goal is to harmonize the billing structures and multiple operators in an automated way.

Planning and governance Urban mobility Planning and governance of urban mobility can be aided by blockchain as well, when they involve the equitable and verifiable distribution of the use of infrastructure, such as monitoring adherence of ride-share vehicles to congestion pricing, or the distribution of toll road money or smart parking system money. In any situation where autonomous cars or drones are in use, blockchain may be widely exploited in terms of controlling the flow of traffic, recording operational situations, and managing decentralized webs of vehicles.

## Disaster Response and Crisis Coordination

Urban regions become more exposed to disasters and pandemics of climatic origin and complex humanitarian emergencies. When you have such scenarios, quick response, proper sharing of information, and the deployment of resources are necessary, but usually, a poor data system as well as duplication of efforts, including mistrust of the people, can hamper such a process. Disaster response can be improved through applications of blockchain based on secure sharing of information in real time, verification of relief delivery, and event recording that is tamper-proof and hence accountable (Habib et al., 2024; Shevchuk et al., 2025; Zachariah et al., 2025).

An example is the tracking of emergency assistance and relief material. Using blockchain ledgers, every food packet, medical kit, or housing voucher could be delivered to the recipient and could not be diverted based on corruption and logistical errors. As an example, the United Nations World Food Programme has also employed blockchain technology in its building blocks project, which used blockchain technology to give refugees in Jordan cash-based aid without using intermediaries and also not relying on tracking systems that depend on paper. Figure 4 shows the workflow of disaster relief distribution via blockchain.

*Figure 4. Flow of disaster relief distribution via blockchain*

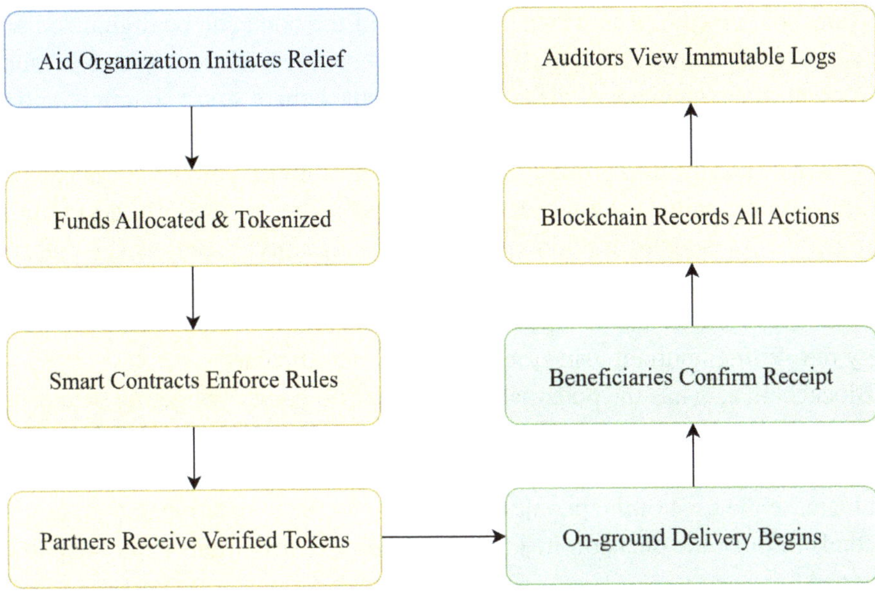


Within cities, the city government can record all important response measures, including sending an ambulance, opening shelters, or sending evacuation notices, in a blockchain ledger accessible to responding agencies and auditable following the crisis. This would make a historical record of emergency actions that cannot be changed, and ultimately lead to next time and institutional learning.

Additionally, blockchain may be used to verify the identity of displaced groups in case of a disaster, so that ill persons, who lack physical IDs, can still receive medical attention or shelter, or monetary support. Other nonprofits have tested blockchain in Indonesia and the Philippines, countries that experience frequent typhoons and earthquakes, and as such, a lack of transparency and trust among donors.

## Urban Finance and Municipal Bonds

Urban finance Municipal finance is a key area of urban development, and can be used by local governments to finance infrastructure, public services, and projects of environmental sustainability. Nonetheless, the municipal bond market (particularly, in developing countries) is most likely to be non-transparent, underdeveloped, or fraught with low confidence among investors. Blockchain opens the potential of a new paradigm of transparent, efficient, and inclusive urban finance, in particular, with the help of the tokenization of municipal bonds and the tracking of expenditure digitally (Biasin & Delle Foglie, 2024; Dehouche, 2025; Dorostkar & Ziari, 2025).

The whole process of issuance and trading of the bond can be digitalized with the use of blockchain technology. This can be implemented by automatic payout of the coupon, and repayment of the principal with the help of smart contracts, and the real-time tracking of such funds will allow the investors to be confident that their money is safe and utilized properly. Such a degree of transparency has the potential to enable municipalities to raise capital at a lower rate, particularly during times when people do not trust traditional institutions. The city of Berkeley, California, considered launching blockchain-based so-called microbonds, enabling citizens to directly invest in neighborhood amenity projects like affordable housing or fire safety retrofitting, without using large financial intermediaries.

Blockchain also has the potential to enable participatory budgeting by converting citizen votes and the allocation of funds to an auditable ledger. This way, the residents will be able to give their direct input in the use of their tax dollars, and it will increase the trust of the people of the nation in the realization that all funding descends through the decision-making and funding distributions path, open to the reader and viewer.

Also, the cities that employ green finance policies like the erection of infrastructure that is resistant to the climate or carbon abatement programs can use the blockchain to monitor the sustainability level and evidence the adherence to the environmental standards. This would especially apply to the exposure of green bonds and ESG (Environmental, Social, and Governance) funds, where the traceability of impact and auditability play a very important role. Table 5 summarizes the blockchain use cases in urban governance.

*Table 5. Blockchain use cases in urban governance*

| Sector | Use Case Example | Blockchain Role |
|---|---|---|
| Land Registry | Title deed digitization | Immutable records |
| Transportation | Smart traffic systems | Transparent coordination |
| Utilities | Energy trading platforms | P2P trustless exchange |
| Public Health | Vaccine supply chain tracking | Provenance assurance |
| Waste Management | Smart bins and collection tracing | Audit trail |

## IMPLEMENTATION CHALLENGES AND TECHNICAL CONSIDERATIONS

Although blockchain offers potent possibilities to raise urban systems' trust, transparency, and accountability, the implementation of the technology does not come without significant challenges. The urban environments are multilayered ecosystems containing legacies, regulatory requirements, and a variety of Stakeholders as documented in Table 6. This part addresses four big obstacles that cities encounter in the process of adopting blockchain technology, as well as practical solutions to offset them. Figure 5 summarizes the key blockchain challenges along with their root causes and their impact on urban governance.

*Table 6. Stakeholder roles in urban blockchain ecosystem*

| Stakeholder Type | Key Roles and Responsibilities |
|---|---|
| Government | Policy, regulation, and infrastructure investment |
| Private Sector | Technology development, deployment |
| Citizens | Data contributors, service beneficiaries |
| Civil Society Orgs | Oversight, ethical watchdog |
| Academia | Research, evaluation, and innovation support |

### Compatibility with Urban Infrastructure

Long-term digital platforms may be the basis of urban systems to provide services such as Geographic Information System (GIS) mapping of services billing, licensing, and citizen records. These legacy systems had no intention of being connected to decentralized technologies, and this has led to major interoperability issues. Existing software might not fit blockchain-based architectures, APIs, and protocols, resulting in information siloes and wasted resources.

In one example, the building permit system of a city could be based on a proprietary data model that is incompatible with a land registry on a blockchain. In the absence of a smooth integration, it would be compulsory to follow the manual reconciliation of the information or build customized connectors, which is time-consuming and error-prone. To overcome this, cities are recommended to implement middleware systems or blockchain platforms that are interoperable (e.g., Hyperledger Fabric, Polkadot, Cosmos) to connect to the existing databases and systems. APIs may be created to interpolate data formats between systems, and department-wide data standardization may enable consistency. Pilot projects ought to be geared towards modular integration- commence with a single or two services and then end up with larger systems. Also, it will be necessary to come up with data government procedures across the agencies to ensure congruent technical processes and eliminate institutional fragmentation.

## Data Privacy and Compliance with Regulations

The leading concept of blockchain involves immutability, in which data initially put on a blockchain cannot be changed, and thus directly challenges the privacy laws like the GDPR in the European Union, focusing on the right of erasure of data (also known as the right to be forgotten), consent, and data minimization. This presents severe compliance issues in urban settings where blockchain may document a person-identifiable information (PII) in exchange services such as identity augmentation or welfare payments.

As an example, data minimization and revocability would be incompatible with the requirement of storing the biometric ID or a tax record of a citizen on-chain, directly. Furthermore, in the case of storing data in a public blockchain, data can be manifested outside the desired jurisdiction, and cross-border data issues become a certain extent. A way out is through off-chain storage and on-chain reference. To get rid of such sensitive information, it can be stored in encrypted, access-restricted databases or cloud stores, and only its hash (digital fingerprint) is sent to the blockchain to check. This guarantees immutability and conceals actual data. Methods of verification, such as the use of zero-knowledge proofs (ZKPs), may permit data verification (i.e., age verification, citizenship) without disclosing all the information. Also, cities should establish policies of governance of privacy towards formulating roles, consent bases, as well as encryption standards to accommodate the national data protection policies.

## Scalability, Energy Consumption, and Cost Implications

A lot of blockchain solutions, especially those of the first generation, such as Bitcoin and Ethereum (before the Merge), suffer from a scalability issue and excessive energy consumption because of the consensus mechanism. Real-time city usage. A real-time application, like dynamic billing of mass transportation or coordinated response during a disaster, may be too much of a transaction load for the blockchain to efficiently process.

In addition, transaction costs are relatively high in public blockchains (a.k.a. gas fees) and can demand substantial resources to house nodes, audit smart contracts, and guarantee availability. This creates some concerns about cost-effectiveness and sustainability issues on the part of the city government, whose budget resources are limited. This can be dealt with by a number of technical and architectural innovations. Cities can select permissioned blockchains (private or consortium), which are more scalable and lower energy-intensive than public blockchains. The faster processing and less energy consumption are possible because of platforms such as Hyperledger Besu, Quorum, or Corda. In the case of public chains, productive scaling solutions (e.g., rollups, sidechains) or Proof-of-Stake (PoS) consensus algorithms make spending and environmental impact minimal. They should use strategic cost-benefit analysis before deployment, not on all services, but on blockchain-only the processes that the government uses, involving high trust and high impact, such as procurement or land records.

## Institutional Capacity and Regulatory Frameworks

The last challenge is the one that is least addressed, and that is a lack of institutional readiness. The majority of the urban governments do not have the internal skills to design and implement, and administer blockchain solutions. Even good-looking pilot projects can be stalled or killed by bureaucratic inertia, inflexible procurement practices, and inexperience in the way decentralized models of governance work.

In addition, blockchain raises a question of regulation. Issues like whether smart contracts are enforceable under the law, the validation of digital signatures, and who is to blame in case of an error in the blockchain are answered by most jurisdictions. The cities should look into capacity-building initiatives among their employees, such as training IT experts, administrators, and legal officers about how blockchain works and how these entities should be governed. Learning and experimentation can be sped up through partnerships with universities, tech hubs, and vendors in the private sector. At the same time, urban areas must collaborate with the national governments to have definite regulatory frameworks on how blockchain can be used in public systems. These are legalizing blockchain documents, standards of compliance in regards to smart contracts, as well as how to go about solving disputes. Experiments with blockchain can be held in regulatory sandboxes, which are already working in Singapore and the UAE: the company performing this experiment can avoid legal risks in a controlled environment.

## Governance Complexity in Multi-Stakeholder Ecosystems

The urban systems imply the presence of various networks of participants, involved in it, such as municipal agencies, utility companies, contractors, citizens, civil society groups, and even international donors. When a blockchain solution is implemented in such a decentralized governance system, the process brings about issues with coordination and ownership. The motifs and interests of individual actors can vary greatly, as well as their degree of technical competence and comfort with openness. Smart contracts can also lead to conflicts regarding the sharing of the data, gaining access, or having control of the smart contract.

An example of this is that a plan to implement a consortium blockchain to manage public infrastructure procurement may need to harmonize governance rules, dispute resolution, and other shared responsibilities, areas in which power imbalances and politics can impede action. In order to address such a complexity, cities ought to establish the contemporary mechanisms of both blockchain consortia governance and blockchain consortia governance that have responsibilities, roles, voting rights, and dispute resolution mechanisms. Such frameworks should be developed in participatory workshops or roundtables with stakeholders involved to establish trust and buy-in, with pilot projects starting with a small, representative group of stakeholders, and working out a model before engaging in wider collaborations. Governance of Blockchain, such as the management of nodes, updating protocols, and hierarchies of decision-making, needs to be thought about initially instead of being added later.

## Ethical Risks and Algorithmic Bias

Smart contracts and algorithmic decision-making in blockchain applications being used in the urban context present questions of ethics, especially when the consequences of automation are eligibility for a service, or allocation of resources. The risk of matrix errors occurs in courts, to cite a recent example, subsidized housing, granny flats, and identity checks.

In addition, blockchain immutability has the potential of making mistakes or having outdated information permanently encoded into it, and injustices might be impossible to correct, and policies might not be able to be changed with time. Once implemented, a smart contract with an unfair logic would not be updated quickly. City projects using blockchain should not take place without the following style of analysis, such as the one applied to public policy or AI. They ought to evaluate the goodness, visibility, and flexibility of smart contract logic. Human in the loop system must be involved to enable discretion or appeal of sensitive decisions. To reduce bias and hold them accountable, regular audits, a citizen feedback loop, and impact assessment of algorithms can be introduced. Also, the implementation of ethical principles (e.g., transparency, explainability, reversibility) should be incorporated into the charters of blockchain projects and procurement regulations at the early phases.

## Citizen Awareness and Digital Literacy Gaps

To increase civic trust through blockchain systems, you need to make sure that citizens are familiar with the technology and that they are comfortable using it. Digital divide and illiteracy are huge issues in most cities, especially in the Global South, isolating or leaving out the majority of the population. Unless there are special measures, blockchain-enabled platforms will be used as the plaything of the elite who are likely to be tech-savvy or well-plasticated.

As an illustration, suppose the participatory budgeting system is transferred to a blockchain application, then the poor or the older members of the population will not be able to vote on the budget since they do not have the necessary smartphones or an internet connection, thus being underrepresented in the civic sphere. Governments need to combine the use of blockchains with digital inclusion policies, including mobile-friendly interfaces, authentications in local languages, and offline authentication options. Trust and increased knowledge among the users can be established through community workshops, awareness campaigns, and association with the local NGOs. Emphasis should not be put on the technical process of blockchain in public education, but rather on its applicability; what the blockchain changes for the citizen. Early testing and feedback, including marginalized communities, can aid the co-design of inclusive tools by addressing a variety of user needs.

## Data Quality and On-Chain Garbage Risk

Blockchain will only guarantee that a document cannot be tampered with, but it does not mean that the information that is submitted is accurate or credible when it is first put in. This contributes to the so-called and much-maligned problem of garbage in, immutable garbage out. In case of corrupted, malicious, or biased data uploaded into a blockchain, it gets fixed in the system and can distort the decision-making process, provoke a reputational setback, or be used to commit fraud.

Using a technical example, when wrong land ownership information is entered and authorized on-chain, it will constitute a permanent record on which legal place takeover decisions can be made, or through which an illegal sale will be facilitated. Cities have to come up with strong data validation procedures and quality control checks prior to the information being written into the blockchain. These are employing proven oracles, auto cross-check using the available databases, and a multi-approval flow. In cases where possible, blockchain ought to be applied with those trusted identity and data certification systems (e.g., notarized uploads, digital signature verification). Also, blockchain designs must comprise metadata relative to the origins of the data, time-stamps, and journey of verification to enable tracing and bringing things right via add-on transactions (excision of initial documentations).

*Figure 5. Blockchain challenges and their impacts on urban governance*

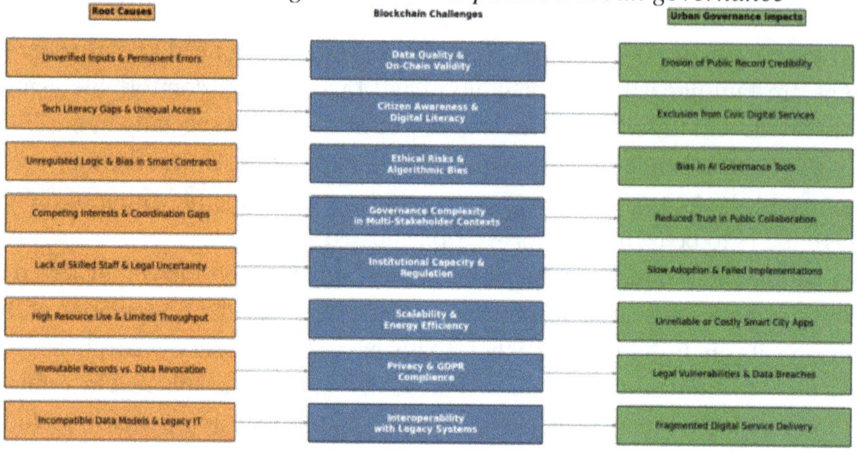


Urban implementation of blockchain does not represent just a technical project but rather a strong socio-political change that concerns governance issues, morals, and fairness. Although the list of challenges is long (the issues of interoperability and privacy, ethical risks, and data quality), these are not impossible to overcome. The risks can be overcome through intelligent planning, inclusive governance, and ethical design, through which cities can realize the promise of blockchain to create transparent, trusted, and people-focused cities of the future. These widened implementation challenges are ignored, and this means that blockchain is not only digitalizing bureaucracy, but it is changing it into the service of the common good.

## CONCLUSION

This can be really transformative, not just service delivery, but also the field of urban governance in general, once blockchains are fully integrated into urban systems. At its heart, blockchain questions the concentration of power of the past and its opacity in governing cities and offers processes, instead, that encourage transparency, auditability, and collective control. With unchangeable data and distributed verification, blockchain can make government actions subject to tamper-free log keeping, whether in land, procurement, or identity management. An effective implementation of this shift has the ability to make citizens have renewed faith in the existence of the public institutions, in particular scenarios where citizens have lost trust due to corruption or inefficiency, as the case may be. In addition, blockchain creates new opportunities for participatory decision-making and the empowerment of citizens. Decentralized applications (dApps) and smart contracts can enable direct participation of the population in the actions: participation in participatory budgeting, consultations on urban planning, and control over the work of municipal services. There is no need now to rely only on the belief of the intermediaries; one can check the decisions on his/her own, can check service delivery rates, and even run and co-govern some parts of urban infrastructure. This helps encourage a less exclusive and more open form of civic engagement, which is enhanced where mobile usage is combined with streamlined interfaces that can reduce the participation threshold.

Nonetheless, such opportunities have to be approached cautiously. The dangers of techno-solutionism, which is the idea that only technology is capable of producing viable solutions to thorny social and political issues, are real. Blockchain, as all-mighty, is not able to replace institutional reform, ethical leadership, and the will of the people. In addition, not every citizen can equally access digital tools or be literate in using them, which is a question of equity and digital inequalities. Unless the implementation is comprehensive, the blockchain might intensify and not mitigate the extant disparities in the engagement with cities and services. In order to effectively gauge the effectiveness of blockchain in enhancing civic trust, cities have to come up with transparent measures and models for assessing the effectiveness. These can be volumes of public audit trails, decreases in personal complaints on services or corruption incidents, citizen satisfaction polls, and acceptances of blockchain-empowered applications. The extent of transparency should be quantifiable, and confidence should be gained by showing better governance results, not by the advancement of technology. Collectively, however, the evidence that has been discussed above is pointing towards the idea that blockchain is not a universal solution, but rather a very effective instrument in the arsenal of an urban policymaker when deployed strategically, responsibly, and with an eye clearly aimed at governance reform. The greatest evidence of blockchain is that it creates institutional integrity, lowers traffic-clogging transactions, and enhances a high level of confidence. However, there is a need to be realistically aware of the implementation issues faced by the cities, especially regarding the cost, capacity, interoperability, and privacy compliance.

The most important recommendation to urban planners and municipal governments is to begin with baby steps: by undertaking pilot projects in one of land titling, procurement transparency, or utility billing, it is most effective to analyze the results and listen to the citizens. They must make an attempt to establish multi-stakeholder coalitions, which would entail technologists, civil society, academia, and proprietary innovators in the private sector. These collaborations would co-design the governance models, establish standards of ethical integrity, and hint at how blockchain implementations are built on a case-by-case basis, making them citizen-friendly. The call to technologists and platform developers is to put interoperability, usability, and security by design first. The solutions also must conform to the current urban workflows and should be flexible in regard to various regulatory and infrastructural requirements. Scalable and open collaborative development, as well as the reduced tendency to vendor lock-in, can be facilitated by open-source platforms and standards-based solutions.

## REFERENCES


Adjorlolo, G., Tang, Z., Wauk, G., Adu Sarfo, P., Braimah, A. B., Blankson Safo, R., & N-yanyi, B. (2025). Evaluating Corruption-Prone Public Procurement Stages for Blockchain Integration Using AHP Approach. *Systems 2025, Vol. 13, Page 267, 13*(4), 267. DOI: 10.3390/SYSTEMS13040267

Akram, W., Joshi, R., Haider, T., Sharma, P., Jain, V., Garud, N., & Singh, N. (2024). Blockchain technology: A potential tool for the management of the pharma supply chain. *Research in Social & Administrative Pharmacy, 20*(6), 156–164. DOI: 10.1016/J.SAPHARM.2024.02.014 PMID: 38423927

Al Barat, M. M., Li, S., Du, C., Hou, Y. T., & Lou, W. (2024). SoK: Public Blockchain Sharding. *2024 IEEE International Conference on Blockchain and Cryptocurrency, ICBC 2024*, 766–783. DOI: 10.1109/ICBC59979.2024.10634422

Alaa, W. (2025). Optimization Solution Proposal for Smart Transaction Security of Smart Blockchain Contracts in E-Banking Applications. In *Sustainable Information Security in the Age of AI and Green Computing* (pp. 295–320). IGI Global Scientific Publishing.

Ali, S. I., Shaikh, M. S., Patidar, P. K., & Pagare, S. (2025). Reimagining Urban Mobility. Leveraging VANETs and Blockchain Technology for Urban Mobility, 29–44. : DOI: 10.4018/979-8-3373-0265-2.CH002

Alves Batista, D. (2024). Enhancing transparency and accountability in public procurement: Exploring blockchain technology to mitigate records fraud. *Records Management Journal, 34*(2–3), 151–170. DOI: 10.1108/RMJ 10 2023 0054/FULL/XML

Asimakopoulos, G., Antonopoulou, H., Giotopoulos, K., & Halkiopoulos, C. (2025). Impact of Information and Communication Technologies on Democratic Processes and Citizen Participation. *Societies 2025, Vol. 15, Page 40, 15*(2), 40. DOI: 10.3390/SOC15020040

Badran, A. (2024). *Delivering Public Service in the Age of Digital Era Governance*. 407–440. : Bahrepour, D., & Maleki, R. (2024). Benefit and limitation of using blockchain in smart cities to improve citizen services. *GeoJournal, 89*(2), 1–14. DOI: 10.4018/979-8-3693-7678-2.CH013

Bellaj, B., Ouaddah, A., Bertin, E., Crespi, N., & Mezrioui, A. (2024). Drawing the Boundaries Between Blockchain and Blockchain-Like Systems: A Comprehensive Survey on Distributed Ledger Technologies. *Proceedings of the IEEE, 112*(3), 247–299. DOI: 10.1109/JPROC.2024.3386257

Biasin, M., & Delle Foglie, A. (2024). Blockchain and Smart Cities for Inclusive and Sustainable Communities: A Bibliometric and Systematic Literature Review. *Sustainability 2024, Vol. 16, Page 6669, 16*(15), 6669. DOI: 10.3390/SU16156669

Burgess, P., Sunmola, F., & Wertheim-Heck, S. (2024). Information needs for transparency in blockchain-enabled sustainable food supply chains. *International Journal of Information Management Data Insights, 4*(2), 100262. DOI: 10.1016/J.JJIMEI.2024.100262

Chen, X., He, S., Sun, L., Zheng, Y., & Wu, C. Q. (2024). A Survey of Consortium Blockchain and Its Applications. *Cryptography 2024, Vol. 8, Page 12, 8*(2), 12. DOI: 10.3390/CRYPTOGRAPHY8020012

Cui, Y., Gaur, V., & Liu, J. (2024). Supply Chain Transparency and Blockchain Design. *Management Science, 70*(5), 3245–3263. DOI: 10.1287/MNSC.2023.4851/ASSET/IMAGES/LARGE/MNSC.2023.4851F4.JPEG

Curry, D. (2025). Limitations of trust and legitimacy in blockchain: Exploring the effectiveness of decentralisation, immutability and consensus mechanisms in blockchain governance. *International Journal of Public Sector Management, 38*(1), 98–117. DOI: 10.1108/IJPSM-12-2023-0368/FULL/XML

Damaševičius, R., Bacanin, N., & Nayyar, A. (2025). Blockchain technology for a trustworthy social credit system: implementation and enforcement perspectives. *Cluster Computing 2024 28:3, 28*(3), 1–41. DOI: 10.1007/S10586-024-04890-W

Dehouche, N. (2025). Blockchain as urban governance infrastructure in private cities: An exploratory review. *Frontiers in Sustainable Cities, 7*, 1594711. DOI: 10.3389/FRSC.2025.1594711

Din, J., & Su, H. (2024). Blockchain-Enabled Smart Grids for Optimized Electrical Billing and Peer-to-Peer Energy Trading. *Energies 2024, Vol. 17, Page 5744, 17*(22), 5744. DOI: 10.3390/EN17225744

Dorostkar, E., & Ziari, K. (2025). Leveraging NFTs for sustainable urban finance: Challenges and opportunities for smart cities. *Cities (London, England), 163*, 106013. DOI: 10.1016/J.CITIES.2025.106013

Ghosh, S., Islam, S. K. H., & Vasilakos, A. V. (2024). Private Blockchain-Assisted Certificateless Public Key Encryption with Multikeyword Search for Fog-Based IIoT Environments. *IEEE Internet of Things Journal, 11*(19), 30847–30863. DOI: 10.1109/JIOT.2024.3415676

Giamberardino, G. G., Gadda, T. M. C., & Nagalli, A. (2024). Using blockchain technology for sustainable public procurement of road works. *Revista de Administração Pública*, *58*(3), e2023–e0073. DOI: 10.1590/0034-761220230073

Giri, A., Sagarnal, A. V., Chinmaya, R., & Dammur, A. (2024). Enhancing Efficiency in Smart Grid Billing with Blockchain Technology and Smart Contracts. *2nd International Conference on Sustainable Computing and Smart Systems, ICSCSS 2024 - Proceedings*, 586–594. DOI: 10.1109/ICSCSS60660.2024.10625244

Habib, A., Alnaemi, A., & Habib, M. (2024). Developing a framework for integrating blockchain technology into earthquake risk mitigation and disaster management strategies of smart cities. *Smart and Sustainable Built Environment, ahead-of-print*(ahead-of-print). DOI: 10.1108/SASBE-12-2023-0376/FULL/XML

Hamoud, D. T. (2025). Security Cooperation in the Protection Concerns of Agriculture Data Using Efficient Signatures and Artificial Bee Colony Manner. In Sustainable *Information Security in the Age of AI and Green Computing* (pp. 439-460). IGI Global Scientific Publishing.

Hasan, F. A., Ashqar, H. I., Alsobeh, A., & Darwish, O. (2024). Blockchain-Based National Digital Identity Framework - Case of Palestine. *2024 International Conference on Intelligent Computing, Communication, Networking and Services, ICCNS 2024*, 76–83. DOI: 10.1109/ICCNS62192.2024.10776538

Ibrahimy, M. M., Norta, A., Normak, P., & Nowandish, H. (2025). Transforming e Participatory Budgeting With Blockchain: Boosting Transparency and Citizen Engagement. *IEEE Transactions on Engineering Management*, *72*, 1376–1403. DOI: 10.1109/TEM.2025.3556191

Karger, E., Rothweiler, A., Brée, T., & Ahlemann, F. (2025). Building the Smart City of Tomorrow: A Bibliometric Analysis of Artificial Intelligence in Urbanization. *Urban Science 2025, Vol. 9, Page 132*, *9*(4), 132. DOI: 10.3390/URBANSCI9040132

Lartey, D., & Law, K. M. Y. (2025). Artificial intelligence adoption in urban planning governance: A systematic review of advancements in decision-making, and policy making. *Landscape and Urban Planning*, *258*, 105337. DOI: 10.1016/J.LANDURBPLAN.2025.105337

Lawal, O. O., & Nawari, N. O. (2024). Blockchain-Enabled City Information Modeling Framework for Urban Asset Management. *Journal of Architectural Engineering*, *30*(3), 04024020. DOI: 10.1061/JAEIED.AEENG-1644;WGROUP:STRING:PUBLICATION

Lax, G., Nardone, R., & Russo, A. (2024). Enabling secure health information sharing among healthcare organizations by public blockchain. *Multimedia Tools and Applications, 83*(24), 64795–64811. DOI: 10.1007/S11042-024-18181-4/FIGURES/4

Lee, J., & Yang, B. (2025). Enhancing smart city infrastructure with a geospatial blockchain-based addressing system. *Cities (London, England), 159*, 105757. DOI: 10.1016/J.CITIES.2025.105757

Ma, X., Li, J., Guo, Z., & Wan, Z. (2024). Role of big data and technological advancements in monitoring and development of smart cities. *Heliyon, 10*(15). Advance online publication. DOI: 10.1016/J.HELIYON.2024.E34821/ASSET/369ACF92-71A7-4F1C-BCDE-215A81607B66/MAIN.ASSETS/GR6.JPG PMID: 39165964

Mehmood, R., Yigitcanlar, T., & Corchado, J. M. (2024). Smart Technologies for Sustainable Urban and Regional Development. *Sustainability 2024, Vol. 16, Page 1171, 16*(3), 1171. DOI: 10.3390/SU16031171

Meneguzzo, S., Selabi, E. G. K., Favenza, A., Gatteschi, V., & Schifanella, C. (2024). Enabling Citizen Sustainable Behaviors in Urban Mobility through Blockchain and Tokenization. *Blockchain Technology in the Automotive Industry*, 245–279. DOI: 10.1201/9781003450306-17/ENABLING-CITIZEN-SUSTAINABLE-BEHAVIORS-URBAN-MOBILITY-BLOCKCHAIN-TOKENIZATION-SILVIO-MENEGUZZO-ELVIS-GERARDIN-KONJOH-SELABI-ALFREDO-FAVENZA-VALENTINA-GATTESCHI-CLAUDIO-SCHIFANELLA

Miron, R., Hulea, M., Muresan, V., Clitan, I., & Rusu, A. (2025). Integrating Blockchain Technology into Mobility-as-a-Service Platforms for Smart Cities. *Smart Cities 2025, Vol. 8, Page 9, 8*(1), 9. DOI: 10.3390/SMARTCITIES8010009

Mlika, F., Karoui, W., & Ben Romdhane, L. (2024). Blockchain solutions for trustworthy decentralization in social networks. *Computer Networks, 244*, 110336. DOI: 10.1016/J.COMNET.2024.110336

Mustafa, G., Rafiq, W., Jhamat, N., Arshad, Z., & Rana, F. A. (2025). Blockchain-based governance models in e-government: A comprehensive framework for legal, technical, ethical and security considerations. *International Journal of Law and Management, 67*(1), 37–55. DOI: 10.1108/IJLMA-08-2023-0172/FULL/XML

Oh, S. E., Kim, J. H., Kim, J. Y., & Ahn, J. H. (2025). Food Safety Distribution Systems Using Private Blockchain: Ensuring Traceability and Data Integrity Verification. *Foods 2025, Vol. 14, Page 1405, 14*(8), 1405. DOI: 10.3390/FOODS14081405

Piccardo, G., Conti, L., & Martino, A. (2024). Blockchain Technology and Its Potential to Benefit Public Services Provision: A Short Survey. *Future Internet 2024, Vol. 16, Page 290, 16*(8), 290. DOI: 10.3390/FI16080290

Przeybilovicz, E., & Cunha, M. A. (2024). Governing in the digital age: The emergence of dynamic smart urban governance modes. *Government Information Quarterly*, *41*(1), 101907. DOI: 10.1016/J.GIQ.2023.101907

Quan, B. L. Y., Wahab, N. H. A., Al-Dhaqm, A., Alshammari, A., Aqarni, A., Razak, S. A., & Wei, K. T. (2025). Recent Advances in Sharding Techniques for Scalable Blockchain Networks: A Review. *IEEE Access : Practical Innovations, Open Solutions*, *13*, 21335–21366. DOI: 10.1109/ACCESS.2024.3523256

Rahman, F., Titouna, C., & Nait-Abdesselam, F. (2024). Fundamentals of Blockchain and Smart Contracts. *Blockchain and Smart-Contract Technologies for Innovative Applications*, 3–37. DOI: 10.1007/978-3-031-50028-2_1

Rasha, R. (2025). Combining Fog Computing and Blockchain Based on the Internet of Medical Things to Preserve Patient Information Privacy. In *Sustainable Information Security in the Age of AI and Green Computing* (pp. 525–546). IGI Global Scientific Publishing.

Shamsan Saleh, A. M. (2024). Blockchain for secure and decentralized artificial intelligence in cybersecurity: A comprehensive review. *Blockchain: Research and Applications*, *5*(3), 100193. DOI: 10.1016/J.BCRA.2024.100193

Shevchuk, R., Lishchynskyy, I., Ciura, M., Lyzun, M., Kozak, R., & Kasianchuk, M. (2025). Application of Blockchain Technology in Emergency Management Systems: A Bibliometric Analysis. *Applied Sciences 2025, Vol. 15, Page 5405, 15*(10), 5405. DOI: 10.3390/APP15105405

Šilenskytė, A., Butkevičienė, J., & Bartminas, A. (2024). Blockchain-based connectivity within digital platforms and ecosystems in international business. *Journal of International Management*, *30*(3), 101109. DOI: 10.1016/J.INTMAN.2023.101109

Takahashi, T., Zhihao, Y., & Omote, K. (2024). Emergency Medical Access Control System Based on Public Blockchain. *Journal of Medical Systems*, *48*(1), 1–10. DOI: 10.1007/S10916-024-02102-X/TABLES/2 PMID: 39298041

Tang, M., Dai, W., Yin, C., Hu, B., Chen, J., & Liu, H. (2024). Spatial Planning Data Structure Based on Blockchain Technology. *ISPRS International Journal of Geo-Information 2024, Vol. 13, Page 290, 13*(8), 290. DOI: 10.3390/IJGI13080290

Wang, M., Zhu, T., Zuo, X., Ye, D., Yu, S., & Zhou, W. (2024). Public and Private Blockchain Infusion: A Novel Approach to Federated Learning. *IEEE Internet of Things Journal, 11*(10), 17525–17537. DOI: 10.1109/JIOT.2024.3360129

Wid, J., Razzaq, R., & Tahayur, D. (2024). Blockchain and cryptography framework of e-apps with big data. *Journal of Education for Pure Science, 14*(3).

Yuan, F., Huang, X., Zheng, L., Wang, L., Wang, Y., Yan, X., Gu, S., & Peng, Y. (2025). The Evolution and Optimization Strategies of a PBFT Consensus Algorithm for Consortium Blockchains. *Information 2025, Vol. 16, Page 268, 16*(4), 268. DOI: 10.3390/INFO16040268

Zachariah, M., Avanesh, N. M., & Raghupathi, K. (2025). Application of blockchain technology in disaster risk management. *The Role of Blockchain in Disaster Management*, 87–110. DOI: 10.1016/B978-0-443-13472-2.00004-8

## KEY TERMS AND DEFINITIONS

**Blockchain:** A decentralized, immutable digital ledger technology that records transactions in a secure and transparent manner across distributed nodes.

**Consensus Mechanism:** A protocol used by blockchain networks to achieve agreement among distributed nodes about the validity of transactions.

**Decentralization:** The distribution of authority and decision-making away from a central entity, ensuring that no single node controls the blockchain system.

**Immutability:** The property of blockchain that ensures once data is recorded and verified, it cannot be altered or deleted.

**Smart Contracts:** Self-executing code stored on a blockchain that automatically enforces the terms of an agreement when predefined conditions are met.

**Tokenization:** The process of representing physical or digital assets as cryptographic tokens on a blockchain, allowing fractional ownership and traceability.

**Transparency:** The ability of stakeholders to access, view, and verify transactions on the blockchain in real time, enhancing accountability.

**Urban Governance:** The framework of rules, institutions, and practices that guide decision-making and service delivery in cities.

# Chapter 10
# The Future of Secure Communication in Urban Environments: Challenges and Innovations

**V. Nivas Kumar**
https://orcid.org/0009-0003-6080-3999
*Jawahar Engineering College, India*

**T. P. Anish**
https://orcid.org/0000-0002-4308-9645
*R.M.K. College of Engineering and Technology, India*

**M. G. Dinesh**
https://orcid.org/0009-0009-7643-5338
*Easa College of Engineering and Technology, India*

## ABSTRACT

*Secure communication in urban environments is becoming increasingly vital as cities embrace smart technologies, IoT, and digital infrastructures. This chapter surveys the challenges and innovations associated with ensuring secure communication in modern urban settings. It highlights key issues such as scalability, real-time constraints, and the integration of legacy systems. Furthermore, the chapter discusses emerging solutions like AI-driven threat detection, federated learning, zero trust architectures, and quantum-resistant cryptography. The need for interdisciplinary collaboration is emphasized to tackle both technological and regulatory challenges. As cities become more interconnected, securing communication networks becomes*

DOI: 10.4018/979-8-3373-8133-6.ch010

*crucial to maintaining the privacy, integrity, and resilience of urban systems. This chapter outlines the future directions and the role of innovation in addressing these pressing security concerns.*

## INTRODUCTION

The modern urban environment is characterized by critical services and infrastructure that are increasingly dependent on digital networks of communication in order to deliver functionality. The nature of urban life is based on stable and assured communication, such as running public transport, traffic flow, emergency response organization, medical services, financial services, and smart city systems. Cities become hyper-connected, and the technologies 5G, IoT, edge computing, and AI, and the amount of data that is exchanged between the public and the private network devices are increasing exponentially. This is not the flow of data and the connectivity that makes such growth efficient and innovative, but it compensates severely with integrity, confidentiality, and availability problems of communication systems. These locations are very vulnerable to cyber-attacks because of the population concentration in cities, the presence of significant infrastructure, and the fact that they support very interdependent systems. Any malfunction in communication networks may prove to be counterproductive due to the cessation of transportation services, disruption of a power grid, disruption of health care services, or hijacking or emergency response systems (Kaneti et al., 2025). These kinds of threats demonstrate the importance of a high level of cybersecurity in the real-time communication environment, in which even temporary vulnerabilities can lead to large-scale and long-term consequences (Adejumo, A., and Ogburie, C. 2025).

### Motivation

Smart cities are complicated systems and designs of gadgets that are constantly interacting with each other to enhance the living standard, and thus appealing to cybercriminals. These vulnerable areas may be used as an example to halt gridlock traffic control systems or big-scale financial fraud systems. Consequently, the technical requirement of urban communication networks' resilience is not a problem; instead, it is an issue of national security and population safety. Governments of the countries, technology firms, cybersecurity researchers, as well as policy makers, are putting their hands in ensuring that the urban communication networks are safe and resilient in the event of these threats. It entails enacting encryption regulations, creating network tracking and threat detection capabilities, creating cyber incident action plans, and creating regulatory provisions that enact high-security requirements within the realms of digital services (Hammed, 2025). It is also marked by an increase in the use of AI-facilitated security systems to respond to a threat in a shorter time. Smart cities, although already becoming smart, urban centers that apply the newest technologies cannot afford to ignore the safety of digital communication networks. These networks are critical to the sustainability of delivering the most vital services, and the guarantee that people place in the digital infrastructure and security against cyber-attack is paramount (Ganapathi, P., & Shanmugapriya, D. 2019).

## Definitions and Scope

This chapter explores this critical issue of secure communications in urban spaces, both in the real world and within the virtual world, in terms of physical structure and the complex digital mechanisms upon which the cities already existing are founded. The defendable process of the information exchange supporting the five fundamental principles of security that are confidentiality (ensuring that the information is not accessed by unauthorized entities), integrity (providing that the information is not changed), availability (meeting the requirement of the presence of systems and services), authentication (defining the identity of the entities that communicate with each other), and non-repudiation (ensuring that the information cannot be denied by the concerned entities) is known as secure communication. Within the context of city environments, the transmission of information between many systems and devices is known as safe communication. These are infrastructures and cloud or edge computing platforms, IoT sensors, autonomous vehicles, components, smart grid, and mobile phones of the public services.

The communication systems in the urban areas are very dense, heterogeneous, and dynamic, and hence very demanding. Its incorporation of modern smart devices (new wireless technologies) and software platforms, and old wired infrastructures and old protocols is merged. More and more such systems are powered by artificial intelligence (AI) that is capable of making real-time and fast decisions when the security, privacy, and safety of the general population are at stake. These layers provide the complexity of safe communication in urban areas, with a multi-layered concern. On the technical front, it has protocol-level solutions that incorporate protocol solutions of generic cryptographic schemes, secure routing schemes, intrusion detection systems, and real-time encryption techniques that have provided defense against networks. Operation level implies that cities are resilient, with resilient architectures, monitoring capabilities, threat detection, and fail-safes to maintain the most critical services despite the cyberattack (Sandhu, K. 2021). Not, however, to mention, of course, that it is not only a technical stratum, but also a social side of it. Standards and rules that are written and structures must exist in such a way that the security best practices are consistently and regularly applied through the public and the private sector, and this could not have been done in a vacuum without industry, regulators, or policy makers. We discuss the human factors, which are also crucial in terms of ensuring that the personnel are well trained, we are encouraging public awareness, and we are instilling moral concerns into AI-driven systems. We will touch on these interrelated facets, technical, operational, and societal, in this chapter to undertake an intensive survey of the tactics, issues, and future directions in ensuring the security of the urban communication systems, both of cryptographic protocols and massive architectural and regulatory directions.

## BACKGROUND AND CONTEXT

Over the last several decades, there has been an impressive growth in the area of communication in urban areas. The first description of cities was made in regard to the analog telephone network and radio-based communications systems that were conducive to voice communications and rudimentary messaging services. The legacy systems began to become very complicated digital ecosystems of interacting apparatuses and advanced networking technologies when urbanization began to gather speed, and demands for more sophisticated services became more complex. Mobile telecommunications and broadband internet have been the object of this evolution. The existing urban infrastructure was designed in such a way that there was a high-speed internet connection and a mobile network that ensures faster and reliable communication that is more available. This transition was so significant in order to stay at pace with the ever-increasing demands of the ever-expanding cities, which required effective communication in areas such as the provision of services to the people and business activities. The very high rate and the high increase in the density of urban population, among others, and the escalating demands of ubiquitous connectivity have led the cities to embrace the state-of-the-art wireless network and smart network paradigms.

### Development of Communication in Urban Areas

The introduction of 5G can be viewed as one of the most drastic developments in the development process. The characteristics of the next generation network technology are Ultra-low latency, huge bandwidth, and millions of devices to be connected. All these features have made 5G into a key enabler of smart cities, self-driving cars, remote healthcare, and real-time surveillance infrastructure that will depend on high-speed, consistent, and secure communication infrastructures. The concept of the Internet of Things (IoT) also helped to further evolve the urban communication systems that are able to interconnect billions of connected objects to the urban environment (Talari et al., 2017). The IoT comprises environmental devices, smart meters, smart traffic lights, surveillance video cameras, and wearable health trackers that generate colossal amounts of data that are central to making the urban services run effectively. The implementation of the IoT device data can be used to maximize energy consumption, to improve traffic flow, to enhance public safety, and to monitor the environment, etc., to make the cities smarter and more responsive to the residents.

These developments are being supplemented by the edge computing that is carrying processing power nearer to data sources. The time-critical applications like autonomous driving, emergency response, and traffic management, and edge nodes are significant because real-time decisions need to be made based on local information, instead of transmitting all the controls to the centralized cloud server. Decentralization minimizes the latency, efficiency, and resilience of responsiveness of urban systems. Major challenges have, however, been raised with these new advanced technologies. More active and diverse networks support modern cities' communication and incorporate the old networks in the modern digitalized ones. This has further complicated the efforts of assurance to ensure that urban communication networks are getting harder. As the amount of information passing through the urban areas becomes larger and larger, the threat of cyber-attacks, data leakage, and computer outages also becomes more significant. These networks must safeguard huge volumes of sensitive information that is transferred using those (Sharma & Gupta, 2024). That is end-to-end encryption, secure access controls, real-time intrusion detection, and strong network designs. The city is forced to address these new communication networks to ensure that its security is not jeopardized in the new digital era, together with its privacy and effectiveness.

## Security Requirements in Urban Communication

As the communication systems that support the urban areas are more interconnected and replaceable than ever before, there is a call for sound security mechanisms. Secure communication is not only the encryption of data, but also the entire domain of values aimed at securing the entire process of the information exchange lifecycle. The basic security requirements consist of confidentiality, which provides a sense that only the authorized individuals have access to the data. Integrity so as to ensure that the information does not get distorted or altered in transit, authentication to determine the identity of parties communicating, and non-repudiation to ensure that the users do not refute that they carried out the actions or messages they conveyed to them. The emergency response coordination, traffic control, and driverless car navigation have to be able to operate with minimum latency. Protection and performance conflict, which is referred to as latency, can be brought about by strong encryption and elaborate security measures. The city networks are also huge and varied, and they present special challenges. End-to-end security of a system is a very complicated task with millions of devices that are connected, different standards and protocols, and diverse manufacturers. Most of these gadgets have low processing power. Thus, the traditional security systems are extremely challenging to install at the cost of functionality. The urban communication systems must also be resilient to both intentional and unintentional cyber-associated attacks and system breakdown. They must propagate responsive security models capable of responding to future threats on the fly. With that, the light, scalable, and smart security solutions play a key role in ensuring trust and reliability in the current urban centers. The holistic method of securing the networks will be significant in ensuring that the next smart cities are successful, given that urban communication is still dynamic.

## URBAN COMMUNICATION SYSTEMS' THREAT LANDSCAPE

With cities increasingly turning into globalized digital networks, there is an ever-growing number of cybersecurity risks to them (Untawale, 2021). Mobile devices and Wi-Fi hotspots in the streets bring all the urban communication networks into one, be it autonomous vehicles and intelligent infrastructure, and provide an enormous potential to be innovative and efficient, as well as a high risk of attack by cybercriminals. One of the most popular risks to consider in such environments is Eavesdropping or the illegal capture of sensitive information on the way it is carried through networks. The most susceptible of them are those of the public Wi-Fi networks that are prevalent in cities and usually offer little to no encryption and very low security.

### Cybersecurity Threats

Attackers are able to tap personal data or financial information, or login credentials or confidential messages, and these are loosely secured connections that can be easily tapped by attackers, compromising both the privacy of personal and organizational data. The other threat that is related to cybersecurity is a Man in the Middle attack (MITM), which is a type of attack where the attacker intercepts the communication between two parties without their awareness (Yamini, B et al., 2024). This method allows the attackers to steal user credentials, financial transaction details, or even critical control signals of smart systems. For example, in a smart city, some MITM attacks on smart grid, surveillance system, or automated public service command and control data can cause their operations to be disrupted. A Distributed Denial-of-Service (DDoS) attack is a particularly dangerous threat to urban communication infrastructures. These are attacks that flood a server or network with enough traffic to make the server or network unavailable to legitimate users. A properly coordinated DDoS attack can disable transportation infrastructure, emergency services, medical care, or energy supply and result in mass disruption and even endanger lives. The second and more critical concern is spoofing attacks, where cybercriminals falsify the identity of a device or service, posing as a legitimate service or device. Specifically, it is crucial in systems in which the credibility of the device identity is crucial, e.g., an autonomous vehicle network or smart traffic management system. To illustrate, hacked signals by a hacker might steer self-driving cars to a traffic jam, a car crash, or mayhem on the urban roads. Moreover, the urban communication networks comprised of mobile and vehicular networks are not similar to the classical fixed line networks because they are dynamic, decentralized, and ever-changing.

These features render them more exposed to cyberattacks, and guarding a constantly migrating endpoint is much more complex. There are common malware attacks, unauthorized access, and signal hacking of the mobile communication devices employed in communicating with the smart city services. Vehicular Ad Hoc Networks (VANETs) are also vulnerable to data spoofing, alteration of messages, and GPS jamming since they provide real-time communication among cars and road infrastructure. The impacts of such attacks can be either road accidents or emergency service disruptions. As this landscape is such, cybersecurity is never a choice, but on the contrary, a necessity. In the absence of effective security that would help to mitigate the effects of a cyber-attack, these can be catastrophic, not only to the digital infrastructure but also to the physical infrastructure of the cities themselves. They will be dealt with considering the risks, and this will entail both the technical solutions as well as the regulatory policy and continuous monitoring of any threats to the future of urban communication networks.

## Physical and Environmental Threats

The other common cybersecurity risks to urban communication security are physical and environmental risks, which, however, should not be ignored. The urban communication systems are also significant in the physical infrastructures of the data centers, fiber optic cables, cell towers, power lines, routers, and network switches. Any intended attack has the capacity to bring down this infrastructure seriously. Physical damage to fiber lines, vandalism of cell towers, or an attack on power substations can put entire segments of the communication network of a city out of commission. The impacts of these attacks are much more far-reaching than communications since they also involve transportation systems, financial networks, emergency services, and public utilities and systems on which modern cities rely are closely interconnected. Or to take an example, an attack on just one large data center can result in the shutdown of internet-related services across groups of government departments, hospitals, banks, and public services, and the economy will be impacted, and safety and panic among the masses will be the outcome.

Fiber optic cables that are frequently buried in the ground or along sensitive routes are also very prone to a cut or broken line, which will instantly disconnect an urban centre from regional or national networks. Moreover, destruction of cell towers, which provide mobile phone and wireless communications, would also interfere with individual communications, mobile banking, and navigation systems, among others. This is the reason why it is significant to have security for digital systems as well as physical assets. Although deliberate attacks are certainly a threat to the resilience of urban communication networks, environmental and natural threats are also very serious threats. Natural disasters such as earthquakes, floods, hurricanes, wildfires, and severe storms can severely damage critical infrastructure. For example, hurricanes can take down power lines and cell towers, flood underground fiber networks, and burn down relay stations or edge computing nodes. Such events can be especially disastrous in cities with dense populations and complex infrastructure. Communication failure that complicates rescue operations, slows emergency response, and leaves citizens confused or unable to access critical information can result from natural disasters. It was during the COVID-19 pandemic that environmental threats were proven to be not only natural disasters, but also public health crises, which put strain on communications networks due to a sudden spike in demand for digital services such as telemedicine, online education, and remote work. Yet, to maintain operational continuity and be resilient in these physical and environmental threats, communication networks must be redundant, disaster-tolerant, and resilient. All of them involve the implementation of backup systems, establishing locations of data centers which are geographically dispersed or having more than one pathway of the network's major data, or investing in high physical security at the main points of infrastructure. Besides that, the renewable sources of energy and off-grid solutions are useful in keeping the operation going even during power outages. Smart cities should incorporate physical security, environmental risk management, and sound infrastructure design as a constituent of their future as an urban planning, policy, and technology provider collaboration. This allows them to maintain urban communication systems operational, resistant, and trustworthy to physical sabotage or natural catastrophe (Bhuvanya, R et al., 2025).

## Privacy Concerns

Privacy can be called one of the most burning and difficult issues of urban communication, and one of the most burning and difficult issues beyond technical and physical threats. Smart cities today are increasingly relying on surveillance systems, smart sensors, and data-driven services that are installed in both public areas and private ones. As much as all these technologies have been praised as measures to enhance efficiency in the city, their dominant resources and enhance the level of public safety, they come at an invisible cost, which is the huge amounts of personal data that are being collected, stored, and analyzed. The intelligent cities actively collect a huge volume of sensitive data on individuals, such as location, movement, communication records, buying habits, and biometric data (like faces or fingerprints) on a regular basis. To illustrate, artificial intelligence monitors potential threats in the public space, smart transport systems track the paths of commuters, wearable devices track personal health indicators, and surveillance cameras track their personal health data, and wearable devices will track their physical location. Naturally, such systems may include such benefits as faster emergency help or better traffic control, yet they are usually operated with minimum transparency and no external audit. The issue here is raised as to how one can guard the individual privacy rights and still address the demand of urban innovation and security. The threat of abuse is extremely high in cases when personal information gathered in cities will be utilized without any serious privacy protections and well-defined regulations.

Another misuse is commercial exploitation, e.g., by businesses profiling individuals to sell them to targeted advertisements or to influence consumer behavior based on personal information. The second threat is unauthorized profiling, which is the collection and analysis of sensitive data about people without their consent and can be used to reinforce the social biases that already exist or utilize them to discriminate. In technical, ethical, and even social aspects, the problem of urban privacy is a threat. As population density in cities rises and digital systems continue to be integrated into every aspect of life, people are losing control over the way their data is being collected, used, and shared. The majority of urban residents are unaware of the amount of data they are accumulating about themselves, or have other worthwhile alternatives as to how they can escape predatory tendencies in data collection. The ethical challenges posed by the continuously growing level of the dearth of control over individual information are serious threats to the bare minimum of independent and free lives in the contemporary urban environment.

In the multidimensional approach that involves the application of technology, policy, and civic participation, the urban communication in an urban setting must be privatized. In all the cities, technically, privacy-preserving technologies like data anonymization, encryption, and decentralized data storage may be applied. It is, however, required that the policymakers develop clear legal frameworks that explain who owns the data, what consent should be provided by the users, how long data can be stored, and how surveillance is restricted. Finally, civic involvement and community discussion should be considered to ensure the voice of residents in the digital agenda of the city and hold the institutions responsible. Integration of the two endeavors can, however, be employed in the creation of urban communication processes that are capable of bringing about both technological innovation and conserving and upholding the privacy rights of every individual.

## CENTRAL TECHNOLOGIES IN THE SECURE URBAN COMMUNICATION

### 5G and Beyond

The introduction of the 5G technology transformed the character of the city communication, and a new generation of applications and services previously impossible and unfeasible are now feasible. The smart city technologies, such as autonomous vehicles, remote healthcare and surgery, real-time traffic management, augmented and virtual reality, and industrial automation, are supported by 5G, which is enabled by its ultra-reliable low latency communication (URLLC), enhanced mobile broadband (eMBB), and massive machine type communication (mMTC). These uses are high data throughput, high speed, and highly secure data transmission, critical, and 5G is an important enabler to the urban digital transformation in such applications. One of the most innovative capabilities that 5G introduces to the table is network slicing, a network feature that enables network operators to create multiple virtual networks or so-called slices, even on a shared physical infrastructure. A slice can be customized to align with the needs in performance, reliability, and security.

As an example, a highly reliable low-latency slice of public safety communications can be deployed, and a slice customized to entertainment services, such as high definition video streaming, can be done. In the event that it is important to have a special secure communications channel dedicated to such important services as emergency response, healthcare, and infrastructure management, the versatility of this solution will allow the cities to do so without affecting the performance of other, less important applications. However, with 5G, that will be far more capable and complex, and the area of attack, the total number of points a malicious actor can attempt to obtain unauthorized access to, also increases. With the transition towards distributed architectures of the industry, where more intelligence and processing are moved to the network edge, new trust models are needed that must be secure. The end-to-end encryption, mutual authentication between devices and services, advanced intrusion detection, and real-time threat monitoring in both core and edge are needed in 5G networks, unlike the previous generation of networks, where much of the security is centralized. With this model being decentralized, many more diverse devices, applications, and paths of communication have to be secured. The vision of 6G that is currently being studied and is set to be commercially implemented is even more radical. 6G is projected to bring new levels of performance with potentially new technologies such as terahertz (THz) communication to support ultra-high data rates, native artificial intelligence (AI)-based networking capabilities with artificial intelligence literally installed into network management and optimization, and the merging of sensing and communication capabilities.

The potential of such innovations was possible, which would enable the application of holographic communication, more advanced robotics, and large-scale digital twins planning and management of smart cities. However, new security dilemmas have emerged due to these developments. As AI is integrated into the networks, it will use more frequency bands, increase the number of device ecosystems, and need flexible, adaptive, and intelligent security systems. This will therefore necessitate a shift in attitude to more dynamic security as opposed to passive security, which will be in a position to predict, identify, and counter an attack before it can lead to destruction. The security base will play a crucial role as much as the realization of technical performance milestones in a 6G future, so that a new generation of urban communications networks is robust and resilient. Figure 1 provides central technologies in the secure urban communication.

*Figure 1. Central technologies in the secure urban communication*

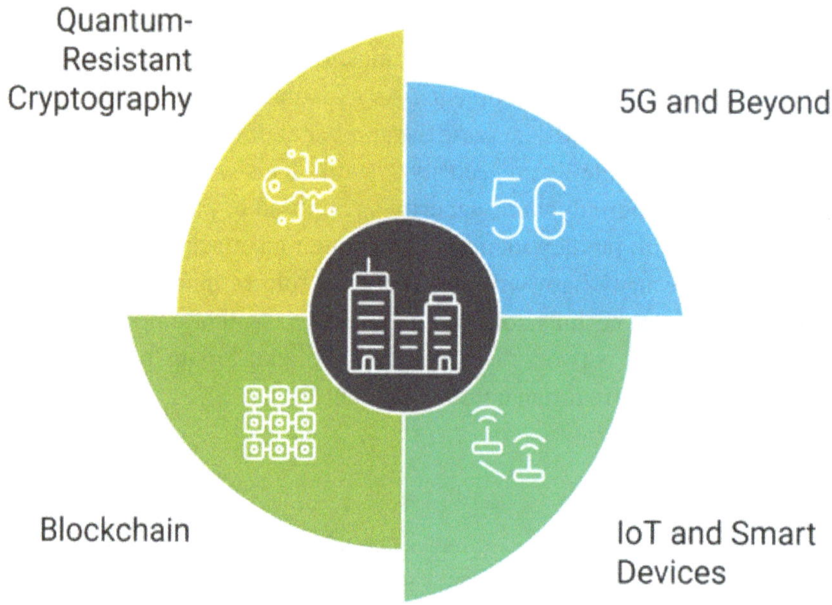


## Internet of Things (IoT) and Smart Devices

The current-day urban ecosystem is built on the IoT, with the existing environment, energy, transport, security systems, and even comforts of living being largely unknown in the past (Eswaran & Khang, A. 2024). Cities are becoming smarter places with billions of connected devices (sensors, cameras, smart meters, traffic lights, connected vehicles, wearable devices, and home automation systems) that are capable of capturing, analyzing, and acting on real-time data to make them more efficient, sustainable, and improve living conditions. However, such a landscape of IoT devices is enormous and non-homogeneous, and it comes with substantial vulnerabilities that may compromise the security and robustness of urban communication networks (Mehmood et al., 2017). Regrettably, due to the design of most IoT devices, which is to be low-powered, the amount of memory and energy is limited, resulting in few resources to run standard, resource-intensive security controls such as complicated encryption algorithms or multi-level authentication frameworks. To address this issue, researchers and engineers have developed lightweight cryptographic procedures and secure onboarding schemes that offer vital security without notifying the resource-constrained hardware. These are the solutions that are required so as to allow even the smallest devices to safely enter and work within the larger network ecosystem. Despite these innovations, the current IoT deployment is still sending too many devices to the world without default or weak credentials, old firmware, or unable to update over the air (OTA). Because of this, they, in particular, are attractive to attackers. The moment the IoT devices are hacked, they can be utilized in any form of wicked activities. To illustrate, they might be forced to participate in botnets in order to carry out distributed denial of service (DDoS) attacks that are able to bombard a target with traffic of thousands or millions of devices, rendering the critical city services unusable.

In other instances, users can be spied on by attackers, monitored, or have their sensitive personal information stolen through compromised gadgets. Further, the protection of the IoT infrastructure can be interrupted, which impacts the provision of essential city functions (e.g., energy delivery, traffic control, operation, healthcare delivery, etc.) on a large scale (Park et al., 2018). The need to find a solution that secures IoT endpoints is necessary in order to gain resilience and comprehensive security of the city's communication networks. It is not content with the attainment of the device, but security has to be exercised in the ecosystem. It requires default device-level protection, where it ensures safe boot-ups, equipment that is tamper-resistant, and regular updates to firmware, network-level control over aberrant behaviour, and cloud-level control and coordination of action among distributed systems. Also, it should have a good regulatory and policy framework that would offer minimum security standards to the manufacturers and service providers of the IoT. That may involve the capacity to make security certs mandatory, more stringent update and patching policies, and updates that allow users to customize default settings and see what is going on with the device easily. With the shift towards the IoT, the cities are increasingly reliant on it, and the protection of such devices is no longer the prerogative of technical challenges but the foundation of the performance, safety, and reliability of the contemporary smart city. The equipment, which is supposed to provide an urban advantage, can be the weakest link in the chain of security of the urban area without general protection.

## Blockchain and Distributed Ledger Technologies

Through blockchain and other distributed ledger technologies, the distributed ledger technologies provide a solution for enhancing trust, transparency, and security of the urban communication systems. The concept of blockchain enables the decentralization of control and removal of centralization of power to provide safe transactions and tamper-proof documentation in various applications in the city. That is why blockchain can be particularly handy in the situation of several mistrusted participants who interact, where all transactions can be proven, unchangeable, and traced (Shayea et al., 2025). Blockchain would offer a trusted program, such as a smart energy grid to smart cities, whereby the purchasing and selling of energy between the producers and the consumers would be registered without the middleman. The supply chain logistics are also significant as they will allow the city administrations and businesses to monitor goods and services in real-time in a transparent manner. The other big use of blockchain is the verification of digital identity, whereby citizens, devices, and services verify each other in a secure manner to reduce the likelihood of identity theft or identity fraud (Duaa, 2025). It removes single points of failure, thereby increasing the vulnerability of cyber-attacks and data breaches to the urban systems.

The ability to decentralize identity management and enable the latter to authenticate safely to the urban services without the central server is one of the largest benefits of blockchain that can decouple both the IoT devices and the users. However, it is particularly so in large, mixed environments, where centralized systems can become a bottleneck or point of attack. But blockchain has not been experiencing its potential without its ills, however, and especially in terms of its scalability and energy consumption, especially in large-scale urban or IoT applications (Raj et al., 2022). Mainstream public blockchains (such as cryptocurrency) are expensive in terms of consensus; they consume enormous processing and energy. To overcome them, certain researchers are working on permissioned blockchains that only trusted actors can participate in and coming up with lightweight consensus mechanisms unique to the application of the IoT and smart cities (Subhashini et al., 2023). Such innovations are to be made such that blockchain can be more scalable, more efficient, and find its application in real-world urban applications with which cities can build a more reliable and trustworthy digital ecosystem.

## Quantum-Resistant Cryptography

The imminent threat of quantum computing has also created interest in cryptographic algorithms that will be able to withstand attacks by quantum machines. A strong quantum computer can make many of the currently used encryption schemes, such as RSA and ECC, obsolete. Therefore, researchers are currently trying to create and standardize the post-quantum cryptographic (PQC) algorithms that are immune to classical and quantum attacks. For urban environments that use long-term infrastructure and secure archival, the switch to quantum-resistant cryptography is important. Incorporation of these algorithms into citywide systems requires being compatible with the existing protocols and supported by the hardware vendors.

## URBAN-SPECIFIC CHALLENGES

### Scalability and Heterogeneity

One of the unique features of the urban communication systems is the enormous scale and diversity. A smart city of the present day can consist of millions of interconnected devices that can be sensors, cameras, vehicles, wearables, and industrial systems, all of which generate data at any time. The scale and complexity of such a large and varied ecosystem demand framework of communication that are scalable and safe at every level. Another complexity is the variety of devices, which are different in terms of the hardware capabilities, software stacks, and communication protocols. The security of such a discontinuous landscape is extremely hard to maintain. The largest problem is the interoperability since the machines purchased by various companies could use their own standards, and secure communication and mutual authentication may be an option instead of a feature. This type of lack of standardization can result in the creation of silos of communication, incompletely bridged security protocols, and security monitoring blind spots. The capability of balancing between attaining scalability and interoperability, and on the one hand, without losing the high levels of security, is the attribute that requires specially-designed modular, flexible, and lightweight security solutions for urban environments. Figure 2 describes Urban-specific challenges.

*Figure 2. Urban-specific challenges*

## Mobility and Dynamic Topologies

It is a highly mobile environment with vehicles, transport systems, drones, and mobile users continuously moving in urban centers. It creates dynamic topologies wherein the network is reconfigured at a very high and unpredictable rate. The old security solutions are unable to accommodate such a change, and this renders them vulnerable and consumes time insofar as communication is concerned. In particular, the Vehicular Ad Hoc Networks (VANETs), which can be used to facilitate the vehicle and the roadside infrastructure communicating with one another, are highly susceptible to message spoofing, position, and denial of service attacks. Urban logistics and surveillance are also not areas where drones and autonomous robots are uncommon. These mobile nodes must establish secure identifications with centrally located systems and peer devices, without prejudice to the efficiency of the operation. These entities are constantly moving; the huge disparity between the signal strengths and the handoff processes demands a safe routing process, light encryption, and real-time authentication tools that are able to operate within highly dynamic environments.

## Real-Time Constraints

Numerous urban systems, such as emergency response management, traffic management, and industrial control, require real-time low-latency communication. Typical security features like encryption, authentication, and anomaly detection do, however, introduce latency. It is a gigantic trade-off of speed and security, and this is very specific where time is of the essence, and any kind of physical damage or any form of stagnation in the processes can be caused by delay. One of the most significant issues to this day is whether the systems that would guarantee a high level of security and the stringent needs of latency could be developed. The lines of approach currently in use, hardware-accelerated cryptography, context-aware security policies, and edge computing, are the ones that are being promised and are not yet deployed and standardized. The integration of the urban communication system demands a high level of security implementation as to be inextricably bound with the very essence of the design, in that the integrity of the data and the safety of the user are secured without any reduction in the real-time responsiveness.

### Legacy Systems and Integration

The old systems have generally been decades old in city systems. These may be outdated telecommunication systems, public safety systems, and industrial control systems that were not even targeted by modern-day cybersecurity attacks. The old encryption used in legacy systems to interact with new smart city systems has severe security concerns, as the old systems are not patchable, and modern authentication standards are absent. The task is to upgrade or retrofit the systems without any service interruption and excessive cost. Bridging solutions, including secure gateways and protocol converters, are able to minimise the risks, but they bring new points of vulnerability. Long-term solutions will involve strategic planning, investment in modernization, and the phased-out of insecure legacy infrastructure with a continuity of critical services.

## EMERGING SOLUTIONS AND INNOVATIONS

### AI and Machine Learning for Detection of Threats

As cyber threats in the urban communication systems become more advanced, static and rule-based security solutions are becoming less and less adequate. In turn, artificial intelligence (AI) and machine learning (ML) have become powerful devices for the creation of adaptive security systems that can change with the threats. These systems are capable of handling high levels of traffic and patterns of behaviors to determine anomalies that may indicate malicious activity - the unauthorized access, data leak, or a distributed denial-of-service (DDoS) attack. The artificial intelligence predictive analytics will be able to identify the possible weaknesses or vectors of attack beforehand, before they are exploited. As an illustration, ML models have the ability to monitor the cities of IoT networks and label the devices that do not behave normally or do not transmit large quantities of data. Real-time data can be trained on such tools, and they get better over time. In very dynamic cities, context-sensitive security enforcement can become scalable with AI since human supervision is not applicable at the scale and speed of human activities. However, the issue is that even the AI models themselves can still be vulnerable, and opponents may attempt to deceive them through various technologies such as data poisoning or adversarial attacks.

## Federated Learning and Edge Learning

Unlike the centralized urban systems, the decentralized nature of the urban systems renders federated learning (FL) and edge learning especially desirable when it comes to the need to ensure security and privacy. The data in conventional machine learning has to be centralized so that training can occur with severe privacy and bandwidth concerns. However, federated learning allows training AI models across a few devices or nodes located in a decentralized manner without necessarily transferring raw data to the cloud. Each participant trains a local model and only transmits the updated parameters, that does not disclose any confidential data, and they can learn jointly. Edge learning takes a step further and enables inference and model updates in real-time at the network end where the data is produced. This would mean that in an urban environment, the detection of threats can operate in a decentralized form, locally, and without a persistent connection to centralized cloud servers, identifying and reacting to threats. This is particularly true in applications where latency may be a very important consideration, e.g., in traffic management, smart grids, and emergency services. By utilizing FL and edge learning, cities will be able to implement privacy-preserving security models that abide by the sovereignty of the user data but remain able to offer good decentralized threat detection functions. The technologies are also effective in removing congestion in the network and reducing the chances of failure and attack on the centralized point of failure or attack. Figure 3 presents emerging solutions and innovations in smart cities.

*Figure 3. Emerging solutions and innovations*

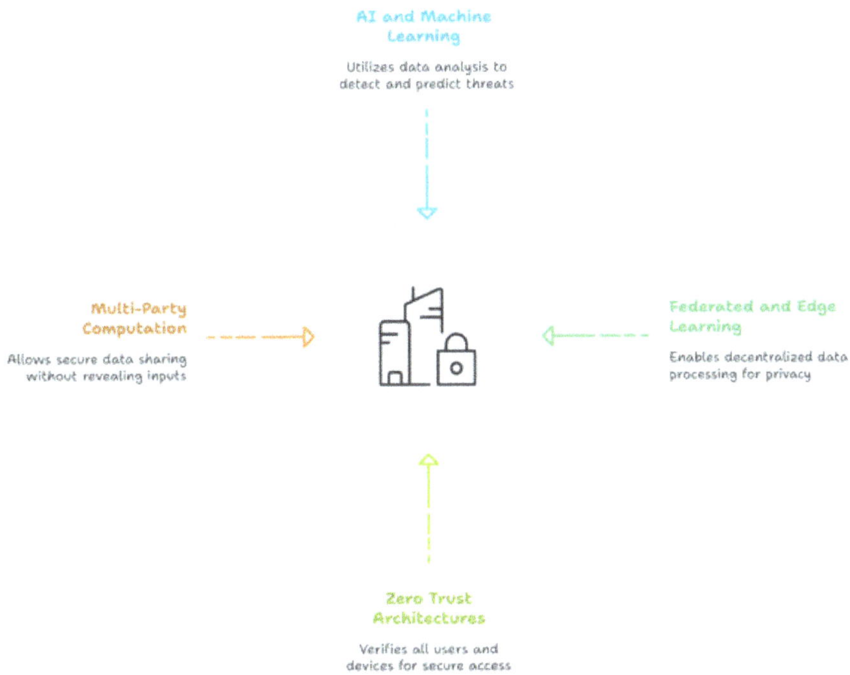


## Zero Trust Architecture (ZTA)

The classic security models assume that threats are external to the network, and this is why it takes the form of trust but verify. As compared to the scenario of Zero Trust Architecture (ZTA), which is anchored on the concept of never trust, always verify. This model is increasingly becoming applicable in urban regions where interaction is conducted between unequal and typically untrustworthy spaces, including public Internet, third-party devices, and infrastructure owned and operated by citizens. In a Zero Trust model, the authentication, authorization, and verification of every user, device, and service are done in real-time and all the time based on the prevailing circumstances before a user is allowed to access any resource. This type of access control is fine-grained, moves access policy dynamically, and offers micro-segmentation of networks, which restricts the harm that a compromised component can inflict. As cities grow and with their interconnection, zero trust models will be necessary as a continuous and adaptive security at scale.

### Multi-Party Computation and Homomorphic Encryption

The aspects of privacy and security are normally conflicting as long as there is data to be relayed between one department or agency to another within the city context. Secure Multi-Party Computation (SMPC) and Homomorphic Encryption (HE) are cryptographic schemes that allow multiple parties to compute on a common dataset without access to the original inputs. The approaches are especially useful in cooperative urban analytics like shared surveillance feeds, integrated traffic control systems, or health tracking, when the interested parties may need to operate the sensitive information without breaching the privacy. SMPC enables functions to be computed in a coordinated manner, with each entity having no knowledge besides the result. However, with homomorphic encryption, it is possible to perform computations using data that is encrypted, and encrypted results are obtained and decrypted to produce the final result. The recent advancement in optimization and the use of hardware acceleration, though computationally heavy, is influencing the implementation of these technologies in smart cities in reality.

## FUTURE DIRECTIONS

### Integration of Quantum Communication Networks

With threats from new technologies such as quantum computing looming over the classical cryptographic techniques, the development of quantum communication networks is emerging as a fast-developing, promising way of improving urban security. Quantum Key Distribution (QKD), an important part of these networks, utilizes the laws of quantum mechanics to allow for the unconditional key exchange, meaning that any attempt at eavesdropping will be noticeable immediately. In the future urban landscapes, QKD might be implemented into the core of metropolitan fiber-optic networks, ensuring safe connections between the vital nodes, such as data centers, hospitals, and governmental offices.

While the process of creating quantum internet infrastructure is still in its infancy, pilot projects in such cities as Beijing, Vienna, or Tokyo prove that urban deployment is possible. The issue is how to scale these systems, how to make them compatible with the classical networks, and how to pay the huge cost of deployment. However, as quantum hardware matures and costs go down, cities could start embracing quantum communication as a layered defense, especially for those sectors that require maximum confidentiality, such as finance, law enforcement, and emergency response.

## Role of Digital Identity and Secure Authentication in Urban Settings

The city communication networks are now depending on strong digital identity networks to be able to provide safe communication between people, appliances, and services. The consumers of the services are constantly surveilling themselves, not just in the real world but also in the virtual world through the application of public Wi-Fi, smart transportation systems, and e-government websites, as well as health services. A secure and sound authentication environment is very urgent for the establishment of trust and discouragement of unauthorized access. The trends indicate that the decentralized identity systems would be executed with the help of such technologies as the blockchain and the public key infrastructure (PKI). Through such models, the individual will have better control of his or her information and identity and will minimize the use of centralized databases that would be the victims of cyberattacks. In addition to that, the biometric authentication, multi-factor authentication (MFA), and behavioral analytics will have a larger contribution to the improvements of the urban identity systems. The interdependence between the digital identity and the mobile devices and wearable technologies may result in the interaction between the citizen and the urban services becoming frictionless and safe simultaneously, as it raises some grave issues of privacy and information control.

## Challenges and Innovations in Policy and Regulations

Communication technology has developed very fast in the urban environment, causing the frontline in policy development and in the regulation systems. The idea of urban communication protection does not imply the use of technical means only, but clear legal provisions, collaboration at the international level, and flexible management. The regulatory processes should answer such questions as data sovereignty, cross-border data flows, encryption standards, and also liability in the case of a cyber incident. It is probable that the direction of the policy in the future will include the idea of privacy by design, compulsory cybersecurity legislation on critical infrastructure, and responsibility for data abuse. Security and ethical issues should be taken into consideration at the stage of planning smart cities projects and involve both public and private stakeholders. The regulations should also be adapted to address the emerging ethical and legal issues by including new paradigms such as autonomous vehicles, drones, and AI-based decision-making systems.

## CONCLUSION

The necessity to guarantee security in the urban environment and the problem of the smart city era, the era of all-around connectivity, and the era of growing digital reliance, is a significant undertaking. A list of susceptibility to advanced cyberattacks, bodily framework, and confidentiality threats has been on a scalding frenzy alongside the flourishing gadgets, data, and flowing frameworks. The communication systems ensuring confidentiality, integrity, and availability are becoming more and more demanded due to the fact that cities are turning into complex digital ecosystems. The problems encountered in the metropolitan communication systems are diverse; some of them include scalability, heterogeneity, integration of old systems, and real-time problems. These are increased due to the new threats, such as quantum computing and greater vulnerability to data breaches due to unprotected IoT device networks. Nevertheless, the promising innovations in the sphere are on a wave. Such innovative technologies as AI-based threat detection, federated learning, zero-trust architecture, and quantum-resistant cryptography are an appealing promise against the dynamically decentralized nature of modern urban systems. Simultaneously, secure multi-party computation and homomorphic encryption establish the basis on which a privacy-guaranteeing partnership between different industries and stakeholders can take place. Although technological developments are carried out, secure urban communication cannot be fully dependent on innovation. It entails the necessity of the collaboration of an interdisciplinary nature, i.e., the collaboration of the technologists, policymakers, urban planners, legal experts, and civil society. This kind of collaboration is significant in the construction of robust regulatory systems, the creation of inclusive digital identities, and ensuring that the security solutions are morally upright and acceptable within society.

In the future, quantum communications, strong digital identity infrastructures, and adaptable governance will play a significant role in the development of secure and resilient cities of the future. The future is not conclusively simple, but the key to securing communication in the city lies in the capability to merge technology development and strategic alliance in a world where everyone knows each other.

## REFERENCES


Adejumo, A., & Ogburie, C. (2025). The role of cybersecurity in safeguarding finance in a digital era. *World Journal of Advanced Research and Reviews, 25.*

Bhuvanya, R., Mariammal, G., Sivakumar, K., Ganga, M., Anish, T. P., Swetha, S., & Subramanian, R. S. (2025). Revolutionizing Urban Planning: The Role of AI and Predictive Analytics in Sustainable City Development. *Leveraging Urban Computing for Sustainable Urban Development*, 303-322.

Duaa, T. (2025). Security Cooperation in the Protection Concerns of Agriculture Data Using Efficient Signatures and Artificial Bee Colony Manner. In *Sustainable Information Security in the Age of AI and Green Computing* (pp. 439–460). IGI Global Scientific Publishing.

Eswaran, U., & Khang, A. (2024). Application of Internet of things (IoT) and sensors technologies for agriculture. In *Advanced IoT Technologies and Applications in the Industry 4.0 Digital Economy* (pp. 158–172). CRC Press.

Ganapathi, P., & Shanmugapriya, D. (Eds.). (2019). *Handbook of research on machine and deep learning applications for cyber security*. IGI Global.

Hammed, M. (2025). A Critical Reliable Model for Promoting Patient Medical Wireless Sensors Information Security. *Procedia Computer Science*, *263*, 17–24.

Kaneti, V. R., Yamini, B., Nagarajan, S., Adaikkammai, A., Gracious, L. A., Subramanian, R. S., & Girija, P. (2025). Smart Transportation Systems and Sustainable Urban Mobility. In *Revolutionizing Urban Development and Governance with Emerging Technologies* (pp. 261–288). IGI Global Scientific Publishing.

Mehmood, Y., Ahmad, F., Yaqoob, I., Adnane, A., Imran, M., & Guizani, S. (2017). Internet-of-things-based smart cities: Recent advances and challenges. *IEEE Communications Magazine*, *55*(9), 16–24.

Park, E., del Pobil, A., & Kwon, S. (2018). The role of internet of things (IoT) in smart cities: Technology roadmap-oriented approaches. *Sustainability*, *10*(5), 1388.

Raj, E. F. I., Appadurai, M., Darwin, S., & Rani, E. F. I. (2022). Internet of things (IoT) for sustainable smart cities. In *Internet of things* (pp. 163–188). CRC Press.

Sandhu, K. (Ed.). (2021). *Handbook of research on advancing cybersecurity for digital transformation*. IGI Global.

Sharma, P., & Gupta, H. (2024). Emerging Cyber Security Threats and Security Applications in Digital Era. In *2024 11th International Conference on Reliability, Infocom Technologies and Optimization (Trends and Future Directions)(ICRITO)* (pp. 1-6). IEEE.

Shayea, G. G., Tameemi, H. A., Khaleel, Y. L., Habeeb, M. A., Hussein, N. A. H. K., & Albahri, A. S. (2025). A Systematic review of metaverse cybersecurity: Frameworks, challenges, and strategic approaches in a quantum-driven era. *Mesopotamian Journal of CyberSecurity*, *5*(2), 770–803.

Subhashini, R., & Khang, A. (2023). The role of Internet of Things (IoT) in smart city framework. In *Smart Cities* (pp. 31–56). CRC Press.

Talari, S., Shafie-Khah, M., Siano, P., Loia, V., Tommasetti, A., & Catalão, J. P. (2017). A review of smart cities based on the internet of things concept. *Energies*, *10*(4), 421.

Untawale, T. (2021). Importance of cyber security in digital era. *International Journal for Research in Applied Science and Engineering Technology*, *9*(8), 963–966.

Yamini, B. MAY, P. M. A., Shobana, R., TP, A., & Nalini, M. (2024, December). Cybersecurity: Strategies, Sector-Specific Challenges, and Future Prospects. In *2024 4th International Conference on Ubiquitous Computing and Intelligent Information Systems (ICUIS)* (pp. 1338-1345). IEEE.

# Compilation of References

Aala Kalananda, V. K. R., & Komanapalli, V. L. N. (2023). A competitive learning-based Grey wolf Optimizer for engineering problems and its application to multi-layer perceptron training. *Multimedia Tools and Applications*, *82*(26), 40209–40267. DOI: 10.1007/s11042-023-15146-x PMID: 37362670

Abdulhameed, S., & Rashid, T. A. (2022). Child drawing development optimization algorithm based on child's cognitive development. *Arabian Journal for Science and Engineering*, *47*(2), 1337–1351.

Abushgra, A. A. (2022). Variations of QKD Protocols Based on Conventional System Measurements: A Literature Review. *Cryptography*, *6*(1), 1. Advance online publication. DOI: 10.3390/cryptography6010012

Achaal, B., Adda, M., Berger, M., Ibrahim, H., & Awde, A. (2024). Study of smart grid cyber-security, examining architectures, communication networks, cyber-attacks, countermeasure techniques, and challenges. *Cybersecurity*, *7*(1), 10. DOI: 10.1186/s42400-023-00200-w PMID: 38707764

Acharya, S., Ghosh, D., Swapnarekha, H., Mishra, M., & Nayak, S. (2023). Integrative data analysis and automated deep learning technique for ovary cancer detection. In *Computational Intelligence in Cancer Diagnosis* (pp. 43–65). Academic Press.

Adejumo, A., & Ogburie, C. (2025). The role of cybersecurity in safeguarding finance in a digital era. *World Journal of Advanced Research and Reviews, 25.*

Aderibigbe, O.-O., & Gumbo, T. (2024). Smart cities and their impact on urban transportation systems and development. In *Emerging technologies for smart cities: Sustainable transport planning in the Global North and Global South* (pp. 105–129). Springer.

Adjorlolo, G., Tang, Z., Wauk, G., Adu Sarfo, P., Braimah, A. B., Blankson Safo, R., & N-yanyi, B. (2025). Evaluating Corruption-Prone Public Procurement Stages for Blockchain Integration Using AHP Approach. *Systems 2025, Vol. 13, Page 267, 13*(4), 267. DOI: 10.3390/SYSTEMS13040267

Ahmad, K., Maabreh, M., Ghaly, M., Khan, K., Qadir, J., & Al-Fuqaha, A. (2022). Developing future human-centered smart cities: Critical analysis of smart city security, Data management, and Ethical challenges. *Computer Science Review, 43*, 100452. DOI: 10.1016/j.cosrev.2021.100452

Ahmed, B., Shabbir, H., Naqvi, S. R., & Peng, L. (2024). *Smart Agriculture: Current State, Opportunities and Challenges*. IEEE., DOI: 10.1109/ACCESS.2024.3471647

Ahmed, S. T., Hammood, D. A., Chisab, R. F., Al-Naji, A., & Chahl, J. (2023). Medical Image Encryption: A Comprehensive Review. *Computers, 12*(8), 160.

Akinade, A. O., Adepoju, P. A., Ige, A. B., & Afolabi, A. I. (2024). Cloud Security Challenges and Solutions: A Review of Current Best Practices. *International Journal of Multidisciplinary Research and Growth Evaluation, 6*(1), 26–35. DOI: 10.54660/.IJMRGE.2025.6.1.26-35

Akram, W., Joshi, R., Haider, T., Sharma, P., Jain, V., Garud, N., & Singh, N. (2024). Blockchain technology: A potential tool for the management of the pharma supply chain. *Research in Social & Administrative Pharmacy, 20*(6), 156–164. DOI: 10.1016/J.SAPHARM.2024.02.014 PMID: 38423927

Aksoy, B., & Salman, O. K. M. (2020). A New Hybrid Filter Approach for Image Processing. *Sakarya University Journal of Computer and Information Sciences, 3*(3), 334–342.

Al Barat, M. M., Li, S., Du, C., Hou, Y. T., & Lou, W. (2024). SoK: Public Blockchain Sharding. *2024 IEEE International Conference on Blockchain and Cryptocurrency, ICBC 2024*, 766–783. DOI: 10.1109/ICBC59979.2024.10634422

Al Duhayyim, M., & Mohamed, G., H., S. Alzahrani, J., Alabdan, R., Aziz, A. S. A., Zamani, A. S., ... & Alsaid, M. I. (2022). Sandpiper Optimization with a Deep Learning Enabled Fault Diagnosis Model for Complex Industrial Systems. *Electronics (Basel), 11*(24), 4190.

Alahe, M. A., Wei, L., Chang, Y., Gummi, S. R., Kemeshi, J., Yang, X., & Sher, M. (2024). Cyber security in smart agriculture: Threat types, current status, and future trends. *Computers and Electronics in Agriculture, 226*, 109401. DOI: 10.1016/j.compag.2024.109401

Alam, T., Gupta, R., Nasurudeen Ahamed, N., Ullah, A., & Almaghthwi, A. (2024). Smart mobility adoption in sustainable smart cities to establish a growing ecosystem: Challenges and opportunities. *MRS Energy & Sustainability : a Review Journal, 11*(2), 304–316.

Al-Dhaqm, A., Ikuesan, R. A., Kebande, V. R., Razak, S., & Ghabban, F. M. (2021). Research challenges and opportunities in drone forensics models. *Electronics (Basel), 10*(13), 1519.

Ali, S. I., Shaikh, M. S., Patidar, P. K., & Pagare, S. (2025). Reimagining Urban Mobility. Leveraging VANETs and Blockchain Technology for Urban Mobility, 29–44. : DOI: 10.4018/979-8-3373-0265-2.CH002

Ali, I. A., Bukhari, W. A., Adnan, M., Kashif, M. I., Danish, A., & Sikander, A. (2024). Security and privacy in IoT-based Smart Farming: A review. *Multimedia Tools and Applications*, •••, 1–61. DOI: 10.1007/s11042-024-19653-3

Ali, M. N., Senthil, T., Ilakkiya, T., Hasan, D. S., Ganapathy, N. B. S., & Boopathi, S. (2024). IoT's Role in Smart Manufacturing Transformation for Enhanced Household Product Quality. In *Advanced Applications in Osmotic Computing* (pp. 252–289). IGI Global.

Almalki, F. A., Alsamhi, S. H., Sahal, R., Hassan, J., Hawbani, A., Rajput, N., Saif, A., Morgan, J., & Breslin, J. (2023). Green IoT for eco-friendly and sustainable smart cities: Future directions and opportunities. *Mobile Networks and Applications, 28*(1), 178–202.

Almeida, F. (2023). Prospects of cybersecurity in smart cities. *Future Internet, 15*(9), 285.

Alves Batista, D. (2024). Enhancing transparency and accountability in public procurement: Exploring blockchain technology to mitigate records fraud. *Records Management Journal, 34*(2–3), 151–170. DOI: 10.1108/RMJ-10-2023-0054/FULL/XML

Alwar, B., Edgardo, H., & Faustino, E. (2024). Integrating IoT and Artificial Intelligence for Sustainable Smart City Development: A Case Study Approach. [Information Technology Engineering Journals]. *ITE Journal, 9*(2), 80–90.

Al-Zubaidie, M., & Jebbar, W. A. (2024). Providing security for flash loan system using cryptocurrency wallets supported by XSalsa20 in a blockchain environment. *Applied Sciences (Basel, Switzerland), 14*(14), 6361. DOI: 10.3390/app14146361

Al-Zubaidie, M., & Muhajjar, R. A. (2024). Integrating trustworthy mechanisms to support data and information security in health sensors. *Procedia Computer Science, 237*, 43–52. DOI: 10.1016/j.procs.2024.05.078

Al-Zubaidie, M., Muhajjar, R. A., & Shihabe, L. A. (2024). Computer Networking and Cloud-Based Learning/Teaching Environment Using Virtual Labs Tools: A Review and Future Aspirations. *Mesopotamian Journal of Computer Science, 2024*, 176–203. DOI: 10.58496/MJCSC/2024/015

Al-Zubaidie, M., & Shyaa, G. S. (2023). Applying detection leakage on hybrid cryptography to secure transaction information in e-commerce apps. *Future Internet, 15*(8), 262. DOI: 10.3390/fi15080262

Amiri-Zarandi, M., Dara, R. A., Duncan, E., & Fraser, E. D. (2022). Big data privacy in smart farming: A review. *Sustainability, 14*(15), 9120. DOI: 10.3390/su14159120

Amiri-Zarandi, M., Hazrati Fard, M., Yousefinaghani, S., Kaviani, M., & Dara, R. (2022). A platform approach to smart farm information processing. *Agriculture, 12*(6), 838. DOI: 10.3390/agriculture12060838

Ang, K. L.-M., Seng, J. K. P., Ngharamike, E., & Ijemaru, G. K. (2022a). Emerging technologies for smart cities' transportation: Geo-information, data analytics and machine learning approaches. *ISPRS International Journal of Geo-Information, 11*(2), 85.

Art. 5 GDPR – Principles relating to processing of personal data. (n.d.). General Data Protection Regulation (GDPR). Retrieved May 25, 2025, from https://gdpr-info.eu/art-5-gdpr/

Asimakopoulos, G., Antonopoulou, H., Giotopoulos, K., & Halkiopoulos, C. (2025). Impact of Information and Communication Technologies on Democratic Processes and Citizen Participation. *Societies 2025, Vol. 15, Page 40, 15*(2), 40. DOI: 10.3390/SOC15020040

Asthana, S., Mahindru, R., Zhang, B., & Sanz, J. (2025). *Adaptive PII Mitigation Framework for Large Language Models* (No. arXiv:2501.12465; Version 1). arXiv. /arXiv.2501.12465DOI: 10.48550

Atik, C. (2022). Towards comprehensive European agricultural data governance: Moving beyond the "data ownership" debate. *IIC-International Review of Intellectual Property and Competition Law, 53*(5), 701–742. DOI: 10.1007/s40319-022-01191-w

Atiyah, R. G., & Razzaq, R. H. (2024). Intermediary decentralized computing and private blockchain mechanisms for privacy preservation in the Internet of medical things. *Mesopotamian Journal of CyberSecurity, 4*(3), 152–165.

Awaad, M. H., & Jebbar, W. A. (2014). Prolong the lifetime of WSN by determining a correlation nodes in the same zone and searching for the best not the closest CH. *International Journal of Modern Education and Computer Science*, *6*(11), 31. DOI: 10.5815/ijmecs.2014.11.04

Awaad, M. H., & Jebbar, W. A. (2015). Extending the WSN lifetime by Dividing the Network Area into a Specific Zones. *International Journal of Computer Network and Information Security*, *7*(2), 33–39. DOI: 10.5815/ijcnis.2015.02.04

Azizi, N., & Haass, O. (2023). Cybersecurity issues and challenges. In *Handbook of research on cybersecurity issues and challenges for business and FinTech applications* (pp. 21–48). IGI Global.

Babu, B. S., Kamalakannan, J., Meenatchi, N., Karthik, S., & Boopathi, S. (2022). Economic impacts and reliability evaluation of battery by adopting Electric Vehicle. *IEEE Explore*, 1–6.

Badran, A. (2024). *Delivering Public Service in the Age of Digital Era Governance*. 407–440. : Bahrepour, D., & Maleki, R. (2024). Benefit and limitation of using blockchain in smart cities to improve citizen services. *GeoJournal, 89*(2), 1–14. DOI: 10.4018/979-8-3693-7678-2.CH013

Bahl, A., Kandpal, S., & Rajendran, R. K. (2024). Innovative Strategies for Urban Construction Optimization in the IoT Era. In *The Climate Change Crisis and Its Impact on Mental Health* (pp. 213–226). IGI Global.

Bakirci, M. (2024). Smart city air quality management through leveraging drones for precision monitoring. *Sustainable Cities and Society*, *106*, 105390.

Balasubramaniam, A., Paul, A., Hong, W.-H., Seo, H., & Kim, J. H. (2017). Comparative analysis of intelligent transportation systems for sustainable environment in smart cities. *Sustainability*, *9*(7), 1120.

Beard, R. W., & McLain, T. W. (2012). *Small unmanned aircraft: Theory and practice*. Princeton university press.

Beigi, P., Rajabi, M. S., & Aghakhani, S. (2022). An overview of drone energy consumption factors and models. *Handbook of Smart Energy Systems*, 1–20.

Bellaj, B., Ouaddah, A., Bertin, E., Crespi, N., & Mezrioui, A. (2024). Drawing the Boundaries Between Blockchain and Blockchain-Like Systems: A Comprehensive Survey on Distributed Ledger Technologies. *Proceedings of the IEEE*, *112*(3), 247–299. DOI: 10.1109/JPROC.2024.3386257

Bhatia, A., Bitragunta, S., & Tiwari, K. (2025). Enhanced Lightweight Quantum Key Distribution Protocol for Improved Efficiency and Security. *IEEE Open Journal of the Communications Society*, *6*, 926–943. DOI: 10.1109/OJCOMS.2025.3528718

Bhuvanya, R., Mariammal, G., Sivakumar, K., Ganga, M., Anish, T. P., Swetha, S., & Subramanian, R. S. (2025). Revolutionizing Urban Planning: The Role of AI and Predictive Analytics in Sustainable City Development. *Leveraging Urban Computing for Sustainable Urban Development*, 303-322.

Biasin, M., & Delle Foglie, A. (2024). Blockchain and Smart Cities for Inclusive and Sustainable Communities: A Bibliometric and Systematic Literature Review. *Sustainability 2024, Vol. 16, Page 6669, 16*(15), 6669. DOI: 10.3390/SU16156669

Binas, D. A., Tzanakakis, P., Economopoulos, T. L., Konidari, M., Bourgioti, C., Moulopoulos, L. A., & Matsopoulos, G. K. (2023). A Novel Approach for Estimating Ovarian Cancer Tissue Heterogeneity through the Application of Image Processing Techniques and Artificial Intelligence. *Cancers (Basel)*, *15*(4), 1058. PMID: 36831401

Boopathi, S. (2024b). Enabling Machine Control Through Virtual Methods: Harnessing the Power of 5G. In *Advances in Logistics, Operations, and Management Science* (pp. 50–74). IGI Global. https://doi.org/DOI: 10.4018/979-8-3693-1862-1.ch004

Boopathi, S. (2024b). Sustainable Development Using IoT and AI Techniques for Water Utilization in Agriculture. In *Sustainable Development in AI, Blockchain, and E-Governance Applications* (pp. 204–228). IGI Global.

Boopathi, S., Arigela, S. H., Raman, R., Indhumathi, C., Kavitha, V., & Bhatt, B. C. (2022). Prominent Rule Control-based Internet of Things: Poultry Farm Management System. *IEEE Explore*, 1–6.

Boopathi, S., Siva Kumar, P. K., & Meena, R. S. J., S. I., P., S. K., & Sudhakar, M. (2023). Sustainable Developments of Modern Soil-Less Agro-Cultivation Systems: Aquaponic Culture. In *Advances in Environmental Engineering and Green Technologies* (pp. 69–87). IGI Global. https://doi.org/DOI: 10.4018/978-1-6684-4118-3.ch004

Boopathi, S. (2024a). Advancements in Machine Learning and AI for Intelligent Systems in Drone Applications for Smart City Developments. In *Futuristic e-Governance Security With Deep Learning Applications* (pp. 15–45). IGI Global.

Boopathi, S., & Khang, A. (2023). AI-Integrated Technology for a Secure and Ethical Healthcare Ecosystem. In *AI and IoT-Based Technologies for Precision Medicine* (pp. 36–59). IGI Global.

Borrero, J. D., & Mariscal, J. (2022). A case study of a digital data platform for the agricultural sector: A valuable decision support system for small farmers. *Agriculture, 12*(6), 767. DOI: 10.3390/agriculture12060767

Breen, J., Allen, K., Zucker, K., Adusumilli, P., Scarsbrook, A., Hall, G., & Ravikumar, N. (2023). Artificial intelligence in ovarian cancer histopathology: A systematic review. *NPJ Precision Oncology*, *7*(1), 83. PMID: 37653025

Bronson, K. (2018). Smart farming: Including rights holders for responsible agricultural innovation. *Technology Innovation Management Review*, *8*(2), 7–14.

Broo, D. G., Bravo-Haro, M., & Schooling, J. (2022). Design and implementation of a smart infrastructure digital twin. *Automation in Construction*, *136*, 104171.

Burgess, P., Sunmola, F., & Wertheim-Heck, S. (2024). Information needs for transparency in blockchain-enabled sustainable food supply chains. *International Journal of Information Management Data Insights*, *4*(2), 100262. DOI: 10.1016/J.JJIMEI.2024.100262

Burlacu, M., Boboc, R. G., & Butilă, E. V. (2022). Smart cities and transportation: Reviewing the scientific character of the theories. *Sustainability*, *14*(13), 8109.

Canca Ortiz, J. D., Navarro Carmona, B., & Andrade Pineda, J. L. (2022). Design and Assessment of an Urban Circular Combined Truck–Drone Delivery System Using Continuum Approximation Models and Integer Programming. *Sustainability*, *14*(10), 13459.

Canca, D., Navarro-Carmona, B., & Andrade-Pineda, J. L. (2022). Design and assessment of an urban circular combined truck–drone delivery system using Continuum approximation models and integer programming. *Sustainability*, *14*(20), 13459.

Castro, F., Impedovo, D., & Pirlo, G. (2023). A Medical Image Encryption Scheme for Secure Fingerprint-Based Authenticated Transmission. *Applied Sciences (Basel, Switzerland)*, *13*(10), 6099.

Chatterjee, R., Chung, K.-M., Liang, X., & Malavolta, G. (2022). A Note on the Post-quantum Security of (Ring) Signatures. In Hanaoka, G., Shikata, J., & Watanabe, Y. (Eds.), *Public-Key Cryptography – PKC 2022* (pp. 407–436). Springer International Publishing.

Chavhan, S., Gupta, D., & Gochhayat, S. P., N, C. B., Khanna, A., Shankar, K., & Rodrigues, J. J. (2022). Edge computing AI-IoT integrated energy-efficient intelligent transportation system for smart cities. *ACM Transactions on Internet Technology*, *22*(4), 1–18.

Chen, X., He, S., Sun, L., Zheng, Y., & Wu, C. Q. (2024). A Survey of Consortium Blockchain and Its Applications. *Cryptography 2024, Vol. 8, Page 12, 8*(2), 12. DOI: 10.3390/CRYPTOGRAPHY8020012

Chen, H., Yang, B. W., Qian, L., Meng, Y. S., Bai, X. H., Hong, X. W., & Feng, W. W. (2022). Deep learning prediction of ovarian malignancy at US compared with O-RADS and expert assessment. *Radiology, 304*(1), 106–113. PMID: 35412367

Chen, R., Li, Y., Yu, Y., Li, H., Chen, X., & Susilo, W. (2020). Blockchain-Based Dynamic Provable Data Possession for Smart Cities. *IEEE Internet of Things Journal, 7*(5), 4143–4154. DOI: 10.1109/JIOT.2019.2963789

Choudhary, R., Mantri, S. P., Barse, M. V. A., & Chitnis, S. (2024). Leveraging AI in Smart Agro-Informatics: A Review of Data Science Applications. [IRJAEM]. *International Research Journal on Advanced Engineering and Management, 2*(06), 1964–1975.

Cui, Y., Gaur, V., & Liu, J. (2024). Supply Chain Transparency and Blockchain Design. *Management Science, 70*(5), 3245–3263. DOI: 10.1287/MNSC.2023.4851/ASSET/IMAGES/LARGE/MNSC.2023.4851F4.JPEG

Curry, D. (2025). Limitations of trust and legitimacy in blockchain: Exploring the effectiveness of decentralisation, immutability and consensus mechanisms in blockchain governance. *International Journal of Public Sector Management, 38*(1), 98–117. DOI: 10.1108/IJPSM-12-2023-0368/FULL/XML

Cyriac, R., & Thomas, J. (2024). Smart Farming with Cloud Supported Data Management Enabling Real-Time Monitoring and Prediction for Better Yield. In *Intelligent Robots and Drones for Precision Agriculture* (pp. 283–306). Springer Nature Switzerland., DOI: 10.1007/978-3-031-51195-0_14

Damaševičius, R., Bacanin, N., & Nayyar, A. (2025). Blockchain technology for a trustworthy social credit system: implementation and enforcement perspectives. *Cluster Computing 2024 28:3, 28*(3), 1–41. DOI: 10.1007/S10586-024-04890-W

Das, D., Chaterjee, P., Ghosh, U., & Blakely, B. (2025). Secure and Privacy Aware Data Sharing Approach for Smart Electric Vehicles. *IEEE Consumer Electronics Magazine*, •••, 1–7. DOI: 10.1109/MCE.2025.3529398

Das, P., Ramapraba, P., Seethalakshmi, K., Mary, M. A., Karthick, S., & Sampath, B. (2024). Sustainable Advanced Techniques for Enhancing the Image Process. In *Fostering Cross-Industry Sustainability With Intelligent Technologies* (pp. 350–374). IGI Global.

de Araujo Zanella, A. R., Da Silva, E., & Albini, L. C. P. (2020). Security challenges to smart agriculture: Current state, key issues, and future directions. *Array (New York, N.Y.)*, *8*, 100048.

De Guimarães, J. C. F., Severo, E. A., Felix Júnior, L. A., Da Costa, W. P. L. B., & Salmoria, F. T. (2020). Governance and quality of life in smart cities: Towards sustainable development goals. *Journal of Cleaner Production*, *253*, 119926. DOI: 10.1016/j.jclepro.2019.119926

Deep, G., & Verma, J. (2023). Embracing the future: AI and ML transforming urban environments in smart cities. *Journal of Artificial Intelligence*, *5*, 57.

Dehouche, N. (2025). Blockchain as urban governance infrastructure in private cities: An exploratory review. *Frontiers in Sustainable Cities*, *7*, 1594711. DOI: 10.3389/FRSC.2025.1594711

Demestichas, K., Peppes, N., & Alexakis, T. (2020). Survey on security threats in agricultural IoT and smart farming. *sensors, 20*(22), 6458, DOI: .DOI: 10.3390/s20226458

Dhanalakshmi, M., Tamilarasi, K., Saravanan, S., Sujatha, G., Boopathi, S., & Associates. (2024). Fog Computing-Based Framework and Solutions for Intelligent Systems: Enabling Autonomy in Vehicles. In *Computational Intelligence for Green Cloud Computing and Digital Waste Management* (pp. 330–356). IGI Global.

Dhanya, D., Kumar, S. S., Thilagavathy, A., Prasad, D., & Boopathi, S. (2023). Data Analytics and Artificial Intelligence in the Circular Economy: Case Studies. In *Intelligent Engineering Applications and Applied Sciences for Sustainability* (pp. 40–58). IGI Global.

Din, J., & Su, H. (2024). Blockchain-Enabled Smart Grids for Optimized Electrical Billing and Peer-to-Peer Energy Trading. *Energies 2024, Vol. 17, Page 5744, 17*(22), 5744. DOI: 10.3390/EN17225744

Dorostkar, E., & Ziari, K. (2025). Leveraging NFTs for sustainable urban finance: Challenges and opportunities for smart cities. *Cities (London, England)*, *163*, 106013. DOI: 10.1016/J.CITIES.2025.106013

Duaa, T., & Hammed, A. (2024). Enhancing electronic agriculture data security with a blockchain-based search method and e-signatures. *Mesopotamian journal of Cybersecurity*, 4(3), 1-21.

Duaa, T. (2025). Security Cooperation in the Protection Concerns of Agriculture Data Using Efficient Signatures and Artificial Bee Colony Manner. In *Sustainable Information Security in the Age of AI and Green Computing* (pp. 439–460). IGI Global Scientific Publishing.

Dui, H., Zhang, S., Liu, M., Dong, X., & Bai, G. (2024). IoT-enabled real-time traffic monitoring and control management for intelligent transportation systems. *IEEE Internet of Things Journal*.

Durairaj, M., Jayakumar, S., Karpagavalli, V., Maheswari, B. U., & Boopathi, S. (2023). Utilization of Digital Tools in the Indian Higher Education System During Health Crises. In *Multidisciplinary Approaches to Organizational Governance During Health Crises* (pp. 1–21). IGI Global.

Elassy, M., Al-Hattab, M., Takruri, M., & Badawi, S. (2024). Intelligent transportation systems for sustainable smart cities. *Transportation Engineering*, *16*, 100252.

Ellis, E., & Paustian, K. (2024). Importance of on-farm research for validating process-based models of climate-smart agriculture. *Carbon Balance and Management*, *19*(1), 16. DOI: 10.1186/s13021-024-00260-6

Eswaran, U., & Khang, A. (2024). Application of Internet of things (IoT) and sensors technologies for agriculture. In *Advanced IoT Technologies and Applications in the Industry 4.0 Digital Economy* (pp. 158–172). CRC Press.

Fabrègue, B. F. G., & Bogoni, A. (2023). Privacy and Security Concerns in the Smart City. *Smart Cities*, *6*(1), 586–613. DOI: 10.3390/smartcities6010027

Falcon, E., & Mordant, N. (2022). Experiments in Surface Gravity–Capillary Wave Turbulence. *Annual Review of Fluid Mechanics*, *54*(1), 1–25. DOI: 10.1146/annurev-fluid-021021-102043

Farahani, H., Boschman, J., Farnell, D., Darbandsari, A., Zhang, A., Ahmadvand, P., & Bashashati, A. (2022). Deep learning-based histotype diagnosis of ovarian carcinoma whole-slide pathology images. *Modern Pathology*, *35*(12), 1983–1990. PMID: 36065012

Ferrag, M. A., Shu, L., Yang, X., Derhab, A., & Maglaras, L. (2020). Security and privacy for green IoT-based agriculture: Review, blockchain solutions, and challenges. *IEEE Access : Practical Innovations, Open Solutions*, *8*, 32031–32053. DOI: 10.1109/ACCESS.2020.2973178

Ferris, J. L. (2017). Data privacy and protection in the agriculture industry: Is federal regulation necessary? *Minnesota Journal of Law, Science & Technology*, *18*, 309.

Fetteha, M. A., Sayed, W. S., & Said, L. A. (2023). A lightweight image encryption scheme using dna coding and chaos. *Electronics (Basel)*, *12*(24), 4895.

Gajjela, C. C., Brun, M., Mankar, R., Corvigno, S., Kennedy, N., Zhong, Y., & Reddy, R. (2023). Leveraging mid-infrared spectroscopic imaging and deep learning for tissue subtype classification in ovarian cancer. *Analyst*, *148*(12), 2699–2708. PMID: 37218522

Gautam, S., Gautam, A. S., Awasthi, A., & N, R. (2024). Regulatory Frameworks and Policies. In *Sustainable Air: Strategies for Cleaner Atmosphere and Healthier Communities* (pp. 49–52). Springer.

Geng, Y., Li, Y., & Deng, C. (2024). An Improved Binary Walrus Optimizer with Golden Sine Disturbance and Population Regeneration Mechanism to Solve Feature Selection Problems. *Biomimetics*, *9*(8), 501. DOI: 10.3390/biomimetics9080501 PMID: 39194480

Gharavi, H., Granjal, J., & Monteiro, E. (2024). Post-Quantum Blockchain Security for the Internet of Things: Survey and Research Directions. *IEEE Communications Surveys & Tutorials, 26*(3), 1748–1774. *IEEE Communications Surveys and Tutorials*. Advance online publication. DOI: 10.1109/COMST.2024.3355222

Ghoniem, R. M., Algarni, A. D., Refky, B., & Ewees, A. A. (2021). Multi-modal evolutionary deep learning model for ovarian cancer diagnosis. *Symmetry*, *13*(4), 643.

Ghosh, S., Islam, S. K. H., & Vasilakos, A. V. (2024). Private Blockchain-Assisted Certificateless Public Key Encryption with Multikeyword Search for Fog-Based IIoT Environments. *IEEE Internet of Things Journal*, *11*(19), 30847–30863. DOI: 10.1109/JIOT.2024.3415676

Giamberardino, G. G., Gadda, T. M. C., & Nagalli, A. (2024). Using blockchain technology for sustainable public procurement of road works. *Revista de Administração Pública*, *58*(3), e2023–e0073. DOI: 10.1590/0034-761220230073

Gift, M. D. M., Senthil, T. S., Hasan, D. S., Alagarraja, K., Jayaseelan, P., & Boopathi, S. (2024). Additive Manufacturing and 3D Printing Innovations: Revolutionizing Industry 5.0. In *Technological Advancements in Data Processing for Next Generation Intelligent Systems* (pp. 255–287). IGI Global. https://doi.org/DOI: 10.4018/979-8-3693-0968-1.ch010

Giri, R. B., N., Alhamad, A. M., Mamidi, P. L., R., S., & Boopathi, S. (2024). Human-Centered Design Approach to Autonomous Electric Vehicles: Revolutionizing Mobility. In *Advances in Logistics, Operations, and Management Science* (pp. 91–109). IGI Global. https://doi.org/DOI: 10.4018/979-8-3693-1862-1.ch006

Giri, A., Sagarnal, A. V., Chinmaya, R., & Dammur, A. (2024). Enhancing Efficiency in Smart Grid Billing with Blockchain Technology and Smart Contracts. *2nd International Conference on Sustainable Computing and Smart Systems, ICSCSS 2024 - Proceedings*, 586–594. DOI: 10.1109/ICSCSS60660.2024.10625244

Godwin Immanuel, D., Solaimalai, G., Chandrakala, B. M., Bharath, V. G., Singh, M. K., & Boopathi, S. (2024). Advancements in Electric Vehicle Management System: Integrating Machine Learning and Artificial Intelligence. In *Advances in Web Technologies and Engineering* (pp. 371–391). IGI Global. https://doi.org/DOI: 10.4018/979-8-3693-1487-6.ch018

Gómez, J. E., Marcillo, F. R., Triana, F. L., Gallo, V. T., Oviedo, B. W., & Hernández, V. L. (2017). IoT for environmental variables in urban areas. *Procedia Computer Science*, *109*, 67–74.

Gopal, M., Lurdhumary, J., Bathrinath, S., Priya, A. P., Sarojwal, A., & Boopathi, S. (2024). Energy Harvesting and Smart Highways for Sustainable Transportation Infrastructure: Revolutionizing Roads Using Nanotechnology. In *Principles and Applications in Speed Sensing and Energy Harvesting for Smart Roads* (pp. 136–165). IGI Global. DOI: 10.4018/978-1-6684-9214-7.ch005

Grauer, J. A., & Morelli, E. A. (2015). Generic global aerodynamic model for aircraft. *Journal of Aircraft*, *52*(1), 13–20.

Groos, D., & Van Veen, E. (2020). Anonymised Data and the Rule of Law. *European Data Protection Law Review*, *6*(4), 498–508. DOI: 10.21552/edpl/2020/4/6

Gupta, B. B., Gaurav, A., Marín, E. C., & Alhalabi, W. (2023). Novel Graph-Based Machine Learning Technique to Secure Smart Vehicles in Intelligent Transportation Systems. *IEEE Transactions on Intelligent Transportation Systems*, *24*(8), 8483–8491. DOI: 10.1109/TITS.2022.3174333

Gupta, M., Abdelsalam, M., Khorsandroo, S., & Mittal, S. (2020). Security and privacy in smart farming: Challenges and opportunities. *IEEE Access : Practical Innovations, Open Solutions*, *8*, 34564–34584. DOI: 10.1109/ACCESS.2020.2975142

Gyamfi, E. K., ElSayed, Z., Kropczynski, J., Yakubu, M. A., & Elsayed, N. (2024, April). Agricultural 4.0 leveraging on technological solutions: Study for smart farming sector *2024*. In *IEEE 3rd International Conference on Computing and Machine Intelligence (ICMI)* (pp. 1-9). IEEE, DOI: DOI: 10.1109/ICMI60790.2024.10585910

Gyamfi, E. K., Kropczynski, J., Johnson, J. S., & Yakubu, M. A. (2024, May). Internet of Things Security and Data Privacy Concerns in Smart Farming *2024*. In *IEEE World AI IoT Congress (AIIoT)* (pp. 0575-0583). IEEE, DOI: DOI: 10.1109/AIIoT61789.2024.10578972

Habib, A., Alnaemi, A., & Habib, M. (2024). Developing a framework for integrating blockchain technology into earthquake risk mitigation and disaster management strategies of smart cities. *Smart and Sustainable Built Environment, ahead-of-print*(ahead-of-print). DOI: 10.1108/SASBE-12-2023-0376/FULL/XML

Hammed, M. (2025). A Critical Reliable Model for Promoting Patient Medical Wireless Sensors Information Security. *Procedia Computer Science*, *263*, 17–24.

Hammed, M., & Jebbar, W. A. (2025). Blockchain-Powered Dynamic Segmentation in Personal Health Record. *Mesopotamian Journal of CyberSecurity*, *5*(3), 953–976.

Hamoud, D. T. (2025). Security Cooperation in the Protection Concerns of Agriculture Data Using Efficient Signatures and Artificial Bee Colony Manner. In Sustainable *Information Security in the Age of AI and Green Computing* (pp. 439-460). IGI Global Scientific Publishing.

Handley, K. F., Sims, T. T., Bateman, N. W., Glassman, D., Foster, K. I., Lee, S., & Sood, A. K. (2022). Classification of high-grade serous ovarian cancer using tumor morphologic characteristics. *JAMA Network Open*, *5*(10), e2236626–e2236626. PMID: 36239936

Hanumanthakari, S., Gift, M. M., Kanimozhi, K., Bhavani, M. D., Bamane, K. D., & Boopathi, S. (2023). Biomining Method to Extract Metal Components Using Computer-Printed Circuit Board E-Waste. In *Handbook of Research on Safe Disposal Methods of Municipal Solid Wastes for a Sustainable Environment* (pp. 123–141). IGI Global.

Harikaran, M., Boopathi, S., Gokulakannan, S., & Poonguzhali, M. (2023). Study on the Source of E-Waste Management and Disposal Methods. In *Sustainable Approaches and Strategies for E-Waste Management and Utilization* (pp. 39–60). IGI Global.

Hasan, F. A., Ashqar, H. I., Alsobeh, A., & Darwish, O. (2024). Blockchain-Based National Digital Identity Framework - Case of Palestine. *2024 International Conference on Intelligent Computing, Communication, Networking and Services, ICCNS 2024*, 76–83. DOI: 10.1109/ICCNS62192.2024.10776538

Herman, D., Googin, C., Liu, X., Sun, Y., Galda, A., Safro, I., Pistoia, M., & Alexeev, Y. (2023). Quantum computing for finance. *Nature Reviews. Physics*, *5*(8), 450–465. DOI: 10.1038/s42254-023-00603-1

Hernafi, Y., Ahmed, M. B., & Bouhorma, M. (2016). An approaches' based on intelligent transportation systems to dissect driver behavior and smart mobility in smart city. *2016 4th IEEE International Colloquium on Information Science and Technology (CiSt)*, 886–895.

Hussain, Z., Babe, M., Saravanan, S., Srimathy, G., Roopa, H., & Boopathi, S. (2023). Optimizing Biomass-to-Biofuel Conversion: IoT and AI Integration for Enhanced Efficiency and Sustainability. In *Circular Economy Implementation for Sustainability in the Built Environment* (pp. 191–214). IGI Global.

Ibrahimy, M. M., Norta, A., Normak, P., & Nowandish, H. (2025). Transforming e-Participatory Budgeting With Blockchain: Boosting Transparency and Citizen Engagement. *IEEE Transactions on Engineering Management*, *72*, 1376–1403. DOI: 10.1109/TEM.2025.3556191

Ingle, R. B., Swathi, S., Mahendran, G., Senthil, T., Muralidharan, N., & Boopathi, S. (2023). Sustainability and Optimization of Green and Lean Manufacturing Processes Using Machine Learning Techniques. In *Circular Economy Implementation for Sustainability in the Built Environment* (pp. 261–285). IGI Global.

Ismagilova, E., Hughes, L., Rana, N. P., & Dwivedi, Y. K. (2022). Security, Privacy and Risks within Smart Cities: Literature Review and Development of a Smart City Interaction Framework. *Information Systems Frontiers*, *24*(2), 393–414. DOI: 10.1007/s10796-020-10044-1 PMID: 32837262

Iyer, S. S., & Rajagopal, S. (2020). Applications of machine learning in cyber security domain. In *Handbook of research on machine and deep learning applications for cyber security* (pp. 64–82). IGI Global.

Jagatheesaperumal, S. K., Bibri, S. E., Huang, J., Rajapandian, J., & Parthiban, B. (2024). Artificial intelligence of things for smart cities: Advanced solutions for enhancing transportation safety. *Computational Urban Science*, *4*(1), 10.

Jakku, E., Taylor, B., Fleming, A., Mason, C., Fielke, S., Sounness, C., & Thorburn, P. (2019). "If they don't tell us what they do with it, why would we trust them?" Trust, transparency and benefit-sharing in Smart Farming. *NJAS Wageningen Journal of Life Sciences*, *90*, 100285.

Janardhana, K., Singh, V., Singh, S. N., Babu, T. R., Bano, S., & Boopathi, S. (2023). Utilization Process for Electronic Waste in Eco-Friendly Concrete: Experimental Study. In *Sustainable Approaches and Strategies for E-Waste Management and Utilization* (pp. 204–223). IGI Global.

Jebbar, W. A., & Al-Zubaidie, M. (2024). Transaction-based blockchain systems security improvement employing micro-segmentation controlled by smart contracts and detection of saddle Goatfish. *SN Computer Science*, *5*(7), 898. DOI: 10.1007/s42979-024-03239-9

Jebbar, W. A., Razzaq, R. H., & Tahayur, D. H. (2024). Blockchain and cryptography framework of e-apps with big data. *Journal of Education for Pure Science*, *14*(3).

Jeya Sundari, M., & Brintha, N. C. (2023). An Intelligent Black Widow Optimization on Image Enhancement with Deep Learning Based Ovarian Tumor Diagnosis model. *Computer Methods in Biomechanics and Biomedical Engineering. Imaging & Visualization*, *11*(3), 598–605.

Jeya, R., Venkatakrishnan, G. R., Rengaraj, R., Rajalakshmi, M., Pradeep Mohan Kumar, K., & Boopathi, S. (2023). Water Resource Managements in Soil and Soilless Irrigation Systems Using AI Techniques. In *Advances in Environmental Engineering and Green Technologies* (pp. 245–266). IGI Global. https://doi.org/DOI: 10.4018/979-8-3693-0338-2.ch014

Jha, A., & Jha, A. (2024). Securing tomorrow's urban frontiers: A holistic approach to cybersecurity in smart cities. Information System and Smart City, 3(1).

Jha, S. K., & Beevi, S. J. P., H., Babitha, M. N., Chinnusamy, S., & Boopathi, S. (2024). Artificial Intelligence-Infused Urban Connectivity for Smart Cities and the Evolution of IoT Communication Networks. In *Blockchain-Based Solutions for Accessibility in Smart Cities* (pp. 113–146). IGI Global. https://doi.org/DOI: 10.4018/979-8-3693-3402-7.ch005

Jouanjean, M. A., Casalini, F., Wiseman, L., & Gray, E. (2020). Issues around data governance in the digital transformation of agriculture: The farmers' perspective.

Jung, Y., Kim, T., Han, M. R., Kim, S., Kim, G., Lee, S., & Choi, Y. J. (2022). Ovarian tumor diagnosis using deep convolutional neural networks and a denoising convolutional autoencoder. *Scientific Reports*, *12*(1), 17024. PMID: 36220853

Kalusivalingam, A. K., Sharma, A., Patel, N., & Singh, V. (2021). Enhancing smart city development with AI: Leveraging machine learning algorithms and IoT-driven data analytics. *International Journal of Artificial Intelligence and Machine Learning*, *2*(3).

Kandt, J., & Batty, M. (2021). Smart cities, big data and urban policy: Towards urban analytics for the long run. *Cities (London, England)*, *109*, 102992.

Kaneti, V. R., Yamini, B., Nagarajan, S., Adaikkammai, A., Gracious, L. A., Subramanian, R. S., & Girija, P. (2025). Smart Transportation Systems and Sustainable Urban Mobility. In *Revolutionizing Urban Development and Governance with Emerging Technologies* (pp. 261–288). IGI Global Scientific Publishing.

Karger, E., Rothweiler, A., Brée, T., & Ahlemann, F. (2025). Building the Smart City of Tomorrow: A Bibliometric Analysis of Artificial Intelligence in Urbanization. *Urban Science 2025, Vol. 9, Page 132, 9*(4), 132. DOI: 10.3390/URBANSCI9040132

Karunathilake, E. M. B. M., Le, A. T., Heo, S., Chung, Y. S., & Mansoor, S. (2023). The path to smart farming: Innovations and opportunities in precision agriculture. *Agriculture, 13*(8), 1593. DOI: 10.3390/agriculture13081593

Kaur, J., & Dara, R. (2023). Ensuring Privacy in Smart Farming: Review of Regulations, Codes of Conduct, and Best Practices. *Encyclopedia of Digital Agricultural Technologies*, 480-495, DOI: DOI: 10.1007/978-3-031-24861-0_272

Kaur, J., Hazrati Fard, S. M., Amiri-Zarandi, M., & Dara, R. (2022). Protecting farmers' data privacy and confidentiality: Recommendations and considerations. *Frontiers in Sustainable Food Systems, 6*, 903230. DOI: 10.3389/fsufs.2022.903230

Kethineni, K., & Gera, P. (2023). IoT-based privacy-preserving anomaly detection model for smart agriculture. *Systems, 11*(6), 304.

Khalaf, M., Ayad, A., Tushar, M. H. K., Kassouf, M., & Kundur, D. (2024). A Survey on Cyber-Physical Security of Active Distribution Networks in Smart Grids. *IEEE Access : Practical Innovations, Open Solutions, 12*, 29414–29444. DOI: 10.1109/ACCESS.2024.3364362

Khan, A. F., & Ivan, P. (2023). Integrating machine learning and deep learning in smart cities for enhanced traffic congestion management: An empirical review. *J. Urban Dev. Manag, 2*(4), 211–221.

Khatoon, N., Dilshad, N., & Song, J. (2022). Analysis of use cases enabling AI/ML to IOT service platforms. *2022 13th International Conference on Information and Communication Technology Convergence (ICTC)*, 1431–1436.

Khrennikov, A. (2021). Roots of quantum computing supremacy: Superposition, entanglement, or complementarity? *The European Physical Journal. Special Topics, 230*(4), 1053–1057. DOI: 10.1140/epjs/s11734-021-00061-9

Köbel, M., & Kang, E. Y. (2022). The evolution of ovarian carcinoma subclassification. *Cancers (Basel), 14*(2), 416. PMID: 35053578

Kodipalli, A., Devi, S., Dasar, S., & Ismail, T. (2022). Segmentation and classification of ovarian cancer based on conditional adversarial image to image translation approach. *Expert Systems: International Journal of Knowledge Engineering and Neural Networks*, •••, 13193.

Köhler, J., & Jeschke, P. (2021). Conceptual design and comparison of hybrid electric propulsion systems for small aircraft. *CEAS Aeronautical Journal, 12*(4), 907–922.

Koshariya, A. K., Kalaiyarasi, D., Jovith, A. A., Sivakami, T., Hasan, D. S., & Boopathi, S. (2023). AI-Enabled IoT and WSN-Integrated Smart Agriculture System. In *Artificial Intelligence Tools and Technologies for Smart Farming and Agriculture Practices* (pp. 200–218). IGI Global.

Koshariya, A. K., Khatoon, S., Marathe, A. M., Suba, G. M., Baral, D., & Boopathi, S. (2023). Agricultural Waste Management Systems Using Artificial Intelligence Techniques. In *AI-Enabled Social Robotics in Human Care Services* (pp. 236–258). IGI Global.

Kosior, K. (2019). Towards a new data economy for EU agriculture. *Studia Europejskie, 23*(4), 91–107. DOI: 10.33067/SE.4.2019.6

Kumar, M., Kumar, K., Sasikala, P., Sampath, B., Gopi, B., & Sundaram, S. (2023). Sustainable Green Energy Generation From Waste Water: IoT and ML Integration. In *Sustainable Science and Intelligent Technologies for Societal Development* (pp. 440–463). IGI Global.

Kumara, V., & Sharma, M. D., Samson Isaac, J., Saravanan, S., Suganthi, D., & Boopathi, S. (2023). An AI-Integrated Green Power Monitoring System: Empowering Small and Medium Enterprises. In *Advances in Environmental Engineering and Green Technologies* (pp. 218–244). IGI Global. https://doi.org/DOI: 10.4018/979-8-3693-0338-2.ch013

Kumari, S., Tiwari, S., Naithani, K., & Subbiah, P. (2024). Internet of things for smart agriculture: a survey. In *AI Applications for Business, Medical, and Agricultural Sustainability* (pp. 100-121). IGI Global, DOI: DOI: 10.4018/979-8-3693-5266-3.ch005

Kumar, M., & Mondal, B. (2025). A brief review on Quantum Key Distribution Protocols. *Multimedia Tools and Applications*. Advance online publication. DOI: 10.1007/s11042-024-20535-x

Kumar, V., Sharma, K. V., Kedam, N., Patel, A., Kate, T. R., & Rathnayake, U. (2024). A comprehensive review on smart and sustainable agriculture using IoT technologies. *Smart Agricultural Technology, 100487*. Advance online publication. DOI: 10.1016/j.atech.2024.100487

Kuntke, F. (2024). The Role of Privacy in Digitalization—Analyzing Perspectives of German Farmers. In *Resilient Smart Farming: Crisis-Capable Information and Communication Technologies for Agriculture* (pp. 81–107). Springer Fachmedien Wiesbaden.

Lartey, D., & Law, K. M. Y. (2025). Artificial intelligence adoption in urban planning governance: A systematic review of advancements in decision-making, and policy making. *Landscape and Urban Planning, 258*, 105337. DOI: 10.1016/J.LANDURBPLAN.2025.105337

Lata, K., & Cenkeramaddi, L. R. (2023). Deep learning for medical image cryptography: A comprehensive review. *Applied Sciences (Basel, Switzerland), 13*(14), 8295.

Lawal, O. O., & Nawari, N. O. (2024). Blockchain-Enabled City Information Modeling Framework for Urban Asset Management. *Journal of Architectural Engineering, 30*(3), 04024020. DOI: 10.1061/JAEIED.AEENG-1644;WGROUP:STRING:PUBLICATION

Lax, G., Nardone, R., & Russo, A. (2024). Enabling secure health information sharing among healthcare organizations by public blockchain. *Multimedia Tools and Applications, 83*(24), 64795–64811. DOI: 10.1007/S11042-024-18181-4/FIGURES/4

Le, D. D., Dao, M. S., Tran, A. K., Nguyen, T. B., & Le-Thi, H. G. (2023, October). Federated learning in smart agriculture: an overview *2023*. In *15th International Conference on Knowledge and Systems Engineering (KSE)* (pp. 1-4). IEEE, DOI: DOI: 10.1109/KSE59128.2023.10299497

Lee, J., & Yang, B. (2025). Enhancing smart city infrastructure with a geospatial blockchain-based addressing system. *Cities (London, England), 159*, 105757. DOI: 10.1016/J.CITIES.2025.105757

Lee, Y., Youn, J., Nam, K., Jung, H. H., Cho, M., Na, J., Park, J.-Y., Jeon, S., Kang, B. G., Oh, H., & Paek, Y. (2024). An Efficient Hardware/Software Co-Design for FALCON on Low-End Embedded Systems. *IEEE Access : Practical Innovations, Open Solutions, 12*, 57947–57958. DOI: 10.1109/ACCESS.2024.3387489

Lipper, L., Thornton, P., Campbell, B. M., Baedeker, T., Braimoh, A., Bwalya, M., & Torquebiau, E. F. (2014). Climate-smart agriculture for food security. *Nature Climate Change, 4*(12), 1068–1072. DOI: 10.1038/nclimate2437

Li, Q. (2020). Resilience Thinking as a System Approach to Promote China's Sustainability Transitions. *Sustainability, 12*(12), 12. Advance online publication. DOI: 10.3390/su12125008

López, I. D., Grass, J. F., Figueroa, A., & Corrales, J. C. (2023). A proposal for a multi-domain data fusion strategy in a climate-smart agriculture context. *International Transactions in Operational Research*, *30*(4), 2049–2070. DOI: 10.1111/itor.12899

Louati, A., Louati, H., Kariri, E., Neifar, W., Hassan, M. K., Khairi, M. H., Farahat, M. A., & El-Hoseny, H. M. (2024). Sustainable smart cities through multi-agent reinforcement learning-based cooperative autonomous vehicles. *Sustainability*, *16*(5), 1779.

Lu, C., & Wang, F. (2024). Towards Secure Internet of Things-Enabled Intelligent Transportation Systems: A Comprehensive Review. *International Journal of Advanced Computer Science and Applications*, *15*(7).

Lu, C.-Y., Cao, Y., Peng, C.-Z., & Pan, J.-W. (2022). Micius quantum experiments in space. *Reviews of Modern Physics*, *94*(3), 035001. DOI: 10.1103/RevModPhys.94.035001

Maguluri, L. P., Ananth, J., Hariram, S., Geetha, C., Bhaskar, A., & Boopathi, S. (2023). Smart Vehicle-Emissions Monitoring System Using Internet of Things (IoT). In *Handbook of Research on Safe Disposal Methods of Municipal Solid Wastes for a Sustainable Environment* (pp. 191–211). IGI Global.

Maguluri, L. P., Arularasan, A., & Boopathi, S. (2023). Assessing Security Concerns for AI-Based Drones in Smart Cities. In *Effective AI, Blockchain, and E-Governance Applications for Knowledge Discovery and Management* (pp. 27–47). IGI Global.

Mahapatra, S., Raj, S., & Badi, M. (2023). Smart transportation based on AI and ML technology. In *Artificial Intelligence and Machine Learning in Smart City Planning* (pp. 281–299). Elsevier.

Makanadar, A., & Shahane, S. (2023c). Urban mobility: Leveraging ai, machine learning, and data analytics for smart transportation planning-a case study on new york city. *2023 14th International Conference on Computing Communication and Networking Technologies (ICCCNT)*, 1–6.

Makanadar, A., & Shahane, S. (2023a). Smart mobility and cities 2.0: Advancing urban transportation planning through artificial intelligence and machine learning. In *Urban Mobility India* (pp. 23–38). Springer.

Malathi, J., Kusha, K., Isaac, S., Ramesh, A., Rajendiran, M., & Boopathi, S. (2024). IoT-Enabled Remote Patient Monitoring for Chronic Disease Management and Cost Savings: Transforming Healthcare. In *Advances in Explainable AI Applications for Smart Cities* (pp. 371–388). IGI Global.

Marcu, I., Suciu, G., Bălăceanu, C., Vulpe, A., & Drăgulinescu, A. M. (2020). Arrowhead technology for digitalization and automation solution: Smart cities and smart agriculture. *Sensors (Basel), 20*(5), 1464. DOI: 10.3390/s20051464

Maria, H. H., Jossy, A. M., & Malarvizhi, S. (2023). A hybrid deep learning approach for detection and segmentation of ovarian tumours. *Neural Computing & Applications*, *35*(21), 15805–15819.

Mavlutova, I., Atstaja, D., Grasis, J., Kuzmina, J., Uvarova, I., & Roga, D. (2023). Urban transportation concept and sustainable urban mobility in smart cities: A review. *Energies*, *16*(8), 3585.

Ma, X., Li, J., Guo, Z., & Wan, Z. (2024). Role of big data and technological advancements in monitoring and development of smart cities. *Heliyon, 10*(15). Advance online publication. DOI: 10.1016/J.HELIYON.2024.E34821/ASSET/369ACF92-71A7-4F1C-BCDE-215A81607B66/MAIN.ASSETS/GR6.JPG PMID: 39165964

Mayakannan, S., Saravanan, M., Arunbharathi, R., Srinivasan, V. P., Prabhu, S. V., & Maurya, R. K. (2023). Navigating Ethical and Legal Challenges in Smart Agriculture: Insights from Farmers. In *Predictive Analytics in Smart Agriculture* (pp. 175-190). CRC Press.

Mehmood, R., Yigitcanlar, T., & Corchado, J. M. (2024). Smart Technologies for Sustainable Urban and Regional Development. *Sustainability 2024, Vol. 16, Page 1171, 16*(3), 1171. DOI: 10.3390/SU16031171

Mehmood, Y., Ahmad, F., Yaqoob, I., Adnane, A., Imran, M., & Guizani, S. (2017). Internet-of-things-based smart cities: Recent advances and challenges. *IEEE Communications Magazine*, *55*(9), 16–24.

Meneguette, R. I., De Grande, R., & Loureiro, A. (2018). Intelligent transport system in smart cities. *Cham: Springer International Publishing, 1*, 182.

Meneguzzo, S., Selabi, E. G. K., Favenza, A., Gatteschi, V., & Schifanella, C. (2024). Enabling Citizen Sustainable Behaviors in Urban Mobility through Blockchain and Tokenization. *Blockchain Technology in the Automotive Industry*, 245–279. DOI: 10.1201/9781003450306-17/ENABLING-CITIZEN-SUSTAINABLE-BEHAVIORS-URBAN-MOBILITY-BLOCKCHAIN-TOKENIZATION-SILVIO-MENEGUZZO-ELVIS-GERARDIN-KONJOH-SELABI-ALFREDO-FAVENZA-VALENTINA-GATTESCHI-CLAUDIO-SCHIFANELLA

Meziani, L., Radjef, M. S., Perito, M. A., & Hammoudi, A. (2024). Will the development of smart agriculture improve food safety in international markets? A theoretical approach. *Frontiers in Sustainable Food Systems*, *8*, 1440006. DOI: 10.3389/fsufs.2024.1440006

Miao, W., Zhao, X., Wang, C., Chen, S., Gao, P., & Li, Q. (2024). A Gnn-Enhanced Ant Colony Optimization for Security Strategy Orchestration. *Symmetry*, *16*(9), 9. Advance online publication. DOI: 10.3390/sym16091183

Min, S., Harrison, E., Jimenez, H., & Mavris, D. N. (2015). Development of aerodynamic modeling and calibration methods for general aviation aircraft performance analysis-a survey and comparison of models. *15th AIAA Aviation Technology, Integration, and Operations Conference*, 2853.

Miron, R., Hulea, M., Muresan, V., Clitan, I., & Rusu, A. (2025). Integrating Blockchain Technology into Mobility-as-a-Service Platforms for Smart Cities. *Smart Cities 2025, Vol. 8, Page 9, 8*(1), 9. DOI: 10.3390/SMARTCITIES8010009

Mishra, A., Alzoubi, Y. I., & Gavrilovic, N. (2024). Quality attributes of software architecture in IoT-based agricultural systems. *Smart Agricultural Technology*, *8*, 100523. DOI: 10.1016/j.atech.2024.100523

Mishra, H., & Mishra, D. (2024). Sustainable Smart Agriculture to Ensure Zero Hunger. In *Sustainable Development Goals* (pp. 16–37). CRC Press., DOI: 10.1201/9781003468257-2

Mlika, F., Karoui, W., & Ben Romdhane, L. (2024). Blockchain solutions for trustworthy decentralization in social networks. *Computer Networks*, *244*, 110336. DOI: 10.1016/J.COMNET.2024.110336

Mohammed, H. M., & Rashid, T. A. (2020). A Novel Hybrid GWO with WOA for Global Numerical Optimization and Solving Pressure Vessel Design. *Neural Computing & Applications*, *32*(18), 14701–14718. DOI: 10.1007/s00521-020-04823-9

Mohanty, A., Venkateswaran, N., Ranjit, P., Tripathi, M. A., & Boopathi, S. (2023). Innovative Strategy for Profitable Automobile Industries: Working Capital Management. In *Handbook of Research on Designing Sustainable Supply Chains to Achieve a Circular Economy* (pp. 412–428). IGI Global.

Mohsen, B. M. (2024). Ai-driven optimization of urban logistics in smart cities: Integrating autonomous vehicles and iot for efficient delivery systems. *Sustainability*, *16*(24), 11265.

Moshref-Javadi, M., Hemmati, A., & Winkenbach, M. (2021). A comparative analysis of synchronized truck-and-drone delivery models. *Computers & Industrial Engineering*, *162*, 107648.

Moshref-Javadi, M., & Winkenbach, M. (2021). Applications and Research avenues for drone-based models in logistics: A classification and review. *Expert Systems with Applications*, *177*, 114854.

Musa, A. A., Malami, S. I., Alanazi, F., Ounaies, W., Alshammari, M., & Haruna, S. I. (2023). Sustainable traffic management for smart cities using internet-of-things-oriented intelligent transportation systems (ITS): Challenges and recommendations. *Sustainability*, *15*(13), 9859.

Mustafa, G., Rafiq, W., Jhamat, N., Arshad, Z., & Rana, F. A. (2025). Blockchain-based governance models in e-government: A comprehensive framework for legal, technical, ethical and security considerations. *International Journal of Law and Management*, *67*(1), 37–55. DOI: 10.1108/IJLMA-08-2023-0172/FULL/XML

Naveeenkumar, N., Rallapalli, S., Sasikala, K., Priya, P. V., Husain, J., & Boopathi, S. (2024). Enhancing Consumer Behavior and Experience Through AI-Driven Insights Optimization. In *AI Impacts in Digital Consumer Behavior* (pp. 1–35). IGI Global.

Nazir, T., Iqbal, M. M., Jabbar, S., Hussain, A., & Albathan, M. (2023). EfficientPNet—An Optimized and Efficient Deep Learning Approach for Classifying Disease of Potato Plant Leaves. *Agriculture*, *13*(4), 841.

Nguyen, T. L., Nguyen, L., Hoang, T., Bandara, D., Wang, Q., Lu, Q., Xu, X., Zhu, L., & Chen, S. (2025). Blockchain-Empowered Trustworthy Data Sharing: Fundamentals, Applications, and Challenges. *ACM Computing Surveys*. Advance online publication. DOI: 10.1145/3718082

Nishanth, J., Deshmukh, M. A., Kushwah, R., Kushwaha, K. K., Balaji, S., & Sampath, B. (2023). Particle Swarm Optimization of Hybrid Renewable Energy Systems. In *Intelligent Engineering Applications and Applied Sciences for Sustainability* (pp. 291–308). IGI Global.

NP, C. (2020). Challenges of Security and Privacy with Internet of Things in Smart Agriculture. *Akwapoly Journal of Communication & Scientific Research, 5*(1).

Ofori, M., & El-Gayar, O. (2019, December). The State and Future of Smart Agriculture: Insights from mining social media *2019*. In *IEEE International Conference on Big Data (Big Data)* (pp. 5152-5161). IEEE, DOI: DOI: 10.1109/BigData47090.2019.9006587

Ogundare, E. (2024a). Understanding the mediating role of artificial intelligence in urban transportation planning for smart city development and its implications for the United States. *International Journal of Innovative Science and Research Technology*, *9*, 10–5281.

Oh, S. E., Kim, J. H., Kim, J. Y., & Ahn, J. H. (2025). Food Safety Distribution Systems Using Private Blockchain: Ensuring Traceability and Data Integrity Verification. *Foods 2025, Vol. 14, Page 1405, 14*(8), 1405. DOI: 10.3390/FOODS14081405

Oladimeji, D., Gupta, K., Kose, N. A., Gundogan, K., Ge, L., & Liang, F. (2023). Smart transportation: An overview of technologies and applications. *Sensors (Basel)*, *23*(8), 3880. PMID: 37112221

Ollitrault, P. J., Miessen, A., & Tavernelli, I. (2021). Molecular Quantum Dynamics: A Quantum Computing Perspective. *Accounts of Chemical Research*, *54*(23), 4229–4238. DOI: 10.1021/acs.accounts.1c00514 PMID: 34787398

Parashar, A., Mabrouki, J., & Sharma, J. (2024). AI and Smart Technologies for Smart Agriculture Environment. In *Advanced Systems for Environmental Monitoring, IoT and the application of Artificial Intelligence* (pp. 95–107). Springer Nature Switzerland., DOI: 10.1007/978-3-031-50860-8_6

Park, E., del Pobil, A., & Kwon, S. (2018). The role of internet of things (IoT) in smart cities: Technology roadmap-oriented approaches. *Sustainability*, *10*(5), 1388.

Pattani, Nalini, M., Yamini, B., Ambhika, C., & Siva Subramanian, R. (2025). Enhancing early attack detection: Novel hybrid density-based isolation forest for improved anomaly detection. *International Journal of Machine Learning and Cybernetics*, *16*(5), 3429–3447.

Periasamy, J. K., Subhashini, S., Mutharasu, M., Revathi, M., Ajitha, P., & Boopathi, S. (2024). Synergizing Federated Learning and In-Memory Computing: An Experimental Approach for Drone Integration. In *Developments Towards Next Generation Intelligent Systems for Sustainable Development* (pp. 89–123). IGI Global. DOI: 10.4018/979-8-3693-5643-2.ch004

Piccardo, G., Conti, L., & Martino, A. (2024). Blockchain Technology and Its Potential to Benefit Public Services Provision: A Short Survey. *Future Internet 2024, Vol. 16, Page 290, 16*(8), 290. DOI: 10.3390/FI16080290

Ponmalar, A., Muthuram, A., Therasa, M., Priya, V., Sathya, V., Subha, S., & Subramanian, R. S. (2025). Convergence of Advanced Technologies for Sustainable Development and Smart Cities. In *AI and Green Technology Applications in Society* (pp. 189–218). IGI Global Scientific Publishing.

Prabhu, D., & Sudha, L. MR, P. K., Adaikkammai, A., Aparna, P., & Sathya, V. (2025). Machine Learning in Cybersecurity: Challenges, Applications, and Future Directions. *Exploiting Machine Learning for Robust Security,* 25-48.

Prasad, M. S. C., Dhanalakshmi, M., Mohan, M., Somasundaram, B., Valarmathi, R., & Boopathi, S. (2024). Machine Learning-Integrated Sustainable Engineering and Energy Systems: Innovations at the Nexus. In *Harnessing High-Performance Computing and AI for Environmental Sustainability* (pp. 74–98). IGI Global. DOI: 10.4018/979-8-3693-1794-5.ch004

Prasad, C. G. V. N., Mallareddy, A., Pounambal, M., & Velayutham, V. (2022). Edge Computing and Blockchain in Smart Agriculture Systems. *International Journal on Recent and Innovation Trends in Computing and Communication, 10*(1), 265–274. DOI: 10.17762/ijritcc.v10i1s.5848

Prasad, R. D., & Srivenkatesh, M. (2025). A Hybrid Model Ccombining Graph Neural Networks, Reinforcement Learning, and Autoencoders for Authomated Code Refactoring and Optimization. *Journal of Theoretical and Applied Information Technology, 103*(1).

Przeybilovicz, E., & Cunha, M. A. (2024). Governing in the digital age: The emergence of dynamic smart urban governance modes. *Government Information Quarterly, 41*(1), 101907. DOI: 10.1016/J.GIQ.2023.101907

Puranik, T. A., Shaik, N., Vankudoth, R., Kolhe, M. R., Yadav, N., & Boopathi, S. (2024). Study on Harmonizing Human-Robot (Drone) Collaboration: Navigating Seamless Interactions in Collaborative Environments. In *Cybersecurity Issues and Challenges in the Drone Industry* (pp. 1–26). IGI Global.

Quan, B. L. Y., Wahab, N. H. A., Al-Dhaqm, A., Alshammari, A., Aqarni, A., Razak, S. A., & Wei, K. T. (2025). Recent Advances in Sharding Techniques for Scalable Blockchain Networks: A Review. *IEEE Access : Practical Innovations, Open Solutions, 13*, 21335–21366. DOI: 10.1109/ACCESS.2024.3523256

Rahamathunnisa, U., Sudhakar, K., Padhi, S., Bhattacharya, S., Shashibhushan, G., & Boopathi, S. (2024). Sustainable Energy Generation From Waste Water: IoT Integrated Technologies. In *Adoption and Use of Technology Tools and Services by Economically Disadvantaged Communities: Implications for Growth and Sustainability* (pp. 225–256). IGI Global.

Rahman, F., Titouna, C., & Nait-Abdesselam, F. (2024). Fundamentals of Blockchain and Smart Contracts. *Blockchain and Smart-Contract Technologies for Innovative Applications*, 3–37. DOI: 10.1007/978-3-031-50028-2_1

Rai, S., Meschini, M., & Genangeli, S. (2016). *The Implementation of Drones in the Business Model of Photovoltaic Companies* [PhD Thesis]. Copenhagen Business School Frederiksberg, Denmark.

Raj, E. F. I., Appadurai, M., Darwin, S., & Rani, E. F. I. (2022). Internet of things (IoT) for sustainable smart cities. In *Internet of things* (pp. 163–188). CRC Press.

Ravindran, D., Revathi, S., Sowndharya, V., Farzhana, I., Sathya, V., Girija, P., & Subramanian, S. (2025). Unraveling the Quantum Computing Frontier: Advancements, Challenges, and Future Prospects. *Integration of AI, Quantum Computing, and Semiconductor Technology*, 139-158.

Ravisankar, A., Sampath, B., & Asif, M. M. (2023). Economic Studies on Automobile Management: Working Capital and Investment Analysis. In *Multidisciplinary Approaches to Organizational Governance During Health Crises* (pp. 169–198). IGI Global.

Razzaq, R. H., & Al-Zubaidie, M. (2024b). Formulating an advanced security protocol for Internet of medical Things based on blockchain and fog computing technologies. *Iraqi Journal for Computer Science and Mathematics*, *5*(3), 723–734. DOI: 10.30880/ijcsm.2024.05.03.046

Razzaq, R. H., & Al-Zubaidie, M. H. (2024a). Maintaining security of patient data by employing private blockchain and fog computing technologies based on internet of medical things. *Informatica (Vilnius)*, *48*(12). Advance online publication. DOI: 10.31449/inf.v48i12.6047

Razzaq, R. H., Al-Zubaidie, M., & Atiyah, R. G. (2024). Intermediary decentralized computing and private blockchain mechanisms for privacy preservation in the Internet of Medical Things. *Mesopotamian Journal of CyberSecurity*, *4*(3), 152–165. DOI: 10.58496/MJCS/2024/020

Razzaq, R. H., Tahayur, D. H., & Jebbar, W. A. (2025). Sturdy Blockchain Combined with E-apps Repositories Based on Reliable Camouflaging and Integrating Mechanisms. *IJ Computer Network and Information Security*, *17*(3), 35–53.

Regan, Á. (2019). 'Smart farming'in Ireland: A risk perception study with key governance actors. *NJAS Wageningen Journal of Life Sciences*, *90*, 100292.

Relf-Eckstein, J. E., Ballantyne, A. T., & Phillips, P. W. (2019). Farming Reimagined: A case study of autonomous farm equipment and creating an innovation opportunity space for broadacre smart farming. *NJAS Wageningen Journal of Life Sciences*, *90*, 100307.

Revathi, S., Babu, M., Rajkumar, N., Meti, V. K. V., Kandavalli, S. R., & Boopathi, S. (2024). Unleashing the Future Potential of 4D Printing: Exploring Applications in Wearable Technology, Robotics, Energy, Transportation, and Fashion. In *Human-Centered Approaches in Industry 5.0: Human-Machine Interaction, Virtual Reality Training, and Customer Sentiment Analysis* (pp. 131–153). IGI Global.

Riboldi, C. E. (2018). An optimal approach to the preliminary design of small hybrid-electric aircraft. *Aerospace Science and Technology*, *81*, 14–31.

Riboldi, C. E., & Gualdoni, F. (2016). An integrated approach to the preliminary weight sizing of small electric aircraft. *Aerospace Science and Technology*, *58*, 134–149.

Roopaei, M., Rad, P., & Choo, K. K. R. (2017). Cloud of things in smart agriculture: Intelligent irrigation monitoring by thermal imaging. *IEEE Cloud Computing*, *4*(1), 10–15. DOI: 10.1109/MCC.2017.5

S., B. (2024). Advancements in Optimizing Smart Energy Systems Through Smart Grid Integration, Machine Learning, and IoT. In *Advances in Environmental Engineering and Green Technologies* (pp. 33–61). IGI Global. DOI: 10.4018/979-8-3693-0492-1.ch002

Sadr, M. A. M., Zhu, Y., & Hu, P. (2023, February 10). *Satellite Anomaly Detection Using Variance Based Genetic Ensemble of Neural Networks*. arXiv.Org. https://arxiv.org/abs/2302.05525v1

Saeed El Etaiby, Y. (2023). Smart agriculture and future technologies for achieving food security. *International Journal of Family Studies. Food Science and Nutrition Health*, *4*(1), 56–71. DOI: 10.21608/ijfsnh.2024.293384.1006

Sahu, S. K., & Mazumdar, K. (2024). State-of-the-art analysis of quantum cryptography: Applications and future prospects. *Frontiers in Physics*, *12*. Advance online publication. DOI: 10.3389/fphy.2024.1456491

Saida, T., Mori, K., Hoshiai, S., Sakai, M., Urushibara, A., Ishiguro, T., & Nakajima, T. (2022). Diagnosing ovarian cancer on MRI: A preliminary study comparing deep learning and radiologist assessments. *Cancers (Basel)*, *14*(4), 987. PMID: 35205735

Sandhu, K. (Ed.). (2021). *Handbook of research on advancing cybersecurity for digital transformation*. IGI Global.

Sarker, I. H. (2022). Smart City Data Science: Towards data-driven smart cities with open research issues. *Internet of Things : Engineering Cyber Physical Human Systems*, *19*, 100528.

Savin, G. V. (2021). The smart city transport and logistics system: Theory, methodology and practice. *Upravlenec, 12*(6).

Schönfeld, M. V., Heil, R., & Bittner, L. (2018). Big data on a farm—Smart farming. *Big data in context*, 109-120, DOI: .DOI: 10.1007/978-3-319-62461-7_12

Selvakumar, S., Adithe, S., Isaac, J. S., Pradhan, R., Venkatesh, V., & Sampath, B. (2023). A Study of the Printed Circuit Board (PCB) E-Waste Recycling Process. In *Sustainable Approaches and Strategies for E-Waste Management and Utilization* (pp. 159–184). IGI Global.

Selvaraj, J., Lai, W. C., Kavin, B. P., & Seng, G. H. (2023). Cryptographic Encryption and Optimization for Internet of Things Based Medical Image Security. *Electronics (Basel), 12*(7), 1636.

Senthil, T., Puviyarasan, M., Babu, S. R., Surakasi, R., Sampath, B., & Associates. (2023). Industrial Robot-Integrated Fused Deposition Modelling for the 3D Printing Process. In *Development, Properties, and Industrial Applications of 3D Printed Polymer Composites* (pp. 188–210). IGI Global.

Shahid, H., Ashraf, H., Javed, H., Humayun, M., Jhanjhi, N., Al, A., & Zain, M. (2021). Energy Optimised Security against Wormhole Attack in IoT-Based Wireless Sensor Networks. *Computers, Materials & Continua, 68*(2), 1967–1981. DOI: 10.32604/cmc.2021.015259

Shamsan Saleh, A. M. (2024). Blockchain for secure and decentralized artificial intelligence in cybersecurity: A comprehensive review. *Blockchain: Research and Applications*, *5*(3), 100193. DOI: 10.1016/J.BCRA.2024.100193

Sharma, P., & Gupta, H. (2024). Emerging Cyber Security Threats and Security Applications in Digital Era. In *2024 11th International Conference on Reliability, Infocom Technologies and Optimization (Trends and Future Directions)(ICRITO)* (pp. 1-6). IEEE.

Sharma, T., Kumar, M. R., Kaushal, S., Chaudhary, D., & Saleem, K. (2023). Privacy Aware Post Quantum Secure Ant Colony Optimization Ad Hoc On-Demand Distance Vector Routing in Intent Based Internet of Vehicles for 5G Smart Cities. *IEEE Access, 11*, 110391–110399. IEEE Access. .DOI: 10.1109/ACCESS.2023.3311515

Sharma, M., Sharma, M., Sharma, N., & Boopathi, S. (2024). Building Sustainable Smart Cities Through Cloud and Intelligent Parking System. In *Handbook of Research on AI and ML for Intelligent Machines and Systems* (pp. 195–222). IGI Global.

Sharma, V., Tripathi, A. K., & Mittal, H. (2022). Technological revolutions in smart farming: Current trends, challenges & future directions. *Computers and Electronics in Agriculture, 201*, 107217. DOI: 10.1016/j.compag.2022.107217

Shen, M. (2023, October). Privacy Protection Smart Agriculture Based on Functional Encryption. In *2023 International Symposium on Networks, Computers and Communications (ISNCC)* (pp. 1-5). IEEE.

Shevchuk, R., Lishchynskyy, I., Ciura, M., Lyzun, M., Kozak, R., & Kasianchuk, M. (2025). Application of Blockchain Technology in Emergency Management Systems: A Bibliometric Analysis. *Applied Sciences 2025, Vol. 15, Page 5405, 15*(10), 5405. DOI: 10.3390/APP15105405

Šilenskytė, A., Butkevičienė, J., & Bartminas, A. (2024). Blockchain-based connectivity within digital platforms and ecosystems in international business. *Journal of International Management, 30*(3), 101109. DOI: 10.1016/J.INTMAN.2023.101109

Singh, A. K. (2022). Smart farming: Applications of IoT in agriculture. In *Handbook of Smart Materials, Technologies, and Devices: Applications of Industry 4.0* (pp. 1655–1687). Springer International Publishing., DOI: 10.1007/978-3-030-84205-5_114

Sonia, R., Gupta, N., Manikandan, K., Hemalatha, R., Kumar, M. J., & Boopathi, S. (2024). Strengthening Security, Privacy, and Trust in Artificial Intelligence Drones for Smart Cities. In *Analyzing and Mitigating Security Risks in Cloud Computing* (pp. 214–242). IGI Global.

Subhashini, R., & Khang, A. (2023). The role of Internet of Things (IoT) in smart city framework. In *Smart Cities* (pp. 31–56). CRC Press.

Sudaryanto, T., Wahida, H. J., Rafani, I., & Andoko, E. (2022). *Promoting Smart Farming based-Digital Business Technology in the Context of Agricultural Transformation in Indonesia*. FFTC J Agric Policy.

Sullivan, C. S., Gemtou, M., Anastasiou, E., & Fountas, S. (2024). Building trust: A systematic review of the drivers and barriers of agricultural data sharing. *Smart Agricultural Technology, 100477*. Advance online publication. DOI: 10.1016/j.atech.2024.100477

Sundar, R., Srikaanth, P. B., Naik, D. A., Murugan, V. P., Karumudi, M., & Boopathi, S. (2024). Achieving Balance Between Innovation and Security in the Cloud With Artificial Intelligence of Things: Semantic Web Control Models. In *Advances in Web Technologies and Engineering* (pp. 1–26). IGI Global. DOI: 10.4018/979-8-3693-1487-6.ch001

Sun, Y., Hu, Y., Zhang, H., Chen, H., & Wang, F.-Y. (2023). A parallel emission regulatory framework for intelligent transportation systems and smart cities. *IEEE Transactions on Intelligent Vehicles*, *8*(2), 1017–1020.

Tahayur, D. H., & Al-Zubaidie, M. (2025, March). Establishing an optimized searching approach with e-signatures based on blockchain for electronic agriculture applications. In AIP Conference Proceedings (Vol. 3264, No. 1). AIP Publishing. DOI: 10.1063/5.0258784

Tahayur, D. H., & Al-Zubaidie, M. (2024). Enhancing electronic agriculture data security with a blockchain-based search method and e-signatures. *Mesopotamian Journal of CyberSecurity*, *4*(3), 1–21. DOI: 10.58496/MJCS/2024/012

Tahayur, D. H., Jebbar, W. A., & Razzaq, R. H. (2024). Dependable Concealing Algorithm of E-apps Repositories Combined with a Robust Blockchain Approach. *Advanced Research on Information Systems Security*, *4*(2), 32–56.

Takahashi, T., Zhihao, Y., & Omote, K. (2024). Emergency Medical Access Control System Based on Public Blockchain. *Journal of Medical Systems*, *48*(1), 1–10. DOI: 10.1007/S10916-024-02102-X/TABLES/2 PMID: 39298041

Talari, S., Shafie-Khah, M., Siano, P., Loia, V., Tommasetti, A., & Catalão, J. P. (2017). A review of smart cities based on the internet of things concept. *Energies*, *10*(4), 421.

Tameemi, H. A., Shayea, G. G., Khaleel, Y. L., Habeeb, M. A., Hussein, N. A. H. K., & Albahri, A. S. (2025). A Systematic review of metaverse cybersecurity: Frameworks, challenges, and strategic approaches in a quantum-driven era. *Mesopotamian Journal of CyberSecurity*, *5*(2), 770–803.

Tang, M., Dai, W., Yin, C., Hu, B., Chen, J., & Liu, H. (2024). Spatial Planning Data Structure Based on Blockchain Technology. *ISPRS International Journal of Geo-Information 2024, Vol. 13, Page 290, 13*(8), 290. DOI: 10.3390/IJGI13080290

Tatipatri, N., & Arun, S. L. (2024). A Comprehensive Review on Cyber-Attacks in Power Systems: Impact Analysis, Detection, and Cyber Security. *IEEE Access : Practical Innovations, Open Solutions*, *12*, 18147–18167. DOI: 10.1109/ACCESS.2024.3361039

Telang, S., Chel, A., Nemade, A., & Kaushik, G. (2020). Intelligent transport system for a smart city. In *Security and privacy applications for smart city development* (pp. 171–187). Springer.

Tezza, D., & Andujar, M. (2019). The state-of-the-art of human–drone interaction: A survey. *IEEE Access : Practical Innovations, Open Solutions*, *7*, 167438–167454.

Tirlangi, S., Teotia, S., Padmapriya, G., Senthil Kumar, S., Dhotre, S., & Boopathi, S. (2024). Cloud Computing and Machine Learning in the Green Power Sector: Data Management and Analysis for Sustainable Energy. In *Developments Towards Next Generation Intelligent Systems for Sustainable Development* (pp. 148–179). IGI Global. DOI: 10.4018/979-8-3693-5643-2.ch006

Tiwari, A. K., Mishra, H., Nishad, D. C., & Pandey, A. (2023). Sustainable water management in agriculture: irrigation techniques and water conservation. *Dr. Ajay B. Jadhao, 53.*

Tregi, T. G., & Al-Zubaidie, M. (2025). Enhancing Traffic Data Security in Smart Cities Using Optimized Quantum-Based Digital Signatures and Privacy-Preserving Techniques. *Mesopotamian Journal of CyberSecurity*, *5*(1), 256–272. DOI: 10.58496/MJCS/2025/017

Turner, S. W., & Uludag, S. (2017). Toward Smart Cities via the Smart Grid and Intelligent Transportation Systems. *Smart Grid*, •••, 117–166.

Untawale, T. (2021). Importance of cyber security in digital era. *International Journal for Research in Applied Science and Engineering Technology*, *9*(8), 963–966.

Upadhyaya, A. N., Saqib, A., Devi, J. V., Rallapalli, S., Sudha, S., & Boopathi, S. (2024). Implementation of the Internet of Things (IoT) in Remote Healthcare. In *Advances in Medical Technologies and Clinical Practice* (pp. 104–124). IGI Global. DOI: 10.4018/979-8-3693-1934-5.ch006

Upadrista, V., Nazir, S., & Tianfield, H. (2023). Secure data sharing with blockchain for remote health monitoring applications: A review. *Journal of Reliable Intelligent Environments*, *9*(3), 349–368. DOI: 10.1007/s40860-023-00204-w PMID: 37359293

Uppalaiah, B., Reddy, D. M., Govindan, V., & Byeon, H. (2024). Optimizing quality of service forecasting in mobile networks through modified walrus optimization and multivariate approaches. *Edelweiss Applied Science and Technology*, *8*(6), 7878–7901. DOI: 10.55214/25768484.v8i6.3717

Varshney, H., Khan, R. A., Khan, U., & Verma, R. (2021). Approaches of artificial intelligence and machine learning in smart cities: Critical review. *IOP Conference Series. Materials Science and Engineering*, *1022*(1), 012019.

Venkateswaran, N., Kiran Kumar, K., Maheswari, K., Kumar Reddy, R. V., & Boopathi, S. (2024). Optimizing IoT Data Aggregation: Hybrid Firefly-Artificial Bee Colony Algorithm for Enhanced Efficiency in Agriculture. *AGRIS On-Line Papers in Economics and Informatics*, *16*(1), 117–130. DOI: 10.7160/aol.2024.160110

Vijaya Lakshmi, V., Mishra, M., Kushwah, J. S., Shajahan, U. S., Mohanasundari, M., & Boopathi, S. (2024). Circular Economy Digital Practices for Ethical Dimensions and Policies for Digital Waste Management. In *Harnessing High-Performance Computing and AI for Environmental Sustainability* (pp. 166–193). IGI Global., DOI: 10.4018/979-8-3693-1794-5.ch008

Vijayakumar, G. N. S., Domakonda, V. K., Farooq, S., Kumar, B. S., Pradeep, N., & Boopathi, S. (2024). Sustainable Developments in Nano-Fluid Synthesis for Various Industrial Applications. In *Adoption and Use of Technology Tools and Services by Economically Disadvantaged Communities: Implications for Growth and Sustainability* (pp. 48–81). IGI Global.

Villegas-Ch, W., & García-Ortiz, J. (2023). Toward a comprehensive framework for ensuring security and privacy in artificial intelligence. *Electronics (Basel)*, *12*(18), 3786. DOI: 10.3390/electronics12183786

Vladislav, D., Maxim, K., Andrey, M., Viktoria, K., & Olga, K. (2024). Development of Determining a Wireless Client Location Method in the IEEE 802.11 Network to Ensure the IT Infrastructure Security. In A. A. Abd El-Latif, L. Tawalbeh, Y. Maleh, & B. B. Gupta (Eds.), *Secure Edge and Fog Computing Enabled AI for IoT and Smart Cities: Includes selected Papers from International Conference on Advanced Computing & Next-Generation Communication (ICACNGC 2022)* (pp. 241–254). Springer International Publishing. DOI: 10.1007/978-3-031-51097-7_19

Wallace, J., Vukovic, M., Karimovic, T., & Edwards, W. (2025). A High-Performance 5G/6G Framework for Smart Cities Supporting Multi-Level Artificial Intelligence. *2025 2nd International Conference on Advanced Innovations in Smart Cities (ICAISC)*, 1–9.

Wang, M., Zhu, T., Zuo, X., Ye, D., Yu, S., & Zhou, W. (2024). Public and Private Blockchain Infusion: A Novel Approach to Federated Learning. *IEEE Internet of Things Journal*, *11*(10), 17525–17537. DOI: 10.1109/JIOT.2024.3360129

Wiseman, L., Sanderson, J., Zhang, A., & Jakku, E. (2019). Farmers and their data: An examination of farmers' reluctance to share their data through the lens of the laws impacting smart farming. *NJAS Wageningen Journal of Life Sciences*, *90*, 100301.

Wolfert, S., Ge, L., Verdouw, C., & Bogaardt, M. J. (2017). Big data in smart farming–a review. *Agricultural Systems*, *153*, 69–80. DOI: 10.1016/j.agsy.2017.01.023

Wu, J., Zhang, J., Liu, D., & Wang, X. (2023). A Multiple-Medical-Image Encryption Method Based on SHA-256 and DNA Encoding. *Entropy (Basel, Switzerland)*, *25*(6), 898. PMID: 37372242

Wu, P., Zhang, Z., Peng, X., & Wang, R. (2024). Deep learning solutions for smart city challenges in urban development. *Scientific Reports, 14*(1), 5176. PMID: 38431741

Yamini, B. MAY, P. M. A., Shobana, R., TP, A., & Nalini, M. (2024, December). Cybersecurity: Strategies, Sector-Specific Challenges, and Future Prospects. *In 2024 4th International Conference on Ubiquitous Computing and Intelligent Information Systems* (ICUIS) (pp. 1338-1345). IEEE.

Yang, X., Shu, L., Chen, J., Ferrag, M. A., Wu, J., Nurellari, E., & Huang, K. (2021). A survey on smart agriculture: Development modes, technologies, and security and privacy challenges. *IEEE/CAA Journal of Automatica Sinica, 8*(2), 273-302, DOI: .DOI: 10.1109/JAS.2020.1003536

Yang, Z., Zolanvari, M., & Jain, R. (2023). A Survey of Important Issues in Quantum Computing and Communications. *IEEE Communications Surveys and Tutorials, 25*(2), 1059–1094. DOI: 10.1109/COMST.2023.3254481

Yavanoglu, O., & Aydos, M. (2017, December). A review on cyber security datasets for machine learning algorithms. *In 2017 IEEE international conference on big data (big data) (pp. 2186-2193).* IEEE.

Yazdinejad, A., Zolfaghari, B., Azmoodeh, A., Dehghantanha, A., Karimipour, H., Fraser, E., & Duncan, E. (2021). A review on security of smart farming and precision agriculture: Security aspects, attacks, threats and countermeasures. *Applied Sciences (Basel, Switzerland), 11*(16), 7518. DOI: 10.3390/app11167518

Yermachenko, V., Bondarenko, D., Akimova, L., Karpa, M., Akimov, O., & Kalashnyk, N. (2023). *Theory and practice of public management of smart infrastructure in the conditions of the digital society'development: Socio-economic aspects.*

Yuan, F., Huang, X., Zheng, L., Wang, L., Wang, Y., Yan, X., Gu, S., & Peng, Y. (2025). The Evolution and Optimization Strategies of a PBFT Consensus Algorithm for Consortium Blockchains. *Information 2025, Vol. 16, Page 268, 16*(4), 268. DOI: 10.3390/INFO16040268

Zachariah, M., Avanesh, N. M., & Raghupathi, K. (2025). Application of blockchain technology in disaster risk management. *The Role of Blockchain in Disaster Management*, 87–110. DOI: 10.1016/B978-0-443-13472-2.00004-8

Zafar, A. (2025). Reconciling blockchain technology and data protection laws: Regulatory challenges, technical solutions, and practical pathways. *Journal of Cybersecurity, 11*(1), tyaf002. Advance online publication. DOI: 10.1093/cybsec/tyaf002

Zampati, F. (2023). Ethical and legal considerations in smart farming: A farmer's perspective. *Towards Responsible Plant Data Linkage: Data Challenges for Agricultural Research and Development, 257.*

Zamwar, U. M., Anjankar, A. P., & Anjankar, A. (2022). Aetiology, Epidemiology, Histopathology, Classification, Detailed Evaluation, and Treatment of Ovarian Cancer. *Cureus*, *14*(10). PMID: 36415372

Zekrifa, D. M. S., Kulkarni, M., Bhagyalakshmi, A., Devireddy, N., Gupta, S., & Boopathi, S. (2023). Integrating Machine Learning and AI for Improved Hydrological Modeling and Water Resource Management. In *Artificial Intelligence Applications in Water Treatment and Water Resource Management* (pp. 46–70). IGI Global.

Zhang, Z. (2024, August 22). *Deep Analysis of Time Series Data for Smart Grid Startup Strategies: A Transformer-LSTM-PSO Model Approach*. arXiv.Org. https://arxiv.org/abs/2408.12129v1

Zhang, G., Sun, X., & Zhong, S. (2024). The impact of smart city construction (SCC) on pollution emissions (PE): Evidence from China. *Scientific Reports*, *14*(1), 6633. PMID: 38503860

Zhang, J., Campbell, J. F., Sweeney, D. C.II, & Hupman, A. C. (2021). Energy consumption models for delivery drones: A comparison and assessment. *Transportation Research Part D, Transport and Environment*, *90*, 102668.

Zhang, L., Wei, J., & Tu, R. (2024). Temporal-spatial analysis of transportation CO2 emissions in China: Clustering and policy recommendations. *Heliyon*, *10*(2). PMID: 38312644

Zhang, S., Niu, T., Wu, Y., Zhang, K. M., Wallington, T. J., Xie, Q., Wu, X., & Xu, H. (2018). Fine-grained vehicle emission management using intelligent transportation system data. *Environmental Pollution*, *241*, 1027–1037. PMID: 30029310

Zhang, Y., Zhang, Y., Zhang, H., & Zhang, Y. (2022). Evaluation on new first-tier smart cities in China based on entropy method and TOPSIS. *Ecological Indicators*, *145*, 109616.

Zhan, W., Wang, Z., Deng, J., Liu, P., & Cui, D. (2024). Integrating system dynamics and agent-based modeling: A data-driven framework for predicting electric vehicle market penetration and GHG emissions reduction under various incentives scenarios. *Applied Energy*, *372*, 123749.

Zhao, C., Wang, K., Dong, X., & Dong, K. (2022). Is smart transportation associated with reduced carbon emissions? The case of China. *Energy Economics*, *105*, 105715.

Ziyambe, B., Yahya, A., Mushiri, T., Tariq, M. U., Abbas, Q., Babar, M., & Jabbar, S. (2023). A Deep Learning Framework for the Prediction and Diagnosis of Ovarian Cancer in Pre-and Post-Menopausal Women. *Diagnostics (Basel), 13*(10), 1703. PMID: 37238188

Zou, Y., Wu, R., Tian, X., & Li, H. (2023). Realizing the Improvement of the Reliability and Efficiency of Intelligent Electricity Inspection: IAOA-BP Algorithm for Anomaly Detection. *Energies, 16*(7), 7. Advance online publication. DOI: 10.3390/en16073021

# About the Contributors

**Mishall Al-Zubaidie** (Member, IEEE) received a bachelor's degree in computer science from Basrah University, Iraq, in 2004, and a master's degree in the security of the wireless network from Basrah University, Iraq, in 2010. He received his Ph.D. degree from the School of Agricultural, Computational and Environmental Sciences, Faculty of Health, Engineering, and Sciences, University of Southern Queensland, Australia in 2020. He has authored many peer-reviewed research in different journals in the field of communications and network security. In addition, he provided review and evaluation services for more than 1100 research papers in various respected journals. His current research interests are communications and networks security including public-key algorithms, authorising users in electronic health record (EHR), electronic medical record (EMR), and both security, efficiency of the wireless sensor network of health systems, keys exchange/agreement algorithms in protecting patients' data/information and smart city security.

***

**Munir Ahmad** is a seasoned professional in the realm of Spatial Data Infrastructure (SDI), Geo-Information Productions, Information Systems, and Information Governance, boasting over 25 years of dedicated experience in the field. With a PhD in Computer Science, Dr. Ahmad's expertise spans Spatial Data Production, Management, Processing, Analysis, Visualization, and Quality Control. Throughout his career, Dr. Ahmad has been deeply involved in the development and deployment of SDI systems specially in the context of Pakistan, leveraging his proficiency in Spatial Database Design, Web, Mobile & Desktop GIS, and Geo Web Services Architecture. His contributions to Volunteered Geographic Information (VGI) and Open Source Geoportal & Metadata Portal have significantly enriched the geospatial community. As a trainer and researcher, Dr. Ahmad has authored over 50 publications, advancing the industry's knowledge base and fostering innovation in Geo-Tech, Data Governance, and Information Infrastructure, and Emerging Technologies. His commitment to Research and Development (R&D) is evident in his role as a dedicated educator and mentor in the field.

**Anorgul Atajanova** is working as Department Head, Department of Primary Education Methodology, Urgench State Pedagogical Institute, Urgench, Uzbekistan

**Vijilius Helena Raj** did her M.Sc., in Mathematics from Mumbai University, Kalina and Ph.d from Manonmaniam Sundaranar University, Tirunelveli, Tamilnadu. She is associated with New Horizon college of Engineering, Bengaluru since 2000 and currently professor in Mathematics heading the department of examinations. She is actively involved in multidisciplinary research and has published a good number of papers in indexed journals and is a recognized research guide under Visvesvaraya Technological University. Her research interests include graph theory, combinatorics, fuzzy Topology and general topology.

**Erkin Iskandarov** is working in the Department of Pedagogy and Psychology, Urgench State University, Uzbekistan

**Nivas Kumar** is a faculty member in the Department of Electronics and Communication Engineering at Jawahar Engineering College. His academic and research interests span modern communication systems, signal processing, and emerging technologies in ECE. He is dedicated to advancing engineering education and contributing to innovative research in his field.

**Anto Gracious L. A.** is a faculty member in the Department of Computer Science and Engineering at R.M.K. College of Engineering and Technology, Tamil Nadu, India. His academic contributions focus on computer science education and student development. He is actively engaged in guiding projects, mentoring learners, and supporting research initiatives in emerging technologies

**M. Vijayalakshmi** is an Assistant Professor in the School of Computing at SRM Institute of Science and Technology, Tamil Nadu, India. Her research interests focus on computer networks, wireless communication, and emerging computing technologies. She has authored several research publications and actively participates in academic and professional development initiatives.

**M.G.Dinesh** is an Assistant Professor in department of Artificial intelligence and data science at EASA College of Engineering and Technology, Coimbatore. He has completed his under graduate and Post Graduate in Information Technology. He has completed his Ph.D in Information and communication Engineering from

Anna University, Chennai. His research interests include Data mining, Big Data Analytics and Network Security. He has published many papers in International journals and conferences.

**Harshit Mishra** is currently a final-year Ph.D. scholar in the Department of Agricultural Economics at Acharya Narendra Deva University of Agriculture & Technology, Kumarganj, Ayodhya (U.P.). He completed his Master's degree from the same university in 2022. During his academic journey, he has been recognized with several prestigious awards, including the Research Excellence Award, Best M.Sc. (Ag) Thesis Award, Best Oral Presentation Award, and Best Poster Presentation Award conferred by esteemed academic societies. He is the author of two books: "Fundamentals of Agri-Business Management & Intellectual Property Rights" and "Manual cum Workbook of Finance and Cooperation." In addition, he has published over 14 research articles in reputed NAAS-rated, Scopus-indexed, and Web of Science-indexed peer-reviewed journals. His scholarly contributions also include more than 35 popular articles published in both Hindi and English across various reputed magazines, and over 40 book chapters in edited volumes published by renowned international publishers such as Springer Nature, CRC Press, Taylor & Francis Group, Apple Academic Press, and many other reputed academic publishing houses.

**P. Girija** is an Assistant Professor in the Department of Information Technology at Panimalar Engineering College, Chennai, India. Her academic interests include artificial intelligence, data analytics, and software engineering. She is actively involved in teaching, research, and guiding students in emerging areas of information technology.

**R.Mohan Das** received B.E.Degree (2002) in Electrical and Electronics Engineering from CSI College of Engineering, Ketthi and ME Power Electronics (2007) from Karunya University. He received Ph.D. in Anna University-Chennai (2020). He is currently working as associate professor in the Department of Electrical and Electronics Engineering, New Horizon College of Engineering, Bengaluru, Karnataka. His research interests are in PWM techniques, power electronics, and renewable energy sources. He can be contacted at email: mohandas@newhorizonindia.edu

**Asha Bharathi S**, Professor in the Department of Electronics and Communication Engineering, received her doctoral degree from Visvesvaraya Technological University, Belagavi in the year 2022. She has received M. Tech. degree in Digital Electronics and Advanced Communication from National Institute of Technology, Suratkal in the year 2003and BE in Electronics and Communication

Engineering from KVG College of Engineering, Sullia in the year 1996.She has 20 plus years of teaching experience. She has published several research papers in various International journals. She is life member of ISTE and member of IEEE,ISRASE,IAENG. She has reviewed several research articles for IEEE international conferences. She is also the Branch Counselor of IEEE Student Branch and UHV co-ordinator for the college

**S. Gopikha** is an Assistant Professor in the Department of Information Technology at St. Joseph's College of Engineering, India. She holds B.E. and M.E. degrees in Computer Science and Engineering. Her research focuses on artificial intelligence (AI), machine learning (ML), and deep learning (DL) for medical applications, particularly skin cancer classification using dermoscopic images.

**Anish T. P.** is a faculty member in the Department of Computer Science and Engineering at R.M.K. College of Engineering and Technology, Tamil Nadu, India. His academic and research interests focus on computer science and emerging technologies. He actively contributes to teaching, research, and guiding students in innovative projects.

**Arunadevi Thirumalraj**, did her BE in Computer Science Engineering in Government college of Engineering, Bodinayakanur and she has worked as a Research associate in various industrial and academic research institutes for past 6 years. Now she is pursing ME Computer Science Engineering in K.Ramakrishnan College of Technology, (KRCT), Tiruchirappalli. She is actively involved in the field of innovative teaching and Learning. She has publishing a good number of papers in indexed journals.

**Tuqa Ghani Treji** received her bachelor's degree in computer science from the Department of Computer Science, College of Education for Pure Sciences, University of Thi-Qar, Iraq, in 2016. She is currently pursuing a master's degree in cybersecurity. Her research focuses on securing smart city data against quantum computing threats using quantum-resistant key exchange methods, digital signatures that ensure the integrity of big data in urban infrastructures, quantum encryption, quantum signatures, and exchange keys using quantum techniques.

# Index

## A



## B



## C



## D

## T



## U



## V



## W

www.ingramcontent.com/pod-product-compliance
Lightning Source LLC
LaVergne TN
LVHW081530300926
849161LV00006B/1369